The
Transition to Socialism
in China

Mark Selden and Victor Lippit, editors

The Transition to Socialism in China

CONTRIBUTORS:

MARK SELDEN
VICTOR LIPPIT
WILLIAM HINTON
EDWARD FRIEDMAN
ANDREW WALDER

KOJIMA REIITSU
TANG TSOU
MARC BLECHER
MITCH MEISNER
CARL RISKIN

M. E. Sharpe, Inc., Armonk, New York
Croom Helm, London

First published in Great Britain 1982
by Croom Helm Ltd
2-10 St John's Road, London SW11

Library of Congress Cataloging in Publication Data

Main entry under title:

The Transition to socialism in China.

  Includes bibliographical references.
  Contents: Cooperation and conflict: cooperative and collective
formation in China's countryside/Mark Selden—Village in transition/William
Hinton—The transition to socialism in China/Victor Lippit—[etc.]
  1. China—Economic conditions—1976-   —Addresses, essays,
lectures. 2. China—Social conditions—1976-   —Addresses, essays,
lectures. I. Selden, Mark. II. Lippit, Victor D.
HC427.92.T7   338.951'05   82-5503
M. E. Sharpe, Inc. ISBN: 0-87332-212-6   AACR2
           ISBN: 0-87332-216-9 (pbk.)
Croom Helm ISBN: 0-7099-2363-5

Printed in the United States of America

304335

FOR AKIRA, LILI, SEIJI, KEN, YUKIO,

YUMI, TAMIKO, AND TAKURO

Contents

Acknowledgments

This volume originated in a conference on the transition to socialism in China held in Washington, D.C., in March 1980. To the papers drafted for that conference and presented at the 1980 annual meeting of the Association for Asian Studies, we have been fortunate to add contributions from Carl Riskin and Andrew Walder, and a joint study by Tang Tsou, March Blecher, and Mitch Meisner. In addition to learning from the contributors to this volume, our understanding of the issues of the transition has been deepened by the insights of the other participants in the conference, Phyllis and Steve Andors. We would like to express our appreciation to the American Sociological Association, whose "Conversation in the Disciplines" grant facilitated the conference, and to the Committee on Research, University of California, Riverside, for additional financial support toward the preparation of this volume.

M. S. and V. L.

The Transition to Socialism in China

Mark Selden and Victor Lippit
THE TRANSITION
TO SOCIALISM IN CHINA

Mao Zedong's death in September 1976 shattered the uneasy surface accommodation which masked the struggle among competing
factions in the Chinese Communist Party leadership. Within days
of Mao's funeral, Jiang Qing (Mao's wife) and other leading proponents of the Cultural Revolution were thwarted in their bid to control state power. The victors within the Chinese leadership embarked on a wide-ranging reassessment of major issues pertaining
to the theory and practice of revolutionary change and development.
In the course of the next few years this produced a reversal of virtually every major verdict of the Cultural Revolution era, including
the assessment of Mao's own revolutionary contribution.

The dramatic changes in policy and theory in the post-Mao era,
accompanied by the publication of the most extensive official and
unofficial data on the Chinese economy and society to be released
in more than twenty years, make possible, indeed imperative, a
thorough reconsideration of the full range of issues pertaining to
the political and economic trajectory of the People's Republic in
its first three decades. Like all data released since the sixties,
these have of course been preselected to highlight the failures of
politically discredited foes charged with responsibility for former
policy errors and therefore must be used with caution. It is nevertheless the case that we now possess the richest sources of information available to researchers since the 1950s. The contributors to
this volume have initiated a comprehensive effort to address fundamental problems of China's socialist development and to reassess
earlier perspectives and conclusions.

THE HISTORICAL SETTING:
CHINA AT LIBERATION

Speaking from the rostrum at Beijing's Tiananmen Square at the founding of the People's Republic on October 1, 1949, Mao Zedong proclaimed that "the Chinese people have stood up." Indeed they had, and we can be sure that Mao had in mind the following accomplishments, among others:

• Communist-led defeat of Japanese imperialism in China in one of the first successful people's wars. China's victory provided the sounding gun in the wave of anticolonial movements which spread throughout Asia and Africa after World War II.

• The defeat of U.S.-backed Guomindang forces in the Civil War, the establishment of the People's Republic, and the elimination of the privileged position of foreigners in China.

• The completion of the land revolution throughout North China, bringing the destruction of the power of the landlord class by a mobilized peasantry and the achievement of basic equalization of land and wealth.

Whatever its achievements, and they were impressive, the new leadership, which had gained experience in the course of more than two decades of guerrilla warfare and the administration of regional bases, well understood that the Chinese nation now faced a staggering range of problems. The poverty and distress of a war-ravaged agrarian nation, its territory the battleground for competing foreign and warlord armies for a century and more, posed the most immediate challenge.

The first half of the twentieth century in China had been marked by slow growth in population and national income — both grew at approximately 0.5 percent per year — leaving per capita national income roughly constant at about U.S. $60.[1] In 1949, however, in the aftermath of World War II and the Civil War, heavy industrial production had fallen to about 30 percent of the previous peak level, and agricultural and consumer goods output had fallen to about 70 percent of the previous peaks.[2] Hyperinflation had ruined the value of the currency, and economic exchanges were increasingly reverting to barter. The fighting had left the transportation system a shambles, and the Soviet Union, which had declared war on Japan in the closing days of World War II, systematically looted Manchuria of its most modern equipment, removing in all approximately U.S. $2 billion worth of heavy industrial equipment or about half of the capital stock in what had been the leading center of heavy industry in this predominantly agrarian nation.

The problems of wartime disruption overlay more basic structural problems. An arable land area of perhaps 300 million acres had to provide food for a population of more than 500 million. Even before the war-induced declines in production, the entire modern sector had accounted for only 7 percent of national income and could scarcely provide the material inputs the modernization of agriculture would require.[3] As a result, traditional production methods prevailed in agriculture, labor productivity was low, and some 80 percent of China's labor force was needed to provide food and other agricultural products. Transportation links were weak even prior to the wartime disruption, and vast areas of the hinterland were served by only the most rudimentary dirt roads. Outside of Japanese-occupied Manchuria in China's northeast, industry had grown in only a few coastal treaty-port cities which were often more closely linked to foreign economies than to the interior in their external economic relations. The disarticulated economy that these conditions define magnified the problems of economic construction and reconstruction.

These and other problems were exacerbated by the fact that from its birth the new nation, like many revolutionary regimes before and since, faced the antagonism of powerful external enemies and an imposed isolation. The United States, which since 1946 had thrown its weight behind the Guomindang in the Civil War, now sought to perpetuate a divided China through backing the Chiang Kai-shek splinter regime on Taiwan. Within less than a year of the founding of the People's Republic, the U.S.-led blockade deprived China of access to trade, capital, and technology. China was barred from assuming its place in the United Nations and denied recognition as well as trade by most other nations within the orbit of American power. Most critical was the fact that beginning in 1950 China was locked in combat with the United States in Korea. Self-reliance was a virtue born of necessity.

The embattled new state enjoyed three potentially important assets. First, successful leadership of war and revolution over the preceding decade earned the Chinese Communists a national mandate for change such as no Chinese state power had ever enjoyed. Coming in the wake of a century of national humiliation and the undermining of confidence in Chinese values, that mandate rested in part on the widespread conviction that the earlier Guomindang regime had betrayed the basic interests of nation and people. New policies were clearly in order. Moreover, the Chinese Communist Party had sunk deep roots in rural communities throughout the countryside, positioning itself to stand in the forefront of social and economic change as it had already done in the initial rounds of land revolution. Second, China enjoyed the support of the Soviet Union, support which received concrete expression in the 1950 Sino-Soviet Treaty of Friendship and Cooperation and the subsequent extension both of a Soviet nuclear umbrella (of vital importance at the peak of U.S. hostility toward China) and of economic, military, technical, and planning assistance as China embarked on the path of industrialization.

Finally, the new government could build on the residual strengths of a society which, to be sure, had been humbled and shattered over the preceding century of war and disintegration, but which nevertheless had embedded in its collective experience and psyche traditions of productive labor, nationhood, sometimes explosive resistance to oppression, and patterns of cooperation rooted in family, lineage, and village experience. The Party's leadership of the peasant-based anti-Japanese resistance demonstrated the capacity of the peasantry to organize, to mobilize, and to grow in the context of a movement which respected its subsistence needs and local gods and which attempted to locate the foundations for change on such common practices as rural mutual aid and the cohesiveness of village structures.[4]

THE LEADERSHIP VISION OF A NEW CHINA

In late 1947, as the Communists prepared for the major offensive which would soon bring them to the threshold of state power, the leadership delineated a strategic direction which was to prevail over the next five years. How would it be possible to achieve the humane goals for which they had fought for more than twenty years, goals of assuring national independence and building in a poor and backward peasant society a prosperous and equitable nation free from class exploitation? The Central Committee statement, "On the Present Situation and Our Tasks," drafted by Mao, sought to respond to this question and establish the parameters for social change.[5] We see here clearly articulated for the first time a concept of stages of development which proved to be one of the seminal concepts guiding the transition to socialism in China. The resolution set forth measures designed to elicit broad popular support for programs of controlled social change in both rural and urban areas.

In the countryside, "our policy is to rely on the poor peasants and unite solidly with the middle peasants to abolish the feudal and semifeudal system of exploitation...." While stressing the satisfaction of poor-peasant demands for land, the Party sharply criticized ultra-left tendencies which threatened to infringe on middle-peasant interests, policies which would not only create deep rifts within the ranks of the people, but would also conflict with the effort to promote economic growth. Similarly, the document asserted that the essence of a new democratic industrial policy is to "confiscate monopoly capital" and "protect the industry and commerce of the national bourgeoisie." Without proclaiming the initiation of a socialist development strategy at this time, the leadership was preparing the ground for the transition.

With the state controlling the commanding heights of industry following the nationalization of the larger enterprises, and with poor- and middle-peasant leadership in firm control in the villages from 1947, policymakers saw benefits to be reaped from the carefully monitored development of smaller enterprises owned by the national bourgeoisie, petty handicraft production, and the middle- and rich-peasant economy, which would provide resources for accumulation besides contributing to bringing prosperity to the countryside.

By 1949 publicly owned means of production (much of it previously nationalized by the Guomindang regime) may have accounted for as much as 80 percent of China's capital stock, and the state took a central role in banking, trade and transport, but the great majority of small enterprises remained in private hands. Similarly, the land revolution program of "land to the tillers" was oriented toward the creation of independent commodity producers in the countryside. The goal of collectivization remained, but the Central Committee document saw the transformation of the agrarian economy as "developing step by step from individual to collective."

Already in 1947, in fact as early as 1943, the leadership had begun seriously to conceptualize the transition to socialism in China's countryside. It was inspired by Lenin's brief but suggestive writing on cooperation and also, it appears, by careful study of the heavy price which the Soviet people and economy had paid for forced collectivization. China would never repeat those mistakes. Social transformation at each stage would rest on the active participation of the majority, ensuring the popular flavor of social movements, minimizing direct coercion by party and state, and facilitating the combination of social revolution and economic development as in the land revolution. This leadership vision united the Party at the highest echelons on the eve of the founding of the People's Republic.

The strategy for the transition period was one of controlled revolutionary change by stages, each resting on a broad base of popular support and active participation, and each involving testing at the grass-roots level to devise measures appropriate to Chinese conditions and popular consciousness.

THE TRANSITION TO
SOCIALISM IN CHINA

In the years 1947-1952, China basically completed land revolution throughout the countryside along with economic recovery from a century or more of war. Only with the completion of these tasks and the drawing to a close of the Korean War with the July 1953 armistice did the Party proclaim the end of the new democratic phase and the inauguration of its program for the transition to socialism. In August 1953 Mao succinctly set forth the tasks for the new period in the form of "the general line for the transition to socialism":

The party's general line or general task for the transition period is basically to accomplish the country's industrialization and the socialist transformation of agriculture, handicrafts and capitalist industry and commerce over a fairly long period of time.[6]

In this statement the Party highlighted two pressing tasks for the early phases of the transition. The first was economic development, centered on industrialization, to overcome the legacy of poverty and economic stagnation. Second was the long-term, phased transformation from private to socialist ownership — including both collective and state forms of ownership — of the means of production. Both of these projects were already under way. Both would be accelerated with the inauguration of the general line. Both left open the larger and more difficult long-term tasks of ensuring that the new public and collective institutions would indeed be responsive to the authority and interests of the immediate producers, a task which may properly be regarded as the core of the transition process and one to which we will return to treat at greater length below.

At the heart of the first goal was the First Five-Year Plan for Development of the National Economy, spanning the period from

1953 to 1957. That plan, drawn up on the basis of Soviet advice and predicated on extensive Soviet technical and financial assistance, emphasized the dynamic role of large, centralized heavy industrial complexes (notably steel) in initiating China's industrial transformation. In this respect it paralleled early Soviet five-year plans. Simultaneously, however, the socialist transformation of ownership was to proceed with the staged formation of progressively larger and more advanced cooperative forms in agriculture and the gradual extension of state ownership in industry. Here we find the Chinese leadership drawing on its own experience in leading the peasant movement over the preceding decades and charting a path quite different from that which the Bolsheviks had pioneered in the Soviet Union.

Both elements, the change in ownership systems and economic development, are central to socialist development in underdeveloped countries in general and China in particular. But the transition to socialism is ultimately a far more complex process which can be grasped only within a more fully elaborated theoretical framework. In attempting to develop such a framework for assessing the socialist transition in China, we center our discussion first on the implications of change in ownership.

The transition in ownership involves the transfer from predominantly private ownership to cooperative, collective, and state forms of ownership of the major means of production. Stated differently, socialist societies incorporate a mix of private, cooperative or collective, and state ownership forms, and socialist development implies the progressive restriction of private ownership in favor of cooperative or collective and state ownership. The development of collective and state ownership forms, besides eliminating the exploitation and inequality rooted in unequal ownership of the means of production, makes possible (but does not assure) equitable implementation of the socialist principle of remuneration based on labor, "to each according to one's work." It also provides a framework within which economic planning can be implemented, allowing an increasing share of resources to be rationally allocated in accord with society's needs and interests rather than hoping that this end will be served as a by-product of competitive and profit-maximizing behavior.

Socialist development does not require the immediate elimination of all forms of private ownership or of the market, but rather their progressive restriction as cooperative and state systems and

planning networks develop the capacity to expand their scope and
effectively serve popular needs. These strictures are essential if
the transition to socialism is to rest on foundations of broad majority support and if it is to contribute to the economic well-being
of the great majority. Here we pose again the case for stages of
development within the transition. The pace of change, if it is to
rest on popular consciousness rather than state coercion, must be
governed by a complex calculus involving, among other factors,
popular consciousness, the balance of class forces, the capacity of
cooperative and state institutions to manage the economy, and the
economic and technological level of society. The history of socialist experiments and, above all, the collectivization of agriculture has been littered with the corpses of premature or miscalcu-
lated ownership changes which can result only in large-scale coercion to maintain the system, economic reverses, or abandonment
of the changes.

Changes in ownership and economic planning are necessary but
not sufficient conditions for the transition to socialism. In our
view, the sine qua non of the transition to socialism is the process
by which the forms of state or cooperative ownership become invested with the substance of mastery by the direct producers, that
is by industrial workers, peasants, technicians, scientists, teachers, health workers, and other working people. This poses the
most complex, and in many ways the most intractable, theoretical and practical issues of the transition. The transition requires
the formulation and implementation of processes which assure the
direct mastery of working people over the workplace, the state,
and the society at every level. Yet it also involves the creation
of a substantial state bureaucracy to pursue socialist goals and
implement planning. Under these conditions, our concern is with
the process by which values and institutions change to facilitate
the expanded political engagement and to enhance the material and
cultural interests of classes and groups which have been excluded
from the political process and victimized by the workings of the
economic order.

Here we touch upon the central issue of the socialist state. We
may pose this question: If the old exploiting classes (landlords,
capitalists, etc.) no longer exist as classes as a result of expropriation or other forms of transformation of ownership, and no
longer control the means of production, what interests other than
those of the immediate producers might be served by the socialist

state? The answer of course is the interests of those who control
the levers of power of the party-state, that is cadres, managers,
and officials at all levels. Once ownership and control of the principal means of production pass to collective and state, then the
most important social cleavages in society can no longer be comprehended in ownership terms as conventionally defined. They
come to center rather on the question of differential access to the
wealth and power associated with the state, the party, and the collective. Moreover, the importance of this potential state-society
cleavage is accentuated by the fact that the transition to socialism
has everywhere strengthened the power of the state through the
unification of economic and political authority in its hands.

   In short, both the central promise and the central contradiction
within societies engaged in the transition to socialism center on
the role of the state, which can serve at once as a vehicle for advancing and concentrating the interests of the direct producers in
socialist society, and as a roadblock preventing the articulation and
expression of those interests. Examining the process of socialist
transition as a whole brings to the fore a series of contradictions
whose resolution is a necessary condition for realizing the mastery
of the direct producers as the substance of socialist society. In
addition to those contradictions concerning the state, a set of inter-
related contradictions concerns the economy. For without economic
development, even the most ambitious of social reforms in a poor
and backward nation will be doomed to create a poor and backward
socialism. A consideration of both types of contradictions is necessary to clarify the core issues underlying socialist development
in China.

STATE, COLLECTIVE, AND INDIVIDUAL

   What is the appropriate sphere and what are the limits of individual rights and state power? The issues have reverberated
through the centuries-long debate over the nature of the state and
the rights of the individual in Western political discourse. From
the late 1940s, and more explicitly from 1953, the Chinese leadership embarked on a program of large-scale, planned social change
to guide this poor agrarian nation along the road to socialist development. In the period of the transition to socialism in China, the
dimensions of the conflict between the party-state and the individual
have been shaped by Chinese political traditions emphasizing the

prerogatives of the ruler and the narrow scope of individual rights as well as by the legacy of the Leninist party and practices associated with the rise of the Chinese Communist movement, of which the mass line is the most important. In addition, the institutional structures of the People's Republic, with a vast collective sector embracing 80 percent of the population, require that we locate the issues in the matrix of relationships among state, collective, and individual.

Here we note a central problem which would continue throughout the entire period of transition. At the heart of socialist development lies the tension between a vision of the socialist future projected by the leadership in the form of theory and policy directives, and the commitment to the principle that working people, particularly the peasants and industrial workers, must shape that future. Within the Marxist tradition, that tension has historically been embedded within the parameters of the concepts of the dictatorship of the proletariat as put forward by Marx and Engels and developed by Lenin, of democratic centralism and the vanguard party as developed by the Bolsheviks, and of mass line politics linking leadership and masses as refined in China during and after the anti-Japanese resistance. It would be intensified by the urgency of simultaneously accelerating economic development and industrialization. In China's mass line and in the concept of development by stages, this tension is by no means dissolved. These approaches contribute, however, to recognition of the principle that the institutional configurations of socialism must be created by the Chinese people in ways appropriate to their needs and in resonance with prevailing, deeply rooted values associated with family, village, and culture.[7]

Analysis of conflicting approaches to the resolution of this tension, which is formed not only in China but in all socialist states, runs through many of the essays included in this volume. The Party's strategy for the socialist transition in the countryside, for the creation of new social relations and institutions as the first step in overcoming stagnation and exploitation, centered on the formation of progressively larger and more advanced forms of agricultural producers' cooperatives. The cooperatives were to be based on the voluntary participation of members who, with state support, embraced cooperative agriculture and created organizational forms appropriate to their needs. Appropriate to their needs, yet mass line leadership principles involved the mediation of the party and state and assumed the compatibility of popular needs and state interests. The problem, however, lies precisely in the realm of continuing conflicts among individual (and household), collective, and state.

This conflict becomes manifest, for example, in conflicts over the allocation of the surplus as the household strives to expand the realm of consumption, the collective to secure access to the surplus for local accumulation, and the state to appropriate the surplus for national accumulation and other public purposes. Similarly, individual, collective, and state clash repeatedly over the allocation of labor in the countryside. We note, for example, individual pressure to expand the scope of economic activity in the private sector or to have access to urban jobs; efforts by the collective to maintain high participation rates in the collective economy and to expand the scope of collective decision-making in such areas as choice of crop and sideline production; and the attempt by the state to control the scope of population movement and to direct private and collective economic activities according to its own priorities for regional and national economic growth, accumulation, and consumption. Because the power and scope of the party-state has expanded dramatically in China since 1949, and indeed in all socialist states, the danger that cooperative and individual sectors may be squeezed poses one of the central problems of socialist development. The outcome of the issue is of crucial importance for the pace and quality of economic development.

In the mid-fifties, conflict in the countryside between state and individuals centered on the question of the pace and process of cooperative transformation, a process governed in significant part by the ability of the new cooperative institutions to provide increased security and incomes for the majority of the peasantry and, on this foundation of rising productivity and progress toward material well-being, to generate support for the expanded scope and scale of cooperation. For only on such foundations could cooperation become anything but an organization of the state imposed on the peasantry. However, as Mark Selden shows in his essay below, at a critical moment in the transformation of agriculture, the party-state intervened decisively to impose nationwide collectivization in ways which challenged basic principles of the mass-line process. The race to collectivization associated with the 1955-56 "high tide" short-circuited the process of gradual, voluntary transformation. The result was to juxtapose state interests in collectivization and resource centralization with the material interests of a large sector of the peasantry. For the first time in the postliberation period, the Party set in motion a process which can perhaps best be comprehended as social engineering from above in the sense that social change lacked broad-based popular support. The setback to the democratic promise of the socialist transition was profound.

If this analysis is correct, we have uncovered a perhaps surprising pattern of congruence between Chinese and Soviet collectivization processes.[8] And not only of collectivization. Edward Friedman's analysis of Maoism, Stalinism, and Titoism as approaches to the transition to socialism suggests that at critical conjunctures, notably during the socialist high tide, the Great Leap Forward and the Cultural Revolution periods, certain striking similarities between Maoist and Stalinist politics may be observed: particularly the insistence of powerholders at the center that policies be implemented which directly conflict with the material interests of large numbers of people, including a substantial portion of the immediate producers. Friedman casts these issues in a broad framework which goes beyond the comparative study of the socialist transition to illuminate the direct relationships which have shaped the policies and prospects of socialist development in specific countries.

A critical issue for the transition may be posed in this way: What political and economic resources are in the hands of individuals and of cooperative or collective units which can be used to resist arbitrary policies by the party-state, policies in which the center imposes its will at the expense of unwilling localities and individuals? Friedman's analysis suggests that so long as political and economic power remain concentrated in the hands of the party-state center, the potential for despotism and manipulation remains high.[9] This view, associated with proponents of a socialism hospitable to the expanded role of the market and economic decentralization, developed in China in the mid-1950s and then disappeared from view for two decades, only to reappear with new vigor in the late 1970s. In the 1980s it occupies an important though hardly unchallenged position at the center of the reform agenda.

The Cultural Revolution offered an apparent escape from the dilemma of the party-state. Proponents of uninterrupted revolution and continued class struggle did in fact develop a cutting critique of the dangers of bureaucratism, of statist tendencies to monopolize and abuse power which threatened to return China to the "capitalist road." Ironically, however, as Andrew Walder's study of the working class in the Cultural Revolution demonstrates, the arbitrary power of the party-state increased dramatically during the Cultural Revolution. This was the result of processes which included carrying to dizzying heights a cult of Mao Zedong; the failure of the Cultural Revolution to create institutional processes which could provide effective expression to worker demands (one of which would surely have been an end to the twenty-year freeze on real wages); the rejection as "revisionist" of proposals which would have decentralized power to the enterprise level or given greater latitude to collective institutions; and the destruction of the few existing institutional vehicles (however weak) for expressing worker demands such as the trade unions. Ironically, as Walder shows, line managers and Party officials in the factories gained unchecked powers in a movement which began as an attack on bureaucracy. Far from initiating a liberating break with Stalinist industrial policies of centralized authority, Walder concludes, the Cultural Revolution initiated a "profoundly conservative reaction to a proposed set of market-oriented reforms that would move away from the Soviet framework established under Stalin."

The problem of the high-handed wielding of state power is also central to William Hinton's report on thirty years of revolutionary change in Longbow Village, the site of his classic account of the land revolution, Fanshen. This is a story which reveals the potential of rural communities to transform their lives in ways which introduce new economic and technological possibilities and improve the livelihood of everyone. But it is also a story which reveals a pattern of the uses and frequently abuses of state power at the expense of the peasantry. If we read him correctly, Hinton implies a certain continuity between the imperial state and the party-state with respect to the position allocated to the peasantry: "In the real order that determines priorities in China," he concludes, "peasants occupy the lowest rung, just as they always have historically."

We see the immense power of the socialist state as a two-edged sword. To take a single example, one of the levers of party-state control in China is the authority to regulate population movement. Looked at in its most favorable light, this facilitates the ability of the socialist state to prevent the blind flood of population out of the countryside into the cities, where it could form the slums characteristic of capitalist third world countries or absorb resources the state must set aside for capital construction. In China, however, this controlled movement also means, among other things, that peasants cannot leave their native villages in search of work elsewhere (the poorer the region and village, the more onerous the burden); permanent movement from poorer mountainous districts to more prosperous regions as well as movement to the cities is barred; even temporary movements are officially controlled. A worker or peasant who wishes to travel by train or plane to another region or city requires written approval, obtained of course from the local administrative office. The power of the state, in short, extends to virtually every aspect of Chinese life, creating vast potential for the abuse of power. It was above all during the Cultural Revolution, moreover, at the very moment when criticisms of party and state reached a peak, that abuses of state power were carried to disastrous extremes.

Yet in surveying the first thirty years of the People's Republic, we conclude that the power of the state has also been a liberating force for the vast majority of Chinese people. It has been instrumental in assisting working people to free themselves from exploitation based on the unequal ownership of property; it has contributed to women's liberation (the completion of which remains, however, a major task for the socialist transition in China); it has attempted with considerable success to ensure the basic welfare, health, and educational needs of the entire population; and it has initiated and promoted the economic development on which the Chinese people's aspirations for the future depend. This performance, whether gauged against the record of previous Chinese governments or viewed in light of the magnitude of the problems confronted, is impressive. It would be as one-sided to perceive only the destructive or coercive power of the state as it would be to perceive only its liberating characteristics. The tensions between state and society and between state and individual are rooted in the problematic of the transition process. The state creates at once the necessary conditions for continuing this process and the principle obstacles to its attainment.

THE ECONOMICS OF THE TRANSITION

Related at every level to the question of the state in the socialist transition are questions of the economy. The importance of the economic issues is heightened by the fact that each of the socialist revolutions has taken place in an underdeveloped country, making rapid improvements in the material well-being of the population imperative at the very time when the pace of accumulation and of social change must be stepped up dramatically; this problem has been nowhere more acute than in China. The issue, moreover, goes deeper than that of competing uses for available resources, for the allocation issue must be resolved in the context of the institutional transformation which the pursuit of socialist goals requires.

By 1952, China had completed, in the main, a remarkably succesful period of reconstruction, bringing output in nearly every industry back to preliberation peaks, restoring agricultural production, and bringing inflation under firm control. The time had come to turn from reconstruction to construction, bringing to the fore the question of where to find the savings to finance a greatly stepped-up pace of capital formation. Since the ultimate meaning of saving is not consuming, the problem may be rephrased as one of finding sectors of the economy where consumption could be depressed below the level of output.[10] Accounting for only seven percent of national income, the entire modern sector was scarcely large enough to fill this role.

Only the rural agricultural-based economy had the potential to supply the initial resources for accumulation. As Victor Lippit has shown,[11] a conservatively estimated 19 percent of national income had flowed to rural property owners — landlords, rich peasants, and moneylenders — prior to the revolution, constituting a potential fund for development finance. Since these income flows were in exchange for no productive service, they could in principle be rerouted to serve social purposes without adversely affecting production. Diverting these flows to the state would have made them available to finance capital construction, but the land revolution did not in the first instance divert them to the state. Rather, in dividing landlord holdings among poor peasant households and eliminating rent payments and debt obligations, it had the immediate effect of increasing income for the rural poor. The problem for public policy then became how to extract a <u>portion</u> of these peasant gains to finance economic development.

In fact, the state succeeded in extracting slightly over one-half of these gains through taxation and control over the terms of trade between industry and agriculture, still leaving the peasant beneficiaries of the land revolution with substantial improvements in personal income.[12] The contribution of the agricultural sector to development finance, however, did not end with the land revolution. As Kojima Reiitsu shows in his essay in this volume, the extraction of surplus from the villages has remained the single largest and most consistent source of investment finance since the founding of the People's Republic.

For many observers, the fact that resources were flowing out of agriculture rather than serving to improve living standards was masked by the improvement in agriculture's terms of trade since the early 1950s. This improvement obscured the fact that the terms of trade were so unfavorable at the outset that all the improvement to date still leaves agricultural prices unduly low relative to industrial prices, whether considered historically, in terms of embodied labor contents, or in terms of the price relationships competitive markets would establish. Further, Nicholas Lardy has argued in an unpublished paper, "Intersectoral Resource Flows in Chinese Economic Development," that official data on relative prices omit agricultural producer goods, an increasingly important component of rural purchases, and that the prices of such goods compared to agricultural prices are extremely high relative to the price ratios which prevail elsewhere in the world. The result is that China's peasants have borne a substantial, even disproportionate, share of the burden of development. Since the 1950s, the peasantry has received a barely nominal return from this sacrifice in the form of improved living standards. This issue is at the heart of the agonizing reappraisal of collective agricultural accumulation, prices, and income policies which has surfaced in China, particularly since 1978, a reappraisal explored in great depth around the rise and fall of the Dazhai model in the essay Tang Tsou, Marc Blecher, and Mitch Meisner have contributed to the volume.

Reliance on the agricultural sector to bear the burden of modernization was not sustained without efforts to find supplementary forms of development finance. As Kojima observes, one of the recurrent themes in China's modern economic history has been the attempt to find new sources of accumulation in a nation with slender financial resources. The Great Leap Forward (1958-1960) strategy, for example, rested on expanded collective labor investment, that is, capital accumulation pursued by massive labor-intensive projects — especially water conservancy — in the countryside. This was the key to the Great Leap concept of accumulation. But the Great Leap failed. In the end it produced not the desired breakthrough in accumulation and productivity but the gravest economic crisis the People's Republic has experienced.[13] After a period of sharply reduced labor mobilization and economic recovery, elements of this approach to accumulation reemerged during the Cultural Revolution decade (1966-76), albeit with reduced intensity.

Surveying the results of China's monumental effort to intensify rural labor and increase accumulation, one fact stands out: for over twenty years rural output and income, measured on a per capita basis, failed to increase significantly. Not until 1978 did per capita food grain production reach the level attained in 1957.[14] And whereas income from collective labor in the rural areas was 57 yuan in 1957, it rose only to 65 yuan in 1977, about half in food and half in cash.[15] At 1 yuan = $0.65, the gain in cash income was U.S. $2.60 per capita over a twenty-year span, or 13¢ per year, scarcely enough to meet the cash needs of a rural population still desperately poor. Moreover, if this return is measured against labor time expended, the results reveal a decline over twenty years.[16]

For industrial workers too, the pattern of frequent wage increases during the First Five-Year Plan was broken for two decades after 1957, with real wages remaining essentially flat over that span.[17] If the surplus extracted from the countryside was not going to the workers, where was it going? In essence, it was going into a rising volume of accumulation which from the late fifties reached extremely high levels — except for the 1960-65 period when the economic dislocations caused by excessive accumulation forced a temporary reduction in the accumulation rate. The high rate of accumulation, however, did not bring a commensurate increase in the rate of economic growth, a failure reflected in the behavior of the incremental capital-output ratio (ICOR). The ICOR indicates the number of dollars of investment needed to produce each additional dollar of output, and a rising ratio indicates that an ever-greater volume of resources is needed to sustain a given rate of economic growth. The sharply rising ratio in China, a phenomenon which paralleled the experience of other centrally planned economies in the postwar period (see Table 1), meant that practically all of society's incremental output had to be reinvested to sustain economic growth, leaving little or nothing to increase personal incomes.

Between 1952 and 1978 industrial output in China grew by an average of 11.2 percent per year and agricultural output by 3.2 per-

cent.[18]   Given the difficult initial conditions, the industrial performance can be considered excellent and the agricultural one creditable. Together, growth in the two sectors drove the Chinese economy forward at an average annual pace of 4-6 percent in real terms
or 2-4 percent per capita if the average annual population growth
of about 2 percent is taken into account. Yet because an increasing
share of national income was going into accumulation to sustain this
growth, real wages and peasant incomes languished from the late
fifties.

Table 1

Incremental Capital-Output Ratios (ICORs) in
Selected Centrally Planned Economies, 1950-65

Time period	Soviet Union	Bulgaria	Czecho-slovakia	East Germany	Hungary	Poland
1950-55	1.77	1.86	2.61	1.28	4.04	2.75
1955-60	2.53	1.92	3.14	2.70	2.84	3.68
1960-65	3.83	3.89	14.28	6.02	3.65	4.62

Note: ICORs show a statistical relationship between investment and growth
in output; they do not indicate a causal relationship since factors other than investment affect output. The ratios indicated here, therefore, do not prove that
the efficacy of investment has been decreasing in centrally planned economies
or that systemic factors have been responsible for this. Rather, they constitute
one piece of evidence that such is the case, albeit evidence whose significance
is heightened by the fact that it points strongly in the same direction both internationally and over time.
Source: Radoslav Selucky, Economic Reforms in Eastern Europe, Z. Elias,
tr. (New York: Praeger, 1972), p. 4; cited in Anthony Scaperlanda, "Human
Capital and Economic Progress in Eastern Europe," in John Adams, ed., Institutional Economics (Boston: Martinus Nijhoff, 1980), p. 129.

During the First Five-Year Plan period (1953-57), China devoted
24.2 percent of its material output to investment. At the height of
the Great Leap Forward in 1960 this figure reached an extraordinary 39.6 percent, and after dropping in the early sixties it rose
again, reaching an average of 33 percent during the period 1970-
78.[19] Yet industrial growth in the seventies was slower than it was
in the First Five-Year Plan period, reflecting the fact that each
new dollar of investment was yielding smaller returns in added

output. Thus during the First Five-Year Plan period, industrial output grew at an average annual rate of 15.8 percent,[20] giving an ICOR of 1.53 where investment is taken as a percentage of material output and related to industrial growth.[21]   The comparable figure for the 1970-77 period, when the investment rate reached 32.6 percent and industrial output grew by an average of 9.7 percent annually, is 3.26.

Thus the ICOR approximately doubled between the mid-fifties and the 1970s, indicating that twice as high a level of investment was needed for each additional unit of output. These figures are admittedly crude estimates, but the declining efficacy of investment to which they point is unmistakable. The reasons for this, as Carl Riskin points out in his contribution to this volume, are familiar to students of centrally planned economies. The rigidity of economic decision-making, the hoarding of raw materials, uneconomic vertical integration (so plant managers could assure themselves of supplies), and the inflexibility of the system tend to grow disproportionately as the economy expands, decreasing its efficiency.[22]   That China's experience is common to centrally planned economies is shown in Table 1.

The long run interests of the immediate producers surely lie in economic growth. Only a larger national income can ultimately fulfill the material needs of the Chinese people. But consumption gains cannot be postponed indefinitely on the basis of the prior claims of accumulation without severely undermining the incentive to produce and accumulate. In this sense, consumption and accumulation are not parts of a zero-sum game. The problem of accumulation in China, then, is first, who should bear the burden, and second, how to adjust that burden to achieve optimal balance between accumulation and the allocation of resources for other social purposes, including raising popular living standards, but also the allocation of resources for education, health, and culture. A socialist country which is unable to distribute the burden equitably and which fails to move toward satisfying the material aspirations of the immediate producers — which even goes so far as to reject the legitimacy of demands for higher incomes — is surely courting crisis. Recognition of the crisis of accumulation and, the other side of the coin, the crisis of consumption, has contributed in no small part to the policy reversals of the post-Mao period.

Perhaps nowhere is the evidence of reversal more dramatic than in the case of Dazhai, which for more than a decade stood as the model for other production brigades, indeed the entire countryside, to emulate. During this period the slogan "In agriculture, learn from Dazhai" reverberated throughout China, and a close analysis of the rise and fall of Dazhai can reveal a great deal about the forces underlying policy change in post-Mao China. The essay which Tang Tsou, Marc Blecher, and Mitch Meisner have contributed to this volume undertakes just such an analysis, clarifying the reasons for which practically every basic principle for which Dazhai stood has been replaced in subsequent agricultural policy.

According to their analysis, the underlying principle of the Dazhai model is that

the collective unit should assume as many functions as ... feasible in production, distribution, the supply of facilities and services to satisfy individual needs ... and the provision of social welfare while the role of individuals should shrink except insofar as they work through organizational channels for the collective unit.

Other essays in the volume place the Dazhai model in a broader context by making clear the extent to which the subordination of individuals to the collective and the state came to characterize every aspect of social existence in the final years of the Maoist era. But while emphasizing the value of collectivity and community has utopian overtones, suggesting a means of overcoming the isolation, alienation and degradation of individuals which capitalist society often imposes, the reality of China in the period culminating in the Cultural Revolution was anything but utopian. Every aspect of life became politicized, individuals lacked redress against injustice and the arbitrary abuse of power, incomes were kept at extremely low levels, and reason itself was assaulted by the attempt to reduce all social issues to the "two-line" struggle between the capitalist-roaders and the socialist-roaders. Under these conditions, the class interests of working people in all walks of life — their interests in material prosperity, social justice, equality, cultural development, and democratic rule in which all could participate — could scarcely find representation.

The economic organization of any society can be thought of in the first instance as reflecting the interests of dominant classes in that society. In capitalist and precapitalist societies, the dominant classes are composed of those who own disproportionate shares of land and capital and are able as a consequence to receive as income a share of the fruits of the labor of tenants, serfs, workers, slaves, or other direct producers. The institutions and the power of the state in such societies tend to sustain, rationalize, and perpetuate this situation. Socialist development implies the reshaping of economic institutions and production relationships to reflect the dominance of people engaged in productive activity. The revolutionary seizure of power and the transformation of ownership relations is just the start of this protracted process. It is worth recalling that the triumph of capitalism on a world scale required a transition period of 500 years. It would be extraordinary if the essential problems of the transition to socialism were resolved in just three quarters of a century or, in China, in just three decades. Of course they have not, not least of all because the socialist experiment is being attempted in an extremely poor, underdeveloped nation. Moreover, China's participation in the capitalist world economy promises to raise new difficulties of a continuing nature even if, as its promoters contend, such participation adeptly addresses existing problems and contributes to economic growth.

From the earliest stages of the emergence of capitalism as a world system in the sixteenth century, the self-expansive power of capital has projected itself beyond national borders to shape a world economy suited to its needs. Although that power has been shaping or blocking the development process almost everywhere in the Third World during the second half of the twentieth century, its direct impact on the People's Republic during the Maoist era was minimal, a reflection of China's great size — which made a large measure of self-sufficiency possible — the isolation imposed on China by its great-power adversaries, and the deliberate choice (perhaps making a virtue of necessity) of pursuing a policy of self-reliance. In the post-Mao period of reform, however, rapprochement with the United States has made possible a new era of international economic relations which China has begun to exploit avidly.

On the surface, the logic for such action appears compelling. Foreign credits make possible maintaining high accumulation rates even while expanding consumption; technology developed abroad can be "borrowed" and adapted to domestic needs far more rapidly and less expensively than it can be developed from scratch at home; imports of complete factories (e.g., steel, fertilizer) can be used to replace imports of finished products; foreign management methods can be adopted to raise industrial productivity; and foreign tourists provide needed foreign exchange. Integration with the

world capitalist system, however, is not costless because the economic relations involved are not purely instrumental in nature.
That is to say, even if the anticipated contributions to China's development are realized, the economic relations into which China
enters will inevitably have a shaping influence on China itself. The
question is one of the extent and nature of that influence, the degree
of penetration of foreign capital and its overall impact on socialist
development.

Overseas indebtedness gives foreign capital a "legitimate" concern with domestic policies; the need to refinance foreign loans
especially has played a major role in giving foreign capital directly
and through international financial organizations considerable influence over economic policy in Third World countries. Foreign
technology is typically suited to different factor proportions — in
the advanced capitalist countries capital is relatively cheap and
labor dear — so that its use in underdeveloped countries affords
much less employment than native technologies. Foreign technology
and management are suited to the relations between capital and labor that prevail in capitalist countries; using them in a socialist
country may reproduce those relations. And wealthy tourists bring
material culture and other values that may not be suited to socialist
development. The list of hazards can be extended indefinitely, but
the central point should already be clear: participation in the
capitalist world economy involves more than utilizing a convenient
new instrument for economic development since it has the power
to shape the user as well.

This does not mean that a policy of economic isolation offers the
only or the surest path to the socialist transition. To the contrary,
the potential benefits to be derived from participation in the world
economy are substantial. It is, moreover, highly questionable
whether any country in the world can withdraw into its own shell
and pursue its own purposes in isolation for an extended interval.
The issue, rather, is twofold: first, the extent to which Chinese
policy-makers become conscious of and adopt successful countermeasures to the shaping influences of the capitalist world system.
Second, and most important, is whether three decades of socialist
development have strengthened China's economic and political position to a degree that will enable it to cope with world economic
forces. The issue here is precisely parallel to the issue of the use
of the market domestically: both participation in the world economy
and the use of the market are necessary conditions for social and

economic progress, but both have the power to subvert the socialist objectives for which they are employed unless consciously, carefully controlled. Whether the socialist transition will be aided or compromised by the new international economic relations into which China is entering will be influenced significantly by the acuity of public policy in the years to come.

In the first three decades of the People's Republic, however, the decisive issues governing the transition to socialism have primarily been domestic ones. Thus the focus of most of the essays in this volume is on domestic affairs, and many of them, concerned foremost with exploring problem areas, look closely at the diverse ways in which the interests of working people have been compromised by state policies, most clearly during the periods of the high tide of collectivization (1955-56), the Great Leap Forward (1958-1960), and the Great Proletarian Cultural Revolution (particularly 1966-69). We have focused on these contradictions of the transition period not because they have overshadowed or negated the achievements of the People's Republic, but because they have been and remain among the most intractable and important problems which socialist societies must resolve if they are to achieve a measure of their potential.

The interests of working people extend beyond material reward to issues of control of the workplace — obviously within the constraints imposed by objective conditions — and to gaining a decisive voice in decision-making at every level of society. They extend further to the creation of social arrangements which reflect their interest in security, equality, freedom of expression and so forth. The progress of the socialist transition, that is, the restructuring of society to reflect the authority and interest of working people, must be assessed in the light of the full array of their interests and concerns. Yet a series of contradictions confronts all attempts at reordering society to achieve socialist goals.

CONTRADICTIONS OF THE TRANSITION PERIOD

A central element of the transition process is the transformation of individual consciousness, the creation of a consciousness that grasps both itself and the broader society simultaneously. Although the creation of socialist consciousness is an integral part of the transition, those party and state leaders who attempt to force the

pace inevitably find themselves caught up in censorship and manipulation of thought. Thus hierarchy and repression are recreated
in a new form which is ultimately anathema to socialism. We have
already referred to the tension which exists between a leadership
committed to the realization of its vision of socialist society and
the socialist principle requiring the initiative and active participation in social change of the entire working population. Resolving
the contradiction which emerges from this is at the heart of the
question of achieving a genuine socialist democracy, at once the
most urgent and elusive political objective of the transition period.

The immediate pursuit of socialist objectives and the requirements of economic development pose another central contradiction,
one which is often discussed in the socialist literature as the issue
of the appropriate relations between the forces and relations of
production, where the forces of production are associated with development and the relations of production with ultimate socialist
objectives. Thus equality, to choose a major example, is a core
element in socialist ideology, but a premature pursuit of equality
may do great damage to development by undermining incentives to
work. And the claim to legitimacy of a socialist state unable to
meet the material and public service needs of the population, needs
which depend on the success of development, would be severely undermined, bringing into question the entire socialist project.

On the other hand, inequality tends to be self-perpetuating. Thus
well-educated or powerfully situated parents living in urban areas
can give their children educational and other advantages peasant
parents cannot match. Or factory workers can obtain preferential
hiring for their children, and in the absence of an inheritance tax,
those with substantial savings can pass them on to their children
as well. All of these patterns of perpetuating inequality and creating
a constituency for its perpetuation exist in China. Perhaps just as
detrimental to the pursuit of egalitarian social goals in China, moreover, is the emphasis on individual material work incentives, which
has increasingly characterized public policy since the end of the
Cultural Revolution period in 1976. This may be necessary for economic development, particularly as an antidote to the combination
of inflated rhetoric and austerity of the Cultural Revolution period.
But there is no mechanism whereby people's consciousness will
automatically be transformed when the major goals of socialist
modernization have been attained. That is to say, an overriding
emphasis on material incentives will foster materialistic people

as well as higher material output.

Thus the dilemma posed for the transition of whether to pursue socialist goals directly or indirectly is a substantive one. As Carl Riskin's essay helps us to see, the reformers' insistence on economic rationality and the use of the market as an <u>instrument</u> for achieving social goals apparently fails to take into account the extent to which the market may generate its own goals by creating a mode of consciousness inconsistent with the socialist vision. Yet equally telling is Andrew Walder's critique of the industrial policies actually implemented during the Cultural Revolution, policies which by ignoring the legitimate material concerns of workers heightened materialism, which by seeking to spur work effort via mass campaigns made people suspicious of all ideology, and which proved that "vigilante" activity could scarcely make workers the masters of the workplace let alone of society as a whole.

Walder's essay highlights the extent to which efforts to pursue (and even impose) socialist goals directly during the Cultural Revolution tended to be counterproductive, a reflection of the failure of public policy to come to grips with the central contradictions of the age. By contrast, it cannot by any means be assumed a priori that the emphasis on socialist modernization that has come to characterize post-Mao public policy is detrimental to the pursuit of other socialist goals. Consider, for example, another dimension of the problem of inequality. In recent years, incomes in the countryside have evidently been growing more rapidly than those in the cities.[23] The result has been to reduce urban-rural inequality in percentage terms, and the number of brigades classified as "poor" with collective incomes averaging less than 50 yuan per capita dropped from 42.8 percent of the total number of brigades in 1976 to 27.7 percent in 1979, while those with incomes averaging under 40 yuan dropped from 24.2 percent to 8.2 percent of the total.[24]

The post-Mao economic reforms constitute in part a reaction to the excesses of the Cultural Revolution. The legitimacy of material concerns in a population that is still quite poor by international standards has been recognized, and material incentives and individual rewards for productive contributions have been reinstituted as core elements in the new development strategy. Yet the Cultural Revolution leadership was certainly correct to be wary of the power of the market economy to shape society according to its own logic, for the power of the market system to generate its own values, its potential as a kind of Frankenstein to shape the society rather than

serve as its instrument, poses the major threat to the modernization priorities of the 1980s.

The market nevertheless plays a necessary role within an overall
planning framework throughout the socialist transition for reasons
which have been clarified in part by the failure of the Cultural
Revolution to achieve a breakthrough as a strategy of accumulation
and development. That failure is expressed most clearly in the
persistence, even intensification, of social hierarchy, and in the
prolonged stagnation in worker and peasant incomes. The new
strategy seeks long-term rapid growth by restoring the harmony
between development and higher incomes. It also assumes that the
best prospect for addressing the question of hierarchy lies neither
with greater centralization of state power nor with political mobilization but in the expanded role of the market, the locality and the
plant, and a more circumscribed role for the party-state center.
The logic, most fully developed in the theory and practice of East
European socialist reformers, stresses the transfer of real decision-making authority from the state to production units and ultimately to immediate producers themselves. Previous Chinese decentralization measures explicitly rejected the transfer of authority
to the enterprises; administrative control by provincial and local
government officials simply replaced that by central government
officials. It should be stressed in this context that the market is
more than a tool that must be suffered to improve economic performance; it appears to be the only means by which real decision-
making authority can be assumed by direct producers.

Enterprise autonomy requires the creation of conditions in which
enterprises have the financial resources and authority to act independently rather than simply respond to orders issued from above.
This is contingent on the expanded scope of the market. Enterprise
autonomy provides no more assurance of worker control under socialism than it did, say, in the classic laissez-faire economies of
nineteenth century Western capitalism. But it does create a necessary precondition for progress toward worker control and does
address the central obstacle to its realization during the transition
period: the power of the state. The market can also contribute to
enhanced economic efficiency and reduction of the amount of investment needed to sustain economic growth and thus release the resources necessary for improvement in living standards. None of
this should obscure the dilemmas which haunt China's market socialists, the advocates of an expanded market role. As Carl Riskin

points out, China's price structure is far from rationalized and cannot be rationalized in the near future since prices serve many functions other than as allocative guides to decision-makers: prices affect income distribution, overall price stability is an important social goal in its own right, and subsidies for particular prices (e.g., house rents) cannot be readily altered without affecting people's sense of equity.

The market, then, appears as a necessary but dangerously volatile instrument in the socialist transition. Its dual nature constitutes one of the many contradictions that socialist countries inevitably confront in the transition process. Several of the essays in this volume suggest that the market must play a significant role in the transition process to increase economic efficiency, realize socialism's inherent potential for material prosperity, check bureaucratic power and extend the scope for initiative and responsibility among the immediate producers. Carl Riskin, however, highlights the hazards of the market system. Surface appearances to the contrary, we suggest that these two perspectives are not irreconcilable. The market must play a role in the transition to socialism in China and elsewhere; the challenge for socialist planners and citizens is to strike an appropriate balance which reduces the disruptive potential of the market while permitting appropriate scope for the contributions of the market and its role in mediating state power.

In analyzing the problems of state and economy in China's socialist transition, one cannot avoid being struck by the intensity of contradictions on every hand. There is no simple resolution to these contradictions, and certainly no resolution to be found in stressing one-sidedly one of the polarities of which each is constituted. Yet in examining the contradictions which are continually being created and recreated by social practice, we confront directly the key parameters governing the transition to socialism in China. The Great Leap Forward and Cultural Revolution created expectations that China's advance from socialism to communism was imminent. Few such illusions exist today in China or abroad. Our study underlines the ambitious goals which socialism has placed on the human agenda. It points to China's impressive progress in laying the foundations of socialist development in the matter of just a few decades. But above all it considers the twists and turns on the long road ahead if China is to continue the process whereby the forms of state or cooperative ownership become invested with the substance of mastery by the direct producers in a society advancing toward material abundance and the creation of a flourishing culture.

NOTES

1. Dwight Perkins, China's Modern Economy in Historical Perspective (Stanford: Stanford University Press, 1975), p. 134.
2. Alexander Eckstein, China's Economic Revolution (Cambridge: Cambridge University Press, 1977), p. 26.
3. Perkins, China's Modern Economy, p. 119. The figure is for 1933 and excludes a few modern services.
4. This argument draws on findings elaborated in the forthcoming study "Wugong: A Chinese Village in a Socialist State," by Edward Friedman, Kay Johnson, Paul Pickowicz, and Mark Selden, and on an earlier study by Mark Selden, The Yenan Way in Revolutionary China (Cambridge, Mass.: Harvard University Press, 1971).
5. Substantial excerpts from the original text are in Mark Selden, The People's Republic of China, A Documentary History of Revolutionary Change (New York: Monthly Review Press, 1979), pp. 169-75.
6. See Selden, The People's Republic of China, pp. 281-82.
7. This is not to imply that such values are immutable, merely that policy should not violate such norms existing at the specific moment in question.
8. Congruence. Not, of course, identity. Chinese collectivization was completed with little if any direct state violence; it was apparently actively supported by a significant portion of the poor peasantry; and it grew out of a decade of fruitful experience with cooperative agriculture. Nevertheless, as in the Soviet Union, the 1956 collectivization was essentially administratively imposed over the opposition of large sectors of the peasantry.
9. Alec Nove has emphasized the identical point in his critique of the writings of Charles Bettelheim on the transition to socialism. See Political Economy and Soviet Socialism (London: George Allen and Unwin, 1979), chapter 7.
10. If output grows over time, then this condition will be consistent with the growth of consumption. In China's case, however, as the essays by Kojima Reiitsu and Victor Lippit indicate, consumption standards did not improve materially between the end of the First Five-Year Plan in 1957 and the initiation of the reform program in 1977.
11. Victor Lippit, Land Reform and Economic Development in China (White Plains: M. E. Sharpe, 1974).
12. Ibid., p. 123.
13. It was not labor mobilization per se that deepened the crisis but the attempt to use it in place of rather than in addition to more conventional means of accumulation. Thus the Leap was characterized by disregard of economic accounting, reduction of peasant income by state actions which stifled peasant handicraft and sideline production, and other measures leading to waste and a fall in the incomes from which accumulation must ultimately be sustained.
14. See Thomas Wiens, "Agricultural Statistics in the People's Republic of China," in Alexander Eckstein, ed., Quantitative Measures of China's Economic Output (Ann Arbor: University of Michigan Press, 1980), pp. 44-107,

and Nicholas Lardy, "Food Consumption in the People's Republic of China," unpublished manuscript.

15. Victor D. Lippit, "The People's Communes and China's New Development Strategy," Bulletin of Concerned Asian Scholars 13, no. 3 (1981).

16. According to estimates presented by Thomas Rawski, although output per worker in agriculture increased some 10 percent between 1957 and 1975, output per labor-day declined by between 15 and 36 percent in the same interval. "Economic Growth and Employment in China," World Development 7, Nos. 8-9 (August-September 1979): 777.

17. Nicholas Lardy, Economic Growth and Distribution in China (Cambridge: Cambridge University Press, 1978), p. 175.

18. State Statistical Bureau, People's Republic of China, Main Indicators, Development of the National Economy of the People's Republic of China (1949-1978) (Beijing 1979). These figures are generally in line with Western estimates. Thomas Rawski, for instance, estimates industrial growth at 11-12 percent per year between 1957 and 1973. "China's Industrial Performance, 1949-73," in Alexander Eckstein, ed., Quantitative Measures of China's Economic Output (Ann Arbor: University of Michigan Press, 1980), p. 183.

19. Beijing Review, December 21, 1979, p. 10; May 5, 1980, p. 7.

20. Arthur Ashbrook, Jr., "China: Shift of Economic Gears in Mid-1970's," in U. S. Congress, Joint Economic Committee, Chinese Economy Post-Mao (Washington, D. C.: U. S. Government Printing Office, 1978), p. 208.

21. This figure is not directly comparable to ICORs calculated in Western nations, where investment is usually taken as a share of national income and related to the growth in national income. As a consequence of the different basis for calculation, Western ICORs are usually higher.

22. A clear exposition of the systemic problems of centrally planned economies appears in Alec Nove, "Soviet Economic Prospects," New Left Review, No. 119 (January-February 1980). Nove argues (p. 4) that "the basic problem of any centrally planned economy (is) the unmanageably huge number of inter-related decisions to be taken." Since the complexity of industrial systems increases far more rapidly than their size, the decision-making problem grows increasingly acute over time.

23. Beijing Review, May 19, 1980, pp. 23-4, and April 20, 1981, p. 8; FBIS, Daily Report, October 31, 1981, p. L21.

24. Beijing Review, January 19, 1981, p. 22. These figures do not include income from private plots and sideline activities, which are believed to amount to at least one-third of collective income on the average.

Mark Selden
COOPERATION AND CONFLICT: COOPERATIVE AND COLLECTIVE FORMATION IN CHINA'S COUNTRYSIDE

Beginning in the 1960s, China's Great Proletarian Cultural Revolution resurrected international debate on problems of the transition to socialism. Stalin and his Soviet successors had constricted understanding of the transition to matters of formal ownership and productivity, relegating to an ever-receding future such issues as the mastery of working people over the productive process, the scope and form of institutions appropriate to the flourishing of socialist democracy, and the elimination of all forms of privilege and inequality.[1]

The critique of Soviet socialism associated with the Cultural Revolution, but drawing on Maoist theory and practice of uninterrupted revolution which had developed since the 1940s, suggested to many a variety of fresh and hopeful perspectives on the transition. The crux of the matter was and is the question of the state, whose extension and penetration is the logical outcome of the creation of new systems of ownership and organization, and of the attempt by socialist societies to promote and guide industrialization and comprehensive development of a new type. Concentration of economic and political power in the hands of the party-state, whatever its contribution to eliminating inequities of the prerevolutionary social order and initiating rational planning, has the potential to produce state despotism, a new moloch more powerful and hence more dan-

*I would like to express my appreciation for the comments, suggestions, and references provided by Anthony Barnet, Ch'iu Cheng-chang, Kojima Reiitsu, Elisabeth Lasek, Victor Lippit, Carl Riskin, and Vivienne Shue. In preparing this paper I have learned above all from the probing criticisms and insights gathered in our joint research from Edward Friedman whose unpublished paper, "How Do You Know When the Revolution Is Over? Collectivizing Villages and Nationalizing State in China's Hebei Province," was among the first to stimulate my rethinking of the issues posed here.

gerous than the more fragmented social systems it replaced. The Maoist critique of bureaucracy distinctively posed certain of these issues and suggested that uninterrupted revolution was the optimal approach for resolving them.

The present essay reconceptualizes the historical options which leadership and people confronted at a critical stage in the development of Chinese socialism, the cooperative and collective transformation of agriculture, and reflects on the continued salience of those issues for the subsequent course of Chinese development. Close analysis of leadership conflict and grass-roots practice centered on the 1955-56 "socialist high tide" suggests striking new conclusions about both the distinctiveness of the Chinese path and the strength of the legacy of Stalinist approaches to collectivization in particular and socialism in general.

At the center of this analysis, viewed from the perspectives of peasantry and leadership, is the question of the relationship between transformation of relations of production (embracing both ownership systems and the organization and leadership of the production process) and the productive forces, that is, between social change and economic development. More explicitly, we will focus on the interaction of state, cooperative, and individual in a shared search for effective means to promote economic development while attempting to resolve conflicting perspectives over appropriate rates of accumulation, state revenues, and increased peasant incomes.

This approach can be contrasted with much of the existing literature. On the one hand, there is a large body of work by orthodox economists and agronomists which weighs production and income data abstracted from issues of social change. On the other hand, there is a corpus of scholarship inspired by the Cultural Revolution which has focused on political and ideological questions. Notably in the work of Charles Bettelheim, but also in the contributions of many other sympathetic observers of the Cultural Revolution, problems pertaining to development of the productive forces and particularly to the standard of living during the transition faded to the margin of discussion, disappeared entirely, or were assumed to have been basically solved.[2] Questions of economic growth, as well as those of income and livelihood of the people, it appeared, could safely be left to orthodox economists (whether capitalist or state socialist) whose fixation with "hard data," the flow of which in any event ceased after 1957, had led to petrification of that field of inquiry. The uninterrupted revolution, class struggle spearheaded against "capitalist-roaders" in the Party, in the state and among the intellectuals, and ideological transformation — these appeared to be the cosmic issues addressed in most serious analyses of the transition, above all those informed by socialist consciousness. Much of this discussion accepted more or less at face value the interpretation of the Party's half century in terms of the two-line struggle, as defined (and redefined) by the Cultural Revolution leadership of the moment. It followed that Mao, virtually alone among the entire Long March generation which charted the national liberation movement, possessed the vision and courage to conceptualize and lead the socialist revolution. In short, the Cultural Revolution appeared not only as the zenith of Chinese (and world) socialism, but as the negation of much of Chinese as well as Soviet and East European experience which preceded it.

Assuming that this brief tour d'horizon has done violence only to the richness and complexity of the analysis and not to its core propositions, I would like to examine its utility as a method of understanding the political economy of the transition by focusing on a critical stage of development in the Chinese countryside: the formation of cooperatives and collectives from their inception in the early fifties through the "socialist high tide" of 1955-56. For it is the countryside which has been most closely associated with the achievements and unique contributions of the Chinese revolution. It was in the countryside that Chinese revolutionaries first developed independent strategies en route to national power. It was over rural policy that Chinese revolutionary praxis had diverged most sharply from inherited Soviet wisdom in the 1940s and early 1950s. And it was above all over rural policy that Mao eventually broke with many of his closest colleagues in the leadership. Finally, it is the countryside which provides the ultimate challenge to the modernization strategy whose lines have become increasingly clear since 1976. This analysis will attempt to probe the ways in which rural classes reacted to and participated in socio-political and economic change, in particular how they interacted with the Party and state in the course of the cooperative transformation of the countryside.

We will consider the constellation of policy choices pertaining to cooperation with respect to production, accumulation, peasant income, and welfare against the background of the Marxist-Leninist tradition and in light of Chinese conditions and conflicting lines on cooperative formation. At the center of this effort will be an attempt to gauge the significance of cooperative and collective transformation in terms of its impact on productivity, accumulation, and income distribution, on the one hand, and peasant control over processes of production and planning, on the other.[3]

MARX, LENIN, MAO: VISIONS OF THE TRANSITION TO SOCIALISM IN THE COUNTRYSIDE

Before turning to the Chinese countryside, I would like to pose two general issues of social change. First is the problem of whether and how nations such as China and the former colonial areas, with low levels of productivity, capital accumulation, and industrialization, and with a legacy of subjugation to the core countries, can initiate the steep ascent to socialism. Second is the origin and significance to the transition of the cooperative ideal within Marxist thought and practice.

In their sparse writings on socialist society, Marx and Engels provided few specific ideas clarifying their understanding of institutions appropriate to the transition. At numerous points in his analysis of capitalist development, however, Marx offered clues pertinent to understanding the challenge which would arise if and when societies with weakly developed capitalist foundations attempted the transition to socialism. In the Grundrisse, for example, he observed that "The greater the extent to which production still rests on mere manual labor, on use of muscle power, etc., in short on physical exertion by individual laborers, the more does the increase of the productive force consist in their collaboration on a mass scale."[4] In rural China, to develop the productive forces and create socialist relations of production would require the formation of cooperative labor both in the sense that Marx used the term here to describe the capitalist transformation of individual labor, and in the sense of creating socialist forms of ownership, management, and distribution. It would require, that is, changes associated with both capitalist and socialist development. Nations such as China, whose agriculture consisted of a mix of subsistence family farming and petty commodity production could not build on highly developed foundations of cooperative labor (even in the capitalist sense) in erecting a new socialist institutional structure. (We will consider this issue from different perspectives below.)

It is widely known that Marx and Engels anticipated that socialist revolutions would dialectically and inexorably grow out of the contradictions of advanced capitalism, building on the dynamic economic achievements of capitalism and on the accumulated experience of cooperative labor. Less well known is their intense interest in the possibilities of revolution in Russia which would bypass the full development of capitalism. "Can the Russian obshchina, though greatly undermined, yet a form of the primeval common ownership of land, pass directly to the higher form of communist common ownership?" Marx and Engels queried in their 1882 Preface to the Russian edition of "The Communist Manifesto." "The only answer to that possibility today is this," they responded: "If the Russian Revolution becomes the signal for a proletarian revolution in the West, so that both complement each other, the present Russian common ownership of land may serve as the starting-point for a communist development."[5]

This conclusion, which opened the possibility of alternate routes to socialism, was not advanced lightly to raise the spirits of Russian comrades. Marx had learned Russian, closely studied Russian developments, and engaged in lively correspondence with Russian revolutionaries since 1869. And in 1874-75 Engels wrote:

> We see that communal property long ago passed its high point in Russia, and to all appearances is nearing its doom. Yet there exists, doubtless, the possibility of transforming this social organization into a higher form in the event it persists until the time when circumstances are ripe for such a change.... Society would have to be transformed into this higher form without the Russian peasants going through the intermediate step of bourgeois individual private ownership of land.[6]

Engels concluded that Russia had two possible routes to communism, the long painful one through capitalist development, and a direct route building on the foundation of the threatened but still existing village commune. Marx made this explicit in the third draft of his 1881 letter to Vera Zasulich in which he wrote:

> If the revolution occurs in time, if it concentrates all its forces [...], to insure the free leap of the rural commune, then the latter will develop itself before long as an element of the regeneration of Russian society, as an element of advantage compared with the nations enslaved by the capitalist system.[7]

This line of thought was hardly congenial to Lenin, whose Bolshevik Party developed in the course of polemics with Russian populists who did see in the commune the future of a regenerated Russia. For Lenin, the Russian revolutionary path lay through the full development of capitalism which would inexorably sweep aside all remnants of the old rural order. His analysis of imperialism, however, implied other possibilities for colonized peoples to advance. It cast the oppressed nations and peoples of the periphery in the forefront of revolutionary change. Both Lenin's theory and his revolutionary practice widened the scope and importance of political dimensions of the transition, above all the national and class struggles. Lenin never believed that communism in Russia, still less in the colonized nations of the periphery, could be achieved in the absence of revolution in the advanced capitalist countries. He insisted, however, above all in his writings on imperialism, that nations whose productive forces were relatively backward, including the victims of imperialism, stood at the center of world political conflicts and could create conditions for initiating the transition.

The pre-Bolshevik origins of the idea that collectivization was the route to socialist transformation in the countryside remain unclear. What is clear is that the Bolsheviks, a profoundly urban-oriented party with no experience in organizing the peasantry or agriculture, and with a preoccupation with the problems and prospects of the proletariat and industrialization, came to power in 1917 unified in the conviction that collectivization, with landownership in the hands of the state, was the panacea to the dual problems of increased productivity and the formation of socialist institutions in the countryside. Thus in 1917, Lenin proclaimed in his April Theses, the "Confiscation of all estate land. Nationalization of all land in the country under control of local councils of agricultural laborers' and peasants' deputies. Conversion of each large estate...into a model farm under control of agricultural laborers' deputies and on public account."[8] The Bolsheviks ratified Lenin's agrarian program at their April Congress. In September, Lenin went still further in spelling out the implications of his program. After calling for the nationalization of all land he stated that "the disposal of the land, the determination of the local regulations governing ownership and tenure of land, must in no case be placed in the hands of the bureaucrats and officials, but exclusively in the hands of the regional and local Soviets of Peasants' Deputies."[9] Nevertheless, in the struggle for peasant support which followed in the coming months, this vision was thrust aside. Lenin and the Bolsheviks, with no significant organizational roots in the rural areas, advanced a program with quite different implications for agriculture and for the party-peasant relationship. Not only did land hungry peasants seize and subdivide the large estates into individually cultivated microholdings, but as a result of harsh grain requisitioning during the civil war, the immense gulf which had existed between the Bolshevik Party and the peasants gave way to direct conflict between the peasantry and the new state.

In 1919, in an important statement on the preconditions for the socialist transition, Lenin observed that "Socialism means the abolition of classes," and then proceeded to focus on the sensitive problem of the Russian peasantry as a class of petty commodity producers.

In order to abolish classes it is necessary, firstly, to overthrow the landlords and capitalists ... it is necessary, secondly, to abolish the difference between working-man and peasant, to make them all workers. This cannot be done all at once. This task is incomparably more difficult and will of necessity be a protracted one. It is not a problem that can be solved by overthrowing a class. It can be solved only by the organizational reconstruction of the whole social economy, by a transition from individual, disunited, petty commodity production to large scale social production. This transition must of necessity be extremely protracted. It may only be delayed and complicated by hasty and incautious administrative and legislative measures. It can be accelerated only by affording such assistance to the peasant as will enable him immensely to improve his whole agricultural technique, to reform it radically.[10]

Here Lenin touched on the long-term tasks of the rural transformation which would culminate ultimately in the transformation of rural producers from peasants to workers. It is worth noting, however, the conception embodied in the italicized passage, "make them all workers," and implicit in much of Lenin's work, with its connotations of social change directed and carried out from above by the urban-oriented vanguard party. We will consider the implications of process in examining cooperative formation in China.

The same passage, however, emphasizes that political transformation was only the first step in building socialism. Ultimately, the technical transformation of agriculture was inseparable from questions of ownership, ideology, and organization. It held the key to the transformation of the peasantry in socialist society. Two years later, he amplified on the technical/material components of the transition in the countryside.

The only way to solve this problem of the small farmer, to improve, so to speak, his whole mentality, is through the material basis, technical equip-

ment, the use of tractors and machines on a mass scale in agriculture,
electrification on a mass scale. This would remake the small farmer
fundamentally and with tremendous speed.... But you know perfectly well
that to obtain tractors and machines and to electrify our vast country is a
matter that at any rate may take decades.[11]

In these and other passages, and above all in the formulation of
the New Economic Program (NEP) in the late teens and early twenties, Lenin exhibited sensitivity to the necessity for state financial
and technological support to facilitate the gradual, long-term transformation of rural social relations. But just as Lenin and the Bolshevik leadership remained distant from the peasantry and rural
politics prior to 1917, they subsequently showed little interest in
working out appropriate institutional arrangements or charting the
politics of a transitional political process to ensure the development of socialist relations in the rural areas. Stated differently,
neither Lenin nor the Bolsheviks perceived in the peasantry the
revolutionary or creative impulses they sometimes attributed to
the proletariat, bases on which to construct the foundations of socialist society in the vast Russian countryside.

In his final years, Lenin did emphasize the importance of cooperatives as the centerpiece of state policy during the transition to
socialism in the countryside. In 1923, he reiterated "how infinitely
important it is now to organize the population of Russia in cooperative societies."[12] What did Lenin have in mind? Not the peasant
communes (kommuna) which had flowered briefly with some official
support in 1918-19 and which organized production and consumption
on a basis of equal sharing. He did, however, see the cooperative
elements of the New Economic Policy as creating preconditions for
socialist development in the countryside. "All we actually need
under NEP," he argued, "is to organize the population of Russia
in cooperative societies on a sufficiently large scale, for we have
now found that degree of combination of private interest, of private
commercial interest, with state supervision and control of this interest, that degree of its subordination to the common interests
which was formerly the stumbling-block for very many socialists."
Noting that "a social system emerges only if it has the financial
backing of a definite class," Lenin urged state "aid to cooperative
trade in which really large masses of the population actually take
part" (original emphasis). "On Cooperation" is Lenin's clearest,
albeit brief, exposition on the nature of the transition in the countryside. Private ownership and cultivation of the land would con-

tinue throughout the NEP. Simultaneously, on this foundation of capitalist proprietorship, the formation of state-supported cooperatives centering on trade would create the basis for peasant support for and participation in protosocialist institutions and eventually for basic cultural or value changes which would facilitate more advanced socialist forms. Collectivization of agricultural production would become feasible, Lenin held, only at such time when the technological revolution could provide the material basis for rural petty commodity producers to create more advanced forms. Trading cooperatives, however, would create important preconditions for change.

Soviet policy favored this very restricted approach to cooperative formation throughout the 1920s. By 1929, however, only one third of rural households had joined trading cooperatives. The countryside was a sea of subsistence and petty commodity production organized at the household level. Trading cooperatives had developed essentially as appendages of the state. The system was costly. It did not significantly increase the supply of marketable grain. Its primary beneficiaries were the more prosperous peasants.[13] Agricultural production remained almost exclusively in private hands. Petty commodity production and family-based subsistence agriculture reigned supreme. The gulf between city and countryside widened. There is little evidence that Lenin's hope for deepening socialist consciousness among the peasantry was realized during the first decade of Bolshevik rule. Against this background, and driven by the desire to create the preconditions for rapid accumulation and industrialization, Stalin in 1929 initiated the forced collectivization which produced violent clashes between peasantry and state and dealt a blow to the long-term prospects for agricultural development and for a transition based on popular support for socialist construction.

Lenin's strictures to the contrary, beginning in 1929, in Soviet rural development collectivization preceded agricultural mechanization. It was in significant part implemented by state coercion rather than building on peasant consciousness of the need for collective agriculture.[14] Soviet collectivization experience shaped in complex ways the perspective of the Chinese leadership as it sought to frame an agrarian policy for the transition.

China faced material constraints on the socialist transformation of agriculture far more formidable than those encountered by the Bolsheviks, including unfavorable population-land ratios and per capita grain yields just a fraction of those in the Soviet Union. For example, at the time that each launched its first five-year plan, with ambitious industrialization targets, China's per capita grain output was approximately 269 kilograms while that in the Soviet Union was 480 kilograms; and the percentage of marketable grain achieved in the Soviet Union was far higher.[15] The material basis for coopera- tive transformation was important, but it was by no means the only factor which preoccupied the Chinese leadership. We will observe certain important political advantages which the Chinese Commu- nists enjoyed over their Bolshevik counterparts at the time of co- operative transformation.

In 1960 Mao summed up the prerequisites for successful institu- tional change and development:

All revolutionary history shows that the full development of new productive forces is not the prerequisite for the transformation of backward production relations. Our revolution began with Marxist-Leninist propaganda, which served to create new public opinion in favor of the revolution. After the old production relations had been destroyed new ones were created, and these cleared the way for the development of the new social productive forces. With that behind us we were able to set in motion the technological revolution to de- velop social productive forces on a large scale. At the same time we still had to continue transforming the production relations and ideology.[16]

But under precisely what conditions will revolutionary change stimulate — or abort — accumulation and the development of the productive forces? A look at Chinese experience in the land revolution and cooperative movement permits us not only to evaluate succes- sive stages of revolutionary change from this perspective but to as- sess their effect on eliminating or reducing class exploitation and inequality, the nature and degree of participation and support for social change by specific classes, the impact of the changes on the livelihood of the people, and their contribution to strengthening co- operative foundations of rural life.

LAND REVOLUTION AND THE
ORIGINS OF COOPERATION

How was a "semicolonial, semifeudal China" to initiate the as- cent to socialism? In December 1947, Mao Zedong drafted a Central Committee resolution which etched a theory of stages for the new democratic revolution (including land revolution) and the socialist transition which lay ahead.

A new democratic revolution aims at wiping out only feudalism and monopoly capitalism, only the landlord class and the bureaucratic-capitalist class (the big bourgeoisie) and not at wiping out capitalism in general, the upper petty bourgeoisie or the middle bourgeoisie. In view of China's economic backwardness, even after the country-wide victory of the revolution, it will still be necessary to permit the existence for a long time of a capitalist sector of the economy represented by the extensive petty bourgeoisie and middle bourgeoisie.... After the victory of the revolution all over the country, the new democratic state will possess huge state enterprises taken over from the bureaucrat-capitalist class and controlling the economic lifelines of the country, and there will be an agricultural economy liberated from feudalism which, though it will remain basically scattered and individual for a fairly long time, can later be led to develop, step by step, in the direction of cooperatives. In these circumstances the existence and development of these small and middle capitalist sectors will present no danger. The same is true of the new rich peasant economy which will inevitably emerge in the rural areas after the land reform. It is absolutely impermissible to repeat such wrong ultra-left policies toward the petty bourgeois and middle bourgeois sectors in the economy as our party adopted during 1931-34.[17] (my italics)

Mao's scenario bears comparison with that of Lenin's set forth in 1923 in "On Cooperation" but thrust aside in Soviet practice, particularly in Stalin's forced collectivization. By 1947, the Chinese Communists had struck deep roots in the countryside dating from the successful rural policy and practice of the 1930s and 1940s, notably the wartime policies of protecting subsistence while initiating gradual reforms which restricted the power of the landlords and benefited the poorer strata. Following the defeat of Japan, as the Party set about launching a land revolution which would fundamentally alter class relationships and free for investment and peasant consumption the substantial surplus previously captured by the landlord class, it drew on two decades of rural experience and a legacy of strength based on firm linkages between Party and peasantry throughout North China. The Party's historical experience with the land question is significant. It is particularly worth recalling that Mao's long-term concern for protecting middle peasants from appropriation in the land revolution in the Kiangsi Soviet in the twenties and thirties had repeatedly drawn fire from his superiors in the Party who criticized his conservative "rich peasant line." If Mao was among the first Chinese Communists to perceive the revolutionary potential of the poor peasants, his preoccupation with safeguarding the interests of the middle peasantry (small landholder cultivators who were neither tenants nor exploiters of the labor of others) as the key both to securing broad-based support and ensuring the vitality of the rural economy is a continuous theme in his leadership and writings from the early 1930s until 1955.[18]

To be sure, the Party's relationship with the peasantry was rid-dled with conflicts, for example over issues of grain requisition. Nevertheless, at least from its leadership of the anti-Japanese resistance to the land reform and early stages of cooperation, Par-ty-peasant bonds forged with broad strata of the peasantry stand in sharp contrast to the chasm which separated the Bolsheviks from the peasantry, both in the decades before and after 1917. In China those bonds rested above all on the Party's ability to tread a fine line which permitted it to support poor peasant demands for redis-tributive justice at the expense of the landlord class while pro-tecting the material welfare of all peasant producers, including middle and even some rich peasants. In this way the poor peasants in the liberated areas became major beneficiaries of wartime rent reduction and taxation policies and of the subsequent land revolu-tion. Many of them changed their status from that of tenants to freeholding middle peasants and substantially improved their in-come and food consumption. At the same time, the Party's guaran-tee of middle peasant interests made possible the formation of a broadly unified peasantry and permitted the unfolding of a social revolution without seriously disrupting agricultural production and trade.

In the civil war document quoted above, Mao and the Party sought the broadest possible alliance of forces to defeat the Guomindang and destroy the opposition power base in the landlord class. At the same time, the concept of stages in China's transition to socialism, here clearly elaborated for the first time, was based on a hard-headed assessment of relationships among social classes and the level of development of the productive forces. This was a strategy which projected revolutionary transformation but which emphasized simultaneously the commitment to phased development in which each step proceeded on the foundation of broad-based popular sup-port. "All empty words are useless," Mao had observed in 1942 in his first extended foray into political economy. "We must give the people visible material wealth ... we can organize, lead and help the people develop production, increase their material wealth, and, on this basis, step by step raise their political consciousness and cultural level."[19]

As wartime strife ended, the ability of the social system to provide increasing material rewards for the great majority would provide an important yardstick of popular support, above all the support of the large and growing middle peasants. Indeed, we hear with increasing frequency from Party spokesmen, including Mao and Liu Shaoqi, of the necessity to encourage the "rich peasant economy," that is, growth of the productive forces in the individual peasant economy through guaranteeing that the fruits of prosperity achieved by nonexploitative means would not be expropriated.[20] This policy, advanced during and after the land revolution, carried within it the seeds of a conflict which erupted in subsquent debates on rural policy. The issue was this: Was the Party to represent the interests of the poor and landless peasants, including tenants and agricultural laborers, or those of all nonexploiting rural classes? In the short run, the former choice led to the emphasis on redistributive justice, while the latter emphasized protecting the interests of the entire working peasantry including middle and (at times) even rich peasants to support and stimulate increased production and income. The Party sought to reconcile these conflicting definitions of its role by supporting poor and landless peasant demands for expropriation while simultaneously safeguarding the interests of middle (and at times rich) peasants, to ensure that the land revolution would stimulate, not sabotage, the growth of the rural economy. This was the basis for Party leadership of a united front in the civil war against the Guomindang which coincided with the struggle for the land and for subsequent strategies of cooperative formation.[21]

AGRICULTURAL COOPERATION,
TECHNOLOGICAL CHANGE, AND
PEASANT WELFARE

Mao's 1947 address spelled out the long-range commitment to move beyond the land revolution goals of eliminating exploitation and creating a society of roughly equal peasant cultivators to implementation of principles of cooperation. As early as 1943, he had explicitly charted the future of the Chinese countryside in terms of cooperation as a springboard for the realization of "mutual prosperity" (gongtong fuyu) and ultimately as a bridge to collectivization. Mao's first significant discussion of cooperation explicitly invoked the authority of Lenin's brief statement during the NEP period.

Among the peasant masses for several thousand years the individual economy has prevailed with one family, one household, as the economic unit. This kind of dispersed individual economy is the basis for feudal control and causes the peasants themselves to succumb to permanent impoverishment. The only method to overcome such a situation is to gradually collectivize [jitihua], and the only road to achieve collectivization, as Lenin said, is through cooperatives [hezuoshe].[22]

As early as 1943, then, Mao advanced the goal of rural collectivization built on a foundation of effective cooperation. In locating Chinese cooperative practice in the tradition of Lenin, Mao did not of course mention the disjuncture between Leninist theory and Soviet collectivization practice. Nor did he note the fact that where Lenin had looked to marketing cooperatives, China would undertake the more ambitious task of forming production cooperatives. Beginning in 1943 and building on traditional cooperative forms, small-scale mutual aid and agricultural cooperation began to take shape throughout the base areas and guerrilla zones. Mao distinguished the new Chinese cooperatives from the Soviet Union's collectives:

The numerous peasant cooperatives which we have already organized in the Border Region, however, are not yet the cooperatives which in the Soviet Union are called collective farms [jiti nongzhuang]. Our economy is a new democratic one, and our cooperatives [hezuoshe], built using collective labor, rest on the foundation of the individual economy (on the foundation of private property).[23]

China remained, in short, in a new democratic stage in which private property would be protected as the foundation of the economy.

Mao's speeches and writings of this period scrupulously emphasized principles of voluntary participation ("compulsion must never be used") and the necessity to ensure that cooperatives stimulate labor enthusiasm, raise productivity, and contribute to mutual prosperity.[24] The Chinese Communist Party, confronted for two decades with the rigors of guerrilla warfare against enemies with superior arms and dependent on peasant support for its survival, turned to rural cooperation as one approach to the peasantry. The Bolsheviks, by contrast, came to power as an urban party with no significant rural experience or constituency. Bolshevik rural policy from 1917 oscillated between extremes of laissez-faire and heavy-

handed state intervention. Not only did the Soviet trading cooperatives of the twenties leave intact the individual economy in the productive sphere, but they failed to sink deep roots among the peasantry.

Long before the land revolution or the founding of the People's
Republic, Chinese peasants in the liberated areas with limited Party support began to implement voluntary small-scale cooperation
which characteristically built on indigenous forms of mutual aid.
The specific institutional forms of cooperation were not transferred
from Party blueprints to village reality. Still less were they made
in Moscow. Their roots were deeply implanted in Chinese soil and
their forms shaped by the mutual interaction of peasantry and
cadres. This is one important reason why the class struggles and
transformations of land revolution and early cooperative formation,
both resting on broad-based support, could achieve far-reaching
social changes compatible with development of the productive forces
as the rural economy recovered from the prolonged destruction of
war.

According to the most rigorous analysis of the agricultural data,
between 1949 and 1952, the recovery period coinciding with the land
revolution, China's total grain production increased at the respect-
able rate of 7.4 percent annually, rising from approximately 127 to
157 million metric tons. Between 1952 and 1957 grain output continued to increase at the annual rate of 3.4 percent, coinciding with
the formation of elementary and advanced cooperatives.[25] The
continued increase in grain production at a rate exceeding population growth constitutes an achievement for a nation engaged simultaneously in the complex process of cooperative formation.

In the countryside, the possibility of increasing yields while carrying out cooperative formation rested on scrupulous protection
and improvement of the livelihood of the majority. If this could be
achieved, cooperatives suggested an approach to a socialist agriculture which could circumvent the rigidifying and commandist
tendencies characteristic of state-managed economies, while
making use of economies of scale, expanded opportunities for accumulation, and rationalization of agricultural and sideline production. This approach required vesting resources and broad admin-
istrative-technical powers in small face-to-face local communities
functioning within the scope of regional and national planning.

Before turning to an evaluation of China's cooperative transformation in general and the accelerated processes of the "high tide"

in particular, it is well to note major obstacles to successful cooperation. In land revolution the Party had aligned itself with the
poor peasant desire for private landownership and a share of the
wealth amassed by the landlord class, while attempting to restrict
the scope of redistribution and retribution to protect middle and
rich peasant interests. The cooperative movement, to succeed,
required that the peasantry overcome the orientation of household
subsistence and petty commodity producers and embrace a broader
definition of community. Cooperation, moreover, posed formidable
technical problems of administration, leadership, record keeping,
and remuneration in a society in which the scale of production had
been miniscule, literacy was at a premium, and rural accounting
was virtually unheard of. Finally, cooperatives could only be placed
on a firm foundation with the enthusiastic participation of their
members if they outperformed individual farming in both production
and distribution without placing onerous burdens on the great majority of the peasants.

The state would use a portion of its slender financial and abun-
dant leadership and administrative resources to facilitate the difficult transition by supporting highly visible model units and providing economic advantages and incentives to cooperatives. Given the
scope of the problem, however, it could not smooth the way by immediately providing the means for mechanization or even the more
modest improvement of traditional tools, though these goals were
closely associated with the long-range success of the cooperative
program. Unless the new cooperatives quickly produced visible
results; unless, in particular, they outperformed the private sector
to the satisfaction of most participants, the alternatives were a
return to family farming or heavy and sustained state coercion to
maintain the cooperatives. The latter course would inevitably
represent not only the defeat of the cooperative principles of voluntary
participation and community initiative, but would set back development of the productive forces and retard the socialist transition.

Throughout the years 1950-55 a continuing tug of war took place
within the ranks of the central Party leadership and between grass-
roots cadres and the peasantry over the appropriate pace of formation, scale of operation, and nature of cooperative institutions,
particularly with respect to ensuring voluntary participation.[26]
Stated differently, the contemporary documents make clear important tactical differences within an overwhelming leadership consensus that the way forward to socialist development of the coun-

tryside was through the following stages of cooperation:

1. The peasantry, with local leadership provided by the Party and the Youth League, would organize mutual-aid teams and subsequently more advanced and larger cooperatives on the basis of voluntary participation and mutual benefit in accord with local conditions. The principal yardstick of success was the ability of the cooperatives not only to outproduce individual peasants, particularly the middle peasants, but also to ensure that their members' <u>incomes</u> rose more rapidly. The leadership stressed mobilization of the poor peasants, but the support of the highly productive peasants, their ranks greatly enlarged in land reform, was crucial to the success of voluntary cooperation.

2. The state, Party and Youth League would restrict private commercial ventures and attempt to eliminate speculative activity through adherence to marketing and tax policies which extended state control over grain, cotton, oil, and other vital commodities and restricted the scope of individual commercial enterprise.

3. China would <u>eventually</u> follow the Soviet Union — Mao in July 1955 estimated it would require three five-year plans — in completing cooperative transformation with ownership of land, draft animals, and other means of production transferred from individuals to large-scale advanced cooperatives. This was the method of development by stages, from small to large and from rudimentary to advanced forms of mutual aid, cooperation, and eventually collectivization. Significant progress in mechanization and technological development would pave the way for large-scale cooperation of the advanced type, that is collectives, with private land ownership eliminated and remuneration based exclusively on the return to labor.[27]

By the mid-1950s, however, with no immediate prospects of fully mechanized agriculture outside of a small number of state farms and model cooperatives, the Chinese leadership developed an analysis of advancing cooperative stages in step with improved technology. In essence the concept of progression in the relations of production was linked to development of the productive forces in this sequence:

> Temporary mutual-aid teams: traditional agricultural implements.
> Permanent mutual-aid teams: improved agricultural implements.

Elementary cooperatives: new-style animal-drawn
                            implements.
Advanced cooperatives: mechanization and electrification
                            of agriculture, particularly
                            tractors. [28]

The progression rested on an understanding of the importance of perfecting and expanding the scope of voluntary, small-scale cooperation to create a basis in trust, community bonds of solidarity, and managerial and accounting expertise in order to place increasingly larger and more complex cooperatives on a firm footing. This required continually expanding cooperative accumulation to finance new equipment. The leadership envisioned a reciprocally reinforcing process of improved technology whose dissemination would be facilitated by cooperation (groups of peasants could afford to purchase equipment and could use it efficiently) which would in turn facilitate advance to higher forms of cooperation.

Even in the absence of technical transformation, and in very poor regions, cooperatives could contribute to rural accumulation through coordination of such labor intensive projects as water conservancy, forestry, and soil improvement and through the promotion of expanded sideline production. As Kojima Reiitsu has documented, peasant labor accumulation rose throughout the fifties in step with the advance of cooperatives.[29] Where this labor produced good results it provided a powerful impetus for the expansion of cooperatives.

In 1954 Deng Zihui, head of the Party's Rural Work Department, stressed the view that, rather than wait until all the technical preconditions were realized, China would move ahead on cooperativization to pave the way for technological breakthroughs in agriculture. "The first step is to carry out socialist revolution, to organize the individual peasants, to achieve cooperativization and collectivization [jitihua]," he told a Youth League meeting. "The second step then is to carry out the technological revolution, to carry out large-scale mechanization."[30]

The transition to socialism in China's countryside began with land revolution and was followed immediately by staged development of cooperatives. From the early fifties, this process, designed to stimulate rural development, would parallel and reinforce the drive for industrialization focused on heavy industry. Eventually (Mao explicitly targeted 1967), the intersection of these two processes would facilitate the transition to advanced cooperatives with strong technological support. The prospect of immediate economic benefits made possible by mechanization, electrification, irrigation, chemical fertilizer, and large-scale production and rooted in the proven success of cooperative agriculture would then overcome the aspirations to private landownership so deeply rooted in peasant experience and world view. Collectivization would emerge logically out of Chinese development experience and, by providing industry with both large markets and revenues, and facilitating the ability of the state to tap the rural surplus through tax and purchase mechanisms, would in turn reinforce the accelerating industrialization drive. These principles, in the course of experimentation with diverse forms of cooperation, constitute one of China's most distinctive contributions to the transition to socialism.

In summing up these principles in his important July 1955 speech on agricultural cooperation, Mao spoke, I believe, for virtually the entire Party leadership. His speech nevertheless touched off new and controversial directions in the cooperative movement and brought to the surface simmering conflicts within the leadership and between the Party-state and rural society.[31]

How did Chinese experience measure up to these guidelines? The official version of China's cooperative transformation is that it proceeded by stages, each predicated on voluntary participation. A close reading of the evidence from the late 1940s through the summer of 1955 confirms the general implementation of these guidelines. To be sure, Party cadres at all levels periodically attempted to force participation in mutual-aid teams and then in larger and more advanced cooperatives without ensuring adequate preparation. Fulfilling numerical targets for the number and size of cooperatives at times overshadowed the painstaking tasks of building solid cooperative foundations. But where careful preparations had not been made, cooperatives invariably collapsed. It appears that many which gradually grew in size and complexity had found ways to win the support of their members through solid economic and distributive performance. The evidence is overwhelming, however, that in the summer and fall of 1955, central premises of the strategy of voluntary participation were thrust aside as China embarked on the "socialist high tide" culminating in the Great Leap Forward two years later.

Consider the situation in the Chinese countryside in the summer of 1955 prior to Mao's decisive intervention in the debate over co-

operative transformation. For nearly a full decade, beginning in
the early liberated North China areas, the Party had encouraged
gradual voluntary mutual aid and cooperation where, following land
revolution, conditions seemed appropriate. At the same time,
particularly with the start in 1953 of the First Five-Year Plan,
state policy increasingly focused on creating conditions for rapid
industrialization, principally the creation of heavy industry centered on the construction of costly large-scale capital intensive
iron and steel complexes. In China's agrarian economy, confronted
after 1950 by the U.S.-led economic blockade and with no prospect
of large injections of foreign capital, the financing for this ambitious program would come, could only come, from the rural sector.
(The significant Soviet contribution to Chinese industrialization
took the form, principally, of technical assistance. It was financed
by Chinese exports. No large injection of foreign capital took
place.) Agricultural exports provided the lion's share of foreign
exchange to pay for Soviet aid which primarily took the form of
short-term loans.

CONTRADICTIONS IN THE CHINESE
DEVELOPMENT STRATEGY: THE
FIRST FIVE-YEAR PLAN AND
THE COUNTRYSIDE

The Chinese leadership in the early fifties projected two mutually reinforcing strategies to achieve the economic goals of the
transition in the countryside:

1) Cooperativization, to stimulate rural productivity and
   raise accumulation and incomes, but also to facilitate
   state access to a larger share of the agricultural surplus for investment in industry, to obtain foreign exchange and to feed the cities.

2) Urban centered industrialization to create the agricultural producers' goods which would eventually underwrite collectivization and agricultural modernization.

While theoretically mutually reinforcing, in practice the conflict
between these goals posed the central economic dilemma for the
socialist transition: Pressures to realize a modernization vision

which stressed large-scale, capital-intensive heavy industry threatened to starve the countryside of the sources of accumulation required to propel agricultural development and provide the higher peasant incomes which were essential to strengthen cooperatives. Lagging agricultural productivity would inevitably impede industrialization by curbing possibilities for rural accumulation needed to finance industrial projects and by depriving industry of a potential market in the countryside.

Average annual accumulation during the First Five-Year Plan period proceeded at the high rate of 24 percent of national income. Much of this accumulation was siphoned out of the countryside by the state in the form of agricultural taxes and compulsory sales at low state purchasing prices. These funds primarily financed a heavy industrial base and urban construction.[32] By contrast, just 15 percent of state investment was directed to agriculture, where more than 80 percent of the Chinese people labored.[33]

The research of Kojima Reiitsu provides important insight into the consequences of the first plan's strategy for the rural areas. Consider the problem of accumulation for industrialization. The 25 billion yuan income which the state derived from the agriculture-based food and textile industries alone approximately equaled the entire value of state investment in industry during the First Five-Year Plan. The state bought agricultural commodities including grain and cotton cheaply from the countryside and exchanged high-priced industrial goods. Although the price scissors working to the detriment of the countryside was reduced after 1949, prices remained (and still remain) stacked against the peasantry. This enabled the state to reap handsome income of 10.8 billion yuan in light industry in the years 1953-57, while heavy industry registered a 5.3 billion yuan deficit.[34] But the countryside was paying for heavy industry in another way whose consequences for the rural economy and for peasant incomes were far more serious.

Prior to liberation, myriad handicrafts and sidelines made it possible for tens of millions of land poor families to survive. Throughout the early decades of the century, significant sectors of Chinese handicraft industry, notably cotton spinning but also silk, tobacco, and vegetable oil, were undermined or destroyed by the influx of foreign manufactures. Nevertheless, almost without exception, rural households engaged in one or more activity to make ends meet — or attempt to. After 1954, however, state procurement and marketing policies systematically destroyed important

remaining rural handicrafts, particularly handicrafts based on the
processing of agricultural commodities which passed out of the
hands of peasants and into urban factories. Population and labor
control policies, moreover, assured that most of those jobs went
not to peasants but to registered urban workers.

According to the major Chinese documentary study of handicrafts
of the mid-fifties, the number of handicraft workers (including those
in newly organized cooperative shops) dropped in 1954 and again in
1955 in virtually every province. For example: in Heilongjiang
the number of individual handicraft workers declined from 99,953
to 85,836 the following year and 79,172 in 1955; those who joined
handicraft cooperatives increased in this period, but only from
18,439 in 1953 to 20,194 in 1955.[35] Nationally, the number of
handicraft workers dropped significantly from 8,910,000 in 1954
to 6,583,000 in 1956 as individual handicraft was largely eliminated
in favor of cooperative enterprise. In these years the value of
handicrafts fell from 10.3 billion yuan in 1954 to 10.1 billion in
1955 and then increased to 11.7 billion in 1956. I hypothesize that
the decline in part-time handicraft and sideline activity by peasant
producers was still greater. Hidden beneath these aggregate statistics is the demise of important rural handicrafts. The Chinese
study cited above records, for example, a 47 percent drop in the
number of workers in Henan's cotton yarn industry between 1954
and 1955; a 45 percent reduction in households engaged in cotton
spinning in Liaoning between 1949 and 1954; a 90 percent drop in
the number of households employed in sugar refining in Heilongjiang between 1950 and 1954; and a reduction of 34 percent in those
processing vegetable oils in Henan between 1953 and 1954.[36]

The heart of the problem was the conflict between a state bent
on centralizing resources for efficient modern processing and export, and rural handicrafts which would expand rural incomes and
disperse accumulation throughout the countryside. The state won,
with devastating effect not only on the 11 million full-time rural
handicraft workers but on the entire structure of rural income and
employment. In many instances the countryside suffered a double
blow. Not only did resource centralization deprive rural households of vital direct sources of income and jobs, but secondary
effects compounded the damage. Consider native oil pressing, an
industry dispersed throughout the countryside, which made use of
cotton, sesame, peanuts, and other crops to produce oil for lighting
and cooking. When this rural industry was virtually eliminated by

state centralization policies in 1954-55, not only did the countryside lose an important source of jobs and income and find itself more dependent on the state for a scarce staple, but the cycle linking agricultural production, sideline industry, and animal husbandry was broken. In this case, for example, the peanut shells used as pig fodder were lost to the peanut producing localities, and this is but one of several important fodder losses which contributed to the contraction of animal husbandry in the rural areas. Likewise the bran from rice whose milling was also centralized. Centralization meant that the suburban communes near oil pressing facilities would gain access to the processed "waste" materials lost to the great majority of more distant villages. State centralization policies directed toward accumulation and industrialization shattered the natural cycle of the preindustrial economy in eliminating a multitude of rural handicrafts.

At the same time, beginning in 1953, the state progressively circumscribed the scope of petty commerce and transport work which provided important sources of rural income in many (particularly mountain) areas. To be sure, state procurement policies contributed to breaking the grip of former landlords and rich peasants over commerce. And these policies were vital for planned industrialization and ensuring adequate supplies to the cities. Nevertheless, since petty trading was widespread throughout the countryside, the loss of these supplemental income earning activities was felt by all rural classes and communities.[37]

By June 1955, despite problems such as the decline in rural handicrafts, China had made substantial progress along the path of voluntary, staged cooperative transformation, notably in the old North China liberated areas where land revolution was completed first. Since liberation, 65 percent of the peasantry reportedly joined the mutual aid teams; approximately half of these were seasonal, and the remainder operated on a year-round basis. Moreover, beginning experimentally in 1953 and in significant numbers in 1954, particularly in North and Northeast China, elementary producers' cooperatives began to form. The diverse institutional practices of these increasingly ambitious cooperatives, the organization and remuneration of labor, and the breadth and scope of their activities, emerged out of experimentation and repeated summing up of local experience. In this early phase flexibility and practical adaptation to local conditions were at a premium. There was no blueprint to which the experiences of mountain and plain,

Table 1. Cooperative Development in the Countryside, 1950–1958
(Percent of Peasant Households)

	1950	1951	1952	1953	1954	1955 June	1955 Dec.	1956 Feb.	1956 June	1956 Dec.	1958 April	1958 Aug.	1958 Sept.
All mutual-aid teams	11	18	40	39	58	50	n.a.	n.a.	n.a.	n.a.	-	-	-
Permanent MATs	2	n.a.	10	11	26	28	n.a.	n.a.	n.a.	n.a.	-	-	-
Elementary agricultural producers' cooperatives	-	-	0.1	0.2	2	14	59	36	29	9	-	-	-
Advanced APCs (collectives)	-	-	-	-	-	0.03	4	51	63	88	100	70	n.a.
Rural people's communes	-	-	-	-	-	-	-	-	-	-	-	30	98

Source: Shi Jingtang et al., Historical Materials on the Chinese Agricultural Cooperation Movement, pp. 989–1019; Kenneth Walker, "Collectivisation in Retrospect: The 'Socialist High Tide' of Autumn 1955–Spring 1956," The China Quarterly 26 (April–June 1966): 14–18; Frederick Crook, "The Commune System in the People's Republic of China, 1963–1974," in Joint Economic Committee of Congress, China. A Reassessment of the Economy, p. 373; Peter Nolan, "Collectivization in China: Some Comparisons with the USSR," Journal of Peasant Studies 3.2 (January 1976): 193.

grain and animal husbandry regions, large and small villages, etc., were expected to conform.

By June 1955, 14 percent of all rural households, nearly all of these in North and Northeast China, reportedly belonged to elementary cooperatives. These cooperatives functioned year round while preserving individual land ownership rights and providing remuneration on the basis both of land and labor inputs. Progress toward cooperation, however, proceeded by fits and starts, or rather by leaps followed by periods of consolidation and retrenchment. This reflected in part a conscious policy of following each advance by consolidation to ensure that the new cooperatives functioned on a firm basis of economic achievement and voluntary support. It also reflected continuing divisions within both leadership and people over the speed with which new cooperatives could and should be created so as to function effectively, as well as over the size, management, and remuneration methods appropriate to the new cooperatives.[38]

The extensive and frank discussion of cooperative experience in the press and in technical agricultural and economic journals in the years 1953-55 — illuminating not only diverse achievements and models for emulation, but also numerous problems and conflicts — enables us both to pinpoint areas of contention and to gauge the process of discovery which accompanied the search for institutions suited to specific local needs and resources. While we note divisions over speed of cooperative formation, size of unit, form of remuneration, management practices, and concern over rich peasant domination, perhaps the most formidable problem centered on devising policies to ensure the protection and strengthening of poor peasant interests while guaranteeing the welfare of middle peasants, whose contributions to the cooperative were essential to its economic success. This was the central issue if cooperation was to be based on voluntary participation and to ensure mutual prosperity of its members.

The example of Wugong Agricultural Producers' Cooperative, a leading Hebei model of early cooperation (the first small coop was formed there in 1943) illustrates the complexity of the problem. In 1953 Wugong overcame official objections that the experiment was premature and succeeded in organizing one of the nation's largest cooperatives embracing nearly all the more than 400 families in the village. A contemporary article in the <u>Chinese Agricultural Bulletin</u> cited three preconditions for the successful formation of a large-scale cooperative in Wugong: (1) The original small cooperative is run well. (2) A strong popular basis for expansion exists. (3) The change is being made in an area and at a time when a good harvest can be expected. The article then detailed the careful preparatory steps required and the obstacles to creating effective large-scale cooperatives.[39]

By 1953 Wugong had the benefit of a full decade of fruitful cooperation on a small scale and access to preferential technical and administrative support from the state. With the widely hailed formation of the big cooperative, Wugong became the site of the first tractor station in Hebei Province. With all these advantages, between 1953 and 1956 Wugong nevertheless revised the remuneration ratio of labor to land almost yearly, just as its predecessor, the smaller model Geng Changsuo Cooperative, had done earlier. Searching for methods which combined equity with sufficient inducement to ensure middle peasant participation and to assure high levels of productive activity, the village experimented with ratios which shifted the apportionment of income based on land:labor from 60:40 to 50:50 to 40:60.[40]

Cooperatives in the early fifties were small semisocialist islands within a sea of household-based agriculture. The state to be sure attempted to tilt the balance in favor of the cooperatives. But given the severe economic constraints of a nation poised at the brink of subsistence agricultural production, and particularly one whose economic priorities centered on accelerated accumulation for the construction of heavy industry, cooperatives had to prove themselves in economic terms and fast, or see their members exercise the choice of leaving to return to individual farming. This meant that the luxury of a transitional period, in which state subsidies cushioned new cooperatives while complex organizational procedures could be perfected and human relationships amicably sorted out, did not exist.

Mao Zedong explicitly and repeatedly instructed the cooperatives that they must not only improve production but must increase the incomes of 90 percent of their members in the very first year of operation. The translation of such goals into reality necessitated incorporating more prosperous peasants. Not only were these frequently superior farmers, but by definition they had access to draft animals and tools as well as better land. To set too low the return on investment of land and other means of production in order to emphasize the socialist principle "to each according to one's work" was to issue a death warrant for the cooperative. For it ensured that middle and prosperous peasants would seek to withdraw their labor and capital. Yet the opposite extreme, placing too low a value on labor, would intensify class polarization and impoverish poorer cooperative members. The leadership looked to cooperatives as a means of increasing the size of state revenue and the share of marketed agricultural commodities as well as the rate of rural accumulation. Nevertheless, it placed sharp restrictions on cooperative accumulation in order to ensure rising personal incomes as a means of demonstrating the superiority of cooperatives and guaranteeing the support of their members. The economist Xu Dixin made the principle explicit. After noting the 5 percent ceiling on cooperative accumulation stipulated in the 1950s model regulations, he observed that "later on, following the development of production, it may be raised gradually to 10 percent."[41]

The solution proposed by the Party leadership in the early fifties was to move gradually toward distributive systems which provided a higher return for labor while holding steady the return on land as the cooperative expanded its own base of accumulation and the state circumscribed opportunities for private profit. Eventually it would be possible to make the transition to fully socialist cooperatives in which remuneration rested on the principle equal pay for equal work supplemented by the provision of minimum subsistence guarantees for all.[42] To attempt to advance too rapidly, however, was to jeopardize the fragile consensus essential for stimulating productive enthusiasm of the majority of the peasants.

The Central Committee's decision to rationalize the cooperatives in the spring and summer of 1955, resulting in a reduction of 20,000 trouble-plagued units, consolidation of others, and slowing the pace of cooperative formation, emphasized the importance of hewing to the principles of voluntary participation and advancing by stages on the basis of the demonstration effect by sound cooperatives.[43]

MAO ZEDONG AND THE CRISIS OF COOPERATIVE TRANSFORMATION

The end of the debate which had been brewing throughout the previous five years came with Mao's decisive intervention of July 31, 1955, his first major public pronouncement on a controversial policy issue since liberation. The magnitude of the issue

is underlined by the fact that Mao went over the head of the Central
Committee, where he was outvoted, carrying his message directly
to a specially convened meeting of provincial and lower Party secretaries. Before considering Mao's conclusions and their impact
on rural policy, we must locate the problem of cooperation in the
context of national development policy as expressed in the five-
year plan, which assumed final shape in the summer of 1955 and
was publicly unveiled one day prior to Mao's pronouncement on
rural policy.[44]

The evidence is overwhelming that, at the very moment when the
Party finalized its five-year plan, its ambitious targets were already gravely threatened. China's agricultural production performance in the years 1949-1957 was creditable. Nevertheless, where
the state projected grain increases of 9 percent in 1953 and 1954,
in both years the actual increase was less than 2 percent. Cotton
targets were still more demanding — and the shortfall greater. The
state projected increases of 16 and 18 percent for these years, but
the harvest registered declines of 11 percent in 1953 and again in
1954.[45]

From the perspective of the central planners, however, the situation may have looked even grimmer. For the decisive issue is not
output but the quantity of marketable commodities which can be captured for centralized industry and urban consumption. As Ishikawa
Shigeru has documented, while commodity sales of grain and cotton
increased by substantial margins between 1950 and 1956 (2.7 times
in the case of grain), the rate of increase was held back by the increase in peasant consumption, including rising grain and cloth
consumption.[46] In 1954 the state had moved to increase marketed
agricultural commodities through the imposition of enlarged sales
quotas and higher taxes. For the first time the marketed grain
ratio (gross) exceeded 30 percent of annual production. The result,
however, was angry peasant protest. The state had moved too far
too fast in endorsing grain sale quotas. Peasants in some areas
where excessive procurement had taken place faced starvation.
Mao and Zhou Enlai were among those who issued public self-
criticisms. The state increased grain relief and reduced tax quotas. And in 1955 and 1956 the ratio of marketed grain fell sharply
to levels of the early fifties. The problem of accumulation confronting planners committed to the ambitious industrialization
goals of the plan was intensified by the fact that beginning in 1956,
and continuing for the next eight years, China had a net foreign ex-

change deficit with the Soviet Union. Between 1956 and 1964 China repaid Soviet loans in the amount of more than $200 million per year.[47]

The First Five-Year Plan, from the moment it was finalized in the summer of 1955, confronted severe bottlenecks. The heart of the problem lay in the countryside. In his speech and subsequent pronouncements, Mao sought to cut the Gordian knot: Accelerated cooperative formation, he held, would simultaneously solve a range of problems of class antagonism and inequality and also open the way for rapid economic growth. The implicit burden of Mao's message was that only large-scale rapid cooperation would enable China to fulfill the ambitious targets of the five-year plan. The economist Tong Dalin explained one element of the new strategy in this way: "It was precisely because of the lack of tractors that cooperation had to be accelerated. That is to say, we had to create favorable conditions primarily by developing agricultural production, so that the cause of socialist industrialization would be assured of a reliable base, supplying it with enough grain and raw materials."[48]

Lashing out at the decision to reduce the number of cooperatives in the spring of 1955, Mao charged that the leadership ("...some of our comrades, tottering along like a woman with bound feet") had restrained the mass movement at the very moment when the peasantry, above all its poorest strata, was demanding accelerated cooperation. The Party and state tailed behind a peasantry which was ready and eager — as no peasantry in the world had ever been — to carry forward large-scale cooperation which would shortly abolish private ownership of land. This was the burden of Mao's message which he laced with a brilliant mixture of biting sarcasm and detailed attention to concrete issues of cooperativization.[49]

Mao persuasively defined the Chinese road to socialism in the countryside in terms of voluntary peasant organization based on mutual benefit through successive stages from mutual aid to elementary and eventually to advanced cooperatives. "These steps," he concluded, "make it possible for the peasants gradually to raise their socialist consciousness through personal experience and gradually to change their mode of life, thus lessening the feeling of abrupt change. Generally, these steps can avoid a fall in crop production during, say, the first year or two; indeed they must ensure an increase each year, and this can be done."[50] Ironically, it was precisely this process of voluntary participation and staged advance based on mutual benefit which the high tide swept aside beginning in the fall of 1955.

Let us consider more closely the reasons behind the new strategy initiated with the speech and then pressed forward so vigorously by Mao. In addition to presenting an eloquent case for rural coopera- tion (Note: the speech itself called not for collectivization but for the formation of elementary cooperatives), he pinpointed a vital reason for stepping up the pace of transformation: growing class polarization.

What exists in the countryside today is capitalist ownership by the rich peasants and a vast sea of ownership by individual peasants. As is clear to everyone, the spontaneous forces of capitalism have been steadily growing in the countryside in recent years, with new rich peasants springing up every- where and many well-to-do middle peasants striving to become rich peasants. On the other hand, many poor peasants are still living in poverty for shortage of the means of production, with some getting into debt and others selling or renting out their land. If this tendency goes unchecked, it is inevitable that polarization in the countryside will get worse day by day.[51]

Was Mao's characterization emphasizing "capitalist ownership by the rich peasants" correct in capturing the problem and pros- pects of the countryside? Land revolution had eliminated gross exploitation and extremes of wealth and poverty. It had not pro- duced absolute equality; nor could it have without severely under- mining production and dividing the poor and middle peasants. Land revolution had united the great majority of poor and middle peas- ants, creating one of the foundations for cooperative unity. In gen- eral, effective Party leadership in the land revolution made it possible to protect middle peasant interests, greatly enlarge the ranks of the middle peasants, and provide overall stimulus to eco- nomic growth. Yet in reconstituting the system of free purchase and sale of land, the possibility was opened up of renewed pauperi- zation for some and concentration of wealth in private hands.

Let us look further at the question of whether class polarization was growing. The answer hinges significantly on whether state policies directed toward cooperative formation and the extension of state power over market and production had overcome tendencies toward repolarization of rural classes. The most significant evi- dence available, apparently the best evidence of national scope available to the Party leadership on the eve of the high tide, is a 1954 national survey of 16,000 rural families. That survey docu- mented significant inequalities of land, draft animals, and income

Table 2. Land Cultivation and Ownership by Social Classes After Land Revolution and in 1954[1]

Classification at time of land revolution	Share of households as classified during land revolution	After Land Revolution (1947-52)[2]					1954			
		Average household size[3]	Average cultivated area per household (acres)	Average cultivated area per person (acres)	Average owned area per household (acres)	Average owned area per person (acres)	Share of households (percent)	Average cultivated area per household[4] (acres)	Average cultivated area per person (acres)	Average cultivated area per worker (acres)
Poor peasant	57.1	4.2	2.08	0.50	2.02	0.48	29.0	2.29	0.54	1.09
Middle peasant	35.8	5.0	3.17	0.63	3.09	0.62	62.2	3.26	0.65	1.63
Rich peasant	3.6	6.2	4.18	0.67	4.38	0.71	2.1	4.27	0.69	2.07
Former land-lords	2.6	4.2	2.03	0.48	2.00	0.48	2.5	2.18	0.52	1.14
Cooperative members	0.0	5.1	0.00	0.00	0.00	0.00	4.2	2.70	0.53	1.04
All households	99.1	4.8	2.55	0.53	2.49	0.52	100.0	2.63	0.55	1.10

1. Based on a survey of 16,000 households in 25 provinces.
2. Land revolution took place at different times between 1947 and 1952 in the areas surveyed.
3. Household sizes are given for 1954 only. I assume that these figures remain constant from land revolution to 1954.
4. No 1954 data is available for landownership. With the advance of cooperation and restrictions on hired labor the gap between ownership and cultivation rapidly narrowed. By 1954 it is likely that the difference between the two was slight, particularly in North China where cooperative formation was most advanced.

Source: "Concise and Important Materials on the 1954 Rural Income Survey," Tongji gongzuo (Statistical Work) 10 (1957): 31-32.

between poor and rich peasants. And we may state with certainty that substantially wider inequalities existed between regions, though no comprehensive data exists on this subject.[52] The national survey data reveals that at the end of 1954 rich peasant households enjoyed a 1.9:1 advantage over poor peasants in the area of land cultivated, and an income advantage of 1.9:1. Was the problem acute? Above all, was the situation deteriorating? The available evidence suggests that, Mao to the contrary, the answer to these questions is no. The data is revealing.

Landownership and cultivation data in Table 2 permits us to compare the immediate aftermath of land revolution (from 1947 to 1952 depending on the area) with the situation at the end of 1954 when the survey was completed. The survey data indicated that while class inequality existed, the issues were not acute. Moreover, state policy had begun to take effect in narrowing differences. We note first that in 1954 the rich peasant per capita advantage in landholding was significantly less than that for families, on the order of 1.28:1. On a per capita basis the landholdings of both rich peasants and poor were quite small. Moreover, this "rich peasant" class constituted just 2 percent of the rural population compared with 62 percent classified as middle peasants and 29 percent poor peasants.[53] Whatever income earning advantages this small group enjoyed, as the countryside expanded the scope of cooperative agriculture, it surely constituted no political threat. It is difficult to conceive of a group politically more isolated, stigmatized, and vulnerable, unless it is the post-land revolution landlord class.

Most significant is the trend in landownership and cultivation. Between the land revolution and 1954 the rich peasant advantage over poor peasants in cultivated acreage dropped slightly from 1.34 to 1.28:1. The reduction in the gap between poor and rich peasants was probably greater than that revealed in these statistics. At the conclusion of the land revolution the per capita rich peasant advantage in landownership acreage was 1.48:1 (significantly greater in value since rich peasant land was generally of superior quality). Unfortunately we lack national ownership figures for 1954. But did not state policies which restricted tenancy and the use of hired labor reduce the gap between rich peasants and poor?

We are fortunate to possess some particularly intriguing evidence on the question of class polarization offered by Chen Boda,

Mao's secretary and, with Mao, the most forceful advocate of accelerated cooperative transformation during the 1956 high tide. In his February 1956 report on "The Socialist Transformation of China's Agriculture," Chen cited statistical evidence from Baoding Prefecture, Hebei Province, which he presented as indicative of trends in sales since the land revolution.

Table 3. Land Sales in Baoding Prefecture, Hebei Province

Year	Number of acres of land sold
1949	7,315
1950	9,082
1951	19,200
1952	15,237
1953	6,071
1954	1,382

Chen pointed out that "after the launching of the agricultural cooperation movement, the amount of land sold and purchased dropped...." Indeed by 1954 as the cooperative movement shifted into high gear and as strictures against hiring labor took effect, individual land sales dropped to virtually nothing.[54]

This did not of course mean that inequality had been eliminated. Rich peasants continued to enjoy advantages over poor peasants in ownership of means of production and higher incomes. Nationally, their per capita advantage in draft animals was on the order of 2.5:1, in plows 2.22:1. Poor peasants as late as 1954 sold on the average of 4.5 days of labor power per person per year, while rich peasant families hired labor an average of 10.8 days per person per year. Finally, rich peasant per capita incomes were 1.80 times those of poor peasants and 1.35 times those of middle peasants. The point, however, is not only that these differences are extremely small whether cast in international perspective or compared with the pre-land revolution situation, but that already by 1954 it was becoming clear to all classes that cooperativization would soon complete the process of eliminating remaining class distinctions based on differential ownership of the means of production. The writing was on the wall. It was several years since the Party had

Table 4. Ownership of the Means of Production and 1954 Income of Social Classes and Cooperative Members

Social class[1]	Average household size	Average no. of workers per household	Draft animals			Plows			Net days hired labor		Income	
			(1) per household	(2) per capita	(3) per worker	(1) per household	(2) per capita	(3) per worker	(1) per household	(2) per capita	(1) per household	(2) per capita
Poor and hired	4.2	2.0	0.51	0.12	0.26	0.36	0.09	0.18	-18.7	-4.5	488.7	116.4
Middle	5.0	2.5	1.10	0.22	0.44	0.74	0.15	0.30	-1.5	-0.3	774.4	154.9
Rich	6.2	3.0	1.84	0.30	0.61	1.22	0.20	0.41	66.9	10.8	1297.0	209.2
Former landlord	4.2	2.2	---	---	---	---	---	---	-8.7	-2.1	497.2	118.4
Cooperative members[2]	5.1	n.a.	n.a.	n.a.	n.a.	n.a.	n.a.	n.a.	n.a.	n.a.	704.6	138.2
Average	4.8	n.a.	n.a.	n.a.	n.a.	n.a.	n.a.	n.a.	n.a.	n.a.	692.9	144.4

1. Social classes are the designations made during the land revolution.
2. The authors note that cooperative members' income is not comparable to that of private cultivators since it excludes cooperative welfare guarantees. When the value of welfare is included, the per household income rises from 704.6 to more than 850 yuan, and in per capita terms to more than 165 yuan, that is it exceeds middle peasant levels.
Source: "Concise and Important Materials on the 1954 Rural Income Survey," Tongji gongzuo (Statistical Work) 10 (1957): 31-32.

trumpeted the slogan of the "rich peasant economy." Cooperation was the wave of the future, and it spelled the doom of rich peasant economic advantage.[55]

These conclusions are strengthened by the research of Kojima Reiitsu, Peter Nolan, and Vivienne Shue, which documents the effect of national and local policies expanding cooperation, breaking the grip of the former landlords and rich peasants over commerce, reducing the scope of such private economic activity as trade, speculation and transport, and generally preparing conditions for the reduction of individual inequality.[56]

The most acute rural problems and obstacles to effective cooperative formation were not those of class polarization but of the general poverty of the countryside, the limited availability of improved means of production and skilled technical and administrative personnel, and the tension generated by the high targets and extractive, centralizing policies of the five-year plan and the organizational and other difficulties associated with cooperation. To use Mao's own phrase, did not some of these policies amount to draining the pond to catch a fish? The real (though unstated) urgency behind Mao's call for intensified cooperative transformation lay in the crisis of the five-year plan. Acceleration of cooperative formation, Mao now held, could stimulate productive energies, making possible fulfillment of the plan and opening new possibilities for accumulation.

Mao's speech introduced a critical new element into the discussion of cooperative formation. Earlier leadership analysis of cooperation, including Mao's, while warning of the danger of rich peasant domination, had focused on the necessity to create institutions responsive to the interests both of poor peasants and of middle peasants who constituted the majority following land revolution. In July, however, Mao offered a new class analysis. Cooperation, he held, was a matter of urgency for the poorest "60 to 70 percent of the entire rural population" whom he now designated as "the poor and lower-middle peasants." Mao rightly perceived that the more prosperous peasants (and a small section of the poor) vacillated on the question of cooperation. However, he held that "most of the peasants are enthusiastic about the socialist road...the only way for the majority of the peasants to shake off poverty, improve their livelihood and fight natural calamities is to unite and go forward along the high road to socialism."[57]

Here we discover the origin of a theme whose explosive overtones became clear after 1962 (and particularly during the Cultural Revolution) in Mao's call "never forget class struggle." The accent in Mao's earlier writings and in Chinese practice of cooperation was on the harmony, unity, and mutual benefit required for and reinforced by a successful cooperative strategy leading to mutual prosperity. In introducing the category "poor and lower-middle peasants," he suggested a startling redefinition of rural society: Instead of a countryside perceived as having made substantial progress toward enlarging and strengthening the middle peasantry, this reclassification placed the emphasis on a new and greatly expanded category of have-nots.[58] Mao thus prepared the ground for a new wave of class conflict which could be directed principally against middle and "upper-middle peasants" who were fearful that cooperative formation and particularly collectivization would represent in effect expropriation of their land and a reduction in their income.

THE "SOCIALIST HIGH TIDE" IN THE COUNTRYSIDE

Throughout late 1955 and the spring of 1956 Mao threw his prestige and authority behind a radically accelerated program of cooperation. The three-volume compilation of exemplary accounts of cooperative formation, which he edited in the summer and fall of 1955 and published as Socialist Upsurge in China's Countryside, carried this message: If these hundreds of communities and individuals, many of them poverty-stricken and confronted with imposing obstacles to development, can successfully organize and creatively solve the numerous concrete problems which arise, why can't the entire countryside move forward to cooperation.[59]

In the October debates at the Central Committee's Sixth Plenum, which formally committed the Party to accelerated cooperation targets, Mao subjected to withering attack each of the arguments put forward by those who insisted (as he had throughout the preceding twelve years!) on adhering to policies of gradual and voluntary cooperative expansion. Mao's wrath centered particularly on those who cited material preconditions for the transition, specifically those who held that the formation of advanced cooperatives required large-scale mechanization if they were to succeed. He concluded with sweeping declamation that "the masses demand a big expansion...in areas which were liberated late, in mountain

areas, in backward townships and in areas affected by natural
disasters....[even] without funds, carts and oxen or without the
well-to-do middle peasants ... and [without] farm machinery."[60]
There were, in short, no insurmountable obstacles, material, organizational, or psychological, to rapid, large-scale cooperation.
Differences in material conditions, historical, experience, leadership, and consciousness were of little consequence. Cooperation
could and must advance rapidly, based on the "demand" by peasants,
above all by the poorer strata. It must advance everywhere and
rapidly regardless of concrete conditions. As Mao's secretary,
Chen Boda, installed in July 1955 as deputy director of the Party's
rural work department, later observed, Mao had challenged the old
concept originally held by some comrades that without the mechanization of agriculture it would be difficult to realize the large-
scale cooperativization of agriculture.[61]

At this point we must inquire whether Mao had correctly assessed
the mood of poor peasants throughout the countryside as he had so
unerringly done at critical junctures throughout his career. There
is scant evidence to support the claim that in the summer of 1955
the poor peasants everywhere were demanding rapid, large-scale
cooperatives. Yet, in another sense, Mao's forecast was not inac-
curate. Once Mao and a significant portion of the national and local
leadership united behind rapid collectivization, poor peasants
quickly responded, while middle and prosperous peasants vainly
attempted to resist. We need not search far for explanations.

Mao's passionate appeal to take up the cudgels of class struggle
imbued poor peasants with the hope that cooperatives would provide
a second windfall for them by equalizing incomes between poor and
prosperous. Driven forward by a coalition of newly activated poor
peasants and local cadres for whom the painstaking requirements
of staged, voluntary cooperative transformation were extremely
vexing, from the fall of 1955 China telescoped the stages of elementary and advanced cooperatives throughout much of the countryside. Mao noted "a fundamental change" in the last half of 1955, as
constraints on cooperation, even collectivization, melted away.[62]

Mao's July and October 1955 speeches and the response to his
vigorous mobilization from the grass-roots to the Party center
silenced critics and produced a surge of cooperative formation
which swept aside not only his own ambitious targets but the entire
logic of voluntary cooperation by stages based on mutual interest.
The October 1955 enlarged Sixth Plenum of the Central Committee

consolidated Mao's triumph on the issue of cooperation. Like all previous official documents of the cooperative movement, the final resolution is replete with cautioning phrases. Noting "the peasants' predilection for the private ownership of land," for example, it warned that "the amount of dividend which the cooperatives decide to pay on land should remain constant for a certain period, say two or three years," to prevent dissatisfaction or withdrawal by more prosperous peasants.[63]

The real message, however, lay elsewhere, and it was twofold: First, the rate of cooperative formation would be dramatically accelerated. For example, in areas where 10-20 percent of peasant households had already joined cooperatives, the formation of elementary cooperatives would be basically completed by the spring of 1958.[64] More important, for the first time in an official document the Party unequivocally signaled that the semisocialist cooperatives preserving private ownership of land and means of production were but "a transitional form to the fully socialist type," that is collectives.[65] As the cooperative tide swelled from late 1955, the "inconvenience" of the semisocialist form, pressures from above to show "results" in terms of numbers and scale of cooperatives, and the fear of being capped with a "rightist" label encouraged cadres, often with the militant support of the poorest strata, to telescope the stages and to move immediately to advanced cooperatives. Tens of millions moved directly from individual farming or small-scale mutual aid to fully socialist large-scale cooperatives. The careful strictures of earlier directives fell before the belief that speed of transformation and expanded size of unit were the real measures of achievement in the socialist transition. Not until January 1956 when the gradualist opposition was thoroughly crushed and the countryside had plunged ahead toward formation of advanced cooperatives did Mao add qualifications like these: "We should not try to advance anything before the overwhelming majority of the people are satisfied with the advance.... What I mean is that we should always make over 90 percent of the people delighted."[66]

In less than a year the entire countryside passed from a mixed system of private ownership of land and the means of production with varying degrees of small-scale mutual aid and elementary forms of cooperation, to large scale collectivization; from production organized in most cases on a scale ranging from single households to a few dozen households, to one embracing an entire village or even a township and typically involving several hundred families. We may describe this process for most villages as instant collectivization, noting that it was administratively imposed in the absence of the organic development of cooperative institutions rooted within the community.

The "socialist high tide" overturned central premises of the earlier strategy of cooperation. As of June 1955 the 14 percent of cooperative member households were concentrated in older liberated areas in the North. Virtually all of these had less than one year's experience in elementary cooperatives which retained private landownership and paid dividends on the dual basis of contributions of means of production and of labor. In South China land revolution and cooperation had come later. In Guangdong, among the last to complete land revolution, in the spring of 1955, just 5 percent of rural households belonged to cooperatives. And more than 90 percent of these had been established within the last year. They had time neither to consolidate effective working relationships nor to demonstrate model effects for others to emulate prior to the race to universalize advanced cooperatives.[67] Moreover, less than half the rural population, including the vast majority of households in south and central China, had any experience with cooperation even at the level of year-round mutual-aid teams. (See Table 1 above.)

By January 1956, six months after Mao's speech, 59 percent of Guangdong's households reportedly belonged to elementary cooperatives and 4 percent to advanced cooperatives. One month later, official figures listed 93 percent of rural households in cooperatives, and of these 44 percent had joined advanced cooperatives.[68] By the end of 1956 fully 88 percent of rural households in all China had joined collectives with another 8 percent in elementary cooperatives. In a word, China essentially completed the leap to collectivization in just one year. This pace makes the speed of Soviet collectivization look almost glacial by comparison.

Mao's 1955 speeches and the Socialist Upsurge documentary collection issued no call for striking a blow at the more prosperous peasants. Nor did they even hint that the formation of advanced cooperatives with their leveling effect on more prosperous families was anything but a distant goal. But the practice of the movement, the linking of official encouragement with the induced demands of the poor for instant formation of large-scale advanced cooperatives, the preoccupation with size and speed rather than voluntary participation, mutual benefit, and advance by stages, de facto introduced features reminiscent of the expropriation of the land revolution. This time it was not primarily old or new exploiting classes but the middle peasants and labor-short households regardless of class who bore the brunt of these cataclysmic changes.

Elementary cooperatives differed from advanced cooperatives in two important ways, one quantitative, one qualitative. First, the elementary cooperatives were much smaller, with recommended size in 1955 of 25-40 households. By contrast, the advanced cooperatives typically embraced an entire village; in 1956 they tended to range in the scale of 100 to 400 families.[69] Second, and most important, elementary cooperatives preserved private ownership of land and major means of production. That is, they were "semi-socialist" in nature. Remuneration was based on the combination of investment of land and labor while advanced cooperatives abolished private ownership of the major means of production and operated on the principle "to each according to one's work."

The model cooperative regulations promulgated on March 17, 1956, stipulated that "the only way to ensure that the peasants take the road of cooperation voluntarily is by adherence to the principle of mutual benefit." It declared that "The co-operative must not violate the interests of any poor peasant, or of any middle peasant."[70] The state guaranteed middle peasant interests against expropriation in the course of a gradual transition to the advanced cooperative form:

As production develops and the socialist understanding of members grows, the dividend paid on land pooled by members will be gradually abolished. Other means of production brought by members for use under centralized management will, as need arises and with the approval of the owners, be gradually converted into common property, that is, property collectively owned by all the members, after paying the owners for them or taking other mutually beneficial measures.[71]

The clauses which I have italicized underscore the sensitivity of the farmers to protecting the interests of middle peasants in a phased transition process. The formation of the advanced cooperative, like earlier stages, was to rest on voluntary participation of its members, including middle peasants. There would be no payment for land converted into cooperative property, but land dividends would be gradually reduced and those who "voluntarily" contributed other means of production would receive equitable payment, or "other mutually beneficial measures" would be implemented. Article 26 points out that cooperatives which had been established for some time and had sufficient resources would "buy animals belonging to members at normal local prices."[72]

These were fine phrases. But when advanced cooperatives were suddenly formed in 1956, most had no such capital fund and those which did preferred to invest it rather than compensate individual cooperative members. The numerous advanced cooperatives, formed directly from individual farms, of course lacked accumulation funds and were instructed to pay for draft animals and equipment over three to five years. As Peter Schran has observed, however, in the high tide

the great majority of peasants became members of advanced cooperatives suddenly. They thus lost title to most of their land and other farm assets abruptly, and they faced distribution according to labor in combination with two to three times as high a rate of accumulation right away. They were organized at once into units which extended in size well beyond the village. And the units were managed by functionaries who lacked, in addition to adequate skills, the special attention which had favored the development of model cooperatives during preceding years.[73]

Deng Zihui put it this way:

There have been deviations in the application of policy: some co-operatives fixed rather low prices for livestock, farm tools, trees and woods, fruit trees and water conservancy facilities placed under common ownership. Others even put certain means of production under common ownership without compensating the owners. In certain places, small holdings of trees and fruit trees, poultry, domestic animals privately owned by members were erroneously made the common property of co-operatives. What is more, in inducing members to invest in the co-operatives, not a few co-operatives wrongly adopted the method of coercion. They sometimes even froze members' deposits in the bank or credit co-operative or money sent them from other places....[74]

In short, the reality of the transition virtually everywhere was profoundly at odds with that outlined in the model regulations. Poorer peasants joining the advanced cooperatives traded their small plots of land and meager means of production with the expectation that the cooperative would provide immediate income gains as a result of sharing in the higher productivity of middle and more prosperous peasants, and perhaps with the anticipation of longer term stability and insurance against natural disaster.

The situation looked quite different from the perspective of middle and more prosperous peasants, not exploiters but hardworking peasants who were marginally better off than some of their poorer neighbors. Perhaps no one has better captured the fears and ambivalence of these and other groups to the pressures of cooperativization than the documentary novelist Zhou Libo in his epic account of the transformation in a Hunan village, Great Changes in a Mountain Village.[75] Many of these middle peasants were but recently poor peasants, and virtually all, while enjoying a livelihood superior to that of the poorest strata, lived in extremely modest, even precarious, circumstances. The advanced cooperative in most cases meant the transfer without remuneration not only of their land but, despite promises of payment, of their draft animals, groves, wells, and implements. As a result, many middle peasants entered the advanced cooperatives with the expectation of lower incomes, having lost the option of choosing individual or cooperative farming. There was to be sure the hope that the advanced cooperative would provide the rational basis for expanding the productive forces which would eventually bring mutual prosperity at higher levels of production. But this prospect could not have looked bright to most middle peasants facing immediate losses. Indeed, by the early 1980s, China had yet to surpass the rural per capita incomes and grain consumption of the mid-fifties.[76] The majority of those who might have been classified as middle peasants in the mid-fifties still have not surpassed income levels achieved prior to the formation of the advanced cooperatives. It is difficult to escape the conclusion that a significant portion of middle peasants experienced the socialist high tide and formation of advanced cooperatives as a form of expropriation, of nonviolent coercion. Was this not precisely what both Lenin and Mao had eloquently warned against?

The problems were not confined to that considerable group of middle and more prosperous peasants. Consider, for example, the case of elderly people relying on modest income from their land to survive when too old to work. For those without family support, transfer of their land to the collective without compensation deprived them of their basic hope for minimal security and threw them on the mercy of the collective. What were their prospects? Welfare systems did become a national issue in 1956, and the experience of advanced units like Wugong which created successful welfare systems was widely publicized. But with multiple pressures on fragile new cooperatives to increase both accumulation and the distribution shares of their members, to purchase draught

animals and equipment, and to surpass their quotas for grain sales
to the state, welfare systems at this time were precarious at best,
and with the exception of disaster relief, welfare payments were
entirely dependent on local resources and local priorities. Again
looking forward, it appears that despite more than twenty years of
discussion of cooperative provision of the "five guarantees," in
the early 1980s rural support systems for the elderly and infirm
continue to rest primarily on their families. In particular, most
poorer and less advanced units have yet to implement minimally
effective welfare systems.[77]   And state welfare policies do not apply to the more than 800 million rural inhabitants.

The nationwide formation in 1956 of advanced cooperatives eliminated the largest income differentials between rich and poor within
each community, specifically those based on ownership of land and
other means of production, and created the basis for a unified village economy.[78]   Universal collectivization at a stroke "solved" a
series of complex problems of the transition period. It essentially
completed the egalitarian redistributive logic set in motion in the
land revolution (remaining individual differences rested for the
most part on differential labor availability and on the ratio of productive laborers to total household members). It eliminated the
fragmented land tenure system based on private ownership which
the land revolution had actually strengthened and opened new possibilities for agricultural modernization, including effective capital
construction in the fields, rationally planned water conservancy,
forestry, tool renovation, and (eventually) mechanization.

A number of astute analysts of Chinese development, including
Thomas Bernstein, Jack Gray, John Gurley, Kojima Reiitsu, Peter
Nolan, Vivienne Shue, and William Parish and Martin Whyte, have
seen in the high tide the successful implantation of cooperative institutions in the Chinese countryside.[79]   Our study suggests the
necessity to reassess the gains and losses inherent in discarding
the tested policy of cooperation by stages so brilliantly articulated
— only to be immediately discarded — in Mao's 1955 speech. There
the chairman presented cooperative transformation as a process
which would grow naturally out of two events bringing together
maturing relations and forces of production: the consolidation of
cooperatives and the availability of modern inputs for agriculture.

The events of the high tide require assessment of the implications
of telescoping stages for the socialist transition in the countryside.
In less than one year virtually the entire socio-economic structure

of the countryside was reorganized in advanced cooperatives, bringing a considerable expansion in the scale of organized economic life. In a matter of months nearly four hundred million small commodity producers were reborn as cooperative members who had traded their right to ownership of land, draft animals, and tools for a share in the product of unfamiliar and untested large-scale collectives.

In contrast with earlier laborious advance, consolidation, and sometimes retreat — the painstaking efforts to devise cooperative forms suitable to the contours and needs of each community — collectivization proceeded in a celebratory atmosphere of drums and gongs. It is an undeniable fact that in China collectivization was achieved in the absence of both the violence and the economic collapse which characterized Soviet collectivization. Moreover, the system has perpetuated itself in essentials and even achieved production gains over the subsequent two decades. Is this not proof of the wisdom of a strategy which, building on the solid foundations of earlier cooperative experience, seized the appropriate moment to leap forward to achieve nationwide collectivization, thereby accomplishing the transition to socialist organizational forms and accelerating the development of the productive forces?

During the Cultural Revolution the history of the early fifties was interpreted to highlight "two roads" with respect to rural policy: one a capitalist road associated with Liu Shaoqi, Deng Zihui, and much of the top Party personnel responsible for rural policy; the other a socialist road blazed by Mao Zedong with the support of the poor peasants. This analysis can now be seen to contain fatal flaws:

    ***It conceals the fundamental shift in 1955 in Mao's own analysis and strategy of cooperative transformation.

    ***It distorts the leadership consensus around the cooperative path while exaggerating the significance of tactical differences over speed and method. It thus fabricates the existence of a leadership faction opposed to cooperation.

    ***It considers only the question of relations of production, including ownership and management systems and issues of equality, but ignores questions of their relationship to the productive forces, that is, the impact of policy on production.

***It downplays the importance of the Party's previous promise that cooperation would bring mutual prosperity in the form of raising peasant incomes.

***It ignores the question of alliance with the middle peasantry and the importance of achieving unity as a basis for effective cooperation.

***It slights the issues of socialist democracy and coercion which Lenin, Mao, and others had posed clearly since the 1920s.

Bigger, faster, more egalitarian may express aspirations and goals for the formation of socialist communities (though not necessarily the only or the best aspirations). But goals surely are one thing and implementation quite another. Mao had demonstrated the importance of proceeding by stages, gradually, in order to construct firm foundations of organizational experience, cooperative values, appropriate technology, capital accumulation, economic growth, and popular consensus and support in the course of the transition. Faced with the multiple crises of 1955, however, he jettisoned all of these proven principles and carried the Party with him on a new course.

The central issues debated within the Party in the mid-fifties were not socialism versus capitalism, or whether to restore the individual economy or continue to build agricultural cooperatives. The question of the appropriateness of cooperative and collective agriculture <u>was</u> being fought out in a number of East European parties, but not in the Chinese party. Intraleadership differences centered rather on the process and speed of the transition, on how to devise appropriate cooperative institutions under diverse conditions in China's rural society.

There were, to be sure, powerful social pressures toward enlarging the private sector in rural production and commerce. The evidence is overwhelming, however, that by 1955 the state had circumscribed many of the most lucrative opportunities for private profit through restriction of commercial endeavor and elimination of channels for speculation. The initiative clearly lay with the expanding cooperative sector.

Policy failures in this period cannot be attributed to "capitalist-roaders within the Party." In the medium to long run, the only effective means to replace the private sector was to strengthen the economic, political, and organizational foundations of the new cooperatives. In stressing the importance of combining increased cooperative accumulation with higher incomes for the vast majority of members during the early fifties, state policy astutely addressed these requirements. On the other hand, in eliminating a large share of sideline and commercial activity, above all in transferring those activities from individuals to the state rather than to newly formed cooperatives, and in maintaining a price structure detrimental to rural interests, state policies undermined the prospects for successful cooperation.

The economic and leadership crises of the summer of 1955 arose out of the conflicting imperatives of fulfillment of the norms of the five-year plan and of the strategy of voluntary cooperation based on mutual benefit, but above all out of the mounting awareness that, barring a major successful policy change, the targets of the plan could not be fulfilled. The Chinese leadership could have recognized that the planned targets were overly ambitious and scaled them down or shifted investment priorities from heavy industry to light industry and agriculture. Such choices would have reduced accumulation pressures, increased incentives for rural production, left greater resources in the rural areas for cooperative accumulation and the diversification of agricultural and sideline production, and stimulated the cooperatives. This route, however, implied lower industrial growth targets than the plan stipulated at least in the short run. It was rejected. High growth targets for heavy industry remained as sacrosanct in China as they had been in Stalin's Russia in the initial five year plans.

But to achieve these goals new stimuli would have to be applied. Mao concluded that numerous developmental obstacles could be simultaneously overcome by moving directly to collectivization. By mobilizing the poor, eliminating private ownership of land and the remaining income differentials which divided individuals, and by taking advantage of cooperative economies of scale and expanded opportunities for labor mobilization, Mao held, accumulation and growth could be accelerated. Intensified cooperativization, in this view, would stimulate rural productivity, raise the share of marketed agricultural commodities, stimulate rural accumulation, and increase purchasing power, making possible industrial construction. In the autumn 1955-spring 1956 period, Mao threw his authority behind a rural strategy which combined accelerated cooperative formation with greatly increased agricultural production targets advanced in the twelve-year plan for agricultural development.

Putting aside for the moment the question of the feasibility of increasing production on this basis, such a strategy implied a price. This approach to collectivization took place at the direct expense of large segments of the middle peasantry. It is well to recall the warning of one foreign authority on the critical importance of the middle peasant problem:

> In relation to the landlords and the capitalists our aim is complete expropriation. But we shall not tolerate any violence towards the middle peasantry.... coercion would ruin the whole cause. What is required here is prolonged educational work. We have to give the peasant, who not only in our country but all over the world is a practical man and a realist, concrete examples to prove that the cooperative is the best possible thing.... cooperatives must be so organized as to gain the confidence of the peasants. And until then we are pupils of the peasants and not their teachers.... Nothing is more stupid than the very idea of applying coercion in economic relations with the middle peasant.[80]   (italics in original)

The comment seems as apt applied to the Chinese countryside in 1955-56 as it was in the context of the Soviet Union's New Economic Policy more than thirty years earlier. China's collective reorganization of rural economic life in a period of less than one year meant, could only have meant, that a significant portion of the peasantry, particularly more prosperous elements of the middle peasantry, but also many poorer people with little or no successful cooperative experience, accepted membership on the basis of various degrees of coercion and with little opportunity to shape cooperative institutions to their needs. Tens of millions of peasants experienced collectivization as expropriation of their land and draft animals or forced participation in a system which lacked legitimacy.[81]

We can approach the problem from another angle. Until 1955, cooperative formation went hand in hand with the gradual development of the productive forces and technological improvement. Early cooperation facilitated tool improvement and semimechanization and above all expanded opportunities for irrigation and rural capital construction, which in turn strengthened the cooperatives. It proved compatible with rising crop yields, expanding rural accumulation, and higher rural incomes. This mutually reinforcing cycle would contribute in the long run to mechanization and electrification, to the material prerequisites for the smooth transfer of landownership to advanced cooperatives, and ultimately to substantial further gains in production, accumulation, and personal income. In the 1956 rush to collectivization, since tractors and electrification were unavailable for all but a few model units (China manufactured her first tractor in 1959), the leadership groped for a will o' the wisp interim technological solution to cushion the slack of rapid social change: In 1956, the double-wheel, double-blade plow, imported from the Soviet Union where it had proven successful in the broad flat wheatlands, was manufactured on a vast scale. Ironically, in light of his subsequent bitter critique of the Soviet Union, it was Mao who threw his prestige behind this Soviet intermediate technology. The moment had come for a production leap to confirm the wisdom of rapid cooperativization. Mao overrode proponents of preliminary testing and evaluation. He personally intervened to force through immediate large-scale production to meet the surging demand for plows which would inevitably follow from the high tide of cooperativization. The double-wheeler, fully equipped, Mao held, would make possible improvement in the spectrum of agricultural processes from plowing to harvesting and threshing. Where individuals could not afford to purchase full sets of equipment, the new cooperatives could. They would be the beneficiaries of the new intermediate technology.

At the height of enthusiasm for the new technology in January 1956, Mao was pictured with the double-wheeler on the front page of the People's Daily. As he pressed the ambitious production targets of his twelve-year National Program for Agricultural Development, planners allocated fully 29 percent of the nation's steel to produce 3.6 million sets of the plows and the accompanying equipment.[82] In fact 1.8 million double-wheelers were produced in 1956, plows which the peasants immediately derided as "hanging plows" (they remained hung in the barn) or "sleeping plows" when they proved useless under Chinese soil and crop conditions, sinking, for example, deep into the mud of the rice paddies while water buffaloes strained to drag them forward.[83]

The new political priorities of the high tide had triumphed over earlier conceptions of economic-technological imperatives and of the politics of voluntary cooperation. Short-circuiting the intermediate process of regional testing precisely mirrored the elimi-

nation of local experimentation with advanced cooperatives in the
heat of the "socialist high tide." Instantism and giantism (in scale
of organization) were the order of the day. China did indeed "complete" collectivization in 1956, but only by inflicting losses on
agriculture, undermining the voluntary and participatory features
of cooperation, strengthening commandist and adventurist elements
within the Chinese leadership, and creating an increasing distance
between the complex economic, technical, and political problems
of the rural areas and slogans promising instant solutions. Finally,
we note that the politics of the high tide reversed earlier strategies
of uniting poor and middle peasants and, consonant with increased
emphasis on class struggle, tended to drive a wedge between them.

LESSONS OF THE "HIGH TIDE" FOR
THE TRANSITION TO SOCIALISM

Robert Tucker has observed that "breakneck industrialization
with priority for heavy industry, and forcible mass collectivization
of the peasantry would be the twin hallmarks of the revolution from
above that Stalin inaugurated in 1929."[84] In more than a decade of
cooperative formation beginning in 1943 and running through the
summer of 1955 China adopted a very different approach to cooperation and to the countryside. Nevertheless, in the burst of frenetic
activity which produced nationwide collectivization in 1956 we note
certain striking similarities to Stalin's state-imposed collectivization. Before discussing these, however, we must distinguish some
important differences. In China, little state violence took place
during collectivization. The army did not play a significant role
in the process, and there is no evidence of killing or violence.
Despite a brief drop in the number of draft animals and pigs, no
major production sabotage took place. The 1956 harvest was poor,
but the rural economy did not collapse.

When the pace accelerated in response to Mao's call, rational
arguments for voluntary cooperative formation by stages, using
the test of mutual prosperity and deferring collectivization until
fulfillment of preconditions of mechanization and semimechanization, were swept away. Technical problems as well as minor
injustices could be resolved later. The important thing was to
strike while the iron was hot. With the revolution in the relations
of production swiftly accomplished, the preconditions for the technical revolution would then be in place. The Chinese economy

could then achieve rapid advances. Or so it appeared to many. Yet more than twenty years later China continues to pay the price for this and subsequent shortcuts and leaps which impose universal blueprints with scant regard to local conditions and which permit the state to ride roughshod over the interests of large numbers of people.

I would like to look more closely at that price from two perspectives central to the realization of the socialist promise. One is the problem of socialist democracy, the process by which the forms of state or cooperative ownership become invested with the substance of mastery by the immediate producers, in this case by the peasantry. This goal, which ultimately requires mastery by the producers of the highest technological processes as well as institutions of popular expression, cannot of course be achieved rapidly, much less instantly, with the change from private to public ownership systems. At best, ownership changes create the preconditions for and the full realization of socialism's democratic and egalitarian promise. The process of transition is critical in determining whether the outcome strengthens tendencies toward state despotism or reinforces cooperative forms resting on the support of their members and responsible to their needs. The high tide weakened foundations of support for the cooperatives among substantial numbers of peasants, reinforced those arbitrary and manipulative tendencies in the Party and state, and undermined the democratic possibilities inherent in the cooperative form. The long-term viability of cooperatives must hinge on the active support of their members. From this perspective, the instant collectivization and coercive (though not violent) environment of the high tide created lasting problems.

The second and related issue concerns the viability of the cooperatives as economic institutions. Cooperatives must prove their worth both in terms of social justice/equity criteria and superior economic performance measured in productivity, personal income, and security. Chinese cooperatives cannot be said to have passed this test, and the continued debate over their viability and optimum size and form in China in the 1980s makes clear that they must continue to prove their worth. Yet a few decades is but a historical instant in which we can begin to make preliminary judgments on the viability of a social system: witness the centuries required for the transition to capitalism on a world scale and its still uneven penetration and performance.

Looking closely at the data, however, we can venture the judgment that the early economic performance of mutual aid and small-
scale cooperation was encouraging given the magnitude of the difficulties the system confronted. The evidence is more conclusive
that the mobilized collectivization of the high tide and great leap,
born of an urgency to accelerate growth, produced its opposite:
the economy shuddered and moved toward collapse. The incomes
of large numbers of middle peasants, but also those of poorer
classes, declined, often precipitously. The fragile legitimization of
the entire structure was quickly undermined. Many people came
to associate cooperation and particularly collectivization not with
mutual prosperity but with permanent sacrifice and belt-tighten-
ing.[85] Faced with resistance and rebellion, the Party temporarily
eased its pressures for large advanced collective farms and high
rates of accumulation to encourage agricultural growth and gains
in income for the peasantry. The Party's repeated invocation of
the memory of the horrors and hunger of life in the old society
may be understood in part as a response, and an increasingly ineffective one at that, to the perception of declining income shared
by many peasants.

We now know that in the early 1980s per capita income and living
standards in the countryside have not exceeded levels attained in
the mid-fifties prior to collectivization which (with the great leap)
initiated the most precipitous economic reverse experienced at
any time in the history of the People's Republic. Our analysis
suggests that the high tide and subsequent mobilizations which abandoned the close analysis of socio-economic and technical conditions,
which juxtaposed rapid egalitarian social change to tangible material benefits for the majority, and which undermined the basis
for the alliance of poor and middle peasants, bear heavy responsibility for outcomes which undermined the economic fabric and
strained to the breaking point the credibility of cooperative institutions. The view that Mao Zedong alone among Chinese leaders supported the best interests of the peasantry, particularly its poorer
strata, will not hold up. In the years after 1955 the reverse is often
close to the truth.

China's cooperative experience prior to 1955 illustrates the awe-
some complexity of creating a social system which reduces inequality, satisfies peasant subsistence and equity norms, and outstrips
the private sector in increasing productivity and accumulation while
raising peasant incomes. The overall performance of this period

nevertheless provides encouragement for the proponents of cooperative solutions. Whatever the individualistic proclivities of China's hundreds of millions of petty commodity producers, substantial progress was recorded toward formation of cooperatives whose performance in the realm of production, accumulation, and income distribution offered grounds for continued experimentation. The mobilization strategies of the high tide and leap periods, characterized by the impossibilism of economic targets and strengthening of the arbitrary power of the state center over local communities, severely undermined both the economic performance and credibility of the cooperative enterprise.

The objections may be raised that this critique of the Maoist strategy in the high tide and after loses sight of the urgent needs and interests of poorer strata of the peasantry, ignores the dangers of deepening class polarization, and slights the difficult choices open in the face of the imminent collapse of the national economic plan. These arguments cannot be sustained. In the years 1949-1955, as we have shown, voluntary cooperation by stages, backed by the financial, technical, and organizational support of the state, began to address the needs of the poorest strata within the limits of scarce resources and competing claims on them. They did so in ways far more effective than those attempted in the high tide. The long-range solution to the economic problems of the countryside could rest on strengthened cooperative productive power and expanded local accumulation. The result of forcing the issue in the high tide and more drastically during the leap, however, was to undermine both possibilities, an outcome evident by the early sixties.

The initial cooperative strategy lay in gradually raising levels of production, income, and accumulation, then, within the framework of higher stages of cooperation, expanding step by step levels of productivity and the share of members' income based on labor. The shift from elementary to advanced cooperatives, under the best of circumstances, poses an immense challenge. But having demonstrated the viability of cooperation, conditions would be favorable to transfer landownership to advanced cooperatives without suddenly or seriously slashing the income of the middle peasants. The great majority might then experience cooperation as a bridge to mutual prosperity. This was also a route which would encourage the expansion of cooperative accumulation, capital construction, and other diversified economic processes by continuously demonstrating their contributions to peasant income, employment, and welfare. As capital and confidence gradually accumulated in the cooperatives, and as an industrializing state became increasingly capable of providing tractors, chemical fertilizer, and electricity, the conditions for formation of advanced cooperatives would ripen. But not before. Mao's 1955 speech on cooperation stands as a monument to the wisdom of this approach, even as it sounded the trumpet which signaled the onslaught against it. The high tide, and above all the economic and political reverses of the Great Leap Forward of 1958 which extended many of its premises, provide eloquent testimony by negative example to the wisdom of development by stages.[86] The new agricultural policies which unfolded in the early sixties, again after the 1970 North China Agricultural Conference, and particularly since 1978, addressed many of the problems left in the wake of the high tide, the leap, and the Cultural Revolution, all of which exhibit certain common tendencies. In each case, policymakers subsequently confronted the necessity to restore the reciprocal relationship between peasant material welfare and strengthened cooperation, and between poorer and more prosperous strata, through relaxing state controls and encouraging policies to raise peasant incomes within both cooperative and private frameworks more attuned to peasant demands. This, however, is a story which cannot be told here.[87]

In advancing this critique I do not wish to minimize the difficult constraints confronting the leadership. The entire Chinese leadership and not just the Mao group shared with their counterparts in newly independent nations a consensus on the urgency for rapid industrialization, a view graphically reinforced by China's armed confrontation with the United States in the Korean War, by the U.S.-imposed economic blockade, and by the bitter lessons of more than a century in which the imperialist powers rode roughshod over the Chinese nation. Moreover, as cooperation advanced, pressures built toward a comprehensive solution which would overcome the complexities and conflicts inherent in the mixed system. The fact remains, however, that on numerous previous occasions the Party leadership had channeled revolutionary impulses in the service of national interests, including broad unity and protection of the economy. The land revolution did not follow certain policies to their logical conclusion — annihilation of all landlords and rich peasants, absolute equality of land and all means of production, for example — in part because of a broader leadership vision of national development. During the high tide and Great Leap Forward that modicum of restraint was obliterated. In important instances reason was silenced and the primacy of a politics of class struggle overrode both economic calculation and the democratic premises which constituted the finest traditions of the revolutionary movement. In each case, immediate goals were achieved — full-scale collectivization, commune formation — only at the expense of long-term economic and political setbacks which assured that the substance if not necessarily the form of major changes would subsequently be reversed.

CONCLUSION

The mobilization logic of the high tide of 1955-56 carried to swift completion the formation of advanced cooperatives throughout the Chinese countryside. The very fact that their formation was achieved within a year with neither the violence nor the massive sabotage characteristic of Soviet collectivization surely reinforced the conviction among Mao and his closest associates of the efficacy of such approaches to the dual problems of social transformation and economic growth. Mao extended this mobilization strategy in 1958 in the Great Leap Forward and the formation of the communes and again won the support of a large section of the Party leadership and the peasantry. This time, however, the system was pressed to the point of rupture. The fragility of the collective fabric created in 1956 became exposed, and the economy, particularly the agrarian sector, hurtled toward collapse, sped to be sure by the abrupt withdrawal of Soviet technical support and three years of horrendous weather. The attempt to expand rapidly the scale and scope of cooperation to the communes undermined such important bases for cooperation as the reliance on familiar face-to-face relationships and the palpable links between labor and remuneration. Inevitably the boldest innovations of the communes had to be cut back. As China enters the 1980s the commune has yet to fulfill its promise as a socially rooted and economically significant institution. The tendency toward smaller teams and working groups and the enlargement of the private sector favored since 1979, moreover, represents a return to a mix of cooperative and private forms similar in concept and scale to those worked out in the mid-1950s prior to the high tide. If this analysis is correct, and if current policies are sustained, we might expect to see not the further dissolution of cooperation but stabilization. Eventually, cooperative expansion and

movement toward enlargement would become possible, but only
when the means of mechanization and other technologies become
more widely available and the accumulated resources and credibility of small cooperative units have been firmly established.

The high tide-great leap strategies, for all their originality and
boldness, and for all the genuinely heroic achievements of millions
of workers and peasants, set back the prospects of socialism: By
undermining the link between cooperation and mutual prosperity
throughout the countryside; by weakening the democratic and popular foundations of cooperation in rural communities; by weakening
the foundations of economic development and accumulation; by
increasing state manipulation of village and peasantry; by reducing
the overall credibility of the Party and of cooperative institutions;
by establishing a conspiratorial political milieu conducive to the
formation of cliques at the center; by divorcing policy from economic reality and popular welfare; and by projecting a distorted
vision of class polarization and class struggle in the countryside.

In the world of necessity, of extreme scarcity of rural China,
changes in the relations and forces of production must reinforce
the development of the productive forces and yield higher incomes
for most people or risk undermining the new social relationships.
Both the successful formation of rural base areas in the face of
militarily powerful foes during the thirties and forties and the land
revolution rested on this premise which was long shared by Mao,
Liu Shaoqi, and the core Party leadership. That leadership consensus began to unravel in the summer and fall of 1955. The high
tide, great leap, and Cultural Revolution brought into the open
critical issues concerning inequality within socialist society and
the role of class struggle in the transition period. In each, however,
when mobilization strategies juxtaposed the political versus the
economic, public interest versus individual welfare, many came
to perceive revolutionary change in terms of permanent sacrifice
of the individual to Party and state and the perpetual deepening of
class divisions. By contrast, the promise of socialism in general
and cooperation in particular had earlier seemed to lie in mutual
benefit, including improvement in the livelihood of all the people
and the creation of new foundations for community solidarity. The
factional struggles of the Cultural Revolution in particular, many
quite incomprehensible to rural people, dimmed the prospects for
further expansion of the productive forces and peasant incomes and
intensified conflict among state, collective, and individual in ways

which strained the cooperative fabric to the breaking point. But the Chinese experience suggests more hopeful possibilities about the prospects for revolutionary change: The periods of anti-Japaneses resistance, land revolution, and early cooperative transformation produced far-reaching institutional changes conducive to expanded productivity and personal income which rested on broad popular support and resulted in the expansion of horizons of human freedom and community. These periods of creativity and achievement linking revolutionary change to the promise of cooperation and mutual prosperity offer a standard by which to gauge the course of the transition to socialism in China and elsewhere.

NOTES

1. Stalin's mechanical concept of social change in which social relations, institutions, and ideas automatically follow from the level of development of the productive forces took this form in one authoritative pronouncement:

> Every base has its own superstructure corresponding to it. The base of the feudal system has its superstructure — its political, legal and other views and the corresponding institutions; the capitalist base has its own superstructure, and so has the socialist base. If the base changes or is eliminated, then following this its superstructure changes or is eliminated; if a new base arises, then following this a superstructure arises corresponding to it.

Joseph Stalin, Marxism and Linguistics (New York: International Publishers, 1951), p. 9. In a series of important books, the Polish economist Wlodzimierz Brus has focused on the process of achieving socialist forms of ownership beginning with nationalization or the formation of cooperative units. The central issue is the political process of investing new ownership forms with the substance of participation in and mastery of the factories and farms by the immediate producers. Brus raises these issues in the context of a critique of centralized socialism. See in particular his "Socialisation in the Conception and Practice of East European Socialism," in Socialist Ownership and Political Systems (London: Routledge and Kegan Paul, 1975), pp. 27-102. Mao Zedong's most comprehensive contribution to the debate is A Critique of Soviet Economics, Moss Roberts trans. (New York: Monthly Review Press, 1977).

2. My own work underestimated the centrality of the interrelated issues of production, accumulation, and income distribution. I would also cite the work of such informed observers writing in the 1960s and 1970s as Jack Gray, John Gurley, Neville Maxwell, James Peck, and Joan Robinson, and much of the writing on the Cultural Revolution which appeared in the Bulletin of Concerned Asian Scholars and Modern China.

3. Chinese documents delineate elementary and advanced cooperatives (hezuoshe) as the basic socialist units in the countryside in the 1950s, using distinctive Chinese terminology rather than the term used to translate Soviet

collectives (jiti nongzhuang). Advanced cooperatives are in fact, however, collective units which own and operate the land and the principal means of production, and in which remuneration is based on the principle "to each according to one's work." They are comparable to, and were initially modeled after, Soviet collectives, the kolkhozes.

4. Grundrisse: Foundations of the Critique of Political Economy (New York: Vintage, 1973). Italics in original.

5. "Manifesto of the Communist Party," in Robert Tucker, The Marx-Engels Reader (New York: W. W. Norton, 1972), p. 334.

6. Quoted in Wada Haruki, "Karl Marx and Revolutionary Russia," Annals of the Institute of Social Science (University of Tokyo) 1977, no. 18, p. 104. The discussion of the view of Marx and Engels on the commune and the prospects of revolution in Russia is based on Professor Wada's pioneering archival research in the Marx-Engels manuscripts.

7. Quoted in ibid., p. 116. At the elipsis [...] Marx had written, "and if the intelligent sector of Russian society, the Russian intellect, concentrates all the living forces of this country," and then crossed it out. In the letter Marx finally dispatched he asserted that the commune could provide the "point of support of a social regeneration in Russia." But "the poisonous influences that attack it from all sides must be eliminated, and then the normal conditions of a spontaneous development insured."

8. Quoted in Robert Wesson, Soviet Communes (New Brunswick, N. J.: Rutgers University Press, 1963), p. 38.

9. "The Tasks of the Proletariat in Our Revolution," in Alliance of the Working Class and the Peasantry (Moscow: Foreign Languages Publishing House, 1959), pp. 180-81. Italics in original.

10. Lenin, "Economics and Politics in the Era of the Dictatorship of the Proletariat," ibid., p. 318. Italics in original.

11. Lenin, "Report on the Substitution of a Tax in Kind for the Surplus-Appropriation System," Delivered at the Tenth Congress of the R.C.P. (B.), ibid., p. 358.

12. Lenin, "On Cooperation," in Robert Tucker, ed., The Lenin Anthology, (New York: W. W. Norton, 1975), p. 708.

13. See M. Lewin's excellent discussion in Russian Peasants and Soviet Power: A Study of Collectivization (New York: W. W. Norton, 1975), pp. 93-102. Nicolai Bukharin, leading the opposition to collectivization as premature and unworkable in the years 1925-29, stressed his fidelity to Lenin's emphasis on marketing cooperatives which left intact private ownership of the means of production during the transition period. Cf. Stephen Cohen, Bukharin and the Bolshevik Revolution: A Political Biography (Oxford: Oxford University Press, 1980), pp. 193-201. Bukharin anticipated many of the failures and problems of Soviet collectivization; he did not, however, successfully frame an alternative policy which would solve issues of the transition.

14. Lewin, Russian Peasants and Soviet Power. Charles Bettelheim, Class Struggles in the Soviet Union, 1923-30 (New York: Monthly Review Press, 1978).

15. Peter Nolan, "Collectivization in China: Some Comparisons with the USSR," Journal of Peasant Studies 3, no. 2 (January 1976): 24.

16. "Reading Notes on the Soviet Text Political Economy," in Mao,

A Critique of Soviet Economics, p. 51. Elsewhere in the same text Mao argued that the analogous pattern had occurred in early capitalist development: The bourgeois revolutions opened the way for the industrial revolution and the rapid development of the productive forces of advanced capitalism (p. 66).

17. Mao, "The Present Situation and Our Tasks," in Mark Selden, ed., The People's Republic of China: A Documentary History of Revolutionary Change (New York: Monthly Review Press, 1979), pp. 173-174. Mao's concept of stages grew organically out of the Party's experience. It invites comparison, however, with a seminal statement on the subject by Lenin in his 1918 "Speech Delivered at the First All-Russian Congress of Land Departments, Committees of Poor Peasants and Communes," Lenin, Alliance of the Working Class and the Peasantry, especially p. 259. "We know very well that in countries where small-peasant economies prevail the transition to socialism cannot be effected except by a series of gradual preliminary stages. ... We fully realize that such vast upheavals in the lives of tens of millions of people as the transition from small individual peasant farming to the joint cultivation of the land, affecting as they do the most deepgoing roots of life and habits, can be accomplished only by long effort, and can in general be accomplished only when necessity compels people to reshape their lives."

18. I have developed these themes in The Yenan Way in Revolutionary China (Cambridge, Mass.: Harvard University Press, 1971) and in my introduction to The People's Republic of China.

19. Mao, "Economic Problems and Financial Problems," in Selden, The People's Republic of China, p. 715. The full text is available in Andrew Watson, Mao Zedong and the Political Economy of the Border Region: A Translation of Mao's Economic Problems and Financial Problems (Cambridge: Cambridge University Press, 1980).

20. Two articles have analyzed the positions of Mao and Liu on issues related to the rich peasant economy and subsequent charges directed against Liu during the Cultural Revolution. Both make clear Mao's participation in formulating the position of support for the rich peasant economy from the late forties. Kenneth Lieberthal, "Mao Versus Liu? Policy Toward Industry and Commerce: 1946-49," The China Quarterly 47 (July/September 1971): 494-520, and Tanaka Kyoko, "Mao and Liu in the 1947 Land Reform: Allies or Disputants?" The China Quarterly 75 (September 1978): 566-593.

21. Documents and analysis of the question of the "rich peasant economy" are included in Selden, The People's Republic of China, pp. 27-39 and 208-253.

22. Mao Zedong, "Zuzhiqilai" (Get Organized), in Takeuchi Minoru, ed., Mao Zedong ji (Collected works of Mao Zedong), IX, pp. 88-89.

23. Ibid., p. 89. The revised text as presented in the Selected Works, III, p. 159 reads: "We have already organized many peasant co-operatives in the Border Region, but at present they are only of a rudimentary type and must still pass through certain stages of development before they can become co-operatives of the Soviet type known as collective farms."

24. We can trace Mao's impulses toward mutual aid and cooperation back to a pre-Marxist period. In his 1919 essay "The Great Union of the Popular Masses," after noting the approach of "one extremely violent party which uses the method 'do unto others as they do unto you' to struggle desperately to the end with the aristocrats and capitalists" (its leader was "a man named Marx")

the young Mao commented on a more promising alternative which

> does not expect rapid results but begins by understanding the
> common people. Men should all have a morality of mutual aid,
> and work voluntarily.... The ideas of this party are broader
> and more far-reaching. They want to unite the whole globe into
> a single country, unite the human race into a single family....
> The leader of this party is a man named Kropotkin.

Cited in Stuart Schram's introduction to Li Jui, The Early Revolutionary
Activities of Comrade Mao Tse-tung (White Plains: M. E. Sharpe, 1977),
p. xxviii.

25. Thomas Wiens, "Agricultural Statistics in the People's Republic of
China," in Alexander Eckstein, ed., Quantitative Measures of China's Economic Output (Ann Arbor: University of Michigan Press, 1980), pp. 61-63. In
light of the performance in the Soviet Union, Cuba, Vietnam, and a number of
other countries which attempted cooperative solutions to the agrarian problem, China's performance during this period seems exemplary.

26. One of the most serious charges made against Liu Shaoqi and others
during the Cultural Revolution was that they had opposed and sabotaged cooperation in the early fifties. The charges, in my view, are unfounded. The
intraleadership divisions centered rather on the pace of cooperation and the
issue of voluntary participation. Jack Gray has argued the contrary. Those
who urged caution in cooperative formation, he concluded, really opposed cooperation and sought to move the countryside toward individual farming. While
there were surely plenty of advocates of such a future among the peasantry,
particularly among more prosperous households, I see no evidence that this
view enjoyed significant support in the upper ranks of the Party or state leadership. "Had collectivization been slowed up," Gray concludes of the 1955
hiatus, "it would never have taken place at all." This is precisely the point
with which this essay takes issue. See Jack Gray, "Mao Tse-tung's Strategy
for the Collectivization of Chinese Agriculture: An Important Phase in the
Development of Maoism," in I. de Kadt and G. P. Williams, eds., Sociology
and Development (London: Tavistock Press, 1975), p. 41.

27. A prominent spokesman for gradual development by stages was Deng
Zihui, head of the Party's rural work department. See for example, "Zhong-
guo nongye zou shang shehuihuyi gaizao de daolu" (Chinese Agriculture Takes
the Road of Socialist Transformation) in Nongye shehuizhuyi gaizau wenji
(Documents of China's Socialist Transformation in Agriculture) (Beijing:
Caizheng jingji chubanshe, 1955), vol. 2, pp. 13-17. Deng's views closely
parallel those set forward in Mao's major statement on cooperation: "On the
Cooperative Transformation of Agriculture," The Selected Works of Mao
Tse-tung (SW), V, pp. 184-207. In his important 1954 address to the Youth
League, Deng's projected timetable for collectivization, while geared to
progress in semimechanization, was actually faster than that which Mao pro-
posed one year later. Deng spoke of the completion of collectivization within
two five-year plans with large-scale mechanization to be achieved in the third,
"Rural Work During the Transition Period" (July 15, 1954), Current Back-

ground 306 (November 22, 1954): 1-15.

28. Kojima Reiitsu, Chūgoku no keizai to gijutsu (China's Economy and Technology) (Tokyo: Keiso Shobo, 1975), p. 61.

29. Ibid., pp. 61-100.

30. Deng Zihui, "Principles of Agrarian Socialist Transformation, Policies, and Leadership Guidelines, "cited in Xinhua yuebao (New China Semi-Monthly) 24 (1954): 144-150.

31. "On the Cooperative Transformation of Agriculture."

32. Beijing Review 29 (July 11, 1980): 18. See also Nicholas Lardy, "Intersectoral Resource Flows in Chinese Economic Development," prepared for a conference on Agricultural Development in China, Japan, and Korea, Academia Sinica, Taipei, December 1980.

33. K. C. Yeh, "Soviet and Chinese Industrialization Strategies," in Donald Treadgold, ed., Soviet and Chinese Communism: Similarities and Differences (Seattle: University of Washington Press, 1967), p. 334. Agriculture Minister Liao Luyan, in his July 25, 1955, speech to the National People's Congress, defended the priority of heavy industry as the focus for state investment against charges that there was insufficient investment in agriculture. Renmin ribao (People's Daily), July 26, 1955, Current Background 352 (December 1, 1955): 1-8.

34. Kojima, China's Economy and Technology, pp. 36-37. See Tongji gong-zuo (Statistical Work), 1957, no. 17, p. 5, which records a 39 percent rise in the price index of agricultural commodities bought by the state between 1950 and 1956, while the price index of industrial goods sent to the countryside increased by only 10.8 percent. This reduced, but did not eliminate, the gap which continued into the 1980s.

35. 1954 Quanguo geti shougongye diaocha ziliao (1954 National Investigation Materials on Handicraft Industry) (Beijing: Sanlien shudian, 1957), p. 52. China's leading anthropologist, Fei Xiaotong, offered a brilliant, if low-keyed, description of the destructive impact of national policy on rural handicraft and income in a single village in 1957. It was his last publication before being silenced for the next twenty years. See "A Revisit to Kaihsienkung," in James McGough, ed., Fei Hsiao-t'ung: The Dilemma of a Chinese Intellectual (White Plains: M. E. Sharpe, 1979), pp. 39-74. A recent if muted criticism of 1950's handicraft policies is Tian Yun's "Handicraft Industry: Trends of Development," Beijing Review 37 (September 15, 1980): 16-24.

36. State Statistical Bureau, Ten Great Years: Statistics of the Economic and Cultural Achievements of the People's Republic of China (Beijing: Foreign Languages Press, 1960), p. 36; Kojima, China's Economy and Technology, pp. 52-53. Unless otherwise noted, the following discussion of handicrafts draws on Kojima's pioneering research in this area.

37. Dorothy Solinger has explored a number of the issues pertaining to commerce in "Marxism and the Market in Socialist China," in Victor Nee, ed., State and Society in Contemporary China (forthcoming) and in her forthcoming book.

38. Articles in the theoretical journal Xuexi (Study) in the years 1952-55 spell out in rich detail the rationale for and specific measures employed in the gradual, voluntary cooperative transition based on demonstrated ability to contribute to mutual prosperity. See particularly Wu Zhen, "Fazhan nongye

shengchan hezuoshe, bixu caiyong shuofu, shifan he guojia caizhu de fangfa" (To Develop Agricultural Producers Cooperatives It Is Necessary to Use Persuasion, Models, and State Aid), Xuexi, 1954, no. 8, pp. 21-24.

39. Zhongguo nongbao (Chinese Agricultural Bulletin), 1953, no. 4. Even model Wugong could not organize all of the households in the village at this time.

40. In many localities payment based on land and other means of production was as high as 70 percent with only 30 percent based on labor. Cf. Ezra Vogel, Canton Under Communism: Programs and Politics in a Provincial Capital 1949-1968 (Cambridge, Mass.: Harvard University Press, 1968), p. 148. For one painstaking discussion of remuneration issues see He Juan, "On Distribution Relations in the Agricultural Producers' Cooperatives," Xuexi, January 1, 1953, p. 15.

41. My italics. Zhongguo guodu shiqi guomin jingji de fenzi (An Analysis of China's National Economy during the Transition Period) (Beijing: Science Press, 1959), pp. 137-39. Cited in Peter Schran, The Development of Chinese Agriculture, 1950-59 (Urbana: University of Illinois Press, 1969), p. 33.

42. The issue of appropriate ratios for remuneration is discussed in numerous articles in Socialist Upsurge in the Chinese Countryside (Beijing: Foreign Languages Press, 1956), and by Jack Gray in "The High Tide of Socialism in the Chinese Countryside," in Jerome Ch'en and Nicholas Tarling, eds., Studies in the Social History of China and Southeast Asia (Cambridge: Cambridge University Press, 1970).

43. These points are made particularly lucidly in the Renmin ribao editorial of February 28, 1955, "Why Is It Necessary to Emphasize the Work of Consolidation of the Agricultural Producers' Cooperatives?"

44. The intra-Party politics of the high tide are suggestively analyzed in Roderick MacFarquhar, The Origins of the Cultural Revolution: Contradictions Among the People, 1956-57 (New York: Columbia University Press, 1974), pp. 15-91.

45. Kenneth Walker, "Collectivization in Retrospect: The Socialist High Tide of Autumn 1955-Spring 1956," The China Quarterly 26 (April-June 1966). The analysis is based on Walker. The statistics used here are Wiens' more recent series which further underline the gravity of the situation. "Agricultural Statistics in the People's Republic of China," p. 63.

46. Cited in Kojima, China's Economy and Technology, pp. 42-43.

47. Ibid., pp. 45, 49-50. Chen Yun provided a detailed and authoritative discussion of the grain crisis and the state response in his July 1955 address "On the Question of the Unified Purchase and Distribution of Grain" at the National People's Congress. Current Background 339 (1955): 3-14.

48. Tung Ta-lin (Tong Dalin), Agricultural Cooperation in China (Beijing: Foreign Languages Press, 1959), p. 41.

49. I have analyzed Mao's speech in some detail in The People's Republic of China pp. 57-62. The discussion which follows reassesses aspects of Mao's statement and China's cooperative transformation. Edward Friedman's essay in this volume provides additional light on the problems discussed here.

50. "On the Cooperative Transformation of Agriculture," p. 195.

51. Ibid., pp. 201, 202.

52. A 1956 survey of Shaanxi Province revealed the following per capita

income differentials by region: Compared with a provincial average of
64 yuan, the average in the industrial crop region was 126 yuan, in the main
grain producing area 75 yuan, in the hill regions 43 yuan, and in poor mountainous areas 19 yuan. If regional differences in income were on a scale of
greater than five to one, differences between poor and rich villages were
many times higher. Peter Nolan, "Inequality of Income Between Town and
Countryside in the People's Republic of China in the Mid-1950s," World Development 7 (1979): 450. Cooperativization strategies do not directly address
these and other regional and intravillage inequalities which persist in China
in the 1980s, and whose resolution hinges on the outcome of other debates,
including state allocation of financial and technical resources, population
policies, and policies which curb the free movement of labor.

53. This discussion of class polarization draws on personal communications from Edward Friedman.

54. New China News Agency, Beijing, February 2, 1956, reprinted in
Current Background 377 (February 15, 1966): 36-44; cf. Edward Friedman's
discussion of Chen's perspective in his essay in this volume.

55. See for example Deng Zihui, "Mobilize All Peasants and Rural Youths
to Struggle for Cooperativization of Agriculture," Zhongguo qingnianbao (Chinese Youth Journal), April 1, 1954, in Current Background, November 18,
1954, pp. 1-10.

56. Kojima, China's Economy and Technology. Peter Nolan, "Collectivization in China: Some Comparisons with the USSR." Vivienne Shue, Peasant
China in Transition: The Dynamics of Development Toward Socialism,
1949-1956 (Berkeley: University of California Press, 1980).

57. Mao, "On the Cooperative Transformation of Agriculture," pp. 194-95.
Chen Yun, minister of commerce in the early fifties, was among the most important and consistent proponents of the importance of strengthening unity
with the middle peasants in contrast with Mao's new emphasis on satisfying
the demands of the poor and lower-middle peasants. The issue is not unre-
lated to Chen's emergence as the leading architect of China's economic adjustment for the period 1979-1982 and beyond.

58. In his September 7, 1955, inner-Party directive, Mao went so far as to
divide the middle peasants into three categories: lower, intermediate, and
upper middle. The version of the directive printed in 1977 in SW V takes the
unusual step of noting that in practice this proved to be a classification "too
fine for drawing distinctions," pp. 208-09.

59. A translation of the politically more important one-volume abridged
edition was published by Foreign Languages Press in 1956. Jack Gray and
Kojima Reiitsu have used the Socialist Upsurge collection to demonstrate the
viability of Mao's approach to cooperation. My own study of Wugong, Dazhai,
and other model units such as those whose experiences are chronicled in this
collection suggests another interpretation. In the rush to collectivization in
1955-56, the genuine achievements of many of these units could not be rapidly
duplicated by most others which lacked such advantages as outstanding leadership, intravillage unity, long cooperative experience, or access to state financial and technical support which could not be made generally available. Cf.
Jack Gray, "Mao Tse-tung's Strategy for the Collectivization of Chinese Agriculture," and Kojima, China's Economy and Technology.

60. Mao, "The Debate on the Co-operative Transformation of Agriculture and the Current Class Struggle," SW V, pp. 216-17.

61. Chen Boda, "Under the Red Flag of Comrade Mao Zedong," Hongqi (Red Flag) No. 4 (July 16, 1959). See also MacFarquhar, The Origins of the Cultural Revolution, p. 18, and Friedman, op. cit. It is instructive to compare the tone and implications of Deng Zihui's writings between 1953 and 1956 with those of Chen Boda. Both were actively engaged in the campaign to develop cooperatives. Deng Zihui, however, attempted to address concretely the specific doubts and hesitations about cooperation of different sectors of the peasantry while emphasizing the importance of voluntary cooperation and mutual benefit. Deng likewise criticized the problems which result from commandism and excessive haste in cooperative formation. Chen Boda's speech of February 2, 1956, "The Socialist Transformation of China's Agriculture," is a prototype of approaches to immediate, wholesale collectivization. Two aspects of Chen's approach stand out sharply from much of the discussion of the period. First, where Deng and others had stressed the dual and complex nature of the peasantry, Chen emphasized the revolutionary qualities of the peasantry, qualities he traced back to the "semiproletarian" character of the majority of semitenants and poor peasants which Mao had pointed to in his 1926 analysis of classes in Chinese society. Second, Chen stressed the dominant role of the state in leading the transition: "...our socialist transformation of agriculture is a revolution above to below, led by the state in which the governmental power is in the hands of the working class." What was essential for Chen was "to give active leadership to ensure the consciousness of the masses and mobilize them..." not to "Passively wait for the masses or let the masses take whatever action they see fit." Chen's emphasis on top down leadership and immediate collectivization, the lack of sympathy for voluntary cooperation, and the absence of appeal to peasant material interests in striking ways evokes Stalinist approaches to collectivization, Current Background, February 15, 1956, pp. 36-44.

62. Socialist Upsurge in China's Countryside, p. 8.

63. "Decisions on Agricultural Cooperation," adopted at the Sixth Plenary Session (Enlarged) of the Seventh Central Committee of the Chinese Communist Party, in Robert Bowie and John Fairbank, eds., Communist China 1955-1959: Policy Documents with Analysis (Cambridge, Mass.: Harvard University Press, 1962), p. 110.

64. Ibid., p. 115.

65. Ibid., p. 109.

66. Cited in John Starr, Continuing the Revolution: The Political Thought of Mao (Princeton: Princeton University Press, 1979), p. 195. Deng Zihui in early 1956 continued to call on cooperatives — but perhaps no longer with much conviction — to ensure that 90 percent of their members improved their income in the very first year.

67. Vogel, Canton Under Communism, pp. 146-56.

68. Ibid., p. 155.

69. Kenneth R. Walker, Planning in Chinese Agriculture: Socialisation and the Private Sector, 1956-1962 (London: Frank Cass, 1965), pp. 16-17.

70. "Model Regulations for an Agricultural Producers' Cooperative," in

Tung Ta-lin, Agricultural Cooperation in China, pp. 96, 99.

71. Model Regulations for an Agricultural Producers' Cooperative (Beijing: Foreign Languages Press, 1956), p. 7.

72. Ibid.

73. Schran, The Development of Chinese Agriculture, p. 34.

74. "Changes in China's Rural Economy and Problems in the Agriculture Cooperative Movement," Speech at the Third Session of the First National People's Congress, New China Advances to Socialism (Beijing: Foreign Languages Press, 1956), pp. 125-26.

75. Beijing: Foreign Languages Press, 1957.

76. United States Department of Agriculture, People's Republic of China: Agriculture Situation Review of 1979 and Outlook for 1980, June 1980, p. 40. These conclusions are confirmed by the as yet unpublished research findings of Nicholas Lardy and Benedict Stavis.

77. I am indebted to Edward Friedman for his suggestions concerning the general framework of the welfare question discussed above. A positive example, drawing once again on Wugong, will illustrate dimensions of the problem. In 1979 the most prosperous team in Wugong (with per capita income surpassing 200 yuan, the village ranks in the top five percent of rural units) implemented an unusually progressive new welfare system. The collective for the first time assumed a measure of responsibility for the aged regardless of need or of family ability to provide income. The new system guarantees the value of 120 labor days (presently valued at 126 yuan) to each individual seventy-five years of age or older. The plan is gradually to lower the age requirement and raise the income provision in subsequent years so that eventually the elderly receive a guaranteed income at levels approaching those of active workers. As the state began to recognize clearly in 1979, the solution to the welfare problem is critical to the long-range success of cooperation. It vitally affects the success of planned birth programs which encourage one child and thus reduce the likelihood of familial support for the aged and infirm. Many other units whose economies are far more fragile and which lack Wugong's political unity have at best weakly developed welfare programs.

78. Left untouched in the process — indeed frozen by official policies stressing labor control and self-reliance — were substantial differentials between city and countryside and between localities based on difference in resource endowment, transportation access, and distance from the city and the market such as those separating mountain from suburban communes. And of course there were differences in quantity and quality of labor power between families.

79. In addition to works previously cited, see William Parish and Martin Whyte, Village and Family in Contemporary China (Chicago: University of Chicago Press, 1978) and Thomas Bernstein, "Leadership and Mass Mobilisation in the Soviet and Chinese Collectivisation Campaigns of 1929-30 and 1955-56: A Comparison." The China Quarterly 31 (July-September 1967): 1-47.

80. V. I. Lenin, "Report on Work in the Rural Districts Delivered at the Eighth Congress of the R.C.P. (B), Alliance of the Working Class and the Peasantry, pp. 276, 282-83. I have substituted the word cooperative for "kommunia" in the original translation. A good introduction to the dismal record of Soviet cooperative

formation in the decade prior to forced collectivization is M. Lewin's <u>Russian Peasants and Soviet Power: A Study of Collectivization</u>. Deng Zihui underlined the point in an important 1954 article, "China's Agriculture Takes the Road of Socialist Transformation," p. 16: "Leninism teaches us: In petty commodity agrarian economy, in carrying out the socialist transformation, we absolutely must not use force and methods of expropriation to collectivize (<u>gongyuhua</u>) the property of the peasantry. This would be a violation of the party's basic policy toward the peasants."

81. Jack Gray's hypothetical example of family budgets, introduced to demonstrate quite different points about the cooperative movement, bears out this hypothesis. In Gray's example, derived from actual cases described in <u>Socialist Upsurge in China's Countryside</u>, 60 percent of income is based on inputs to land, 40 percent to labor (pp. 55-61). Gray's three articles on the socialist upsurge period creatively reconstruct the internal logic of the upsurge, the view so to speak from Mao's desk, based on a close reading of the several hundred case studies provided in the <u>Socialist Upsurge</u> collection. At one critical moment, however, Gray steps back from this reconstruction to raise serious problems about its results. Commenting on the <u>Upsurge</u> collection, he observes that it "represents an experimentalist idea, and contradicts the notion of gradualism. It is enough that the manifold particular problems of co-operativization and cooperative working have all been solved <u>somewhere</u>. They are therefore capable of solution everywhere. This is acceptable on the level of the leadership and the cadres; but it is not a substitute for gradualism at the level of the farmers, who can only be convinced, in the last resort, by their own practical experience over a series of agricultural seasons; and who must <u>get used gradually</u> to a new form of discipline and a new concept of shared profit. This is the nub of the politics of the cooperative movement; it sets an irreducible minimum period for success, and in the event most Chinese farmers were not given this minimum" (pp. 115-16). (Italics in original.) Precisely. Yet Gray's work as a whole is devoted to explaining the logic and success of the transition and of Mao's analysis. The logic that the performance of model units, typically the beneficiary of special financial and leadership support, proves the viability of national policies, is unacceptable.

82. The text of the twelve-year program is presented and discussed in Selden, <u>The People's Republic of China</u>, pp. 358-63.

83. This discussion draws heavily on data presented in Kojima, <u>China's Economy and Technology</u>, pp. 62-64. See also Leslie Kuo, <u>The Technical Transformation of Agriculture in Communist China</u> (New York: Praeger, 1972), pp. 192-93.

84. <u>Stalin as Revolutionary, 1879-1929: A Study in History and Personality</u> (New York: W. W. Norton, 1973), p. 406.

85. James Petras and Mark Selden address in preliminary fashion this problem and a number of related theoretical issues of the transition in "Social Classes, the State and the World System in the Transition to Socialism," <u>Journal of Contemporary Asia</u> XI.2(1981): 189-207.

86. The cooperative transformation of agriculture in general and the high tide-great leap in particular became the subject of intensive study in China and Hong Kong in 1980. Among the more significant attempts at reinterpreta-

tion are Yang Junshi, "Zhongguo de nongye jitihua wenti" (Problems of China's Agricultural Collectivization), Dousou (Awake) 39 (July 1980).
The "Resolution on Certain Questions in the History of Our Party since the Founding of the People's Republic of China," adopted by the Sixth Plenum of the Eleventh Central Committee on June 27, 1981, noted (for the first time in an official document) that "from the summer of 1955 onwards, we were over-hasty in pressing on with agricultural cooperation and the transformation of private handicraft and commercial establishments; we were far from metic-ulous, the changes were too fast, and we did our work in a somewhat summa-ry, stereotyped manner, leaving open a number of questions for a long time." The document does not, however, explicitly hold Mao Zedong responsible for the attendant problems in this area. Beijing Review 27 (July 6, 1981): 16.

87. This is a major theme of a forthcoming study: "Wugong: A Chinese Village in a Socialist State," co-authored by Edward Friedman, Kay Johnson, Paul Pickowicz, and Mark Selden. These issues are explored in detail by Tang Tsou, Mitch Meisner, and Marc Blecher in their essay in this volume.

William Hinton
VILLAGE IN TRANSITION

Thirty years ago the sounds heard in Longbow Village were country sounds — cocks crowing in the darkness before dawn, the creak of giant millstones as they were pushed around their stone beds by hand, the cries of a bean curd peddler in the alley, the hoarse bellow of the village chairman announcing a meeting through a megaphone from the tower of the expropriated Catholic church. The loudest sound of all then, and one that still haunts memory, was the crashing of the massive wooden wheel hubs against the beams of the heavily laden carts as they traveled the frozen ruts of the north-south track in winter. From the distance it sounded like some tireless, nether-world kettledrummer, or the busy pounding of a phantom carpenter knocking together a hollow barrel.

Today the dominant sound heard in Longbow is no country sound but the shrill wailing of steam locomotives in the railroad shops testing their eerie voices against a background roar of army tanks racing across the proving grounds on the flanks of Great Ridge Hill and the accompanying cacaphony of truck, bus, and jeep horns on the road as frustrated drivers try to make their way through the handcarts, donkey carts, tractor-drawn wagons, bicycles, pedestrians with carrying poles, and ordinary strollers that flow in a constant stream in both directions.

Inside the village a lesser background roar rolls from the big grinder of the brigade's own cement plant, while from the long shed that was once a meeting hall the high whine of carborundum on steel shreds the air as young women, working in shifts around the clock, polish sawblades that will be exported to Tanzania.

The tower of the old church has long since been torn down. The brigade leaders have installed a loudspeaker on the roof of the two-storied, block-long brigade headquarters. When this crackles to life their booming voices can be heard in the farthest fields. Other

villages still announce time by broadcasting that solemn hymn to
Mao Zedong, "The East Is Red." Not Longbow. What blasts forth
here before dawn to wake people up, at noon to summon them from
the fields, and at sundown to signal that the day's work is done, is
a lively Shanxi rock tune rendered on a double-reed horn (an oboe-
trumpet cross) and several Chinese snakeskin fiddles. Inside the
village the amplified jam session wrung from this ensemble makes
eardrums ache. Out on the garden land of the First Production
Team, half a mile away, it sounds like a wedding dance for elves,
leprechauns, cow demons, and snake gods.

Cocks still crow in Longbow and peddlers still hawk bean curd
in the alley, but their calls no longer command the attention they
once took for granted. There are too many locomotives in the railroad yards.

Today the road that flanks Longbow to the east is no cart track
but an improved asphalt highway that is the main north-south artery
of the whole southeast Shanxi region. Across the highway, less than
one hundred yards from the village entrance, lies the railroad that
links Zhengzhou, in distant Henan, to Taiyuan in central Shanxi.
The repair shops that service this whole line have been built on
land that once belonged to Longbow's Fourth Production Team.

Between the highway and the railroad hundreds of adobe and reed
shacks have been thrown up to house the thousands of railroad construction workers who are building an east-west line through the
region. This will cross the existing line less than a mile north of
Longbow at the site of Changzhi North Station, making it one of the
busiest junctions in the country.

Going south along the tracks from the railroad repair shops one
comes to the Changzhi City Cement Plant with several hundred
workers. South again and a little to the east, but still on Longbow
land, lies the Taihang Sawblade Works, with 5,000 workers and
almost twice that many family members. The railroad, the highway, the industrial plants, and the workers settlements have taken
over one third of Longbow's cropland. In the meantime the population dependent on the land has doubled. In 1948 there was a tilled
acre for every man, woman, and child. Now with only 530 acres
for 2,200 people there is less than a quarter of an acre per person.

This drastically compressed yet burgeoning community no longer
counts as part of rural Lucheng County, but has been transferred
instead to the territory of Changzhi City, a municipality of 300,000
that administers a long finger of land stretching northward from

the old city line that is zoned industrial and now includes the power plant at Yellow Mill, the coal mine at Shigejie, the coal mine at Wuzhuang, and the huge smelter and furnace complex known as Changzhi Steel.

What all this adds up to is a Longbow Village that is no longer rural. It is suburban, a community in transition from agriculture to industry where the way of life is undergoing not only socialization but urbanization and industrialization all at the same time. This may not be a typical situation in the Chinese countryside, but it is something that is happening everywhere that industry is taking hold, and the process here may be taken as a symbol of the future of the nation.

In the last few years Longbow has been remarkably successful both in farming and in industrial sidelines. Whereas in 1948 grain yields averaged less than 10 bushels to the acre, they now average 100.

If one third of the land area had been lost, this loss has been made up to a certain extent by the enormous increase in nightsoil available to the community from the industrial population. Not only this, but workers and their families have created a demand for fresh vegetables that has made it possible to shift one sixth of the land that remains from grain to vegetable production, a more intensive and more profitable use for the land than planting it to corn and wheat.

With the capital derived in part from the transfer of the land — villages receive the value of three years crops for transferred acreage — four thriving local industries have been built: a cement plant producing 15 to 20 tons of cement a day, a sawmill that saws 10,000 board feet a day, a woodworking shop that makes handles for saws, and a polishing shop that finishes steel blades for the Taihang Sawblade Works. These industries employ only 12 percent of the labor power of the village but bring in about 70 percent of the income.

The returns from all enterprises, both agricultural and industrial, have underwritten not only a rising standard of living in terms of housing, clothing and food, but greatly expanded social services as well. Every child in Longbow now goes to the eight year school. Every family receives medical care under a cooperative plan that costs $.50 per person per year for doctors' services and provides drugs at one-half the market price. Everyone is entitled to a free bath every week and a haircut every month. Grain is ground for all at a central location at reasonable fees, and there is a library, a political night school, a drama group, and a large contingent of stiltwalkers — to mention but a few of the extracurricular activities. All this adds up to a prosperous, thriving community that is just now embarking on some major experiments in farm mechanization that are bound to have an impact on the whole of China.

Most of this striking prosperity and progress has taken place only in the last five years. After the land reform in 1948 there was a big spurt in production that raised the yield of grain from 10 to 20 bushels to the acre. In the mid-fifties, after the land was pooled and the whole village became a cooperative brigade, production again rose a certain amount — from 20 to about 30 bushels to the acre. But after 1958, production slid off to a level below 30 bushels, and no amount of political rectification or mass mobilization was able to change the picture again until recently.

The question that concerned me over the years was why? Why should an apparently healthy cooperative community like Longbow, after some remarkable initial successes, stagnate for fifteen years and then suddenly spurt forward in the seventies. The upsurge was not owing to any basic economic or social reorganization, for nothing of this sort occurred after the villagewide cooperative was formed in 1956 and this cooperative joined the Horse Square Commune in 1958. One had to look elsewhere for answers. The search, I felt, could reveal something of the real social and political conflicts in China and bring out both the strengths and the weaknesses of the unique agricultural system there.

It is taken for granted by millions in China that the cooperative organization of agriculture is the only way out for Chinese peasants and that it has tremendous potential both for production and rising standards of living. To prove this there is the example of Dazhai Brigade, held up as a model for many years.

Dazhai is a small settlement in Shanxi Province less than a day's journey by jeep from Longbow. It became famous because, after its people formed a producers cooperative in 1953, they put the welfare of their community ahead of individual self-interest, put agricultural production ahead of sidelines or trade, where returns were more immediate, and worked together to transform the badly eroded loess deposits on the slopes of Tigerhead Mountain into highly productive, terraced fields where the yields of corn, beans, and millet now rival the best in the world. After Mao Zedong called attention to this brigade in 1964, peasants all over China began to study it. Here and there they were able to apply the lessons learned and reach or even surpass the levels of prosperity and community service pioneered by Dazhai.

The peasants of Longbow studied Dazhai, read about Dazhai, heard speeches about Dazhai, and sent delegations to Dazhai on three different occasions, but failed again and again to learn the proper lessons, or if they learned them, to apply what they had learned. This was not unusual. Rhymes have been written about such failures:

> Moved when you see it.
> Moved again when it is explained.
> Motionless when you get back home!
>
> At the meeting, wholeheartedly for it.
> On the way home, halfheartedly for it.
> Back home, no heart for it. It is forgotten!

When Longbow peasant activists returned from Dazhai they continued to farm their heavy, level alkaline land much as they always had before and with the same indifferent results. They sent their best labor power, their most skillful and competent people, out to work at various sidelines where cash wages could be earned. With the exception of a brick kiln, which is standard equipment in villages all over China, they failed to develop any sidelines of their own. They hauled other people's freight down the highway in flat-carts, unloaded public goods at the railroad station by the ton, cut steel bars at the steel mill at so much per bar, and generally dispersed their effort in any direction that brought in a dollar.

These, at least, were collective efforts. The income received was turned in to the brigade and the people involved earned work points in their production teams. This gave them a claim on a share of the crop and a share of total cash income when accounts were settled in the fall.

Outside the collective sphere quite a few brigade members went in for speculation. The most notorious example of this was Li Hongchang, a bachelor, a bully, and a rascal until he reformed and became a model team leader in 1976. Before that when he ran out of funds he rode freight trains into Henan Province, bought dried sweet potatoes there, swapped them pound for pound for wheat back in Longbow, and sold the wheat for twice what the sweet potatoes cost him. A four day trip into Henan brought in more cash than a month's work in the field. Why study Dazhai when a killing could be made on the road?

Other people added extra rooms to their houses so that they could rent them out to the railroad builders or to the "temporary" workers from Henan who came to Changzhi City looking for work when their crops failed at home. Rents were regulated by the brigade, but householders could always get around that by asking for key money in advance. One Longbow peasant, Li Hongen, opened an inn and made money not only on the rent and the key money that he charged his boarders but on the night soil and kitchen waste they left behind in his courtyard.

There were both objective and subjective pressures pushing people into such questionable enterprises. On the objective side there was the stubborn alkalinity of Longbow soil, which no one had yet found a way to ameliorate. Hard work on the land almost never yielded more than ten pounds of grain a day. Ten pounds of grain were worth only about $.50, half of which had to go for expenses. Hence a day on the land brought in, at the most, $.25. By working outside one could earn at least $.50 and sometimes quite a bit more, and the whole amount earned was income. Living in the middle of one of the fastest growing industrial districts in the nation, the temptation to seek outside work was overwhelming.

The obvious solution to this problem was to raise the earnings from field work by increasing yields. The most widely accepted method for this on land that could not be improved by spreading it out as at Dazhai was irrigation. Everyone knew that "irrigation is the life blood of agriculture." The slogan had been put forward by Mao Zedong himself. Unfortunately irrigation didn't work in Longbow. The more the peasants watered the land the harder and more alkaline it got. Water brought up salt instead of washing it down. When the sun dried the water out the land cracked into blocks, tearing apart the roots of young plants. To irrigate was to invite disaster. Every fall the city authorities mobilized Longbow people to increase the irrigated area by means of winter labor in well digging, canal building, and land leveling. Community leaders agreed, but when spring came very little progress was evident. People were voting with their feet against irrigation, and the city officials were calling them backward.

"Backward" Longbow peasants annually put forth a token effort on irrigation works but looked elsewhere for real income, as we have seen. This tendency was reinforced by uncertainty over the future of the land. How much of it would be diverted to industrial use? Why break your back on irrigation works when a factory might well be placed right in the middle of it anyway? The Taihang Sawblade works ruined an irrigation ditch that people had expended tens of thousands of labor days to build. Longbow Brigade was compensated for the pumping station that was uprooted but not for the labor expended.

As industrialization accelerated, life around Longbow developed a sophisticated, cosmopolitan style that tended to raise expectations and divert attention further from hard work on the land. Among the 30,000 railroad workers and their families who lived along the tracks or rented rooms in Longbow courtyards, there were hundreds who had worked on railroad construction in Africa. They brought home radios, tape recorders, and hand calculators that could not be bought anywhere else in China. When they needed cash they sometimes parted with these treasures, and someone acquired a windfall that could be parlayed into a small fortune.

The railroad workers included Koreans from the Northeast, coal miners from Fushun, and mechanics from Tianjin. They wore clothes, displayed hair styles, sang tunes, and used words different from those Longbow people were used to. But close contact changed local customs in inconspicuous ways that added up. After a few years Longbow people found themselves already "superior" to peasants who lived only a few miles away from the railroad in what they came to regard as backcountry. It became almost impossible to marry a Longbow girl unless one was willing to move into Longbow because the sophisticated young women there would not leave home, certainly not for any village without quarter-hourly bus service to Changzhi City and twice daily train service to Zhengzhou and Beijing.

Longbow cadres found it increasingly difficult to hold meetings because there was always some play being performed or some film being shown nearby — if not at the railroad shops then at the construction headquarters, if not at the headquarters then at the Sawblade Plant or at Changzhi North Station. Film watching became a habit that had a devastating effect on both cultural and political life, at least until the novelty wore off. But this took several years. Some Longbow children even became dissatisfied with the brigade's excellent new school. The brigade leader's daughter, entirely on her own, transferred to the high school run by the construction headquarters for railroad workers' children. Her father beat her for it until his arms gave out, but she refused to transfer back!

These were some of the objective economic and social factors that made it difficult for Longbow people to concentrate on agriculture. Dazhai peasants had no alternative. If they failed to transform Tigerhead Mountain they had to leave home. In Longbow one could neglect the land, live at home, and still be better off than most of the peasants in the backcountry, but not without violating all the guidelines for rural brigades that had been worked out over twenty years of socialist construction, and not without damaging the collective foundations and mutual security of the whole community, which, in the long run, could be disasterous for many individuals.

The subjective factors that stood in the way of agricultural development were equally formidable. A Chinese rural cooperative is a complex social organism that includes both collective and private spheres of production, ownership, and distribution. Gross income is split among the state, the collective, and the individual, and the individual income is distributed in part according to work performed, as wages or a share of the crop, and in part on the basis of need in the form of free services and guaranteed supplies. The proper balance between all of these things is hard to arrive at and once established is subject to change as the economy develops. There is a continuing, built-in struggle over the size of the public and private sphere, over how much to invest versus how much to consume, over how much income should be earned and how much should be supplied free. Deviations toward one extreme or the other are called "Right" or "Left" depending on whether they promote individual enrichment and polarization, or leveling that reduces everyone to an equal level of poverty. Both are bad for morale, bad for production and unstable to boot, but the pendulum of policy tends to swing between them without any permanent resting place because the whole situation is so dynamic.

In Longbow over the years there were political tendencies, most of which came from above, that pushed people toward ultra-"Left," equalitarian excesses, and then, in the course of correcting these, toward extremes of individualism.

An early big swing to the "Left" came at the time of the Great Leap (fall 1958) when, in the first flush of enthusiasm for communes, production was pooled on a countrywide scale. People were urged to build a 10,000-mu square and a 10,000-pig farm where science, technology, and economies of scale were supposed

to create astonishing production breakthroughs. In 1959 Longbow
people transported all their manure to a 10,000 mu square of land
that belonged to another village, only to see the project collapse
before spring planting got under way. As a result they had no manure for their own cropland and had to get through the year on a
catch crop of turnips.

The 10,000-pig farm never materialized. But an inspection team
of higher officials demanded to see something, so Longbow people,
in the course of one night, built a ceremonial gate replete with red
banners and huge congratulatory slogans that announced completion
of the project. The officials never took time to drive through the
gate, which was fortunate, for there was nothing behind it.

These grandiose projects collapsed along with the huge communes
that inspired them, primarily because the level of production
reached at that time would not support collective effort at that level.
The fine crops of 1958 created the opportunity for a "leap" but it
could not be consolidated, especially in the years of bad weather
that followed. In some places the ensuing retreat came close to a
rout. There were pressures to abandon levels of cooperation that
had already proved sound. Leading members of Longbow Brigade
gave up their hard work for socialism and set out to enrich themselves as they had once been encouraged to do after land reform,
before their cooperative was built.

Xinfa, the brigade chairman at that time, began to speculate in
houses, buying old houses cheap, fixing them up, and selling them
at a profit. This was legal, if not laudable, for a brigade leader.
Trouble developed when he began to "borrow" public funds to make
down payments and the accounts got mixed up. He was dismissed
from office and assigned to raising pigs for the brigade.

Wang Wende, in charge of public security and famous as the first
man ever divorced by his wife in Longbow, spent his spare time re-
claiming wasteland wherever a small patch could be found. He
planted private corn at the juncture of roads and on the banks of
irrigation canals. This opened the way for others who began to neglect the community fields for what they hoped would be more profitable private plots. Yields throughout the brigade fell.

The Socialist Education Movement, initiated by Mao in 1963, put
a stop to these trends and reestablished the principle that working
peasants as a class could only prosper if they put "public first, self
second." The banner of Dazhai was raised on a national scale, and
hundreds of thousands went there to learn what self-reliant, pro-

tracted effort in the transformation of nature could do. But studying Dazhai and applying its lessons were difficult, and before Longbow peasants could digest what had been learned the Cultural Revolution began.

The Cultural Revolution raised many questions, not only about the overall direction to be taken by the rural economy, but about the concrete steps to be taken enroute, questions that revolved around the proper balance between public and private that lay at the heart of the entire conflict. The Cultural Revolution raised these questions but never answered them in any convincing way because the mass organizations that arose, first in the schools, later in government offices, and finally in factories and rural brigades, split into irreconcilable factions that fought each other for positions of power and completely lost sight of the policy questions involved. The split originated at the highest level, inside the Central Committee of the Communist Party itself, where "radicals" like Chen Boda backed certain student organizations against "conservatives" like Tan Zhenlin who backed an opposition in self-defense. Opportunists like Lin Biao and Mao's wife, Jiang Qing, fanned up the conflict from both sides, creating an atmosphere of confusion and uncertainty that enabled them to consolidate a position of power from which to threaten the whole system.

Longbow peasants followed the lead of local high school students and split into two factions, each of which felt that victory for the opposition meant the end of the revolution. Actually both were made up of hardworking peasants and cadres who split more along old clan and neighborhood lines than over any political issue. Two organizations named Stormy Petrel (after the bird in Gorki's famous poem "Storm") and Shangan Ridge (after a battle in the Korean War) formed in the south end of the village that had once been dominated by the South Temple Association, while five organizations named Mao Zedong Thought Red Guards, Defend Mao Regiment, Truth Fighting Team, Defend the East Red Guards, and Expose Scheme Fighting Corps formed in the north end that had once been dominated by the North Temple Association.

The southenders became "rebels" who moved to overthrow the brigade administration by occupying the brigade office and seizing the seals. The northenders stood fast as "loyalists" who defended the cadres in power, opposed the seizure carried out by the southenders, overthrew their short-lived administration, and restored most of the original brigade committee members to their posts.

The restored cadres, propelled by a factional wind in the region
and the province that denounced all opposition as enemy inspired,
proceeded to suppress the "rebels" as "landlords, rich peasants,
reactionaries, and counterrevolutionaries." Their leaders were
arrested, beaten, and driven into flight. When they ran through
their grain, their grain coupons, and the hospitality of relatives in
distant counties, they returned to Longbow only to be beaten and
driven out again. The conflict went on for years. It tore the village
apart and made a mockery of any plans for increased production
or enlarged social services.

In January 1968 the factions that grew up at the regional level,
known as Red and United, confronted each other in civil war. Before
the People's Liberation Army could impose peace, 800 people had
been killed and thousands wounded, buildings had been shelled and
smashed, vehicles destroyed, thousands of tons of grain burned,
and production brought to a standstill. Whatever happened in Longbow Village, it was less extreme than that which happened in Changzhi City, the Southeast Region of Shanxi, or Shanxi Province as a
whole. At least in Longbow nobody killed anyone.

The most dynamic figure to emerge out of all this struggle was
the young poor peasant Wang Jinhong, a Deng Xiaoping of Longbow.
He earned this title because in the course of the Cultural Revolution
he was three times raised to a position of power and twice overthrown, as was Vice-premier Deng in Beijing.

Wang Jinhong was born into the Shi family in Longbow's north end
in 1944. His parents were so poor that they despaired of feeding
him and abandoned him in a cornfield. He was picked up by his
mother's sister who was married to a peasant named Wang but had
no son of her own. Brought to the Wang home by this stepmother
whose husband died soon afterward, the Shi Family child lived a
hard life. Carrying heavy loads by pole so bent his back that he became duo (humped). His head was thrust permanently forward so
that he looked, when he walked, as if he could not wait to get where
he was going, an impression that was true to his character, for he
was eager, inquisitive, impatient, and very smart.

In 1958, at the age of sixteen, Wang Jinhong volunteered to study
electricity at a training class set up by the state-owned power company and spent four years thereafter as a power plant construction
worker on various construction sites in North China. When the
Soviet Union broke with China in 1962, terminated all contracts,
and pulled out its experts, power plant construction closed down

temporarily, and Jinhong was laid off and sent home. He became electrician to Longbow Brigade and leader of its Youth League. In 1966, just as the Cultural Revolution began, he was chosen vice-secretary of the Longbow Party Committee. His older brother, Shi Shuanggui, was the secretary. With some justification people began to call Longbow the "Shi Family Kingdom."

When the "rebels" from the south end seized the seals, the brothers Shuanggui and Jinhong were overthrown. When the "loyalists" from the north end threw the "rebels" out, Jinhong was restored to office and took his brother's place as secretary. This was April 1967.

Wang Jinhong led the village through the years of factional strife that followed and was responsible for the persecution of the leading members of Stormy Petrel and Shangan. The group around him, particularly the militiamen under their flamboyant captain Guo Xiaohong, abused their power, "repaired" (beat) people for little or no reason, wasted brigade funds on lavish entertainment, and pursued illicit affairs in flagrant violation of community standards. Production, as might have been expected, did not improve, and when in 1971 a work team was dispatched to Longbow by the revived Party committee of Changzhi City, Jinhong was blamed for everything that had gone wrong. He and his assistants were removed from office and suspended from the Party. In the first shock of this disgrace Jinhong ran away. Persuaded to return home by Changzhi City leaders, he took up work as a carpenter building houses for other peasants, then headed up the small repair shop which the brigade built at the edge of the highway to take advantage of the many breakdowns that occurred near the village. His skill brought trade from far and near and the shop prospered.

The people who replaced Wang Jinhong and his group as brigade leaders — a coalition of north- and south-enders who wanted to heal the factional split — were unable to unite the community without the participation of the suspended Party leader. The work team had called Jinhong's group a "black gang." Wearing this title proudly, the "black gangers" stuck together and defied the rest of the village. As hard feelings escalated, production stagnated. The truth of the matter was that Jinhong was technically the most skillful man in Longbow and politically the most effective. His years in power plant construction had served him as a university. He came home with notebooks full of sketches, measurements, and calculations. He had mastered electricity, welding, engine repair, and multistory construction. He had also mastered some political economy. Many young people in the village followed Jinhong whether he was in office or out. When he was out they tended to lose interest in the affairs of the brigade and concentrate instead on learning some of the skills that Jinhong had to teach.

All this became clear to the Party secretary of the commune, He Xuezhen, who came to live in Longbow for a few months in 1973 in an effort to learn why production there continued to stagnate. Secretary He decided that Jinhong, whatever mistakes he might have made in the past, was important to the future of the brigade. In the course of many long discussions with the brigade leaders and members, he won a majority to his view. After Jinhong criticized himself for the factional excesses of the sixties, he was restored to full Party membership and was then elected to the post of brigade chairman.

This proved to be a turning point for Longbow.

The new leading group brought together the most talented and dedicated people that the community had produced. Wang Jinhong and leaders like old Zhao Guizai, the resistance fighter who had been the brigade's first chairman in 1948, Bei Xinfa, the Party secretary of that year, later assigned to pig raising, and Li Zhengen, brother to the persecuted leader of Shangan Ridge and an able accountant, put their differences aside and concentrated on making some sort of breakthrough in production.

The first thing on the agenda was the question of Longbow's alkaline soil. Two developments over the years had provided clues to a possible solution. The first was the effect on the soil in the vegetable gardens of the large quantities of coal ash that came from the factory workers' kitchens in the form of "sanitary manure," a word used for any kind of domestic waste. As the proportions of coal ash in the soil built up, water percolation improved, alkalinity tended to be washed down, and when the sun came out after a rain, fewer and fewer cracks appeared.

The second was the effect on the soil around the new power plant near Yellow Mill of the ashes that fell from the plant's tall chimney. In a wide circle around the plant ashes turned the crops and soil gray. At first people protested this pollution and demanded that the power company install a scrubber in the stack. But as time went on observant people began to notice that the "polluted" land grew better crops with each passing year. Clearly the coal ashes were transforming the soil in some miraculous way.

Wang Jinhong made a study of these phenomena, then set the Longbow school children to work at an experiment. In order both to earn some money and to learn something about farming, the school children customarily planted an acre of ground. In 1973 they hauled large quantities of coal ash — the power plant clinkers — from Yellow Mill by handcart and spread them on their plot. The effect was remarkable. Crop yields almost doubled. After that Jinhong mobilized the whole community to haul ashes during the winter and spread them on the land at the rate of 100 tons to the acre. Each production team made a plan for transforming a portion of their ground each year. Once the soil was treated with a sufficient amount of coal ash, irrigation, far from causing harm, guaranteed the crop and raised yields as it was supposed to do. After that, digging wells, building water channels, installing pumps, and leveling land so that water could be evenly applied became a major off-season task. Seeing a way forward, Longbow peasants adopted the Dazhai spirit of self-reliance and hard work with enthusiasm. The results, in terms of bushels per acre, were remarkable:

1970	28 bushels	1973	48 bushels	1976	54 bushels
1971	33 bushels	1974	60 bushels	1977	67 bushels
1972	40 bushels	1975	65 bushels	1978	68 bushels
				1979	100 bushels

Now that there was something important to do on the land, the whole question of sidelines had to be reexamined. The wages that could be earned unloading freight at the railroad station, hauling goods on the road, or cutting steel bars at the steel mill did not look so big when compared to the income made possible by doubling, possibly even tripling, yields. Wang Jinhong called back the able-bodied men who were working outside and assigned them to the reconstruction of the fields. Then he looked around for sideline projects that could use the partial labor power of groups like the teen-aged girls. Sawblade polishing, which the sawblade works wanted to contract out, turned out to be a practical solution. It took a lot of skill, a lot of patience, but not a lot of strength. And so Longbow Brigade set up a plant for polishing sawblades that operated twenty-four hours a day, employed about thirty young women on three shifts, and earned for the brigade each day more than six times what the young women could have produced for the brigade in the fields.

Making saw handles of wood was another task that the sawblade plant wanted to contract out. This too was a job for people with less than full labor power. Longbow set up a saw handle shop that also employed young women. To ensure adequate supplies of wood, the brigade then bought a power bandsaw that could handle logs of any size and was equal in efficiency to any power saw in the world. The men who operated this saw earned for the brigade eighteen times what they could have produced in the field.

The final project that Wang Jinhong led the brigade to set up was the cement mill. Originally Jinhong had bought a big cylindrical grinder in order to turn phosphate rock, which could be bought by the carload in its raw state, into fertilizer. But once this grinder was put to work, it became clear that it could go into year-round operation grinding cement. So a plant was built replete with kiln, elevator, primary grinder, and secondary grinder that could turn a mixture of limestone rock from Great Ridge Hill, coal ashes from the power plant, and yellow earth from the fields into cement. Every day it produced from fifteen to twenty tons of cement and earned for the brigade twelve times what the operating crews could have earned working in the fields. Most of the cement was sold at very attractive prices to outside buyers. A certain amount, however, was reserved for the construction on Longbow land of a major reservoir for runoff water and of concrete-lined channels to carry water to the fields. These prevented seepage, saved water, and in the long run raised yields.

These sideline industries enabled the brigade to pay off all its debts, build up an accumulation fund that could be used to construct buildings, extend community services, underwrite culture and recreation, and finance experiments in the mechanization of field work.

This last item has become a point of concentration for Longbow since 1977. Wang Jinhong, a highly skilled mechanic, machinist, and metal worker, has long been fascinated by the challenge of farm mechanization. He has analyzed the process of crop production in Longbow and picked out certain key points as areas for a breakthrough. When I spent the summer there in 1977 he met with me almost daily to discuss machinery and asked me such questions as: How would you lift grain onto the second floor of the warehouse? How would you irrigate a cornfield? What method would you use for drying corn shelled out of the field?

I described the grain augers that I use on my farm in Pennsylvania, explained how a center pivot irrigation system works, and

suggested that he experiment with a coal-fired dryer for the corn.
Now most people in China, when they hear about some modern
method of farming, will say, "Some day we'll have that." But not
Jinhong. When I made a sketch of an auger, he said, "I'm going to
start building one tomorrow." And he did. In ten days he made a
grain auger, primarily from scrap metal that he had been collecting
for years in the yard behind the brigade office. As soon as he
grasped the principle of center pivot irrigation, he said, "I'm going
to build one tomorrow." And he did. Within a month he had created,
again primarily from scrap, a center pivot pipe that turned in a
circle under its own power. When I described the grain dryer, he
said, "I'm going to make one of those if it takes me all winter."
And he did, using a method of indirect heating so that coal smoke
and soot could not contaminate the grain. So far as I know such a
method has not been used before. Jinhong worked it out by trial
and error in the winter of 1978. Today grain dryers designed and
built in Longbow are appearing in far off counties of Shanxi Province, and their fame has reached Beijing.

In 1979 Jinhong launched a hundred-acre experiment in the
mechanization of corn based on the idea of using two people for the
job, an 80-fold increase in labor efficiency in one season. For this
he borrowed a corn planter, a corn picker, and a field cultivator
that had been sitting in the warehouse at the Provincial Institute
of Farm Mechanization for years. Given some support from above,
Longbow Village could probably absorb the labor power released
by these machines by setting up a plant to manufacture the grain
augers, grain dryers, and center pivot pipes that Jinhong has designed.

Whether such support will be forthcoming remains to be seen.
So far Jinhong has encountered both help and resistance from the
higher levels of government. There is extreme reluctance in some
circles to push forward with the mechanization of field crops grown
by peasants as distinct from those grown by salaried workers of
state farms, because of the enormous dislocation of the population
that this must inevitably set in motion. In spite of much lip service
to the idea that the common people are the motive force of history,
there is almost no recognition of the role that peasants themselves
must play in developing farm machines suitable to conditions in
China. Higher cadres assume that somewhere engineers will develop or import ideal prototypes, that these will be manufactured
by industrial departments and then sold to waiting peasants. Un-

likely as this scenario seems, it nevertheless lies behind much of
the failure of industry to develop ties to peasant agriculture and
the extreme difficulties encountered by peasants when they try to
obtain the supplies they need to create the simplest machines.
Longbow has a few bundles of welding rod only because one of the
educated youth assigned there has a sister in the supply department
of the city industrial bureau and Jinhong can bargain with her,
using cement as a chip. Bronze allocated by the province to Longbow was expropriated by the machine shop hired to make nozzles
from it on the sole grounds of possession — "We've got it. What
are you going to do about it?" A minor Changzhi City official in
charge of entertaining foreign guests replaced a Longbow peasant
on an excursion to see the Twelve-Nation Farm Machinery Exhibit
in Beijing on the grounds that this was "foreign affairs."

In the real order that determines priorities in China, peasants
occupy the lowest rung, just as they always have historically. Any
official at any level takes precedent over a peasant when there is
an opportunity to travel, to study, or to receive an honor. Anything
created by a peasant who lives in the administrative sphere of a
higher official, if it will enhance the latter's career, can be moved,
removed, manipulated, or expropriated by that official just as if he
were the lord of a feudal fief.

Jinhong invented a coal-fired grain dryer but a local factory that
helped to make it got first prize for it. An improved second dryer
made by Longbow peasants was taken away to be exhibited somewhere. It was never returned and no compensation was paid.

All this is justified as part of the new revolutionary order regulated by democratic centralism, but because the democratic side
of the equation is so undeveloped, it bears an uncanny resemblance
to the bureaucratic absolutism of the old empire.

The cadres of today exhibit a strong tendency to copy or rather
to recreate the patterns of thought and organization typical of the
old Chinese scholar-officials, who recognized only one profession
— governing — who assumed the right to establish control over
every aspect of social and private life, who were quite satisfied
with traditional techniques and clamped down hard on initiative and
innovation, finding ways to monopolize that which they could not
stamp out. They lived in real fear of assuming responsibility and
usually managed to saddle on some subordinate who could serve
as a scapegoat the blame for anything that went wrong.

These are harsh conclusions, but they describe quite accurately many middle-level cadres who tend to be completely unsettled by the revolutionary implications of mechanization. Of course there are also enlightened cadres who are struggling against such tendencies. The developing democracy at the village level also provides some counterthrust. Cooperative brigades have leverage against bureaucratic interference because of the very real autonomy they enjoy as self-reliant productive units in command of their own resources. The best of them have shown a remarkable ability to survive and develop in spite of indifferent or even hostile leadership.

As Jinhong once explained to me, "There are very few people in China who can do anything about mechanization. I am one of them. As a brigade leader I have land, labor power, money, and materials. What I don't have I can usually find some way to get. Who else has such leverage? The supply departments have materials but no labor power. The factories have labor power but no materials. The mechanization office has nothing but a sign on the door. What can those fellows do but talk?"

All over China there are brigades like Longbow and innovators like Jinhong. In the higher levels of government there are individuals who support them when they can. These forces can prevail over bureaucratic inertia and hesitation, but it will not be soon and it will not be without sharp struggle. There is even the possibility that the heritage of two thousand years of centralism will crystallize the status quo for decades to come and ensure that the hoe continues to be, as it has always been in the past, the primary implement of agricultural production.

Victor Lippit
SOCIALIST DEVELOPMENT IN CHINA

1. INTRODUCTION

During the Cultural Revolution period in China, lasting from
1966 to 1976, a distinctive new program of development emerged.
Based on a determination to avoid the bureaucracy and elitism of
the Soviet Union, on the one hand, and the inequality, poverty, and
social injustice of capitalist nations, on the other, Chinese policymakers charted an historically unprecedented course in pursuit of
economic development and socialist construction. Fortified in
their quest by the lessons learned from the Great Leap Forward,
they sought to carry on economic development in ways which would
infuse the form of public ownership of the means of production
with the substance of social control by the direct producers, primarily workers and peasants. Their efforts to wed economic development and the transition to socialism were widely acclaimed
by radical intellectuals throughout the world.

Yet with the change in leadership initiated by the death of Party
Chairman Mao Zedong in October 1976, a crescendo of criticism
was directed at the policies he had supported from the late 1950s,
policies which had culminated in the program of the Cultural Revolution period. This program, shaped by the so-called "Gang of
Four" led by Jiang Qing, Mao's wife, was almost totally discarded
in the ensuing period, and by 1980 the entire Cultural Revolution
was being treated officially as a national catastrophe. In every
sphere, the policies which marked it were discarded, often to be

*This essay is a chapter from my forthcoming book, The Economic Develop-
ment of China. An earlier draft was presented at the California Regional Seminar,
Fall 1980, Center for Chinese Studies, University of California, Berkeley. I
would like to thank all those who provided me with constructive criticisms of
the earlier draft and Mark Selden especially for his detailed comments.

replaced by their diametric opposites. These dramatic reversals and the new information accompanying them have highlighted in unprecedented fashion the issues of the transition to socialism and of socialist economic development.

In part because the issues have never before been raised with such force and clarity, theoretical literature on both socialist economic development and the transition to socialism is sorely lacking. To analyze these processes in China, therefore, it is impossible to rely on a preexisting analytical framework. Thus a brief detour will be necessary to establish such a framework before proceeding to an assessment of China's historical experience and empirical reality. In attempting to establish such a framework, I would like to focus on the class-specific nature of economic development and on the contradictions which characterize the socialist transition. I will argue that in several critical respects, the Cultural Revolution policies violated the norms of socialist economic development and failed to find satisfactory resolutions for the central contradictions characterizing the transition to socialism. The policy reversals of the post-Mao reform period emerge from this analysis as necessary measures, but as measures which generate their own problems and contradictions that will have to be resolved in their turn if the transition to socialism is to be carried through successfully in China.

2. ECONOMIC DEVELOPMENT AND
   CLASS INTEREST

Many of the classical economists were keenly aware of the role of classes and class structure in furthering or hindering economic development. According to David Ricardo, for example, the wages of direct producers in industry and agriculture would always tend toward subsistence while the capitalists and landlords contended for the surplus they produced. Since Ricardo believed the capitalists would invest their income while the landlords would use theirs for luxury consumption, economic development depended on the success of the capitalist class.

From the time of the neoclassical economists, however, economic analysis has generally ignored the existence of classes, and this has been as true of economic development as of any other branch of the discipline.[1] As a consequence, some of the most essential issues in development have been obscured. Indeed, except for the now-rare cases of direct colonial control or overt neocolonial intervention, whether economic development takes place or not depends in the first instance upon the interest of the dominant class or classes. If development does take place, more-over, the general characteristics of the development process depend on the interest of the dominant class or classes.[2]

Economic development is the process whereby capital accumulation and technical change become institutionalized — carried on regardless of which particular individuals are in charge of making economic decisions — and lead to rising per-capita income. Socialist economic development is simply development carried out in ways that serve working people: workers, peasants, teachers, health workers and all those whose primary economic role is participation in socially useful labor. The principal beneficiaries of capitalist economic development, by contrast, are those who own the means of production. Although the distinction between capitalist and socialist economic development cannot be elaborated fully here, the failure of the development literature to clarify the class nature of economic development makes at least a cursory presentation imperative. The model of socialist development that emerges from the following analysis is a "pure" one and as such is not matched by the empirical reality of any particular country's experience. It is necessary, however, to develop the pure model in order to provide a benchmark against which the Chinese ex-perience can be evaluated.

Assessing China's development experience in relation to a model of pure socialist development, however, can provide only one part of the basis for understanding the transition to socialism in China, since the criteria that emerge are essentially static ones. To grasp the dynamics of the transition process, it is nec-essary as well to analyze the contradictions inherent in the process of socialist transformation. Thus, for example, central planning is — quite rightly — generally regarded as a principal component of socialist economic organization, but it is not imme-diately evident how this can be reconciled with control by working people over the production process, which has been advanced with equal legitimacy as a socialist principle. The transition to so-cialism in any country is marked by a series of confrontations with contradictions such as this one, and progress in the transi-tion is determined by successful resolution of the contradictions.

The procedure I will follow here then is to begin by clarify-ing the distinction between capitalist and socialist economic de-

velopment. The model of pure socialist development which
emerges will provide the basis for assessing China's development
experience. In two principal regards, I will argue, China has devi-
ated from the socialist development model; these are in the failure
of real wages and incomes to rise in industry and agriculture from
the mid-fifties to the mid-seventies, and in the failure of Chinese
policy to deal satisfactorily with the persisting social and economic
hierarchy. These failures, and the dynamics of the socialist
transition process generally, can best be understood in the light of
the principal contradictions that confront all countries undergoing
the transition process. A discussion of these contradictions and
their resolution in China will therefore follow. The essay concludes with an analysis of the economic policy changes implemented since Mao's death in 1976 from the perspective of the
criteria for socialist development and the contradictions inherent
in the socialist transition.

3. CAPITALIST ECONOMIC DEVELOPMENT

Since the main contours of development everywhere reflect the
interests of the dominant classes, the early stages of development in
capitalist countries characteristically produce these general features:

1) growing inequality
2) the perpetuation and even intensification of poverty in a large
   part of the population
3) substantial unemployment and underemployment
4) neglect of the people's welfare within the limits set by the
   need to assure the reproduction of labor and the preservation
   of social stability
5) large-scale displacement of population and the exploitation
   of the countryside to the advantage of the urban economy
6) a hierarchical ordering of society and the labor process with
   the subordination of the direct producers to the owners of
   capital and land

These general features of early capitalist development, it should
be emphasized, are characteristic tendencies; they are not universal, and certain ones change as the development of capitalism
progresses. Thus the growing systemic requirements of a developing capitalist economy eventually include a more educated

labor force and a great increase in technical and professional manpower. These requirements usually reverse the tendency toward growing inequality after development has reached a certain point. Further, the nature of development in a particular country may occasionally create a countervailing force relatively early in the course of development. If a sizable portion of the labor force is drawn from agriculture into industry, for example, national income distribution may appear more equal despite a growing gulf between workers and industrialists simply because the gulf between peasants and industrialists is larger still.

While these reservations should be kept in mind, the features of capitalist development itemized above are indeed the norm, as the empirical evidence presented below will indicate. In the 1960s, a number of writers observed that per capita income growth was not a satisfactory indicator of economic development, that what was really critical in development was declining poverty, inequality, and unemployment (see, for example, Seers, 1973). Although this proposition expresses a worthy humanitarian critique of the widespread failure of Third World development to deal with these critical social issues, it misses the point that all these shortcomings are systemic features of capitalist economic development. In the early stages of capitalist development, for reasons which are systemic rather than coincidental, working people are often the victims rather than the beneficiaries of social change.

If, on the other hand, the dominant classes are composed of working people, then each of these capitalist development characteristics will be replaced by its opposite. That is to say, socialist economic development is characterized by growing equality, disappearing poverty, shrinking unemployment-underemployment, sharply improved popular welfare, relatively balanced urban-rural development, and the sharp curtailment of social and economic hierarchy. The clarification of these propositions requires pausing a moment to clarify the class nature of economic development.

It is quite natural for the class in power to implement policies which are in its own interest. A capitalist class will try to direct to itself as large a share of the national income as it can, consistent with maintaining the ability of the system to reproduce itself. Since this class constitutes a small proportion of the population, any degree of success will imply widening income disparities. Further, insofar as income is being channeled mainly to those who already have more than their share, reductions in poverty are likely to come about slowly, if at all. Finally, social hierarchy is an essential element securing the authority and control of the capitalist class, while unemployment enhances that authority by weakening the position of the direct producers and, not incidentally, their wage demands as well.

There is ample theoretical and empirical support for the position that economic development is a class-specific process. In his discussion of primitive accumulation, for example, Marx (1961: part VIII) shows that for capitalist production and reproduction to get under way on a regular basis, it is necessary to form concentrated clumps of capital capable of financing investment, on the one hand, and a class of people bereft of the means of self-support — peasants deprived of land or artisans of tools — on the other. Capital and wage labor form the poles of a unity necessary for capitalist production to proceed.

In his classic article "Economic Development with Unlimited Supplies of Labor," W. Arthur Lewis (1963) approaches the question of capitalist accumulation from a perspective which is quite different. Combining methods of neoclassical economic analysis with the class perspective of the classical period, he shows that as long as surplus (unemployed or underemployed) labor[3] exists, the capital accumulation process will channel the increment in national income to the capitalists, while real wages remain flat. Whether we use Marxian or neoclassical analysis, poverty, unemployment, and inequality would appear to be intrinsic elements in early capitalist development.

With the exception of a few special cases,[4] these theoretical findings are amply confirmed by empirical analyses of early capitalist development. Irma Adelman, who has carried out the most extensive studies on the relationship between income distribution and economic growth, writes (1979: 314):

The relationship between levels of economic development and the equity of income distribution is ... asymmetrically U-shaped, with more egalitarian income distributions being characteristic of both extreme economic underdevelopment and high levels of economic development. Between these extremes, however, the relationship is, for the most part, inverse: up to a point, higher rates of industrialization, faster increases in agricultural productivity, and higher rates of growth all tend to shift the income distribution in favor of the higher income groups and against the low-income groups.

In a recent study of seven Asian countries — Pakistan, India, Bangladesh, Sri Lanka, Malaysia, Indonesia, and the Philippines — which together account for about 70 percent of the rural population of the nonsocialist developing world, the International Labour Office (1977: 9-15) noted worsening distribution of income and declining real income of the rural poor to be persistent tendencies over a period ranging from ten to twenty-five years.

In each case ... it was found that the proportion of the population below the "poverty line" has been increasing over time. ... In most of the countries for which measurements could be obtained real wages either remained constant or there appeared to have been a downward trend. (p. 10)

It is certainly not the case that the increasing poverty of many of the poor is mainly due to general stagnation in Asia, or, worse, economic decline. On the contrary, all but one of the seven countries surveyed have enjoyed a rise in average incomes in recent years, and in some instances the rise has been quite rapid. Only in Bangladesh have average incomes fallen, and the interesting question there is how, despite the decline in the average, the upper income groups were able to improve their living standards. In a sense, Bangladesh is the most dramatic illustration of what is happening in the rest of Asia: in countries where average incomes have increased, the poor have tended to become poorer and the rich richer; in Bangladesh, where average incomes have fallen, the rich have nevertheless become richer while the incomes of the poor have fallen faster than the average. (p. 15)

The results described here are not anomalous; they flow logically from the inherent nature of capitalist economic development.

4. ECONOMIC DEVELOPMENT IN CHINA, 1949-1976

The brief description of capitalist economic development presented here was meant to demonstrate the class-specific nature of the development process and also to provide the contrasting backdrop against which the discussion of socialist economic development can proceed most meaningfully. Socialist economic development can take place where the classes of direct producers (peasants and workers especially) and other working people are dominant. Such classes will be concerned with eliminating poverty, reducing unemployment, promoting equality, enhancing public welfare, and combating hierarchy as a matter of their self-interest, as a matter of course. These concerns will typically be incorporated in any development strategy they pursue.

Consider, by contrast, the exploitation of women and child workers in the early development of England, the United States,

Japan, and (prerevolutionary) China, in all of which they constituted the majority of the factory labor force (for Japan and China
see Lippit, 1978b: 68). The women factory workers were typically young women from farm families too poor to support them
prior to marriage; poverty forced them to work in the factories
under appalling conditions. There was no particular reason for
the capitalist class to protect them and every reason to exploit
them. In a nation where the direct producers are dominant, however, such a situation would be untenable. The women and children in question would be the leading class's own women and
children, and allowing their exploitation would be acting contrary
to its own interest. Where socialist economic development pre-
vails, therefore, we would expect to find women workers protected
and child labor eliminated. The extent to which policies which
reflect the interests of working people are actually implemented
in the socialist countries determines the extent to which their development programs can in fact be considered socialist.

In conventional usage, countries where the means of production
are predominantly publicly owned are referred to as socialist, and
one can hardly object to a meaning which is conveyed by common
usage. But as Paul Sweezy (1971: 4) has properly pointed out,
public ownership is a juridical form and in itself cannot express
fully the class relations which underlie it. The essence of socialism is ultimately the control by working people — whether
engaged in industry or agriculture, or carrying out intellectual,
service, or other socially useful tasks — over their own productive
activity and indeed over their own lives. It is only in the sense of
deepening control by working people and the shaping of economic
activity to conform to their interests and those of the entire population that we can talk of a "transition to socialism" in countries
where the means of production have already been socialized.

The general criterion for socialist economic development is
whether the strategy pursued and policies implemented serve the
class interests of the working people. As I have indicated, this
implies that the pure socialist model of development will differ
markedly from the pure capitalist model in each of the features
enumerated. Socialist economic development, reflecting the class
interest of the vast majority of the population which must work for
a living, will have the following general features:

1) relative equality

2) the elimination of poverty (malnutrition, lack of medical care, etc.)
3) virtually full employment
4) significant improvement in people's welfare, reflected in rising real wages as well as improving social services
5) accompanying industrialization with rural development so that the entire working population benefits from growth
6) the sharp curtailment of social and economic hierarchy

In China, most of these features of socialist economic development have been present. There are, however, two notable exceptions: the failure of the people's living standards to improve over a prolonged period from the mid-fifties to the mid-seventies, a period in which substantial increases in agricultural and industrial production occurred, and the failure to curb social and economic hierarchy. These failures were of such importance, however, as to jeopardize the entire transition to socialism. The failure to improve living standards reflects both a faulty development strategy and the ability of the Party and state leadership to impose its preferences over mass aspirations for greater material prosperity. The enhanced authority of state and Party leadership, unsuccessfully attacked in the Cultural Revolution, also underlies the new forms of hierarchy that have replaced traditional forms of class rule and state power in modern China. These points can be developed best in the context of an analysis of the main features of Chinese development between 1949 and 1976.

5. THE DYNAMICS OF SOCIALIST TRANSITION

In contrast to the growing inequality in income which characteristically marks the early stages of capitalist development, China established a relatively high degree of equality soon after the success of the revolution and has sustained it since then. The single most important factor underlying income inequality in capitalist countries is the unequal ownership of property; the socialization of industry and land reform in agriculture eliminated this factor in China. Table 1 below, for example, shows the distribution of income among the peasants of Hunan Province before and after the land reform.

Table 1

Per Capita Income of Peasants in Hunan Province

Income, 1952 yuan	1936	1952	1956[b]
Per capita[a]	69.71	70.44	83.2
Poor peasants	59.2		83.5
Middle peasants	78.8		86.2
Rich peasants	118.8		102.6
Landlords	127.3		75.3

Notes:

a) Listed in the source as "per household," an evident error.

b) Differences in the consumption of major items which correspond to the income differences indicated are specified in Vivienne Shue, Peasant China in Transition (Berkeley: University of California Press, 1980), pp. 315-316.

Source: Nai-ruenn Chen, Chinese Economic Statistics, p. 433; based on data published by the Hunan Provincial Statistical Bureau.

Although differences among peasants persisted (and still do), what is most striking about these data is the narrowness of the differentials between the "poor" and the "rich," a narrowness which verges on the extraordinary whether contrasted with the income differentials which existed in prerevolutionary China (see, for example, Fei and Chang, 1945) or in capitalist Third World countries today.

In urban areas, the elimination of the private ownership of houses (now permitted again) and the more expensive consumer durables like automobiles provided a counterpart to the equalization of incomes resulting from the socialization of property. Although the highest-paid workers could earn as much as three times the income of the lowest-paid ones (and still can), this reflects in part differential wages over the working-life cycle. That is to say, people begin working at the lowest wages and seniority plays a significant role in the raises they receive. Further, most necessities (housing, utilities, medical care, public transport, and so forth) are heavily subsidized, so the difference in real incomes is much less than the difference in money wages would appear to indicate. As far as differences between workers on the one hand and managers and engineers on the other are concerned, Riskin (1975: 218) finds the most highly paid managers and engineers received 2.7 times the average worker's wages and 1.6 times the most highly paid worker's wage in a sample of ten factories in the early 1970s. These differentials are extremely low by international standards. In general, the high degree of equality in income in China conforms to the expectations of the socialist development model.

In the elimination of poverty, too, the Chinese practice has been in accord with the socialist model. China's per capita GNP (gross national product) in 1979 was equivalent to U.S.$253 (BR, 10/27/80: 16). While international income comparisons of this kind suffer from a number of well-known defects, this figure is a legitimate indicator of the low average income level. Despite the low average income, however, and the fact that many of the remote parts of the countryside especially remain quite poor, the relatively equal distribution of the national income and the heavy subsidies for essential living requirements like housing and medical care have virtually eliminated the types of extreme poverty that are everywhere visible in the capitalist third world.

Structural unemployment and underemployment in capitalist countries is associated with lack of access to the means of subsistence; increasing employment opportunities in China, by contrast, reflect both public policy and increased access to the means of subsistence. This is nowhere more clear than in the agricultural sector. Land reform in China redistributed a reported 44 percent of the arable land area of the country to poor and landless peasants (Lippit, 1974: 95); although this estimate appears to be somewhat on the high side, the redistributed land constituted a sizable share of the total. The subsequent collectivization of agriculture and the formation of the communes created socialist institutions capable of absorbing productively all of the surplus labor in the Chinese countryside. Although the number of workers in mining, manufacturing, and utilities increased from under 15 to almost 40 million between 1957 and 1975, industrial labor force growth accounted for only 17.5 percent of the estimated increase of 148.5 million in China's labor force (Rawski, 1979a: 770); non-agricultural labor as a whole accounted for about one-third of the increase. Most of the increase, therefore, had to be absorbed in the rural sector. Agriculture, including water conservancy and land improvement as well as farming and animal husbandry, absorbed an increase of 97.3 million workers during this span, or approximately two-thirds of the overall labor force increase (Rawski, 1979b: 125); the agricultural sector was able to do this even while the average number of labor days worked each year by Chinese peasants increased from well under 200 in the early 1950s to 250 by the mid-1970s (Schran, 1969: 75; Rawski, 1979a: 767).

In the urban areas it is true that unemployment has often been circumvented by draconian means, including restrictions on migration from rural areas and sending young people out to the countryside involuntarily. The former policy appears to have been the only means to forestall the development of the urban slums and poverty that characterize less developed capitalist countries (capitalist LDCs). The second policy, however, highly unpopular and dismantled in the post-1976 reform movement, seems to have contributed, perversely, to the only significant elements of unemployment to reappear following the end of the First Five-Year Plan period (1953-57), by which time, according to the heads of the State Bureau of Labor, the unemployment inherited from the prerevolutionary society had been virtually eliminated (interview published in BR, 2/11/80: 13-16).

The new unemployment had two sources. Many of the young people sent to the countryside returned to the cities illegally, and thus could not usually obtain regular urban jobs. Estimates of their number vary from several hundred thousand to several million, but even if the upper estimates are correct and the proportion of those unable to work high, the resultant unemployment rate out of an urban work force approaching 100 million would have been quite moderate in comparison to the unemployment rates which characterize capitalist LDCs (Rawski, 1979b: 127). The second source of unemployment to which the rustication-of-youth policy gave rise appeared, ironically, when it was abolished. Most of the young people flooded back to the cities in the late 1970s, and their return coincided with a bulge in the number of high school graduates (expected to end in 1982).[5] As of April 1980, this meant that high school graduates in Shanghai had to wait about six months for their job assignments. Conditions in other major cities were similar, but except for this clearly transitory phenomenon, employment in China remains essentially full.

A host of imaginative measures has been adopted to deal with the temporary bulge in the labor supply, including the vigorous encouragement of urban cooperatives, the development of the service sector, and the revival of individual handicraftsmen and service workers. Measures such as these contributed to the new urban employment of 26.6 million people between 1977 and 1980, with 9 million new workers both in 1979 and in 1980 (BR, 9/22/80: 34; 5/25/81: 3). The net figures are smaller because those leaving the labor force must also be taken into account, but the achievement in opening up employment opportunities remains a remarkable one for an underdeveloped country with total urban employment of about 104 million. The situation in China contrasts with average labor underutilization rates of close to 30 percent in capitalist underdeveloped countries, rates which have been increasing over the past three decades (Todaro, 1977: 167).

Accompanying industrialization with rural development so that the entire working population benefits from the growth process has also been a hallmark of Chinese development. The people's communes provide an institutional framework for mobilizing rural resources and indeed for carrying out an all-round rural development strategy. The "barefoot doctor" system and conventional medical services make medical care and public health available in the countryside to a degree that is probably unprecedented in countries with comparable income levels per capita. Providing agricultural inputs is one of the major foci of industry, and the development of rural, small-scale industry — which employs some 28 million people in commune and brigade factories out of a total rural labor force of about 300 million — contributes further to all-round development. For China as a whole, Nicholas Lardy (1978) demonstrates conclusively that tight governmental control over the central planning process made possible the systematic redistribution of real resources from wealthier regions to poorer ones, from more industrialized regions to less industrialized ones, over the entire period since 1949.

Despite China's real accomplishments in rural development, however, the stagnation in real incomes in the countryside for two decades starting in the mid-fifties indicates serious limitations on the success of the program. Since a parallel lag characterized industrial wages in the same period, however, and since their common cause transcended urban-rural relations, it will be more appropriate to take up the two lags in the discussion of popular welfare, to which I turn next.

In certain respects a deep concern with popular welfare has made China an exemplary case of socialist economic development. The elimination of child labor and protection for women workers — indeed for all workers — have been hallmarks of Chinese development, with basic schooling made almost universal, hours of work limited, maternity benefits arranged, inexpensive day-care provided, and so forth. Stable prices have also characterized

Chinese development until the late 1970s (the inflationary problems which appeared at the end of the decade will be taken up in
the next section). Price stability has an important influence on
popular welfare since it is the weakest members of society who
suffer most from price fluctuations and the owners of property
who most typically benefit. Prices in China were basically stable
in the 1950s, and after a modest increase by the early 1960s were
again stable to the mid-70s. This performance stands in marked
contrast to that of all the capitalist LDCs and to Japan in the
Meiji era, 1868-1912 (Lippit, 1978b: 73-4).

One can also point to the provision of pensions for all state-
sector employees, the medical care provided free or for nominal
charges, the widespread subsidies of necessities, and the guarantees that all citizens have of the most basic requirements of life.
In spite of all this, however, average incomes remain extremely
low, so that raising them must be a vital component of improving welfare. In a capitalist context it would be quite natural to see public policy or corporate power restraining the
real incomes of working people, but in a socialist country,
where the working people are presumably in control, the failure
of real incomes to rise from extremely low levels requires
close examination.

In 1957, per capita income from collective labor in the countryside was 57 yuan, half in cash and half in kind.[6] It fell sharply
during the Great Leap Forward, recovered up to 1965, and thereafter rose slightly to 65 yuan in 1977. Thus over a twenty-year
period, real income rose by 8 yuan, equivalent to U.S.$5.20 (at
the exchange rate of 1 yuan = U.S.$0.65); cash income over the
twenty-year period rose by half that amount or $2.60 per person.
Since we know that over the same interval the collective labor
effort per person increased sharply, the real income per hour
worked actually fell.

Between 1952 and 1956, the real wages of industrial workers
rose by 19 percent but in 1975 remained at practically the same
level they had attained in 1956 (Lardy, 1978: 175). There is a
striking parallel here with the experience in the countryside, a
parallel which can scarcely be considered coincidental. Note that
according to Table 1, peasant income per capita in Hunan Province
rose by 18 percent between 1952 and 1956, a period during which
peasant incomes throughout the countryside were generally rising.
Thus, up to 1956-57, the incomes of peasants and workers were

rising, but after that time they failed to increase significantly.

This suggests that Chinese policy may have downgraded the importance of improving the incomes and well-being of workers and peasants from around the end of the First Five-Year Plan. The qualification "may have" is an important one, because it would be quite improper to abstract the national incomes policy from the various national and historical forces that inevitably constrained it. If national income had not increased, if China had become involved in a major war, or, most importantly, if no viable alternative strategy of development had existed, then limiting real income gains would have been inevitable. In fact, however, none of these potential constraints was operative.

Between 1957 and 1977, GNP rose by an estimated 191 percent and GNP per capita rose by an estimated 89 percent (Ashbrook, 1978: 208). While these estimates are subject to considerable error, it is quite clear that the gains in national income and income per capita were substantial. More important, however, is the fact that an alternative strategy for raising national income existed, a strategy capable of raising people's incomes even while developing the national economy. Indeed, as I will discuss below, just such a strategy was being implemented in the post-Mao era. Thus, the long period of limited income gains for people who by any standard are very poor suggests that a socialist development policy was not being implemented in this respect.

An even more serious deviation from the pure model of socialist development existed in the perpetuation of social and economic hierarchy despite serious concern with this problem on the part of many people and official efforts to confront it in a number of respects. Among the most notable of these is the "two participations," according to which managers participated in actual production activity and workers in management. Further, one basic thrust of the Cultural Revolution was aimed at preventing the consolidation of bureaucratic authority as a power over the people and the congealing of the bureaucratic stratum into a ruling class. Nevertheless, the basic problem of hierarchy in a socialist society could not be addressed in this fashion.

Central planning has long been properly regarded as a key element in socialism. Its use implies that production decisions will be based not on private profitability but on social utility, taking the entire society into account. Putting central planning into practice, however, leads to many well-known difficulties, difficulties with which all of the socialist countries are struggling today. One set of difficulties involves the overall efficiency of the economic system, from the standpoint of allocation of resources, choice of technique, and meshing production with consumer needs and desires. In a world of scarcity, central planners must find a way to take into account the principle of opportunity cost — the principle that the real cost of using resources in a particular way is the alternative production for which they might have been used — but have difficulty doing so.

From the standpoint of the elimination of hierarchy as well, however, central planning raises another set of difficulties. As a system of economic coordination and allocation, it requires a hierarchical social and economic ordering. Further, in the party-state that emerged in China since the Revolution, political, social, and economic authority merged into what was essentially a single hierarchy, creating a great weight above the working classes (peasants, workers, and all those engaged in socially useful labor). This situation is hardly consistent with the pure socialist model's criterion of worker interest and worker control.

Both sets of problems can be addressed in part by the limited introduction of market exchange; economic reform has moved in this direction in parts of Eastern Europe, notably in Hungary and Yugoslavia, slightly in the Soviet Union, and with increasing vigor in China since the death of Mao. Prior to 1976, however, market decentralization was for the most part anathema in China. A limited rationalization of the economic planning system was carried out with the administrative decentralization of 1957-58, but this ultimately could not come to grips with the most basic problems.

The attack on bureaucracy and the emphasis on control by the direct producers which marked the Cultural Revolution could not lead to substantive results without some form of market decentralization. As Alec Nove (1979: 122) points out, "If a market does not indicate what the customers . . . want, then some other person or institution must." There is no way that workers producing say sulfuric acid can reasonably determine the level of social need and make allocation decisions accordingly. Ultimately central planners must make such decisions in the absence of markets.

Under such circumstances, the Cultural Revolution could produce no more than an illusion of worker authority. Control over the major economic levers remained highly centralized, and the integrated social, economic, and political hierarchy that stood above ordinary people remained intact despite changes in institutional forms and in individual positions within it (Walder, 1982). Ultimately, establishing a leading role for the direct producers and other working people as autonomous social actors required reform of the economic system. The perpetuation of hierarchy limited the realization of socialism in China. This can be grasped most clearly perhaps through an analysis of the contradictions confronted by all countries attempting the transition to socialism.

6. THE DYNAMICS OF SOCIALIST TRANSITION

As I have indicated, the essence of socialism lies deeper than state ownership of the means of production, for a variety of production relations are possible under the veil of state ownership. It is possible, for example, for the same hierarchical relations of production that characterize capitalism to exist in state-owned enterprises; under such circumstances, with workers experiencing the same subordination and alienation under state ownership as under private, to distinguish between the systems by calling one socialist is hardly meaningful.

This is especially true if we consider the moral content that has been associated historically with the idea of socialism, which has evoked people's commitment not only because of their class interest — and at times in spite of it — but also because they saw fraternity, equality, and justice as intrinsic to socialism, because they saw socialism as a system in which the full potentialities of human beings could be realized. To define socialism exclusively in terms of juridical forms, ignoring this ethical thrust, does violence to the broader meanings with which history has imbued the term.

The transition to socialism is the process by which working people come to gain control over their own lives at the workplace and at every level of the economic, political, and social institutions which govern their existence. At the same time, it is the process by which rational social consciousness imbued with the spirit of justice comes to shape social decision-making and resource allocation. Both are made possible by the public ownership of the means of production; neither are guaranteed by it.

Although ideally the two will be mutually reinforcing, contradictions between them will often prevail. I would like to analyze here
three principal forms such contradictions may assume and a
fourth contradiction of equal import, noting as I do that under
particular circumstances other contradictions may emerge more
intensely. Progress in the transition to socialism is determined
by how successful the resolutions to these contradictions, which
repeatedly emerge in new form, prove to be.

The first contradiction is that between the immediate producers
and society. Adam Smith saw the pursuit of individual benefit
under the market relations of capitalism as tending to work to the
benefit of all, as though social welfare and harmony were being
created by an "invisible hand." It has often been remarked with
keen insight, however, that each pursuing his own benefit in the
market does not invariably benefit others, that the effects of such
pursuit can as readily be understood in terms of the working of an
"invisible foot" booting the less fortunate in the scramble for
personal gain as of an invisible hand. Granted that this is true
of capitalism, it is by no means clear that control by working
people over their own productive activity will take into account
adequately the interests of the entire society.

Consider, for example, a commune which produces sufficient
grain for its own needs. From the standpoint of the immediate
producers it might be entirely reasonable to turn to other pur-
suits: building houses for the members instead of terracing new
fields, enjoying more leisure, growing other crops, and so forth.
Yet at the same time an unslaked demand for grain may exist in
the cities and on other communes set in a harsher environment or
focusing on the production of cotton or other cash crops. Moreover, grain exports may be needed to supply the foreign exchange
necessary to permit importing industrial goods needed for China's
economic development. To specify the role of producer control
in the achievement of socialism has obvious merit, but it grasps
only one pole of the contradiction.

It is my purpose here to indicate the principal contradictions
rather than to specify appropriate resolutions, for these must
change as actual conditions change and as the contradictions are
recreated in new forms. It may not be inappropriate, however,
to indicate the broad framework within which this first contradiction must be resolved, for this will help to clarify the analytical
approach. In the example I have presented, rational social con-

sciousness must be embodied in central planning and producer
control in the authority of the commune and its subordinate units
to dispose of their own resources and to organize their work activity as they see fit. A successful resolution of the contradiction
between the two most certainly requires a mix of central planning
and market allocation, the latter of which is a necessary condition
for investing the producing unit with real decision-making authority. As I shall argue more fully below, excessive centralization
marked public policy prior to the post-Mao reforms, impeding the
transition to socialism as well as generating serious economic
difficulties.

The second basic contradiction stems from the fact that the consciousness which a socialist system may ultimately engender is
also needed for the transition itself. Some revolutionary intellectuals and Party leaders have a vision of society and a sophisticated consciousness which grasps the self and society simultaneously, which grasps the self in society. It is appropriate, indeed
necessary, for them to take a leadership role in raising the consciousness of the rest of the population, which is commonly absorbed in personal affairs and personal benefit. But there is no
sharp line dividing such leadership from censorship and thought
control, and the victims are working people as well as intellectuals.

Thus the second basic contradiction defining the transition to
socialism emerges. On the one hand, it is incumbent on those
with an advanced consciousness to assume a leadership role in
propagating it via all the forms of social communication, including
education, the press, the arts, and so forth. On the other hand,
such activities are open to evident abuse; those who claim to be
disseminating "correct thought" do so by virtue of their political
and social power which bypasses completely the question of the
legitimacy of their ideas. Moreover, the ethical thrust of socialism, which is a quite inalienable part of the concept, man-
dates a respect for the individual, for free expression and for
equality, and an abhorrence of hierarchy, manipulation, and thought
control, all of which conflict with control by the direct producers
in any event. Leadership is necessary, but thought control by a
self-constituted elite is anathema to socialism.

The third contradiction is that between the leaders and the
masses, between party cadres and the bureaucracy which public
ownership of the means of production and the enhanced state power

of a revolutionary regime tend to spawn, on the one hand, and the mass of the working population, on the other. If this contradiction is not successfully resolved, it is possible for a cadre-bureaucratic stratum to form a distinct class, based largely on its preferential access to the power and resources of the state, in opposition to the classes made up of working people. The result will be a new social formation that, although distinct from capitalism, aborts the transition to socialism. Elements in the formation of a cadre-bureaucratic stratum as a distinct class include (1) the appropriation of a significant share of the economic surplus for its own use, thereby widening differences between its interest and that of the direct producers, (2) the loss of control by working people over its activities, and (3) the development of institutional mechanisms that maintain the class status of its descendants. Events appear to have led in this direction in the Soviet Union. The situation in China is much more ambiguous; there the issue of new-class formation remains to be determined.

In China, cadre status has not by and large been a source of personal enrichment. It is true, on the other hand, that ordinary people have had little or no control over the selection and activity of cadres, but tentative steps toward democratization have marked the reform period which began in the late seventies, including, as discussed below, the popular election of factory and local government officials on a trial basis. It is still too early to tell how far this movement will go. Reforms in education to the contrary, especially the reinstitution of the examination system for admission to higher education, tend to favor children from educated urban households, including cadre households. Whether this will prove to be a mechanism of maintaining class status remains to be determined. Overall, whether a cadre-bureaucratic class will be formed in China remains an open question; the result may depend in large measure on the extent to which the efforts to encourage democracy take root.

The fourth contradiction, emphasized by Marx in his analysis of the dynamics of social change, is that between the forces and relations of production. Emphasizing equality and downplaying material incentives runs the risk of slowing economic development to such an extent as to endanger the entire transition process. Relying on modes of consciousness that are still incipient to motivate economic behavior may, by breaking the link between direct work effort and reward, be counterproductive, benefiting primarily those

who are cynical or lazy, or who are simply not strongly motivated.
On the other hand, if compensation according to labor is emphasized, people's highly unequal natural endowments and social opportunities (e.g., of urban dwellers as opposed to rural ones) may
spontaneously generate inequality and a new hierarchy of wealth
and position. Thus, giving priority to developing the forces of
production runs the risk of undermining socialist relations of
production, whereas prematurely stressing socialist relations may
undermine the development of the forces of production, threatening
the viability of the socialist transition.

Once public ownership of the means of production has replaced
private ownership, a necessary but surely insufficient condition
for the achievement of socialism, the period of transition to socialism is defined especially by the four basic contradictions I
have outlined, and progress toward socialism can be measured in
terms of the resolutions of these contradictions, resolutions that
are themselves constantly changing in the course of development.
To analyze the transition to socialism in China, it is necessary to
examine how each of these contradictions has been resolved. It
is not possible to do so exhaustively here, but even a brief discussion should help to highlight some of the most critical issues
raised by Chinese practice.

The first contradiction, that between people's control over their
own work activity and the social interest, is expressed in many
forms, but perhaps most sharply in the form of the contradiction
between worker (and peasant) control and central planning, where central planning represents the social interest. Prior to the post-Mao
reforms, industrial decentralization in China had never placed
substantive decision-making authority in the hands of producing
units. The major decentralization of 1957-58 simply transferred
authority over most enterprises from ministries in Beijing to
provincial and local governments. Economic decision-making remained bureaucratized, removed from the producing units themselves. And although decision-making power at the enterprise
level by no means assures worker control, it is a necessary condition for it.

The Cultural Revolution sought to deal with this contradiction,
but in ways foredoomed to failure. Although the authority of workers within the enterprise was supposed to have been enhanced, the
major decisions continued to be made outside the enterprise.
Consider, for example, the problems encountered by the Beijing

television picture tube plant in securing adequate quality control
in and supplies of the glass casings it requires to manufacture
picture tubes. Refused permission by the economic bureaucracy
to manufacture the casings itself, it was forced to halt production
for a total of three years and ten months during the seven-year
span from 1973 to 1979 inclusive owing to its suppliers' inability
to meet its requirements. The suppliers in their turn suffered
from repeated redesignation of which plants were to be responsible for supply and to which municipal or ministry bureaus they
would be responsible. The procedures to be followed when quality
control issues arise capture the flavor of just how bureaucratic
the whole process is.

The Beijing picture tube plant is subordinate to the Beijing Broadcasting and
Television Company, which is under the leadership of the Beijing Electronic
Instruments Bureau. As for the glass casing plant, it is subordinate to the
Beijing Glass Manufacturing General Plant, which is under the leadership of
the Beijing Municipal Light Industry Bureau. For this reason, in the event of
quality disputes arising between the glass casing manufacture and picture tube
manufacture, the procedure involves a whole series of contacts from the workshop to the picture tube plant, then to the Broadcasting and Television Company, the Instruments Bureau, the municipality, the Light Industry Bureau, the
glass manufacturing general plant, the glass screen manufacturing plant and
finally the relevant workshop or team. ... Hence, whenever a problem of
quality arises, it results in the plant stopping production for several months
(Jingji guanli [Economic Management; in Chinese], 8 [August 15, 1980]: 15-17.
Translated in FBIS, Daily Report, October 3, 1980, p. L13).

Under these circumstances, with the enterprise completely
hemmed in by the bureaucratic hierarchy, worker control, even
had it been successfully implemented during the Cultural Revolution period, would have been limited to finding ways to best com-
ply with production and other orders issued by the authorities.
In fact, as Andrew Walder (1982) has shown, the ironic consequence
of the Cultural Revolution's anti-bureaucratic reforms was to
"concentrate power in the hands of the hierarchy of leaders that
started with the plant director and stretched down to the shop
floor." By 1971, the revolutionary committees responsible for
enterprise management and ostensibly instruments of mass power
were brought under the control of the top military or Party leaders
in each plant.

The membership of revolutionary committees evolved without elections. ...
(The committees were) composed of pliant delegates who had survived the pre-

vious years of investigation and purge by not rocking the boat. They met irregularly, at the choosing of the committee head. There were no provisions
for regular elections, for accountability to workers, for democracy within the
committee itself (Walder, 1982: 231).

Thus the twenty-year Maoist period culminating in the Cultural
Revolution did not in fact resolve the contradiction between worker
control and social interest and could not in principle do so. Two
basic conditions must be met for this to happen: first, real decision-making authority must be given to the producing units (in
agriculture as well as in industry), and second, within each unit
working people must assume a central role. The first condition
implies an important role for the market. While planning would
remain responsible for the overall dimensions of the system (the
shares of consumption and investment, the direction of investment,
etc.), insofar as it impinges on individual enterprises the planning
system must strive as far as possible to rely on indirect means of
control, such as manipulating relative prices to encourage (dis-
courage) the production of certain products or the use of certain
raw materials or intermediate products. Definite if limited
steps toward meeting both conditions have been adopted in the
post-Mao reform period; these will be discussed further below.

The second contradiction is posed by the discrepancy between
the consciousness of the leaders and the consciousness of the
masses, the need to raise the latter and the manipulative, hierarchical implications of doing so. During the numerous campaigns which marked the Maoist period and during the Cultural
Revolution especially, consciousness-raising was pushed to a
fever pitch. The central thrust of the Cultural Revolution, which
sought to transform the social superstructure of institutions and
consciousness to match the socialist changes that had taken place
in the economic base of society, made consciousness-raising the
order of the day. At the same time, it highlighted the contradictions such efforts embody.

During the Cultural Revolution, a small group of people, the
"Gang of Four" and its close associates, assumed responsibility
for determining what was "correct" thought, which ideas would
be publicly admissible, and perhaps most significantly, assessing
the implications of holding contrary views. In their judgment,
cadres seeking to restore a modicum of material incentives,
peasants seeking to increase their income through exploitation of
their private plots, professors who favored examinations, violin-

ists who played Western classical music, and many, many others
were, in effect, capitalist-roaders threatening the transition to
socialism — they were potential or actual counterrevolutionaries
who had to be suppressed, struggled with, and transformed. Not
all survived the process.

The experience of the Cultural Revolution highlights the pitfalls
of consciousness-raising. Those who led the process themselves
developed no clear class analysis of contemporary Chinese society. With the conclusion of land reform and the collectivization of
agriculture, the old class categories of landlord and rich peasant
ceased to have meaning, yet even the children of the former landlords and rich peasants continued to have their old class status
ascribed to them and were discriminated against accordingly.
Similar treatment was accorded the children of former capitalists,
even though the socialization of industry was carried through
smoothly, leaving no possibility of capitalist restoration by the
late 1950s. Further, not only were the initial class categories
abused, but the ill treatment of all those who had a different vision
of how to carry out the transition to socialism was legitimized by
terming them "capitalist-roaders." The Marxian conception of
class which the Gang of Four pretended to use is based on people's
relations to one another in the production process. The Gang of
Four's misuse of the Marxian conception assigned people on the
basis of their ideas (the very opposite of Marx's materialist conception) to classes which in fact had long since ceased to exist.

Charles Bettelheim, perhaps the sharpest critic of the post-
Mao reforms and a strong supporter of the Cultural Revolution,
acknowledges as a critical shortcoming the failure of the Cultural
Revolution to develop a coherent class analysis. He presents the
following example of the misuse of class concepts (1978: 95):

In 1976 an article entitled "A Great Victory" (Jen-min Jih-pao, April 10) declared that Teng Hsiao-ping's social base was made up of "the capitalist-
roaders in the party" who were connected with the bourgeoisie and the unreformed landlords, rich peasants, counter-revolutionaries, bad elements, and
Rightists in society" (Peking Review, 1976, no. 16)...in 1977 Hua Kuo-feng,
who had accepted this "analysis," declared in his report to the Eleventh Congress, with Teng Hsiao-ping by his side, that the (Gang of) Four were "typical
representatives within our party of landlords, rich peasants, counter-revolutionaries, and bad elements, as well as of the old and new bourgeois elements...(Peking Review, 1977, no. 35).

Although the new leadership has subsequently toned down its rhetoric and dropped such obviously archaic categories as "landlord" and "rich peasant" in determining the class status of rural residents, it too has yet to make a meaningful analysis of the class question in contemporary China.

The class conflicts of contemporary "socialist" societies lie in fact in a different arena altogether. The issue is whether those who have access to the power and material resources of the state will come to constitute a distinct class superior to the immediate producers and all those engaged in socially useful labor. There are powerful systemic forces leading in this direction, and unless the issues are clearly grasped and appropriate countermeasures taken, the transition to socialism will be cut short. In China, the outcome is still to be decided. The members of the Gang of Four, who took on themselves the task of raising the consciousness of the rest of the nation, simply failed to understand what in fact is most basic. The inadequacies of their analysis and the abuse of their authority bring into sharp focus the pitfalls of consciousness-raising.

Yet the contradiction cannot be resolved by assuming the need away. Creating an awareness in people that they are part of a society whose members are mutually responsible for one another is important in the socialist transition. Ideas do have consequences. The consciousness underlying self-seeking behavior, racism, sexism, and so forth must be attacked in a socialist society. This is not always easy to do while maintaining principles of free speech and expression, but that is what resolving the second contradiction requires.

As for the third contradiction, that between leaders and masses, the emphasis on the "mass line" in China showed a certain awareness of the problem and suggested an approach to its resolution. Here the issues are of power, participation, and material interest rather than of consciousness. In one sense, the Cultural Revolution, despite its theoretical weaknesses, stood as an attempt to prevent this contradiction from resolving itself in the formation of distinct, antagonistic classes. The "two participations" (a longtime revolutionary principle but stressed especially during the Cultural Revolution) and the May 7 cadre schools — which sent most persons with administrative and social responsibility to the countryside for a period of six months or more of physical labor, study, and reflection — are representative of a variety of efforts to institutionalize the attempt to forestall the emergence of a new

elite class, an attempt which was also reflected in the effort to
heighten mass consciousness in ways inimical to elitist control.

Yet all of these efforts failed to come to grips with the problem
of hierarchy in China, a problem inextricably intertwined with the
complex role of the state in socialist development. As a leveling
force eliminating old class distinctions and upholding social
justice, the state must play a central role in the transition to socialism. At the same time, the concentration of nearly all social
power in the state gives those with access to its authority and resources a distinctly privileged position. Ultimately, the failure to
address the problem of hierarchy in China reflected an inability
to come to grips with the social forces and institutional structures
spawning it. The nation's commitment to centrally planned industrialization and rapid social change under the leadership of the
state and a single dominant party inevitably tended to concentrate
authority at the apex of a social pyramid; overthrowing individual
bureaucrats for holding the "wrong" ideas, characteristic of the
Cultural Revolution, offered no solution to the systemic problems.
Mao was correct in seeing that the conditions giving rise to the
contradiction between leaders and masses would constantly re-
generate it in the course of socialist transition, but quite wrong
in believing it could be resolved, even temporarily, by a series of
cultural revolutions.

The fourth contradiction, that between the forces and relations
of production, appeared in a form that makes interpretation of the
empirical reality ambiguous. Over the 1952-1976 period, industry
grew at a rate of about 11 percent per year, and the growth in grain
output of about 2.4 percent per year (State Statistical Bureau,
1979) outpaced population growth of slightly over 2 percent by a
narrow margin. But the agricultural performance was bought with
massive increments in labor use in the face of sharply declining
labor productivity, which measured on a labor day basis fell by
between 15 and 36 percent between 1957 and 1975 (Rawski, 1979a:
776-777), and despite a massive increase in material inputs as
well, agricultural output failed to respond commensurately. In
industry, extremely high rates of capital investment — about 33
percent of material output in the 1970s compared to 24 percent in
the First Five-Year Plan period (BR, 12/21/79: 10) — were required to produce the output gains, making it necessary to limit
consumer goods output and wage increases. The significance of
poor allocative efficiency in China lay primarily in the fact that

an increasing quantity of resources was necessary to produce a given increment in output. The use of these resources for investment limited the amount that might otherwise have been available to improve people's living standards.

As in the Soviet Union, China's initial gains in economic growth reflected in the main a sharply stepped-up investment rate. As centrally planned economies become more complex, however, systemic factors come into play to reduce their efficiency. The most significant of these is the relegation of economic decision-making to an administrative hierarchy removed from the points of production. The case of the Beijing picture tube plant cited above demonstrates the nature of the problem clearly. The system vanquishes flexibility, timeliness and, perhaps most important, the initiative and ingenuity of the cadres and workers responsible for production. The systemic nature of the problem is reflected in the pressures for economic reform which have appeared in all of the centrally planned economies, even though the pressures have generally encountered strong resistance and have usually led to limited action or to no action at all.

One of the conditions for the development of the productive forces in centrally planned economies is a genuine decentralization which shifts economic responsibility to the enterprises or other units responsible for production rather than merely to local government officials. This can be done only through the incorporation of some elements of market economy in the planning system. Although the market system does have the power to generate its own values and to influence the process of social development, the point in socialist transition is to control these elements rather than to dismiss the market system altogether. The consequence of the Maoists' refusal to incorporate market elements (beyond a bare minimum) was, on the one hand, an economic performance insufficient to raise real incomes significantly either in industry or in agriculture and, on the other, a perpetuation of economic decision-making by an administrative hierarchy removed from the direct producers.

The fear that the use of the market economy would undermine socialist consciousness and give rise to greater inequality and other social ills is not without foundation. Rejecting its use, however, as the one-sided stress on the relations of production and the proper forms of consciousness dictated, appears to have seriously undermined the development of the productive forces; this is reflected in education, training, and the motivational system as well as in the aggregate economic performance.

The lack of material rewards to those who worked well was just one part of the process. Equality was often pursued as a levelling matter; in education, examinations were eliminated and standards reduced to what the most ill-prepared could master, while in the workplace, those with superior technical or managerial skills tended to lose their authority. Now it is quite correct that entrance examinations tend to favor those with urban, intellectual backgrounds and to place the children of peasants and workers at a disadvantage. Thus it was not improper to seek to remedy this. The problem of the Cultural Revolution stemmed from the one-sided pursuit of the remedies here and in practically every aspect of social life. The consequence in education was a poorly educated generation and the limited development of the technical skills China sorely needs. For China as a whole, the one-sided stress on social relations of production limited the development of productive forces and prevented people's material lives from improving.

Another aspect of the contradiction between the forces and relations of production emerges when the issue of participation in the capitalist world economy is raised. Such participation offers access to capital, technology, foreign exchange, markets, training, and so forth which would not otherwise be available; the potential boost to the development of the forces of production is enormous. At the same time, participation in the capitalist world system increases a nation's vulnerability and dependency. Perhaps still more important, participation in the world system can only be on its terms, terms which mold the participant accordingly. Thus China must increase its exports to pay for the capital and technology it acquires abroad. Exports, to be competitive on world markets, often require foreign-type managerial methods and institutions. Under these conditions, the production relations characteristic of capitalism will tend to be reproduced.

Further, although the enterprise tends to be an engine of development under capitalism, it is of course a blind agent in that its profit-seeking and expansion of capital become ends in themselves. If the Chinese enterprise becomes like its Western counterpart, an independent engine of accumulation, then the planned direction of the economy to serve social ends will be undermined and a system of values justifying this will develop. Yet the simplified reaction to the dilemmas posed by participation in the world economy which characterized the Maoist era, when China by and large remained aloof from it, limited economic development. It may well have had perverse effects on consciousness as well, contributing to the insularity which played a part in the rule by ideologues and undermining confidence in socialism by restricting gains in real income. The contradictions posed by participation in the world economy, which I have subsumed here under the contradiction between the forces and relations of production, can be resolved successfully only by treading a fine line between their polarities.

In each of the four principal contradictions that mark the transition to socialism, Chinese policy was wanting. Progress in the transition requires finding ways to serve individual interests while serving the social interest as well, avoiding censorship and authoritarian control over intellectual life while deepening people's social consciousness, reconciling the need for leadership with the power and authority of ordinary people, and fostering the development of the forces of production and socialist relations of production simultaneously. China's policies since the death of Mao can best be understood as an attempt to find new resolutions for each of these contradictions, and as an attempt to correct the two principal deviations from the pure socialist model of development: the failure of real incomes to improve materially and the persistence of social hierarchy.

7. ECONOMIC DEVELOPMENT SINCE 1976

The economic and social policies pursued since 1976 have sought to make China's development conform to the socialist model and at the same time to correct the one-sided resolutions of the principal contradictions implemented under the Gang of Four. As such, these new policies are essential to furthering the transition to socialism in China. However, the principal contradictions continually reproduce themselves in new form; there are no permanent resolutions. The new policies, moreover, marking as they do a sharp reaction against previous extremes, show some signs of swinging to opposite extremes. If these tendencies persist, counterweights to the new policies will have to be found in time to sustain the socialist transition. To demonstrate these rather abstract propositions, it will be necessary to examine the set of economic policies that has been implemented since 1976.

China is putting primary emphasis on the development of the productive forces in an effort to achieve the so-called four modernizations — of industry, agriculture, science and technology, and national defense — by the end of the century. The target for national income is a per capita GNP of 1,000 (1980) U.S. dollars by the year 2000, roughly a quadrupling from the 1979 level of U.S.$253. The four modernizations are to be carried out primarily through bringing into full play the initiative of basic decision-making units — individuals, enterprises, and collectives — even while central planning establishes the broad priorities and parameters of economic activity.

According to arguments presented by Chinese economists (see Xue, 1980 and 1979, for example), socialist economic organization can avoid the macroeconomic problems of capitalism through conscious direction of the economy, yet at the same time benefit from the more purposive activity of the direct producers acting in their own self-interest. Basic decentralization of the economy in 1958 transferred authority from ministries in Beijing to lower governmental authorities — provinces, prefectures, and counties — but retained, as I have indicated, a bureaucratic structure with which enterprises had to contend.

Under the administrative decentralization, for example, a firm which developed an innovation capable of reducing production costs but which had to be embodied in new capital equipment could not simply proceed with its introduction. It would have to get the approval of the appropriate administrative body, which in turn would have to approach the administrative superior of the machinery-producing enterprise whose cooperation was sought. The latter enterprise would tend to be distinctly unenthusiastic because such "custom" assignments could be carried out only at the cost of lowering overall output quantity, upon which its success was primarily judged. The new equipment was likely to be obtained only after a long delay.

To circumvent such problems, enterprises have tended to try to produce as much of their own requirements as they can. The result has been excessive vertical integration and duplication of facilities built and utilized on an uneconomically small scale. Many works have enumerated the efficiency problems of the Soviet economy (see Nove, 1977, for example), and although partially decentralized administration in China has reduced such problems in comparison to the Soviet Union, they remain substantial nonetheless.

To remove the layer of bureaucracy that intervenes between economic units' perception of their needs and their ability to fulfill them, China is increasingly permitting a devolution of powers and the partial introduction of market forces. Many firms, for example, can now accept new employees by examination rather than have them assigned by the state labor bureaus, although the bureaus still determine the pool of eligible employees. Firms which meet their production plans have increased leeway to produce and market unplanned items, as well as to purchase inputs directly from suppliers. A larger share of above-plan profits can now be retained by firms to finance investment or provide employee bonuses and benefits. In 1980-81 these changes were distinctly experimental, but the early results were generally favorable. As might be expected, however, a number of problems did arise; these forced a slowdown in the pace of reform but not a halt.

The most serious problem was one of rising prices in a nation which had escaped serious inflation for close to thirty years. The free markets for nonstaple agricultural produce, the rights of enterprises to develop new products and negotiate their own contracts, new pricing flexibility, the switchover to emphasizing profits in plan fulfillment, and the unanticipated budget deficits associated with loosened economic control all put upward pressure on prices. The rise in retail prices was officially indicated to be 6.7 percent for 1980 (BR, 5/18/81: 17), but among Chinese people the rate was widely believed to have been much higher. On December 7, 1980, the State Council, recognizing the seriousness of the situation, issued an edict strictly limiting price increases. The effect of this, however, was to limit the flexibility and decentralization that economic reform was intended to bring. The pace of economic reform is likely to continue to be limited by efforts to forestall inflation.

In agriculture as well as in industry, however, market forces are still being given greater play. Instead of ordering all communes to plant grain, for example, including those whose natural conditions may be unsuited for grain, the government can raise the price of grain, reduce the cost of inputs, or adjust the relative prices of grain and alternative crops until the desired outcome is attained. Thus in 1979 the price of grain was raised by 20 percent and that of above-quota grain to 50 percent more than the base price, even while pressures on all regions and communes to grow grain regardless of natural conditions was eased. Guizhou, for example, whose hilly terrain and moist, mild climate make it especially suitable for tree crops, is being permitted to specialize accordingly (BR, 10/14/79: 7). Yet in 1979, grain production rose an unparalleled 9 percent to 332.12 million tons, an increase of 27.37 million tons (BR, 9/22/80: 31), and although poor weather brought a decline in 1980 to 318.2 million tons (U.S. Department of Agriculture, 1981: 6), the crop was still the second best on record and a new plateau seemed to have been reached. Spurred by a sharp increase in cash crop production, the gross value of agricultural output rose in 1980 by 2.7 percent despite the grain decline (Ibid.: 1).

One of the prominent features of reform in the agricultural sector has been the widespread introduction of the contract system for subunits of the production teams (the teams average 30-40 households), usually small groups of households or individual households. The households may be given complete responsibility for production in certain fields, for example, and required to turn over an agreed-upon amount of the harvest to the collective. Any excess (sometimes just a portion of the excess) they may keep or sell, and they are responsible for making up the difference if output falls short of the amount contracted for (the system is often referred to as the "responsibility" system). The land, trees, major implements, and so forth remain collectively owned under the contract system, but much of the actual farm work is divided among smaller units. The system has a number of important implications for collective agriculture.

First, it allows for much greater flexibility in organizational forms, which can correspond more closely to differences in the level of development of the productive forces. In suburban communes, which are usually highly mechanized and have well-developed brigade and commune industries, the contract system is less useful (and less used); work is more socialized, with a greater division of labor dictated by the technology and equipment employed. In relatively poor, remote mountain villages, on the other hand, where individual households may be widely separated and a lack of equipment makes division of labor meaningless from a productivity standpoint, the contract-responsibility system makes it possible to carry on production with smaller units, often individual households, to maximize incentives, and to adhere closely to the socialist principle of distribution according to labor. At the same time, it cannot be denied that this practice has the potential to undermine the collective ethos and to blur the distinction between capitalist and socialist organizational forms. Like most of the reform measures, the contract system in agriculture promises to raise output and incomes but also carries within it seeds of disruption. Whether these will sprout depends on the ability of public policymakers to perceive incipient problems and to find the delicate mix of policies that will preserve the positive features of the reforms while inhibiting their negative ones.

The use of material incentives in industry and agriculture forms part of a comprehensive strategy to decentralize and debureaucratize the economy. Despite the rhetoric of the Cultural Revolution extolling worker control, in fact the rigid avoidance of most market forms and material incentives left almost all major decisions in the higher rungs of the planning hierarchy, depriving enterprises and individuals of the possibility for initiative. Instead of orders from above determining what to produce or plant — and how to produce and plant it — enterprises or communes have increased leeway to respond independently to market signals, but market signals which are carefully orchestrated by the central planners wherever the public interest is at stake. The intention is to create conditions where the personal interests of the economic actors will indeed be harnessed to the achievement of national social goals.

In industry, 46 percent of wage-earners received wage increases in 1977, 4 percent in 1978, and 40 percent in 1979. Wages of workers and staff members in state-owned enterprises rose by 7.6 percent in real terms in 1979 and 6.1 percent in 1980, when they reached an average of 762 yuan; the wages of workers and staff members in urban collectives rose by 7.1 percent in real terms in 1980 to an average of 624 yuan (BR, 5/19/80: 24; 5/18/81: 20). In agriculture, per capita income from collective labor rose from 65 yuan in 1977 to 74 yuan in 1978, 83.4 yuan in 1979, and 85.9 yuan in 1980 (BR, 5/18/81: 19). Each of the single-year increases in 1978 and 1979 exceeded the increase in the entire twenty-year period between 1957 and 1977 of 8 yuan. In addition to the increased income from collective labor, the income from private plots increased sharply as a consequence of the revival of rural markets and sharp increases in the state purchasing prices of pork, eggs, and so forth; peasant income from private plots reached an estimated 30-40 yuan per capita in 1979. The substantial increase in urban and rural incomes led to a sharp rise in the demand for consumer goods; in real terms retail sales rose in 1979 by 12.4 percent and in 1980 by a further 12.2 percent (BR, 5/19/80: 21; 5/18/81: 17). In the first nine months of 1980, retail sales of consumer goods in the countryside increased by 16 percent over the like 1979 period; the increase for the nation as a whole was 13 percent (BR, 11/17/80).

The increase in the sale of consumer goods required a new stress on the development of light industry. Reversing a consistent pattern of heavy industry's growth surpassing that of light industry, 1979 saw light industry's output grow by 9.6 percent as compared to heavy industry's 7.7 percent (BR, 5/12/80: 12); the shift became more pronounced still in 1980, when the gain in light industrial output was 18.4 percent compared to a 1.4 percent increase for heavy industry (BR, 5/11/81: 23). So much importance is attached to increasing consumption, moreover, that a marked drop in the investment rate is also under way. According to national income accounting practices used in the socialist countries, the accumulation rate in China dropped from 36.5 percent of national income (net material product plus the value added by sectors like transportation which serve the material-producing sectors directly) in 1978 to 33.6 percent in 1979 and a planned 30 percent in 1980 (BR, 9/22/80: 32). Of the funds allocated to capital construction, the portion set aside for worker housing, science, education, culture, and so forth rose from 17.4 percent in 1978 to 27 percent in 1979 and 33.7 percent in 1980 (BR, 5/11/81: 26).

With the drop in the accumulation rate, growth is to be sustained — and in agriculture accelerated — by two principal means. The first involves combining material incentives with turning authority over to production units and attempting thereby to unleash entrepreneurial initiatives that heretofore have had limited means of expression. The second involves stepping up the pace of technological progress. This entails increasing scientific and technical education markedly, as well as restoring the status of scientific and technical research. It also entails a deliberate effort to tap the world's storehouse of scientific and technical knowledge by cultivating economic and other relations with advanced capitalist countries. China appears to have attained the same kind of self-confidence Japan reached after the turn of the century in permitting an inflow of foreign capital without fearing that its national purposes will thereby be subverted. Whether this self-

confidence will ultimately prove justified depends in large measure on the leadership's clear perception of the effects of involvement in the capitalist world economy and its timely adoption of
countermeasures to forestall the most damaging ones (for a discussion of these issues see the essay by Mark Selden and myself,
"The Transition to Socialism in China," in this volume).

It is important to grasp China's new economic policies as part
of an integrated development strategy. It is also important to see
in them an attempt to remedy defects perceived in China's deviation from the pure model of socialist development. I have argued
that the two principal defects were the failure to materially improve people's living standards and the failure to limit the social,
political, and economic hierarchy that weighed on the entire working population. I have already presented evidence that after two
decades of stagnation, worker and peasant incomes have begun to
leap upward. Similar gains have marked the construction of
housing for workers and staff; 1979 saw the completion of 62.6
million square meters of housing, a record level 66 percent over
the 1978 figure, and a further increase to 82.3 million square
meters, a gain of 31.6 percent, took place in 1980 (BR, 10/22/80:
34; 5/18/81: 20). It is clear that the long neglect of people's living standards has been brought to an end.

The question of hierarchy is a much more complex one. We
can see clearly that the limited introduction of market relations
in the economic sphere, the sharp curtailment of censorship, and
the flowering of the arts and local cultures are all part of — to
borrow a phrase from an American president — getting the government off people's backs. Obviously a hierarchy which is as
deeply rooted in the nation's history and institutions as is China's
is not going to be removed overnight. But the fact that the moves
against hierarchy are pervasive and consistent suggests that a
substantive change may be in progress. One of the recent experiments at the enterprise level indicates just how significant the
institutional reforms may prove to be.

In five factories in Beijing, factory directors have assumed
responsibility for their enterprises under the direction of the
factories' congresses of workers and staff rather than under the
direction of the Communist Party (BR, 11/17/80: 3). Great power
had been concentrated in the Party committees and in their first
secretaries especially, and they always tended to be intervening
in the administrative affairs of the factories. Under the reform,

the Party committee is to stay out of enterprise administration except to see that Party policies and state laws are carried out. The congress which replaces it is directly elected by the workers and staff. It is to be

the organ of power for the enterprise and has the right to make decisions on: the orientation and policy of production and management, long-term and annual plans, measures for major technical renovation, important rewards and punishments for workers and staff members and the setting up, revision or abolition of regulations for the whole factory. It elects a director and discusses the list of deputy directors recommended by the director, and then submits the names to the higher leading body for appointment ... the director assumes full responsibility for the management of the enterprise. He submits major programmes to the congress for examination and is responsible for their implementation (BR, 11/17/80: 3).

Although this reform is experimental and the extent to which it will be implemented uncertain, it indicates at least that curtailing the role of the Party and state in favor of enhanced grass-roots participation and control is on the reform agenda.

Thus it is clear that the two principal deviations from the pure socialist model of economic development are being addressed. Since the new development model is an integrated and pervasive one, however, it is proper to ask whether some of the features of Chinese development which previously conformed to the pure socialist development model will be affected as well. Questions have been raised concerning the new strategy's impact on equality especially, and these deserve consideration.

The use of the market and material incentives has a strong potentiality for generating inequality. The question of potentiality, however, I would like to reserve for the concluding section, and to limit the discussion here to the empirical evidence we have. It is quite clear that in China today those who are more productive are getting paid more, but the effect of this on equality is ambiguous; it tends to widen the gap among workers, but may reduce the gap between workers and managers. Bonuses tend to increase equality when cadres and managers do not receive them or receive only the factory average, as is often the case.

At the Shanghai Machine Tool Factory, for example, a factory which has 6,000 workers and specializes in the manufacture of grinding machines, there are eight wage grades: [7]

Table 2

Wage Structure of the Shanghai Machine Tool Factory

Wage grade	1	2	3	4	5	6	7	8
Monthly income (yuan)	42	49.4	57.5	66.9	77.8	90.6	105.4	123

Source: Data gathered by the author on a personal visit to the factory April 4, 1980.

The grades are the same as those which existed during the Cultural Revolution. Since the Cultural Revolution, wages have been increased three times by moving people to higher levels; the average wage is currently 68 yuan. The chief engineer, who is also the factory director, receives 254 yuan per month. The 550 technicians range from 44 to 106 yuan per month; the 100 engineers generally receive 106-145 yuan, and most assistant directors earn 145 yuan. The income of the director and assistant directors has not increased since the Cultural Revolution. Thus the wage increases have narrowed the gap between them and the workers. This effect has been reinforced by the use of bonuses.

Bonuses amount to 15 percent of the factory's payroll; the average bonus is a little over 10 yuan per month — higher for workers, less for cadres. Workers with production norms receive more bonuses than those without them. The average bonus for individual production work, based on norms for output, quality, consumption of materials, and safety, is 7-8 yuan per month. Some workers can get as much as 15 yuan; very few fail to get any bonus at all. Those with no production norms usually receive 4-6 yuan. At the end of the year the factory management divides the surplus left over in the bonus fund equally among all the workers. Once or twice a year, bonuses are given for work team performance in intraplant competitions for quality, safety, and so forth. There is some differentiation between more and less productive workers, but the system narrows the gap between managers and cadres on the one hand and workers on the other.

On a broader, national scale, the evidence also points toward the maintenance of equality. In 1979 and 1980, as I have indicated, incomes and retail sales in the countryside grew more rapidly than those in urban areas, decreasing urban-rural differentials in percentage terms. Within this context, the natural tendency of communes with locational advantages to prosper prior to others

must be regarded as secondary. If in the future the differences
among communes continue to widen and resolute public policy
measures are not taken to reduce them, then this could later become a significant source of inequality. We cannot know what
public policy will be in the future, but the evidence we have from
the present indicates that equality remains a vital concern.

The increase in the purchase prices of agricultural products
put into effect in March 1979 immediately created anomalies in
the price structure because retail prices initially remained unchanged. Whether the story that peasants who sold eggs to the
state could then buy them back at lower prices in state stores and
resell them to the state is true or not, it is clear that some adjustment in retail prices was in order. On the other hand, raising
food prices, on which people's welfare critically depends, would
seem to be inconsistent with following the socialist development
model. The way in which the quandary was handled reveals a
continuing commitment to equality as well as to people's welfare.

From November 1, 1979, price increases at the retail level
were put into effect for pork (33 percent), beef and mutton (about
the same), eggs (32 percent), vegetables (slightly), aquatic products (33 percent), and poultry and milk (varying amounts). But at
the same time,

To ensure that the living standards of the workers and urban residents will not
be affected by the rise in prices, the state grants a 5-yuan monthly subsidy to
each worker and government employee, including those who have retired and
apprentices, totaling 100 million in all. Those in the pastoral regions get an
8-yuan subsidy since they consume more meat. It is estimated that the price
hikes will bring in about 5,000 million yuan for the state each year while the
subsidy given by the state amounts to more than 6,000 million yuan (BR,
11/9/79: 4).

The solution to the quandary was to increase the sales price, but
to do so in a way that would on the whole more than fully compensate people for the extra cost and at the same time improve
the distribution of real income by raising all incomes an equal
absolute amount rather than an equal percentage amount. The way
this was handled makes it quite clear that even while rationalizing
the pricing system, the government is determined to protect the
people against the harm wrought by inflation.

The question of equality is a complex one; a reduction in the
gap between workers and managers may be associated with increasing differentiation among workers, and a reduction in the gap

between peasants and workers may be associated with increasing
differentiation in the countryside as some communes prosper
earlier than others. The evidence we have, however, suggests
that equality remains an important objective of state policy, and
that material incentives and market forms have not thus far led
to any substantive increases in inequality. At the same time, the
new economic strategy as a whole is clearly moving toward correcting the neglect of mass living standards and reducing the
weight of hierarchy, the principal deviations from the socialist
model which characterized Chinese development up to 1976. Current successes, however, cannot prevent new contradictions from
arising, or the reappearance of old ones in new form.

8. THE TRANSITION TO SOCIALISM
IN CHINA

The dynamics of socialist transition, it will be recalled, are
shaped in large measure by the recurrence and resolution of four
principal contradictions, contradictions (1) between producers and
society, (2) between the need to elevate social consciousness and
the oppressive hierarchy such efforts tend to generate, (3) between
masses and leaders, and (4) between the forces and relations of
production. The events that have transpired since 1976 can be
understood as the working out of these contradictions. Since these
contradictions characterize the entire transition period, however,
the outcome can only be to recreate them in new forms.

One-sided resolutions of all these contradictions characterized
the 1966-76 Cultural Revolution period; had all the resolutions of
that time been allowed to congeal, there is no way China could have
effectively carried out the transition to socialism. Despite os-
tensible support for the mass line at an official level, prior to
1976 the direct producers were subjected to a considerable extent
to externally imposed goals and subordinated to an administrative-
bureaucratic hierarchy. The policy reversals which followed
Mao's death reasserted the rights and interests of working people
as individuals, led to the partial restoration of basic rights of free
speech and expression, weakened the concentration of power and
authority in society, and helped bring the development of the forces
of production into balance with the development of socialist relations of production.

Despite the clear logic underlying the integrated strategy of re-

form and modernization responsible for these reversals, the
strategy has met with considerable hostility from critics on the
left who argue that far from clearing the way to socialist transition it actually blocks the path. Possibly the most important
issue raised by the critics concerns the role of the market.

Writing in another context long before the market reforms
were implemented, Paul Sweezy (1971: 4) argued that

the trend toward capitalism is built into the present system [referring to
Czechoslovakia]: control of enterprises in the enterprises themselves, coordination through the market, and reliance on material incentives — these three
factors, taken together, make inevitable a strong tendency toward an economic
order which, whatever one may choose to call it, functions more and more like
capitalism.

Charles Bettelheim responds in the same work (pp. 18-20) that
market relations are surface phenomena, and that their significance can be grasped only in relation to "the basic social relationships, the class relationships," that underlie them. The basic
class relationships, according to Bettelheim, are production relationships. Nevertheless, Bettelheim agrees (p. 40) "that the
advance toward socialism requires that commodity relations dis-
appear"; he argues that ultimately they are an obstacle to producer domination, but that eliminating them is an historical task.
What then is the relation between commodity production, the
market, and the transition to socialism?

I have taken here a position in agreement with Nove (1979:
ch. 7) that is directly contradictory to Sweezy's position. If there
is no market, then a hierarchy must exist to transmit production
orders to the direct producers. To say that the planning hierarchy
represents the class interests of the direct producers is to take
refuge in an abstraction; whether it does or not, control is essentially outside of their hands. This is not to deny a central role
to economic planning in the socialist state; indeed, whether it is
a waste of society's resources to develop a private motor car industry or whether the agricultural sector needs a stepped-up investment pace to avert food shortages cannot possibly be decided
by individual producers or consumers. In such major decisions
planning is essential, and it must reflect the class interests of
working people if it is to further the transition to socialism. The
point remains, however, that within the broad parameters established by central planning, the market has a critical role to

play in releasing the initiative and enhancing the authority of the direct producers. The fact that commodity production plays a key role in capitalist society does not mean that it has no role to play in socialist society.

Under certain circumstances, however, the use of market forms in conjunction with individual material rewards may indeed generate contradictions which block socialist transition. It is possible to envision a new hierarchy emerging based on income and wealth, and a growing materialism and self-seeking of individuals displacing socialist consciousness. The emphasis on the forces of production, especially if pushed to an extreme, could seriously undermine the development of socialist production relations.

These possibilities, however, are not inevitable outcomes of the integrated development strategy that has emerged in China since 1976; nor do they constitute sufficient reason for its abandonment. The new strategy appears to offer the only viable means of dealing with the critical shortcomings of China's socialist development. Like any possible strategy, it will generate new contradictions which will have to be successfully resolved in their turn if the transition to socialism is to proceed in China. The outcome of that effort remains for the future to determine.

NOTES

1. The essay of W. Arthur Lewis (1963), discussed below, is a notable exception, and because of (or despite) its class analysis it is widely regarded as one of the most basic theoretical contributions to the development literature.

2. These assertions, basically at odds with dependency theories, which locate the sources of underdevelopment in external aggression or the more subtle impact of world trade and investment, are documented historically for the case of China in my essay "The Development of Underdevelopment in China," Modern China, Vol. 4, No. 3, reprinted in Philip Huang, ed., The Development of Underdevelopment in China (White Plains, N.Y.: M. E. Sharpe, 1980). I do not wish to deny the importance of external forces, merely to assert the primacy, in most cases, of the internal ones.

3. Surplus labor is formally defined as labor whose marginal product is zero. That is to say, if a simple rearrangement of the work process can sustain output at the previous level when a worker withdraws, then we say that surplus labor was present. In practice, the concept of surplus labor is usually extended to cases in which the marginal product of labor is very low.

4. In small countries where a labor-intensive industrial export sector develops rapidly, the shift of a large share of the labor force from agriculture to industry may reduce inequality for reasons elaborated in the text. In such cases, moreover, industrialists tend to be powerful relative to landowners, and

may be able to bring about a genuine land reform, which will be to their interest insofar as it raises agricultural productivity, lowers agricultural prices
(and thus the wages they must pay), and extends rural markets. These factors
may have been operative in Taiwan and South Korea, both of which have among
the most equal income distributions of the less developed capitalist countries.
In the case of Taiwan, the fact that the elite class was composed of mainlanders
bringing "liquid" wealth (they couldn't carry their land) when they occupied the
island in the late 1940s, a class quite distinct from the Taiwanese landowners,
facilitated land reform. As the text makes clear, however, growing inequality
is the norm in the early stages of capitalist development.

5. According to the Head of the General Office of the Shanghai Labor Bureau, 400,000 people were newly assigned to jobs in Shanghai in 1979, an estimated 220,000 were to be assigned in 1980, 150,000 in 1981, and 130,000 in
1982. The number of new senior high school graduates, however, was expected
to drop to about 100,000 in 1983 and less thereafter, greatly easing the employment crisis. Data provided in a personal interview with the author, April 4,
1980.

6. Data provided to the author by Ministry of Agriculture officials.

7. This information and the following information were gathered by the author on a visit to the factory on April 4, 1980.

REFERENCES

Adelman, Irma (1979) "Growth, Income Distribution and Equity-Oriented De-
velopment Strategies," in Charles Wilber, ed., The Political Economy of
Development and Underdevelopment, 2nd ed. New York: Random House.
Ashbrook, Arthur, Jr. (1978) "China: Shift of Economic Gears in Mid-1970s,"
in U.S. Congress, Joint Economic Committee, Chinese Economy Post-Mao.
Washington, D.C.: U.S. Government Printing Office.
BR = Beijing Review (dates indicated in text).
Bettelheim, Charles (1974) Cultural Revolution and Industrial Organization
in China. New York: Monthly Review Press.
_____ (1978) "The Great Leap Backward," Monthly Review 30.3 (July-
August), 37-130.
Chen, Nai-ruenn (1967) Chinese Economic Statistics. Chicago: Aldine.
Fei Hsiao-tung and Chang Chih-I (1945) Earthbound China. Chicago: Univer-
sity of Chicago Press.
Field, Robert M. (1975) "Civilian Industrial Production in the People's Repub-
lic of China: 1949-74," in U.S. Congress, Joint Economic Committee, China:
A Reassessment of the Economy. Washington, D.C.: U.S. Government
Printing Office.
Foreign Broadcast Information Service (FBIS) (1980) Daily Report, October 3,
pp. L10-L15.
International Labour Office (1977) Poverty and Landlessness in Rural Asia.
Geneva: ILO.
Lardy, Nicholas R. (1978) Economic Growth and Distribution in China. Cam-
bridge, England: Cambridge University Press.
_____ (1976) "Economic Planning and Income Distribution in China," Cur-
rent Scene XIV.11.

Lewis, W. Arthur (1963) "Economic Development with Unlimited Supplies of Labour," in A. N. Agarwala and S. P. Singh, eds., The Economics of Under-development. New York: Oxford University Press.

Lippit, Victor D. (1978a) "The Development of Underdevelopment in China," Modern China, Vol. 4, No. 3.

_____ (1978b) "Economic Development in Meiji Japan and Contemporary China: A Comparative Study," Cambridge Journal of Economics 2.1 (March).

_____ (1974) Land Reform and Economic Development in China. White Plains, N.Y.: M. E. Sharpe.

Marx, Karl (1961) Capital, Vol. 1. Moscow: Foreign Languages Publishing House.

Nove, Alec (1979) Political Economy and Soviet Socialism. London: George Allen & Unwin.

_____ (1977) The Soviet Economic System. London: George Allen & Unwin.

Perkins, Dwight (1975) "Growth and Changing Structure of China's Twentieth-Century Economy," in D. Perkins, ed., China's Modern Economy in Histori-cal Perspective. Stanford: Stanford University Press.

Rawski, Thomas (1979a) "Economic Growth and Employment in China," World Development 7.8/9 (August-September).

_____ (1979b) Economic Growth and Employment in China. New York: Oxford University Press.

Riskin, Carl (1975) "Workers' Incentives in Chinese Industry," in U.S. Con-gress, Joint Economic Committee, China: A Reassessment of the Economy. Washington, D.C.: U.S. Government Printing Office.

Schran, Peter (1969) The Development of Chinese Agriculture, 1950-1959. Urbana: University of Illinois Press.

Seers, Dudley (1973) "The Meaning of Development," in Charles Wilber, ed., The Political Economy of Development and Underdevelopment, 1st ed. New York: Random House.

Shue, Vivienne (1980) Peasant China in Transition. Berkeley: University of California Press.

State Statistical Bureau, People's Republic of China (1979) Main Indicators, Development of the National Economy of the People's Republic of China (1949-1978). Beijing.

Sweezy, Paul M., and Charles Bettelheim (1971) On the Transition to Social-ism, 2nd ed. New York: Monthly Review Press.

Todaro, Michael P. (1977) Economic Development in the Third World, 1st ed. New York: Longman.

U.S. Department of Agriculture (1981) Agricultural Situation: People's Republic of China — Review of 1980 and Outlook for 1981. Washington, D.C.

Walder, Andrew (1982) "Some Ironies of the Maoist Legacy in Industry," in Victor D. Lippit and Mark Selden, eds., The Transition to Socialism in China. Armonk, New York: M. E. Sharpe.

Xue Muqiao (1980) "On Reforming the Economic Management System (1)," Beijing Review 5 (February 4).

_____ (1979) "A Study in the Planned Management of the Socialist Econ-omy," Beijing Review 43 (October 26).

Edward Friedman
MAOISM, TITOISM, STALINISM: SOME ORIGINS AND CONSEQUENCES OF THE MAOIST THEORY OF THE SOCIALIST TRANSITION

INTRODUCTION

Maoism, Titoism, and Stalinism are shorthand terms for the three broad notions which have legitimated the policies of the socialist transition in the People's Republic of China.[1] I will try to clarify these three socialist projects by sketching contours of these notions as they were first drawn between 1948 and 1958.

What has struck most observers is the struggle by Titoists and Maoists to avoid the errors, defeats and horrors of diverse aspects of the Soviet Union's experience. But the Stalinist path may have seemed more attractive in the 1950s when Minister of National Defense Peng Dehuai and others were generally incapable of imagining swift economic progress without close ties to the USSR.

The major theorist of the Maoist position was Chen Boda.[2] By 1958, in developing a critique of how capitalism was restored in Yugoslavia, Maoism took the form of new policies to guarantee the transition through socialism to communism. The new commitment was to a mass campaign, labor intensive, anti-economic, change of consciousness approach to the socialist transition.

The target of Chen's 1958 campaign was China's Titoists. Leading Titoists included Zhou Enlai, Chen Yun, and Sun Yefang. Since Chen Boda accepted and built on Stalin's notion of Titoism as capitalist restoration, his Maoism was not the antithesis of Stalinism. Yet because Chen's Maoism shared similar historical origins with Titoism, it also shared key Titoist concerns — a fiery nationalism, bureaucratism as a major obstacle to socialism, a

*This article was revised after criticisms from Mark Selden and Dorothy Solinger. My sincere thanks to both.

need to positively woo the peasantry in the coming transformation.

Maoism was theoretically unique. Yet it built on Stalinist notions and included Titoist concerns. The complexity behind analytic shorthands such as Maoism, Titoism, and Stalinism in China can best be comprehended by relating theoretical distinctiveness to actual historical evolution.

1. TITOISM AS CAPITALIST RESTORATION

In 1948 Tito broke with Stalin. By 1953 Yugoslavia's Titoists had developed a theoretical critique of Stalinism as a terroristic, bureaucratic, overcentralized, antidemocratic path which could not be considered socialist. When Tito's Yugoslavia broke with Stalin's Soviet Union, it also opened up the possibility that Leninist parties controlling the levers of state power and committed to socialism as described by Marx could take a far more humane path than that carved out by Stalin. Tito's quest began to open new vistas for many. Such people began to look more sympathetically at Bukharin's opposition to Stalin's murderous forced draft collectivization.[3] They looked into building on the democratic, popular, egalitarian, and antibureaucratic elements in Marx and Lenin.

Titoist efforts to move in a socialist direction while avoiding the worst features of Stalinism had eventually to concern the revolutionary group coming to power in China which was confronted in 1949 on the establishment of the People's Republic with what seemed to be the same dilemma as Yugoslavia. How should it wield power through a socialist transition to achieve the humane goals for which it had fought, an independent people determining its own destiny and building a flourishing, just, and equitable society without exploitation by classes which owned the means of production, classes which could live a life of plenty while most others went hungry and lost home and family and life itself? How to do all of this in one poor and backward peasant society, in China?

The head of China's Marxist-Leninist-Mao Zedong Thought Institute noted many decades later that

in the beginning, countries which adopted socialism ... adopted the same "pattern" as that of the Soviet Union ... it was quite inevitable.... Later the differences between the forms of organization in the world's socialist countries became greater and greater. In the early 1950s there appeared a form which was quite different from the pattern of the Soviet Union, the autonomous system of Yugoslavia.[4]

But would it be reasonable to expect Mao Zedong and other nationalistic Chinese revolutionaries to be quick to inquire into non-Stalinist socialist strategies? These Chinese Marxists led by Liu Shaoqi had already at the end of the 1930s attempted to make over their Party to avoid the horror of Stalinist inner-Party purge.[5] Mao had made explicit his opposition to centralized statist development of the Stalinist sort. Stalin's loyal Chinese worshiper, Wang Ming, was the major inner-Party opponent mechanically and dogmatically miming the USSR. Mao's indigenous Chinese Leninist-Marxists explicitly distinguished their new patriotic path. It could include almost all China's people in a united front encompassing bourgeois classes — peasants, merchants, and entrepreneurs — who gradually would learn and affirm the superior nature of socialism.

This might have predisposed Mao toward Tito. It didn't. Mao moved in a profoundly anti-Tito direction. Despite all of Stalin's crimes and cruelties, many of which Mao subsequently acknowledged and criticized, Mao came to define Stalin as a legitimate socialist revolutionary successor to Marx and Lenin. Mao came to define Tito as Stalin defined Tito, a traitor to socialism, a friend of imperialism. On the socialist transition, much of the Maoist analysis as it developed between 1948 and 1958 was infused with the need to follow on the misleading dualism that Stalin's way was true to socialism, that Titoism was the enemy's way.

Mao's identification with Stalin's socialist transition may have been overdetermined and inevitable. Mao believed political movements required leaders. In an international struggle, Stalin's Soviet Union emerging victorious over international fascism as the world's number two industrialized military power could play a global anti-imperialist leadership role. Weak, little Yugoslavia, apparently on the verge of national extinction, hardly seemed a natural to become a leading champion of a nonaligned movement of Third World nations. The situation defined the choice for Mao. In 1948 Tito contended that he was an orthodox adherent of Stalin's socialism. There was no alternative Titoist strategy then.

China's revolutionary armies then stood on the steps of China's capital city. Their armed adversary was backed by the rising superpower from America. The government in Washington was already engaged in cold war combat with the Soviet Union which the Soviet government feared could turn into a hot war as America struck with nuclear weapons. Whatever China's new leaders had not learned in decades of murderous combat, they well knew the ultimate danger of isolation when confronted by an armed foe which might try to destroy them. Survival itself dictated holding out more than an olive branch to the United States while making certain of continuing lines of trade and military support from the Soviet Union. To stand with Tito against Stalin meant jeopardizing a lifeline to Moscow while thrashing in perilous waters churned up by a hostile United States. Not to denounce Tito would be to court extinction. Surprisingly Liu Shaoqi's November 1, 1948, statement on the Stalin-Tito issue, "Internationalism and Nationalism," came from a context in which leaders of China's revolutionary movement were quite divided on how to respond to Yugoslavia's plight.

Stalin had diplomatically stood with the Chinese revolution's armed adversary, the Chiang Kai-shek side, to the end. Stalin had instructed Mao not to fight for victory. Stalin's forces had stolen billions of dollars worth of scarce industrial equipment from China's northeast as war reparations from Japan. Stalin was allied to the Wang Ming faction in China's Communist Party which had opposed Mao's group. Any Chinese Maoist patriot had to know that the interests of Mao's China and Stalin's Russia were not always congruent, that Moscow regularly sacrificed vital Chinese concerns (e.g. recognizing the Japanese puppet government of Manchukuo in China's northeast) to Soviet strategic priorities.

Besides, the Soviet economy was a wreck after World War II. Surely there was much to be said for the Tito position which treated both Moscow and Washington as expansionist imperialists with the American side less an immediate threat to Yugoslav independence. This meant comprehending Russian expansionism as a continuation of a centuries old Czarist drive. (Mao too would eventually adopt this view, but not until twenty years later, long after he defined his notion for China's socialist transition as the negation of Tito's policies.)

Mao already differed with Stalin, who saw international politics pitting imperialist America against peace-loving Soviet Russia in Europe, a contest between capitalism and a supposed international proletariat. Liu expressed the view of the whole Mao leadership in focusing on real Third World struggles for independence of imperialism, for

without such national liberation movements which say, weaken and undermine the foundations of imperialist domination, it would be extremely difficult for

the proletariat of the imperialist countries to achieve victory in the struggle
against monopoly capital and to attain its emancipation.

...the victories of the national independence movement of the oppressed nations of the world over imperialists...will deprive these countries of their
colonies, undermine the foundation on which they dominate the world, greatly
weaken the rule of the imperialists in their home countries, and will therefore
lead to these liberations of the proletariat and the peoples of the countries
from the rule of imperialism.[6]

This position, similar to Tito's, seemed a nationalist heresy to
Stalin. Liu and Mao insisted that the patriotic bourgeoisie could
participate in anti-imperialist struggles and side with the forces of
socialism in the colonial and semicolonial world which contained
most of the earth's people and therefore would decide the fate of
the species. Stalin, on the other hand, insisted that the fate of the
first socialist state, his Soviet Union, was the essence of international struggle. The difference was decisive. Mao's Stalinist adversary Wang Ming wrote, as he no doubt told Stalin, that on October 4 and 5, 1941, he and Mao had argued fiercely. "I said anti-
Japanese military operations in China had to be stepped up to deny
Japan any chance of helping the Nazi offensive against the Soviet
Union. Mao objected . . . I intimated that his line was anti-Soviet. . . ."[7]

In short, Mao played the role of a Titoist (putting socialism in
his nation before Moscow's global interests) long before Tito's act
gave the part meaning. Mao naturally put first leading an independent Chinese nation toward socialism. Hence when Tito gave content to the crime of which Mao had long stood accused, it had to
create a crisis within the Chinese leadership. Mao had always
claimed that fighting wars of national liberation was proletarian
internationalism and best advanced the cause of socialism. Tito's
partisans had fought such a war. But Yugoslav national independence lead to a life and death conflict with what Stalin insisted was
proletarian internationalism.

Nonetheless, if China's war-torn economy, hungry people, and un-
fulfilled great dreams were to come alive in a world where the
United States was threatening to blockade and embargo Mao's China,
and if Western Europe and Japan were dependent on the United
States, what alternative was there to turning to Stalin? Observers
of virtually every political stripe agree that Stalin imposed harsh
terms hoping to make China dependent and subservient. Soviet
scholar, L. Z. Kopelev found,

The successes of the Chinese Communists disturbed Stalin. . . . It was in those years . . . that the conflict with Yugoslavia began. . . . Mao, was undoubtedly stronger and more dangerous than Tito. . . . Therefore, . . . Stalin imposed unequal treaty concessions. . . holding fast to the Chinese Eastern Railway, the naval bases at Port Arthur and Dairen and Sinkiang. . . . At the same time there was an attempt to implant Soviet military advisers in all major Chinese army units and institutions. Stalin [wanted to] . . . make it [China] more dependent. [8]

One top Chinese Party leader, Gao Gang, may have tried to link himself and China most closely to Stalin's Soviet Union. Professor James Hsiung finds that Gao bid "for Soviet favor" during the debate over the Tito-Stalin rift by being "outspoken in urging a selfless internationalism bordering on servitude to Soviet supremacy."[9] In contrast to Gao's posture of subordination, and to the eventual policy stated by Liu of keeping open the possibility of a Soviet alliance while maximizing strategic independence, there was a third possibility: to avoid entangling alliances and preserve maximum room for maneuver.

Zhou Enlai may have headed this third group. By May 1949 after approaches to American officials in China by two of his aides, Zhou had a private message sent to the highest executive level in Washington. Zhou's position was that the U.S. diplomatic hostility to China, U.S. military support of Chiang Kai-shek, and a U.S. economic embargo against China strengthened his opponents in China's Communist Party. U.S. policies directed against the new China helped the pro-Soviet Russian group which favored narrow, extreme left, class struggle policies. In contrast, Zhou's group sought the broadest alliance at home with maximum friendly relations abroad so as to preserve, win, and use all available resources to improve the life of China's people in an atmosphere of broad national cooperation.

In Washington this meant Titoism. Zhou's group was seen as opposing singular reliance on the USSR, as seeking a patriotic united front to enhance Chinese independence.[10]

Zhou seems to have held to this policy orientation for the rest of his career. We do not know the origins of the tendency of Zhou's group which kept it committed to broad alliances, gradual development, the avoidance of left extremism, and concern for the material interests of the peasantry. It could have gone as far back as Zhou's first defense of a correct path for the socialist transition against purist leftists out of touch with popular consciousness and possibility.

In 1922 Zhou Enlai lived in Paris and organized radical young Chinese into the Communist movement. He wrote for their journal, Shaonian (Youth). When Chinese anarchists in France contended that Lenin's New Economic Policies spelled death to the Bolshevik Revolution, Zhou defended NEP. He wrote that large industry, banks, modern transportation, etc., had been nationalized in the Soviet Union; land had been put in the hands of the tillers. As a result, the basis for a few owners of private property to exploit the many had been abolished.

Revolution, Zhou argued, was a long-term enterprise. It had to be continued premised on the success of destroying bases of class exploitation. Then, given industrial weakness, war destruction and turmoil, a long process of construction was needed. This is what Lenin's NEP recognized. It recognized that peasants had to be paid fairly to obtain their grain and hold their allegiance. With power securely in the hands of dedicated socialists, a peasant agricultural country had to care about the peasants' market and income. The inherited economic conditions set the limits of possibility and dictated the agenda of Lenin's New Economic Policies.[11]

Whatever the lineup or origins in the Chinese debate over how to respond to the Stalin-Tito split, the outcome was to establish the orthodoxy of Stalin's critique of Tito. Increasingly it became presuppositional to Mao's politics that he was not and would not become another Tito. Liu's essay speaking for the Party leadership gives us the first meaning of that premise for the period of socialist transition.

The Stalinist Soviet Union is defined as a socialist state, one which "has abolished all forms of class exploitation." In contrast, Titoism is defined in terms of continuing class struggle as national and class betrayal. It is a warning to all Communist Parties that representatives of the bourgeoisie can dwell "inside the ranks of the proletariat," that they can jeopardize successful socialist liberation. Drawing on China's experience, Liu stated, "There may appear within the revolutionary ranks such people as Chen Duxiu, Zhang Guotao in China and Tito in Yugoslavia." The revolution can be betrayed by revolutionaries, socialism by socialists. Defecting fractional opponents within the Leninist Party could derail the socialist transition to communism.[12]

Mao's subsequent agenda for preventing capitalist restoration in a socialist state was already embodied in the CCP's approval of the Cominform's June 28, 1948, denunciation of Tito's Yugoslavia:

In domestic policy the leaders of the Communist Party of Yugoslavia are...
breaking with the Marxist theory of classes and class struggle. They deny
that there is a growth of capitalist elements in their country, and consequently,
a sharpening of the class struggle in the countryside. This denial is the direct
result of the opportunist tenet that the class struggle does not become sharper
during the period of transition...as Marxism-Leninism teaches, but dies
down, as was affirmed by the opportunists of the Bukharin type, who propa-
gated the theory of the peaceful growth of capitalism into Socialism.

The Yugoslavs are pursuing an incorrect policy in the countryside and by regarding the individual peasantry as a single entity, contrary to the Marxist-
Leninist doctrine of classes and class struggle, contrary to Lenin's well-
known thesis that small individual farming gives birth continually, daily,
hourly, spontaneously and on a mass scale to capitalism and the bourgeoisie.

... [In Yugoslavia] nationalist elements, which previously existed in a disguised form, managed in the course of the past five or six months to reach a
dominant position in the leadership of the Communist Party of Yugoslavia....
[S]uch a nationalist line can only lead to Yugoslavia's degeneration into an
ordinary bourgeois republic...[13]

Thus even before China's revolutionaries won state power, they
had already committed themselves to the proposition that the true
socialist path was to be distinguished from the capitalistic road
chosen by Tito's Yugoslavia. To stay in power and maintain Yugoslavia's independence from the Soviet Union, the Tito group in 1948
split with Stalin. That Soviet ruler quickly lined up Communist
parties to denounce Tito as a counterrevolutionary traitor who had
restored capitalism in Yugoslavia. The issue was power. The disguise was ideology. China's Maoist rulers would bury the issue
and treat the disguise as reality.

The Yugoslavs still expected the socialist transition in China to
resemble the Yugoslav path. The Yugoslavs looked at the Chinese
as in a situation very similar to their own. They concluded that
Stalin would look at Mao with eyes hypnotized by the actions of Tito.
The Yugoslavs saw "uneasiness in the Kremlin provoked by the appearance of a country [China] in which the revolution had been
victorious under the leadership of its native Communist Party and
which had not been 'liberated' by the USSR."[14]

The Yugoslavs believed that the terms of the economic agreements which Mao and the Chinese leadership negotiated in Moscow
in 1949-1950 "could hardly have delighted Mao."[15] Not only didn't
the Soviet Union offer much aid, let alone free aid or helpful prices,
but the terms of the joint stock companies imposed by the USSR on

the PRC were worse than those imposed on Moscow's Eastern European dependencies. In the Chinese case, the Soviets owned half of all that was produced. In Eastern Europe, the host state owned the products and sold a portion to Moscow at less than the best prices. Moscow could force Beijing to pay for Chinese products at Soviet-imposed prices.[16]   Consequently, as nationalistic Yugoslavs had to break with the USSR to make room for economic maneuver, so would China.

Despite China's endorsement of the Comintern condemnation of Yugoslavia, Tito did not reply in kind. He understood the international pressures which make it so difficult for a nation to act decently; Belgrade offered Beijing normal diplomatic relations, praised the Chinese revolution, and supported Beijing's position at the United Nations.[17]

While backing Mao, Tito opposed Stalin, whose policies Tito found antithetical to the cause of building socialism in Yugoslavia. Stalin's aims were "hegemonistic aims." When one examined the USSR's international pricing policies, the terms of the joint stock companies it imposed, etc., one discovered that Soviet ruling groups acted in a capitalist manner. To accept Stalin's demands was to ensure Yugoslavia's "subordination to the USSR and exploitation of the backward by the advanced...."[18] Such a subservient role conflicted with Tito's commitment

to move rapidly toward industrialization. The Soviet experts urged, first and foremost, that the Yugoslavs put all their emphasis on improving their agriculture and extractive industries and ... avoid any adventurist effort to industrialize rapidly.[19]

Moscow's pressures on Belgrade intensified with the 1948 Molotov Plan. Its "neocolonial features" included "assigning national specializations," leaving Yugoslavia "no place for the development of diversified industry or for raising the standard of living." Tito, rather than accept such dependence, tried to expand trade with the West where better terms existed for Yugoslavia's nonferrous metals. Stalin then turned on Tito, imposed an economic boycott, accused Tito of coddling the Yugoslav peasantry, denounced him as an agent of Western imperialism, and tried to overthrow him.[20]

To survive, Belgrade had to consummate a nasty deal with Washington. Only by closing its borders to Greek revolutionary forces could Yugoslavia assure itself the raw materials (e.g. Ruhr coal to replace Czech coal), capital, and weapons it required to hold and

grow despite strong Soviet pressures.[21] Tito, while committed to
socialist liberation struggles, put Yugoslav independence first.
Yugoslavia could not stand alone against the Soviet Union. It had
to settle with Stalin's Western adversaries.

China's Maoists eventually would blame Tito for his painful
choice among evils. But never to our knowledge did they utter a
word about Stalin, who, fearful of provoking the Anglo-American
camp and giving its hawks a pretext for a strike at the USSR, insisted "The uprising in Greece must be stopped, and as quickly as
possible."[22] The issue was far less a Yugoslav betrayal of Greek
rebels than a politically self-interested choice of blinkers by Chinese leaders which permitted them to scold Tito and sweet-talk
Stalin. It is ordinary realpolitik rationalized as Marxist-Leninist
theory, an approach to theory defined by the Hungarian Marxist
theorist Lukacs as Stalinism.[23] Because Mao's China was not
vulnerable to Stalin's forces the way little Yugoslavia was, Mao
had the privilege of walloping Tito and wooing Stalin while pretend-
ing that it was all in the service of international proletarian purity
rather than a betrayal of Yugoslavia's political sovereignty to the
Soviet empire's power.

2. THE EMERGENCE OF A TITOIST
   ALTERNATIVE IN CHINA,
   1949-1957

Not only did Stalin's power make it impossible for Yugoslavia to
build socialism, the Titoists also found that following the Soviet
Union's domestic policy path meant abandoning socialism. In the
USSR, Yugoslavia's Milovan Dijilas pointed out, "the society is increasingly becoming stratified into hired workers and the highly
paid caste of unscrupulous, turncoat, sly and brutal state-capitalist
bureaucrats."[24] To avoid a "Soviet Bureaucratic Caste," one had
to learn from the lessons of the Paris Commune. Engels had explained in March 1891 that the key decree of the Paris Commune
was that of April 16, 1871. It allowed workers themselves to organize and run factories. Without owners and with worker-level
salaries for managers preventing the development of separate
managerial strata, the alien state was dissolved. Society took command of its own destiny. These self-managed factories would then
join and form coordinating units. With workers' self-management,
the state could not economically exploit workers. Instead, workers'

self-management liberated the people's "creative initiative from below in their struggle against conservative tendencies in socialism and [against] the spineless bureaucratic 'geniuses' who have climbed up on the backs of the Soviet people ..."[25] Thus the Yugoslav Marxist patriots found that their transition to socialism required a new and independent path, not an imposed role as an oppressed party in Moscow's capitalistic international division of labor; it required workers' self-management from below, not the centralized Stalinist bureaucratic road to privilege and stratism.[26]

China seemed to the Yugoslavs to be interested in involving factory workers in factory management. The Chinese system was not yet settled. The Soviet Union was trying to block "the real road to socialism," worker participation, and to force China onto the non-socialist road of one person (the manager) management.[27] China might even end up as Stalin's Russia, overly stressing heavy industry and seizing the investment funds from the peasantry. "The Chinese plan attaches exceptional importance to heavy industry.... The central problem in financing investments is how to increase funds."[28]

But China seemed compelled to subordinate its own preferences for socialist, independent development to the Soviet Union's exploitative, capitalistic imperatives. The Yugoslavs saw the new Chinese rulers as preferring to avoid the evils of Stalinism, yet lacking the power to reject Stalin's requests. In China's foreign trade,

A considerable amount of this business was carried out by order and account of the USSR.... Therefore, thanks to the structure of her exports (access to sterling earnings, purchases through Hong Kong, etc.), China was assigned a special role — to create abroad as many free dollars as possible, that is, to secure foreign exchange to buy definite products. In this way, her foreign trade instead of being an effort in reconstruction and building of the country, had in 1950 the task of solving problems of Soviet policy.[29]

Despite the bad terms imposed on China by Stalin's regime, in a world where the U.S. bloc opposed, blockaded, embargoed, and sabotaged China, Mao could be grateful to Stalin. Mao seems to have concluded that to win better terms, he had to prove to Stalin that China would not take the Yugoslav path, that Mao would not become another Tito.

While Mao was trying to prove China's loyalty to the USSR, Yugoslavia was trying to win China room for maneuver so it would not

end up as a Soviet dependency, a late-born Stalinist society. At the
United Nations, Yugoslavia opposed labeling China an aggressor in
Korea. It opposed the UN embargo on China. Such anti-China policies would, the Yugoslavs believed, actually serve only the USSR;
for the policies "would push China into the arms of the USSR and
support it [the USSR] in its endeavors to become the leading big
power in Asia."[30]

There is no doubt that in policy toward Japan's CP China did
subordinate its policy preferences to Stalin's definition of socialist
interests. For Mao, China's 1950 intervention in Korea was proof
of loyalty to Stalin. Much of the Chinese leadership opposed that
armed move. They did not see intervention serving Chinese ends
or believe that the U.S.-led forces in Korea would attack China.
For them, China had to devote its energies to rebuilding its society
and fulfilling the promise of socialism for China's people. Mao,
however, insisted on going in. He later claimed that this act of
pulling Stalin's chestnuts out of the fires of the Korean War finally
persuaded Stalin that Mao was a proletarian internationalist, not a
Titoist, not a bourgeois nationalist. Mao declared,

After revolutionary victory, [Stalin] then suspected that China was a Yugoslavia, that I would become a Tito. Later, in Moscow ... he did not want to
sign [a treaty].... When did Stalin begin to trust us? It was from our resistance to America and aid to Korea; in the winter of 1950, he believed we
were not Titos, we were not Yugoslavia.[31]

More and more Mao came to identify his cause with negating Titoism. For the Mao-Chen Boda group, to succeed to Marx's mantle
came to mean succeeding to the revolutionary heritage of Stalin, including antagonism to Titoism.

The Titoists nonetheless supported tendencies in China similar
to their own. These seldom emanated from the Mao-Chen Group.
After Stalin died, the Yugoslavs noticed a change in Soviet policy
toward China. Moscow began countenancing a Chinese path to socialism in response to Chinese conditions. What was now to be
avoided was slighting Chinese independence and uniqueness, what
was to be avoided was forcing Beijing to break with Moscow as
Belgrade had done. "Soviet policy towards the People's Republic
of China is dominated by the desire to escape a repetition of the
'Tito affair.' "[32]

The Yugoslavs believed Stalin had helped keep China out of the
UN and used the Korean War to isolate China from the rest of the

world and make it more dependent on the USSR. But then China had broken with Stalin's USSR and opted for peace in Korea, making the concessions which broke the deadlock in the armistice negotiations. China had moved on its own interests and also the best interests of the peoples of the world to be free of the hegemony of the two, opposing cold war military monoliths. China improved relations with India based on Five Principles of Peaceful Coexistence and took great initiatives for peace at the 1955 Bandung Conference of Asian and African nations. China was now taking the road Yugoslavia had traveled on in 1948. All that remained to assure China her independent socialist path was for the United States to come to terms with the Chinese revolution.

It is most doubtful that Mao saw it this way, Tito's way. Mao apparently concluded instead that his efforts had persuaded Stalin of his loyalty, proved Mao wasn't a Tito. Stalin was reciprocating. The Korean initiatives probably had Stalin's backing.[33] As the Yugoslavs noted, Stalin already in 1952 began to give China better terms of aid and trade. They saw that a mission to Moscow led by Zhou Enlai had won an increase in East Germany's machine exports to China. "The Russians reached a bargain with the Chinese at the expense of the Germans."[34]

The most intriguing sign of this Stalin-Mao rapprochement was Stalin's betrayal of a top Chinese leader, Gao Gang. As Khrushchev remembered it,

Stalin decided he wanted to win Mao's trust and friendship, so took reports [of the USSR ambassador to the PRC, Panyushkin] about his conversations with Gao Gang and handed them over to Mao....

...Because of Stalin's betrayal of Gao Gang, we were deprived of a man who'd ...supplied us with valuable information.

...He [Stalin] figured that sooner or later Mao would have learned on his own that Gao Gang had been informing on him.... So Stalin decided it would be better to sacrifice Gao Gang and thereby earn Mao's trust.[35]

Whatever the truth of the charges against Gao, they led to a massive secret police hunt for foreign agents in China's leadership. The job of carrying out that investigation was given to Kang Sheng, who apparently had a similar brutal job in 1943. According to Hu Yaobang, Kang imitated Soviet Stalinist tactics of 1950-52 in Eastern Europe of ferreting out alleged Titoist enemies of Stalinist orthodoxy.

When Hungary, Poland, Czechoslovakia and other East European countries produced great numbers of Trotskyites, Titoists, imperialist spies, nationalists and Zionists and arrested or killed great numbers of Party members under the guidance of the erroneous Stalinist line between 1950 and 1952, Kang Sheng vigorously widened the scope of the first clean-up within the Party between 1951 and 1956 to create numerous framed-up cases and kill a number of comrades by following this erroneous line and taking advantage of the Gao-Rao case and the campaign against counter-revolutionaries in illicit correspondence with Anastas Ivanovich Mikoyan and Laverent Pavolich Beria. For this comrade Deng Xiaoping severely criticized him in 1956.[36]

As Edward Rice reported it, in 1956 "Kang Sheng — 'China's Beria' — was dropped from full membership in the Politburo...."[37]

Maoism as a political force is inseparable from the central power grouplets with which Mao associated himself for various purposes. There was the Chen Boda, Lin Biao, Wang Li, et al. group. There was Wang Dongxing's unit 8341. There was Kang Sheng with his base in the secret police and his allies Jiang Qing, Ke Jingshi, and Zhang Chunqiao. The members of these groups neither liked nor trusted the other groups. Their link was Mao.

Kang returned from the USSR during the Moscow purge trials. He took up work in security police activities. After the 1976 arrest of his political allies, Kang's 1943 secret police terrorism was discussed in the Party in great detail. Actually it had already been outlined earlier in a book by Wang Ming.[38]

Chen Boda too worried in 1943:

The KMT authorities . . . dispatch large numbers of secret agents to penetrate the Communist Party . . . attack it from the inside so as to completely "destroy" it.

. . . several hundred bandit-like anti-Communist secret service corps throughout the whole country . . . force and entice the youth to spy for the secret services, compel them to penetrate the Communist Party . . . mass organizations and intellectual and educational circles.[39]

Whatever the roots of this world view that the Party was full of spies and traitors, of Confucians who were capitalists (the categories and analogies of the later Cultural Revolution period), these capitalist-Confucian-Titoist enemies had to be removed by any means before they killed the true revolutionaries, seized Party power, and brought the revolution to a halt. Chen Boda's categories of 1943 and Kang Sheng's activities of 1943 did in fact prefigure the anti-Titoist categories of 1948 and 1958 and the policies of the Cultural Revolution.

The presuppositions of the Chen-Kang world view were widely shared in both Party and army. People such as Peng Zhen, Liu Shaoqi, Bo Yibo, indeed anyone who had worked in the urban underground or been captured by the enemy police and lived (or even talked before they died) were suspect. The Party warred on itself in bandit-secret society fashion, a blood brotherhood where suspected traitors or families of traitors were assassinated.

As Zhou Enlai's group was predisposed to find clues to the socialist transition in the Titoist transition out of their own long and deep experience,[40] so Chen Boda, Kang Sheng, and their allies had affinities with these nasty aspects of the Stalinist path out of their own real experience in China. This Stalinist virus penetrated so deeply that it remains as cancerous cells in China's body politic.

Nonetheless, in 1956 Kang Sheng was demoted. New stress was put on law and due process and the broadest of united fronts. Nineteen fifty-six was a peak year in China for finding clues to the socialist transition in warm friendship with Tito's Yugoslavia. Zhou Enlai's people came to the fore.

At a theoretical level, this new approach to the socialist transition had its origin in a debate on the nature of that transition over the meaning of Stalin's 1952 text, Economic Problems of Socialism in the USSR.[41] In China with Stalinism a legitimator, even Titoism had to be presented as Stalinism.

Although Stalin was an extreme centralist and not a proponent of anything resembling market socialism, his 1952 essay was used in China by the democrats, decentralists, and marketeers.[42] That is how Marxists generally use Stalin's 1952 essay on Economic Problems of Socialism in the USSR. In contrast to Chen Boda's Maoism, Stalin could be cited in 1952, the end of his career, the summation of his experience, declaring,

such things as cost accounting and profitableness, production costs, prices, etc. are of actual importance in our enterprises. Consequently, our enterprises cannot, and must not, function without taking the law of value into account. . . .

[T]his really is not a bad thing since it trains our business executives . . . to count production magnitudes . . . accurately . . . to look for, find and utilize hidden reserves . . . to lower production costs, to practice cost accounting, and to make their enterprises pay.[43]

There were three major positions in this Chinese debate over the continuing transition. Liu Shaoqi, Yang Xianzhen, et al. contended that the five elements of the economy (from state socialism to individual tillers) could coexist for a long time, each according to the laws of its sector of the economy, but with the guidance and gradual enlargement of the socialist sector.[44] The Chen Boda-Kang Sheng position was that the socialist transition had its own laws. And the Sun Yefang-Chen Yun position was that planning had to be based on the law of value, markets, commodities, etc.

The Yang Xianzhen-Maoist dispute, like the NEP preferences of the Zhou Enlai group and the Stalinist predispositions of Chen Boda and Kang Sheng, have long roots. Dr. Carol Hamrin shows that even before the PRC was established, in a discussion of the significance of the economic institutions of the new democracy, Mao saw the state-owned and cooperative sectors as indicators that China would "avoid a capitalist future and enjoy a socialist future."[45] Yang, on the other hand, insisted that these systems were capitalist and exploitative. "Even the arsenals of the Eighth Route Army and the cooperatives are not exceptions." What mattered was that socialists held power and would use it to build wealth and support for undermining the exploitation. Hamrin reminds us that in the early 1950s, Yang and Chen Boda continued the argument at the Institute of Marxism-Leninism where Yang was vice-president and Chen president. That Chen by 1955 should favor a swift transition to more control from the true and pure center and that Yang — in part combining NEP on peasants and Stalin on heavy industry — should want to bring people along by making larger and more cooperative work organizations also advance people's material interests had origins preceding the Tito-Stalin tiff. Yang mistrusted claims that calling something socialist or revolutionary actually helped real people with the material needs — food, medicine, housing, pensions, etc. — of their daily life. Chen feared that failing rapidly to make institutions ever more socialist would lose the revolution.

The third position, the Sun Yefang-Chen Yun position, was that planning had to be based on the law of value, markets, and commodities.[46] Sun Yefang would build on Stalin's acknowledgement that the law of value regulated commodity circulation and apply it to the collective sector. He argued that it should also in some measure apply to production and the state sector. They would drop the Stalinist idea of insisting that enterprises stress gross output value. Gross targets led to production with little concern for quality, thereby cheating consumers and causing a high rate of product failures. As Chen Boda-style Maoists attacked the Sun Yefang-Chen Yun po-

sition on the general question of market, value, etc., they also took
on both Sun-Chen and Yang Xianzhen-Liu Shaoqi on their claim of a
need for balanced development and especially Yang-Liu's opposition to using administrative fiat to wipe out individual tillage of the
land at a stroke.

Yang saw no reason for forcing peasants to do what they didn't
want to do. As best he could understand Chen Boda's arguments
for coerced collectivization, they were purely ideological. Said
Chen, "We cannot stand with one foot planted on socialist industry
and the other on a small peasant economy."[47] Chen contended that
Party people who opposed forced collectivization were stopping the
revolution at the bourgeois democratic stage, were siding with the
rural rich and opposing the poor, and were thereby choosing the
capitalist road and opposing the socialist road. To Chen, China
must build on its coops, its newborn forces and row against the
current of those who would hold back socialism. "Unless this
second revolution is carried through," Chen concluded, "we cannot
hope for any high growth in our productive forces."[48]

Yang mocked Chen's position. Surely there was no evidence from
the Soviet Union that collectivization gave great impetus to farm
production. Chen's position seemed based on the impropriety of
socialists in power investing in and helping nonsocialist elements.
Yang kidded the purist left. "Is it not undignified for socialists to
eat the food produced by individual peasants?"[49] Yang insisted on
gradual reform out of capitalism; he opposed Chen's notion of acute
class struggle. It made no sense to Yang to claim as Chen did that
the bourgeoisie would change the "socialist political structure into
a capitalist political structure,"[50] that the Chinese state would go
capitalist if it helped individual peasant tillers become more productive and prosperous. Yang's view was that the transformation
to cooperative agriculture had to be long-term. China needed an
extended period of Lenin's New Economic Policies. Chen's Maoism, on the other hand, stood with Stalin. NEP was done. Collectivization was the order of the day.

In criticizing Yang and peasant agriculture, Chen's Maoists argued that "Comrade Yang Xianzhen's 'Theory of Balanced Development' is a reprint of Bukharin's Theory of Equal Development."
In so arguing, they fundamentally reformulated their notion of the
superstructure in the period of the socialist transition. This would
be crucial for later political developments premised on the notions
that "there has never been a case of a moribund class voluntarily

withdrawing from the stage of history," and that "the proletariat can eliminate classes only through cruel class struggle."[51]

Yang had argued that with socialists in state power, controlling army, police, Party, administration, education, law, etc., there was nothing to fear from individual tillers who would be brought by material incentives, family interests and education, by stick and carrot, into socialism.[52] Maoists replied that if a capitalist base existed, it was reflected in the superstructure. State officials who would use capitalist forms had heads full of ideas which threatened progress away from capitalism. This imposed upon socialists a need to continue that class struggle in the superstructure against state powerholders with capitalist ideas. In short, a legitimation for the use of violence to purge Party people with different policy analyses was already built into the debate of Chen Boda's Maoists against the Yang-Liu and Sun-Chen Yun positions at the time of collectivizing agriculture.

Alec Nove shows that this concern for value, market, etc., in Titoism (and, though much, much weaker there, even in Stalinism) results from its being the only practical way to deal with industrialization under conditions of relative scarcity short of a bloated and arbitrary bureaucratic apparatus.[53] That evil is what China's Sun Yefang-Chen Yun group tried to avoid in 1956 as it drew closer to Tito's Yugoslavia and experimented with market related prices.[54]

With collectivization of agriculture and nationalization of industry in 1955-56, the Liu Shaoqi-Yang Xianzhen position lost out. But in association with Yugoslavia, the Chen Yun-Sun Yefang position grew in strength especially when people saw that the haste of 1955-56 created problems — wiping out at a stroke millions of nodes in commercial and sideline networks built up over millennia — such that one had to slow down, pay closer attention to economic realities, to people's material needs and income incentives, to specialization, division of labor, the market, balanced growth and competition.[55] If in 1956 domestic and international conditions facilitated the questioning of Stalinist dogma, if collectivization of agriculture and the administrative takeovers of industry and commerce had caused great problems, and if the Soviet Union was now treating Tito as a socialist, it was not unnatural for Chinese leaders concerned with the need for more democracy and less economic centralization to look to Titoism. On January 10, 1956, Liu Shaoqi told a journalists' delegation from Yugoslavia, both our parties represent the interests of the working people and both carry through socialist construction in accord with Marxist principles.... In the most basic and most important aspects both are the same.[56]

Thus was inaugurated what Klaus Mehnert called "those rapturous dreams of Yugoslav-Chinese friendship of the spring and autumn of 1956."[57] Albania's Stalinist leader, Enver Hoxha, claims to have recorded just how far even Mao went in a direction which Hoxha abhorred.

[W]hen I met Mao in Beijing in 1956...he criticized the "incorrect" activity of Stalin, and especially "Stalin's actions towards Yugoslavia," because according to Mao, Stalin "had made mistakes" and the Yugoslavs were "good Marxist men," and in order to support this "idea" it was precisely the Chinese who were the first and only ones in that period to invite the Yugoslavs to the Congress of the Communist Party of China.[58]

In politics, economics, and theory, China moved toward Titoism. In February 1956, Beijing and Belgrade signed a five-year agreement for cooperation in science and technology. A direct shipping line opened between Rijeka and Shanghai. A trade agreement was signed. The Yugoslav side said it "revealed vast possibilities for the expansion of economic collaboration between the two countries."[59] Yugoslavia imported "oil seed, hides and other livestock products, tin, asbestos, graphite, tea, raw silk and chemicals," while exporting to China "tobacco, agricultural machinery, chemical products, cotton fabrics, medical instruments."[60]

Everything was exchanged from art exhibits and theater delegations to military missions. In October 1956 the Yugoslav military mission, before going to Guangzhou where Minister of National Defense Peng Dehuai had invited it,[61] was honored at a reception in Beijing. Heading the Chinese host side were Zhou Enlai, Chen Yun, and Wu Xiuchuan.[62] The friends of Tito would be the adversaries of Chen Boda's Maoism. These friends included the leadership of China's trade unions who welcomed the broader role of workers as in Yugoslavia. When Chen Boda's line won out in 1966 with the Cultural Revolution, these Chinese leaders of the proletariat would be ousted and denounced as revisionists of the Yugoslav variety.[63]

In early 1956, the Yugoslavs still noted that the Chinese government "attaches exceptional importance to heavy industry"[64] which, as with the USSR, produced the concomitant problems of imbalanced growth neglecting food and the material needs of working people.

But after the Eighth Party Congress of September 1956, the Yugoslavs found a fundamental switch in China's path of economic development. China was breaking with Stalin's type of economic development. Of American academics, Franz Schurmann best and
earliest caught this seizing of the initiative by China's new minister
of commerce, Chen Yun, who cared so much about economic decentralization, material incentive, utilizing the market, and achieving
balanced growth.[65]

The Yugoslavs found that China's state powerholders, confronted
by the dual monsters of growing "centralism and bureaucracy,"
were reconsidering "the future road of Chinese socialist development." In late 1956, military and administrative expenses were
reduced from 32 percent to 20 percent of the state budget. Wages
and living standards would be raised as would be investment in light
industry and agriculture to assure, Zhou Enlai had said, "balanced
economic development." No longer would investment in heavy industry be allowed as in Stalinism to "exert an adverse influence on
the improvement of the standard of living and thus impair the
initiative in socialist construction."[66]

Chen Yun, the major spokesman for this alternative to Stalinism,
had won some fame for devising the policies which ended the raging
inflation which the PRC inherited. He opposed nationalization of
commerce and the administrative collectivization of agriculture.
For Chen, "it is first necessary to take care of the peasants."[67]
This meant concern for rural markets, prices, and consumption
goods. So Chen criticized Stalin for slighting the role of circulation, for overemphasizing production in a one-sided way. And he
criticized Mao for unrealistically seeking impossibly rapid development which, ignoring markets, prices, incentives, etc., would un-
balance the economy in disastrous ways.[68]

As the Yugoslavs saw it, in late 1956 China was abandoning a
Stalinist emphasis on heavy industry, centralization, bureaucratization and party monopoly for policies more consonant with the Titoist critique of Stalinism. China's Eighth Party

Congress devoted particular attention to the measures aiming at further decentralization of the economic, political and cultural life of the country and
the struggle against bureaucracy.... the trend to a certain degree of decentralization...is a sure sign of the wish of the Chinese leadership to eliminate
the weakness of exaggerated centralization.

...Realizing the dangerous tendency of a Party in power to alienate itself from the masses, the conviction ... that the Party is not entitled to "take everything into its hands" and impose its will by means of decrees and "govern the people" is the keynote of the new Party constitution.[69]

The Yugoslavs were not wrong to see 1956 as a year in which Chinese ruling groups sought for their socialist transition alternatives and antidotes — law, democracy, economic decentralization, a market, etc. — to Stalinist deformations which were haunting China. That Chinese alternative to Stalinism would be denounced in 1958 as Titoism.

3. THE RISE OF MAOISM

In China as in Yugoslavia the Marxist heritage had to be assimilated to live in the national body politic. The key person with the task of assimilating a Chinese Maoism to a universal Stalinism was Chen Boda, vice president of the Institute of Marxism-Leninism (later to become president) and of the Academy of Sciences. In 1944 he justified Mao's strategy of peasant revolution and of a broad united front including powerful bourgeois elements by contrasting it with the errors of Trotskyism.[70] Trotskyists insisted that China was capitalist. Therefore a Chinese socialist revolution required a confrontation of capitalism by the proletariat. But, in fact, Chen argued, China was feudal or semifeudal, a point Stalin had made. Therefore Mao was correct that "China is in need of a bourgeois democratic revolution" against "feudal exploitation." Chen's task was to establish Mao's orthodoxy, his Stalinism.

Criticizing self-styled leftists who "substituted their subjective idealism for Marxist materialism," Chen identified with Liu Shaoqi's attack on those who claimed to be "most revolutionary." That left, purist view would undermine the broad alliance against the major enemy of the moment and leave the genuine socialist left engaged in suicidal, sectarian squabbles. "[S]ome comrades ... regard all the political parties and factions of the bourgeoisie and petty-bourgeoisie as 'counter-revolutionary parties'...." In that left view,

we have no friends but only enemies ... ; furthermore, they make no distinction between our main and minor enemies ... present and future enemies.... [T]hey consider that no one should be befriended, no one should be neutralized. All they recognize is opposition.... [71]

In his 1953 monograph <u>Stalin and the Chinese Revolution</u>, Chen Boda quoted Mao in the 1930s in opposition to purist leftists: "You cannot overthrow those in power, so you want to overthrow those who are not in power. They are already out of power, yet you still want to overthrow them."[72]

Hence it was wrong to insist, as these purist leftists did, on a "decisive fight between the two ways in China." What was needed, Chen argued, was a long term struggle against errors left and right.

After the People's Republic was established, Chen set to work with P. Yudin, a Soviet diplomat-theorist, on editing and revising Mao's works better to conform with Stalinist orthodoxy while establishing Mao's own genius. Chen's essay on "Stalin and the Chinese Revolution" reviewed "Stalin's guidance to the Chinese revolutionaries during the past decades." In 1949 it was "assigned as the subject matter for study and discussion in many public and private organizations."[73]

There are many sources of Chen Boda's especially deep and personal ties to Stalin and Stalinism. Apparently in 1949-1950 when Stalin imposed neocolonial terms on China, Chen was very "accommodating to the Soviets at the time of the negotiations which took place in Moscow."[74] Still, foreign policy tactics aside, Chen was mainly camouflaging Chinese innovation with the color of Stalinism. Everything changed when Mao changed and Tito became the enemy and ever bigger collectives became an ultimate good.

Chen would opt for rapid collectivization as an imperative of a proper socialist transition in contrast to the Titoist, NEP, Zhou Enlai approach to gradually building socialism in the countryside by meeting the material needs of tillers of the soil. Soviet Stalinists saw this Chinese Titoist encouragement of peasants to enrich themselves as rightist class betrayal.[75] In 1955, Stalinist allies in Czechoslovakia "laid down a hard-line policy for completing the collectivization of agriculture" based on the "Stalinist ideology of 'intensifying the class struggle.'"[76]

Mao in 1955-56 also embraced this Stalinist orthodoxy, thereby abandoning the theory and policies of his broad, united front approach. This negated the Maoist view, reiterated in 1951 by Chen Boda, which defined a leftist error as denying the need to "unite with middle peasants"[77] (middle peasants being almost a euphemism for peasants who now were doing well and who should be able to continue to do better). Already, as in his April 1952 essay 'In Commemoration of the Twenty-fifth Anniversary of the Publication of Stalin's Great Work 'Problems of the

Chinese Revolution,'" Chen Boda began to sound like a caricature of the purist left he had once so well shown to be counterproductive and potentially narrowly tyrannical. And now the new, harsh, at times brutal three anti- and five anti-campaigns were struggles "determining the path that China is to take."

Instead of stressing that capitalists had been defeated and were not in power and that many could be allied with in the new period, Chen contended,

[T]he representatives of the national bourgeoisie...placed their men in government organizations...and in addition enticed...some of the personnel in our government organs...into becoming their agents. They launched a violent attack against the state, against the working class.... Even after the founding of the People's Republic, they dreamed of clandestinely usurping the working class-led People's Republic.... They dreamed of checking the advance...from New Democratic construction to Socialist development. It is very obvious that the state will be in danger if we do not repel this frenzied assault by the law-breaking elements of the bourgeoisie.

No such "frenzied assault" existed or could possibly exist. But, Chen was moving from Mao's established mode of allying with all those who could be allied with and won over and neutralized in order to isolate an extreme right (a small group) and avoid the adventurism of the left, to a more Stalinist approach in which the situation would be polarized into left and right (a large group) and the state's machinery of violence would be used to smash hypostatized enemies. Chen warned opponents real and otherwise that, quoting Mao, "the people have a powerful state machine in their hands and do not fear rebellion on the part of the national bourgeoisie." As if there were a rebellion to fear! What was developed by Chen was a model of violent two line struggle similar to Stalin's attack on Tito to be applied in the future to resolve domestic issues. "It is possible that this struggle over the choice between the two paths will continue even after the Three Anti- and Five Anti-movements are over."[78]

But where was the enemy class? Certainly it was not the national bourgeoisie. Its weakness made the successful path of Mao's revolution possible.[79] From 1958 on, however, but especially in the Cultural Revolution of 1966 and after, Maoist struggle was supposed to be directed against "the overthrown bourgeoisie" who supposedly were using control of the cultural apparatus to regain power.[80] Chen became the purist left he had once dissected. Chen already in May 1949 called for a "Great Cultural Revolution."[81] That rev-

olution was needed, in Lenin's terms, to wipe out "the remnants of
the middle ages" in the feudal peasantry. This meant, for Chen and
for Mao, that to prevent a capitalist restoration of a landholding
peasantry, capitalist ownership had to cease in the countryside.
China's rulers would have to act soon and surely to see that socialism won in rural China. That concern compelled Mao and Chen
to consider Stalin and Tito on the matter of collectivization of agriculture.

Mao's 1943 talk on "Getting Organized" was central to Chen's
rural policy line. In that talk, Chen found, "getting organized" and
"getting collectivized" were one and the same.[82] Chen always
looked to build on the socialist elements in the situation. He believed in building on "newborn forces."[83] In China after 1949 that
seemed to him first to be the large, bureaucratic capitalist enterprises of the Chiang Kai-shek clique which the PRC had nationalized and now considered to be owned by "the whole people." These
economic forces supposedly owned by "the whole people" (really
state powerholders) were then adjudged the leading elements in
socialist planning.[84]

But Titoists damned these state-owned enterprises as bureaucratic-capitalist elements which could not facilitate a socialist
transition. Chen responded, citing Stalin, that what mattered was
not the organizational form but the content infusing it, that is, the
purposes of powerholders. Everything depended on who was in
power.

In the countryside, a topic he had long studied,[85] Chen stressed
rural coops as the socialist element that had to be built on.[86] It
was in 1943 in "Get Organized" that Mao first forcefully offered
this route as the right one for rural China.[87] Collectivization,
Chen said on February 2, 1956, was "a new, great revolution, a
socialist revolution."[88] Tito's Yugoslavia had doubted the wisdom
of imposing collectivization on a peasantry when the peasants did
not want it or could not materially benefit from it. In 1953, Chen
noted, Tito permitted the abandonment of collectivized agriculture.[89]

Stalin identified forced collectivization as a central element in
his "creative application of Marxism-Leninism."[90] Naturally, as
Doreen Warriner noted in her 1950 book Revolution in Eastern
Europe, the issue of collectivization was a focal point in the Tito-
Stalin dispute at a politico-ideological level.

Tito had been trying to woo Yugoslavia's so-called middle peas-

ants, including the core landowning peasantry of the regions of
Serbia and Croatia.[91] But Stalin's people in Yugoslavia's Communist Party contended that if Tito would not opt for full-scale, rapid
collectivization, this would prove that Tito refused to take the socialist road, that he stood instead with the capitalist elements in
the society which were increasing all the time.[92] Tito, to prove
himself a real Stalinist socialist, then pushed through forced collectivization. It was a disaster. The Yugoslav Party by 1953 backed
out of it and tried to woo the nation's tillers anew.

With Titoists by 1953 legitimizing individual ownership of land
(with strict limits on size of holdings), Mao let it be known that in
the countryside in China there was a struggle in which either capitalism or socialism would win. As a result, Chinese officials forcefully promoted larger coops. Many of these were a mess, and by
the end of 1953 Deng Zihui's people in charge of rural work were
permitting Chinese villagers to return their level of work organization to something smaller, more comprehensible, and more effective.

Mao convinced himself that this expansion and reduction proved
that many Party leaders would not make the break to a socialist
transition. He began to rely more on Chen Boda in rural work and
to create his own private secretariat as a source of policy information and analysis. Thus by 1955 on the issue of collectivization as
a necessary Stalinist act to avoid Tito's supposed path of capitalist
restoration, Mao was already facilitating the creation of a small
group of people immediately committed to the transition toward
communism who comprehended their adversaries on the Party's
policy on collectivization as Titoist revisionists, Party people with
power who would take China down a capitalist road, people who
would stop the revolution at the merely bourgeois democratic stage
of land to the tillers.

Mao, previously the theorist of a unique Chinese path, was now
promoting Stalin on the collectivization of agriculture as a universal
imperative of the socialist transition. "The transition to socialism"
required collectivizing peasant-owned property. "The model of successful agricultural collectivization in the Soviet Union embodies
the beneficial conditions so that our nation's peasants will not take
the wrong road of capitalism, but will take the great, bright road of
socialism," contended the Party's theoretical journal.[93] Apparently
Mao went very far in legitimating his policies in terms of oneness
with Stalin's and a negation of Tito's. This switch by Mao would

come as a surprise to Tito who still saw Mao as similar to himself in no small measure precisely because China had avoided the costly Stalinist path of forced collectivization.[94]

Stalin died in 1953. Khrushchev soon began to try to undo some of the worst of Stalin's deeds. Khrushchev worked for rapprochement with Tito. In 1955 Khrushchev went to Belgrade. Stalinists in the Soviet Union were more than offended by Khrushchev's trip to embrace Tito. They saw it as a betrayal of Bolshevism. "Yugoslav views were pure Menshevism," in this Stalinist perspective.[95]

In China, Khrushchev's trip to Yugoslavia was experienced by many as an ultimate betrayal. Stalin, whatever damage he had done, also had helped China when China was threatened by American might. Tito meanwhile had treated Stalin as the devil, while treating the threat to China, the imperialist Americans, as his savior. For Khrushchev to go groveling to Tito was to betray Stalin, surrender to American imperialism, turn wrong and right into their opposites and threaten to leave China vulnerable. If Tito meant more than Mao to Khrushchev, then China could be left exposed to American force and pressure.[96]

Khrushchev's rapprochement with Tito was proof enough for Mao that Khrushchev might be abandoning the supposedly revolutionary socialism of Stalinism. Mao later claimed never to have accepted Khrushchev's arguments for the reopening to Tito's Yugoslavia. If Tito's successful break was "the most bitter defeat of his [Stalin's] political career,"[97] if Mao was identifying himself as anti-Tito, if the "visit of Khrushchev and Bulganin to Belgrade in the spring of 1955 was a stroke of diplomacy as startling in terms of what had gone before as would be a visit of Eisenhower and Dulles to Peking ...,"[98] then if we but remember Hanoi's feeling of betrayal when Kissinger and Nixon surfaced in Beijing, we will have an idea of how deeply Mao must have felt betrayed by Khrushchev.

For Mao, the duo of Tito and Khrushchev became one as did Mao and Stalin. Mao would act to prove himself on Stalin's side, not Khrushchev's. That commitment related to a fierce coming to a head of Chen Boda's debate with spokesmen for other tendencies (Yang Xianzhen et al.) on the relation of collectivization to the socialist transition. Mao abandoned his prior policy of voluntary, gradual cooperativization, a policy which still held late in July 1955, for an embrace of Stalin's policy of forced, rapid collectivization.[99]

With China's state administration coming to conclusions that sounded like the recent Titoist analysis, Mao began to build and rely increasingly on his own private secretariat, a private government which would not insist on machines and other capital inputs by the state to assure that collectives win economic gains for peasants.

In May 1955 he [Mao] gave an important talk at a cordial meeting with the unit standing guard for him.... You are all good comrades. Only your educational level is a bit low. Make a good effort and you will be able to acquire scientific knowledge....

On May 14, 1955, Mao had asked the members of unit 8341, headed by his bodyguard of two decades, Wang Dongxing, to make that effort and become his own private state administration. He asked unit 8341's members to go to their villages and see what the situation was, especially if it related to the prospects for further collectivization.

In July 1955 Mao spent ten hours over three days including dinner at his place discussing with unit 8341's members their reports from their home villages.

When Chairman Mao read the report of one comrade who described how the poor and lower-middle peasants in his home village had overcome natural adversities by relying on the coop, he was full of praise for the people there and said that was precisely the role an agricultural cooperative should play. Picking up his pen he wrote on the report five brilliant characters meaning "the cooperatives are very fine."

One day when comrades from Hunan and Hubei provinces finished reporting about their home villages, Chairman Mao said ... it took only three hours to learn the conditions of the 60 million people in the two provinces. This was indeed an excellent method. You have served as a link between me and the peasant masses. Gesticulating with three fingers, Chairman Mao said: You have seen the peasants and I have seen you; thus I have seen the peasants indirectly within this bit of distance. You are peasants with arms and class consciousness.[100]

Anyone with any experience dealing with a top powerholder knows how unlikely it would be — once Mao had expressed his convictions, his firm belief that socialism in China required rapid collectivization — that any of those peasant lads would vigorously have contested Mao's convictions. Thus Mao began to rely increasingly on people who would agree with him and dismiss as conservative rightists — and eventually capitalist-roaders — those who saw the facts otherwise.

Talking as if Stalinist collectivization hadn't been a disaster, Mao claimed that Soviet collectivization had increased grain production. He dismissed the views of Party leaders who would not rush into collectivization.

This is to disregard the experience of the Soviet Union. These comrades fail to understand that socialist industrialization cannot be carried out in isolation from the co-operative transformation of agriculture.

Mao ignored the difference between Stalin, who tried to take an existing surplus away from peasants without paying for it, and China where there was no extra surplus to take. Why should more land, tool, and animal collectivization create a surge in production? All the more so collectivization imposed by state fiat.

Mao would silence other Party people who insisted that the Soviet experience argued against "impetuosity and rashness." On "no account shall we allow these comrades to use the Soviet experience as a cover for their idea of moving at a snail's pace." "The road traversed by the Soviet Union is our model." The danger to be avoided was "that polarization in the countryside will get worse day by day." Mao feared Russian kulaks. His proof of this danger in China was "new rich peasants springing up everywhere."[101]

Mao cited no hard evidence to buttress his claims of a kulak threat. The evidence didn't exist. He had distorted the consequences of Stalinist collectivization in the USSR and the rural reality of contemporary China.

To be true to Stalin, Mao had to continue the so-called revolution in the countryside. That is, in contrast to Tito, he had to divide the peasants in each village by classes in a way that would legitimate a continuation of class struggle. That was meaningless in China in 1955 after a very decent land reform had created largely middle peasant villages.[102] What resulted from Mao's call for a collectivization campaign, therefore, was an administrative enrollment of people in collectives and many people thereby wronged, injured, and made enemies. It had little to do with popular consciousness, majority interest, or enhanced productivity, let alone class. Mao was using the people of China as ideological counters. Those people could ill-afford straying from the needed, grueling march to some modicum of prosperity.

Mao would subsequently state the simple truth, "And us?" he asked. "Already during land reform, we had practically done away with the rich peasant economy."[103] There was, in fact, no growing, new rich peasantry. Liu Shaoqi had made this point more gently, stating that land reform had "isolated the rich peasants."[104] One observer, Jack Chen, found that these few isolated rich peasants concerned with everything from their family's future to access to capital which the state controlled, wanted to join the coops. They feared being kept out and isolated.

Since the spring of 1953 and 1954, the period when the country was making the biggest advances in the coop movement, the rich peasants had, in fact, been finding it increasingly difficult to hold their own.

These rich peasants, who had been kept in political and economic check as the coop movement had got into its stride, were finally admitted to the collective farm. They were few in number, their economic and political influence was now negligible. As a matter of fact, they were eager to pool their land and other means of production and glad to get rid of the taint of the old "rich peasant status."[105]

But in 1955-56 Maoists justified collectivization in Stalinist terms as needed to defeat the growing number of rich peasants. Since land sold was taken as a key indicator of increasing polarization, Chen Boda got the data on land sales in Baoding Prefecture in Hebei Province, where he had developed strong personal and political ties. But even the data he presented showed that there was no growing polarization.[106]

Baoding Prefecture Land Sales
1951-1955

Year	Number of mu sold
1951	115,800
1952	91,421
1953	78,450
1954	36,245
1955	8,290

Land sales by 1955 had virtually stopped. There was no tendency toward rural polarization. In like manner, data collected from nine counties in Hunan Province showed a middle peasant China and not a great, growing gap between rich and poor.[107]

Percent of Total Land Owned

Land status	at land reform	1952	1953	1954
poor	56.73	36.46	28.08	28.22
middle	30.25	50.45	58.96	58.07
rich	3.18	3.46	3.63	3.70

The last changes are so miniscule as to be explicable by reporting errors. They are not significant. China's was ever more a middle peasant countryside.

One Chinese analyst of data "Concerning the Problem of Rich Peasants" found that

In areas where land reform is already completed, the number of newly emerged rich peasants is only one percent of the total of peasant households.... So the strength of the rich peasant economy is dropping steadily.... [It is] unnecessary for us to launch another movement like land reform to eliminate the rich peasant economy.[108]

Surely these numbers do not reflect a polarization process demanding drastic surgery.

Mao, however, chose to define away the major, new experienced reality of rural China, a middle peasant majority. His negation of reality came to be called a "major contribution to the Marxist-Leninist theory of class struggle." Village leaders were ordered to collectivize based on class division and class struggle.

Dividing the middle peasants into upper peasants and lower middle peasants, dividing the lower middle peasants again into lower middle peasants among the new middle peasants and the lower middle peasants among the old middle peasants, regarding those among the new middle peasants who rose to the next level of well-to-do middle peasants not as part of the force to be relied upon, and taking the lower middle peasants among the old middle peasants as part of the force to be relied upon....[109]

Real middle peasants who would oppose these policies which injured them could then be labeled capitalist-roaders, thus destroying the broad peasant alliance.

Ignoring this middle peasant reality and building on Mao's new analysis, Chen Boda urged collectivization so that grain and cotton production, two key indicators, would surge forward.[110]

One of Chen's models for this path was Wugong Village in Rao-yang County, Hebei Province, with its 420 households. In 1954, he claimed it had produced 419 catties of grain per mu; in 1955 that had leaped, he said, to 463; it would shortly reach 500.[111] In fact, according to the village accountant's records which I — with Mark Selden, Paul Pickowicz, and Kay Johnson — examined grain yield for 1954 and 1955 was not 419 and 463 catties per mu, but 250 and 300 respectively. It fell to 278 in 1956 after forced collectivization. In 1960, after an intensification of Chen's policies, per capita grain production fell below the 1954 mark. In short, grain production in Chen's model village did not surge forward; during the period in which his policies were in vogue, more work, in fact, won less reward.[112] By his own standards and in his preferred testing ground, Chen's policies failed. Nonetheless, he continued to promote the policies of ever bigger collectives as the only means to assure a true socialist transition toward communism, thereby snapping the tender strands holding building socialism to people's experienced material interests.

The reckless advance and its concomitant problems — waste, income stagnation, decline of sideline earnings, neglect of industrial crops, etc. — permitted rural work director Deng Zihui to criticize "upper levels which were hasty" and to promote balanced, overall development[113] in ways which brought China closer to an appreciation of the Titoist critique of Stalinism, a different notion of socialist transition.

Yet in February 1956 Khrushchev, who had embraced the anti-Stalin Tito, now directly attacked Stalin. If we are right about the importance of this Tito-Stalin issue to Mao, then it is no wonder that Mao chose to defend Stalin in a swift rejoinder to Khrushchev.

At the Twentieth Congress of the CP of the Soviet Union in February 1956, Khrushchev embraced Tito as a socialist, saying,

Lenin wrote "All nations will arrive at socialism ... but not the same way." ... Historical experience has fully confirmed the brilliant words of Lenin's. ... [In] Yugoslavia, unique specific forms of economic management and organization of the state apparatus are arising in the process of socialist construction.

Mao had gone pretty far in identifying with Stalin's notion of Titoism as capitalist restoration when Khrushchev turned the categories topsy-turvy. It could be embarrassing for Mao, Chen Boda, et al. It could give ammunition to their domestic adversaries.

Nonetheless, Mao could not push his disagreements with Khrushchev too far. As in 1948, realpolitik also shaped ideological possibility. In 1956, as an internationally isolated, very poor, and dependent member of the Soviet bloc, China had to stand with Khrushchev and critically accept Tito and opposition to Stalinism. This helped create an atmosphere for the great events of 1956-57 in China, the retreat from incipient Stalinism, and the emergence of Beijing-Belgrade entente, a closer look at Titoist socialist transition which we explored in an earlier section of this essay. Now we must see how the force of Chen Boda-style Maoism which rose between 1953 and 1956 won out by 1958.

4. THE 1956 TO 1958 MAOIST NOTION OF THE SOCIALIST TRANSITION AS NEGATING TITOISM

After Tito blamed Stalinism for the 1956 Hungarian rebellion, Mao turned with a vengeance on Tito's Yugoslavia, and on those in China who would act as Yugoslavia did. These people, Mao argued, "think that China should take a middle course.... This is the Yugoslav way, a way to get money from both sides." That is, it was immoral. Mao then defended alliance with the Soviet Union as inevitable for economic reasons, too.

If China stands between the Soviet Union and the U.S., she appears to be independent, but actually she is not. The U.S. is not dependable.... Illusions of securing a bridge between the Soviet Union and the U.S. and Britain for profit — this kind of thinking is wrong. We do not know how to design a big plant. Who would design large plants for us — such as chemical industry, steel industry, petroleum industry, tanks, airplanes and the manufacture of automobiles?[114]

To be sure, there was much truth to the notion that given obdurate U.S. opposition and hostility to China, that poor, backward, vulnerable nation's options were extremely limited if it wished to develop its economy. U.S. policies made life very difficult for Chinese-style Titoists. In but a few more months Mao would abandon that concern for economic aid from the USSR. What he wouldn't abandon was the search for a theoretical justification which would condemn Tito and Titoism in a way that would also cover the USSR's Khrushchev, the notion of Stalin as a good socialist.

This is surprising to many students of the topic. They very naturally think that Mao might have welcomed Khrushchev's anti-Stalin approach, including praise for China's special path as a legitimate road toward socialism and criticism of Stalin for imposing on China, as in the joint stock companies, colonial terms of relations.[115] But Mao had long identified with the Stalin critique of Tito and had just acted boldly in 1955-56 on Stalin's two general theses that the socialist transition required (1) the extirpation of capitalist elements in the countryside and (2) the continuation of class struggle under the dictatorship of the proletariat. Mao, who had previously been a great innovator stressing particular historical conditions and diverse practice in opposition to those pro-USSR dogmatists in China who held to universal shibboleths from Marx or Lenin or Stalin, had just switched sides. He was making his innovations and China's transition to communism a matter of universal moment. Mao was making himself into China's Stalin, that is, the legitimate successor in the line Marx, Engels, Lenin, Stalin, just when Khrushchev launched his attack on Stalin. Mao was therefore vulnerable in Chinese politics unless he counterattacked Tito and Khrushchev. After all, if Stalin was a bastard and Mao was Stalin's heir, where did that leave Mao in any line of legitimate inheritance? Stalin would have to be kept a legitimate, worthy descendant of Marx or Mao would lose his own claims to the inheritance. These political imperatives helped to distort crudely the new Maoist notions of a socialist transition. The Maoist conception of the socialist transition now added to its history of defending Stalin and Stalinism and betraying Yugoslavia in 1948 opposition to the revolutionaries of Hungary and the Titoism which at first welcomed those heroes and martyrs as adversaries of Stalinism.

Tito praised the Hungarian leadership of Nagy and "the democratization of public life, the introduction of workers' self-management and democratic self-management in general, the regulation of relations between socialist countries on the basis of equality and respect for sovereignty." Tito considered the Nagy leadership of Hungary to be socialist. Khrushchev denounced the Nagy leadership as "the restoration of capitalism."[116] Mao would stand with Khrushchev's Stalinist denunciation of that in the Hungarian experience which was legitimated by the Titoists. What Tito would be for, Mao would be against.

The popular and patriotic rebellion of the people of Hungary, of industrial workers and of farmers as well as party members and intellectuals, led Yugoslavia's Tito and Kardelj one step further in their critique of Stalinism. As shown by the overthrow of the Stalinist regime in Hungary, self-styled socialists who wielded state power in a Stalinist manner were antagonistic to the interests and will of the great mass of the people. Tito claimed that only democratization could save socialism. He asked of Hungary's revolution, where are the roots of Stalinism?

They are to be found in the bureaucratic apparatus, in the methods of leadership and in the so-called one man rule, the ignoring of the role and wishes of the working masses and among the Parties who are opposing democratization....

...People...demanded their elimination and a transition to the road towards democratization.

Kardelj argued that the Hungarians rebelled against the "despotism of a bureaucratic clique." What was at stake was the socialist transition. For Kardelj no transition was possible through the statist bureaucracy of Stalinism: "[T]here can be no progress of Socialism without a parallel development of specific forms of democracy which correspond to the Socialist economic forms." For Titoists like Kardelj, there was only one kind of solution to the problem of economic, technocratic, and bureaucratic centralization and concentration of power. That answer was democracy. Otherwise the conservative new bureaucracy would become entrenched. In conflict with Stalinism's search for scapegoats in alleged remnants of capitalism, a scapegoating which legitimated the total power of the Stalinist bureaucracy's narrowest, ruling core, Titoists called for more use of the market, decentralization, and workers so that great power over all could not be amassed in a few hands.

The absence of any serious analysis of social process in the transitional period, and even more...the fiction that a society building socialism contains no reactionary conservative elements except remnants of the bourgeoisie — this was the characteristic of Rakosi's Hungary.[117]

Titoist opposition to the state bureaucracy's power over people became for Maoists the essence of capitalist restoration.

There was an evolution to the Maoist analysis of Hungary and Titoism. To be sure, the Maoists claimed that until "the leaders of the Communist Party of the Soviet Union accepted our suggestions" to intervene and smash the rebellion, they had "intended to adopt a policy of capitulation and abandon socialist Hungary."[118] Mao urged Khrushchev to crush the Hungarian rebels and then sent congratulations when the USSR's armed intervention succeeded. But by that time Tito too concluded that Hungary had turned counterrevolutionary since Hungarians "hanged and murdered" a few Communists.[119] Most likely, the Yugoslavs opposed as an ultimate danger to their own independence anything that led the Soviet Union's army to march across borders in Eastern Europe.

At first the events in Hungary were used in China to legitimate ongoing new economic policy, broad class alliance, and due process of law. Within the framework of the 1956 concern for legal safeguards and economic decentralization, for the double hundreds policy and Titoism, the Chinese CP could contend,

It is true that certain mistakes have been made [in Hungary].... Politically, it has never thoroughly liquidated the counterrevolutionaries or strictly observed a socialist legal system. Economically, due to unbalanced development of industry [China had just increased the proportion of capital invested in light industry], it has experienced a shortage of consumer goods. Bureaucratism in leadership has damaged its Party's and Government's relations with the masses.[120]

On October 30, 1956, in an official governmental statement on Poland and Hungary, China's leadership affirmed its support for the demands for more democracy, independence, equality, and concern for the material conditions of their citizenry and warned Moscow against big nation chauvinism which damages solidarity among nations.[121]

Mao's view of Hungary changed between February 1957 and June 1958. In February 1957, in alliance with Zhou Enlai, Mao argued that China's problems of bureaucratic antagonism of the population would best be resolved by more liberty, law, democracy, and criticism of Party bureaucrats in combination with genuine alliance with all skilled people — scientists, technicians, critical intellectuals — who could deal with these problems. This approach had been dubbed the "double hundreds" policy.[122]

But by June, Mao abandoned Zhou for Chen Boda and found that intellectuals (the Petofi circle) lay behind the Hungarian revolution and the anti-Stalinist path of Khrushchev and that intellectuals and their economic approach to things were virtually the essence of Tito's capitalist restoration.

Citing the role of the intellectuals of the Petofi circle in the Hungarian Revolution and of supposedly similar people in the USSR in urging more use of price and market and education of talents, Mao persuaded many of his colleagues, from the ideologue of the quick transition, Chen Boda, to the tough pragmatist Chen Yi, that, as Chen Yi eventually put it, Stalin

contributed to the degeneration process. He did not adopt any measures for the elimination of the capitalist vices of the intellectuals. He was impatient to declare that there was no more class struggle in Russia. Stalin did not take notice of a change toward capitalism.... Khrushchev used the intellectuals to restore capitalism.

...We are trying to eliminate the intellectual class.

... The intellectuals must work in the fields and factories to build themselves politically. Because the intellectuals are the new class ... Marx and Engels did not foresee the possibility of the capitalist degeneration of socialism.[123]

The confusions in this formulation are enormous. On the one hand, many jobs in a high technology economy require much education. Yet is the issue of state power or a capitalist economy to be understood in terms of surgeons, electrical engineers, meteorologists, geneticists, architects, geologists, etc.? Surely these various professions do not constitute a ruling stratum. Nor do painters, writers, or musicians. Literate, trained people such as nurses and secretaries hardly add up to a threatening bloc on the verge of state power. Free-floating intellectuals can and do sign up with any and all political tendencies. They are not an independent group. Should people who manage banks, industries, and the like be seen as intellectuals? Should higher administrative authorities who run the state police, personnel bureaus, and planning agencies be considered intellectuals? Such usages of the notion intellectual stretch the term to the point where it breaks with significant meaning. Apparently what Mao had in mind with his notion of a danger to socialism from intellectuals was a combination of economists who insist on the long-term importance of economics, that is, of value, exchange, material incentives, economic accounting, cost effectiveness, and the like, and all professions committed to an orderly and independent search for truth and creativity. In other words, Mao's enemies, dubbed intellectuals, were actually the groups and ideas dedicated to motion in a more Titoist economic direction, and politically to movement toward law, democracy, and liberty. The ene-

mies were the rising forces of 1955-57 that strove against the
bureaucratic centralization of all power. Mao's enemies were the
enemies of Chinese Stalinism. Chen Boda and his friends were
settling accounts with Chen Yun and his allies.

The Chinese Maoist leadership saw Khrushchev as having gone
too far in criticizing Stalin and now conceding to the Chinese defense of Stalin. The Moscow government in January 1957 published
and broadly disseminated the December 1956 Maoist evaluation of
Stalin, "More on the Historical Experience of the Dictatorship of
the Proletariat." Khrushchev told Zhou Enlai in Moscow on January 19, 1957, that the Yugoslavs "called us Stalinists ... to blacken
us, whereas in fact it can only be for us a term of praise and approval."[124] The Yugoslav ambassador to Moscow commented,

The Chinese have thought up the formula that Stalinism is identical with communism and that this is what is really important about Stalin, not what we
found to criticize about him. The Chinese leaders need this attitude to Stalin
primarily for domestic use.[125]

With Khrushchev's defeat of a remnant Stalinist group in mid-
1957, Mao could conclude that the Khrushchev tendency had won
power in the USSR. That is, the Maoists found that Stalinism and
socialism had, as in Tito's Yugoslavia, been defeated.[126] What
seemed called for, therefore, was a theoretical comprehension of
how socialism lost first to Tito's group in Yugoslavia and then to
Khrushchev's in the USSR so that China, armed with foreknowledge,
could continue the socialist transition. That would take Chen Boda
back to the Stalinist condemnation of Titoism.

At a July 1, 1958, meeting marking the thirty-seventh anniversary
of China's Communist Party, Chen Boda told a gathering at Beijing
University that where the scientific discoveries of Marx, Lenin,
et al. are concerned, "the Tito clique echoes the imperialists [and]
curses and distorts it [scientific Marxism] in the most despicable
ways." He then criticized "rightist conservative ideas" in China's
CP, that is, people who argued as Tito did. These people, according
to Chen, believed that unless state planners assured producers wage
incentives and managed investment and commerce to guarantee
overall balanced development, the economy could not surge forward.
They did not believe that mass energy could win production breakthroughs if tractors, irrigation, chemical fertilizer, and scientific
know-how were not available. In contrast, Chen commented, "Mao
Zedong placed the mass development of production in the leading

position and criticized the error of one-sided financial and distributional viewpoints...."

This Maoist reliance on mass energies was presented by Chen
as replacing the developments after the Eighth Party Congress
which the Titoists had applauded.

Persons holding such a rightist view simply confine themselves to financial
problems while neglecting the enthusiasm and creativeness of the masses in
increasing production and practicing economy. They seem to take the view
that instead of governing consumption, distribution and exchange, production
is governed by consumption and distribution and exchange. Such a harmful
rightist viewpoint was essentially a point of departure for the so-called "opposition to reckless advance" thinking in the winter of 1956.

Chen's main stress was again on the need for what he called a
"cultural revolution." This required a willingness to follow a
"helmsman" who would lead the people in "sailing against the current." Then the practice of today could, he concluded, win "the
great tomorrow of communism."

Chen was advocating that the broad united front based on real and
experienced interests be replaced by the notion that enemies were
everywhere. Mao, Chen declared, had shown that to win the "struggle between socialism and capitalism" required "struggle on the
political and ideological fronts; otherwise the results of socialist
transformation as regards ownership could not be consolidated."
This meant reeducating the superstitious peasantry, turning them
into agro-scientists, doing away with a separate strata of scientific
intellectuals, closing the gap between mental and manual labor.
Then all China's counties could be industrialized and the division
between industry and agriculture could end. Chen claimed that in
the Great Leap this was already happening. He claimed that such
worker-technicians now produced "above the international standards," that such peasants had "surpassed the world wheat records
in many cases," that such peasant scientists would "surpass university students and professors in cultural and scientific knowledge." With the Chinese working people armed with Mao's thought,
Chen claimed, "one can visualize the gradual transition of our country from socialism to communism."[127] This Maoist stress on
campaign politics, moral incentives, and despecialization would be
found in neither Titoism nor Stalinism.[128]

Chen's claims were more out of touch with reality than even the
claims about the village of Wugong in 1956 when Chen promoted

immediate collectivization. In 1956 and more so with the Great
Leap, production plummeted as a result of these misconceived policies. China barely escaped mass starvation. Whereas Mao at that
time conceded the need temporarily to carry out Chen Yun-type
policies to save China, Chen Boda insisted on pressing ahead. The
stage was set for a struggle wherein Chen Boda's people, in the
name of Maoism, would try to destroy their adversaries, seen by
them in the image of Tito as threatening to restore capitalism in
China. The Chen Yun-Sun Yefang people, on the other hand, believed that with the Great Leap disaster practice proved that Chen's
anti-Tito policies warred on and split the peasantry, sabotaged
overall economic development, and inhumanly persecuted Party
people who held different policy preferences. As the magnitude of
the Great Leap economic disasters became clear, top Party people
who stood with Mao and Chen Boda in 1958 began to see Chen as the
enemy. More would see it that way after the political disaster of
the Cultural Revolution launched in 1966. But the categories of
conceptualization which formed the Maoist premises of the Cultural
Revolution were basically formed in the pre-1958 period and most
clearly promoted by Chen Boda.

The full critiques of the Yugoslav way promoted by the Chen Boda
group appeared first as an editorial in the national newspaper of
the Central Committee, Renmin ribao (People's Daily), on May 5,
1958, and then in the Party's new theoretical journal, Hongqi (Red
Flag), on June 1 in an essay signed by Chen. Chen contended, in
the language of 1948, that as Lenin responded in his era to the
threat to socialism from revisionists such as Bernstein, so now,
after Leninist parties have taken state power, it was necessary to
defeat the new revisionists, the threats to socialism in the era of
the dictatorship of the proletariat. The modern revisionists, "the
leading group of the League of Communists of Yugoslavia [LCY],"
had, under the pretext of opposing Stalinism, dubbed the state-
controlled economy, what this Maoist group considered to be "ownership by the whole people," as merely state capitalism. The LCY,
Chen Boda wrote, "alleges that proletarian dictatorship must inevitably lead to 'bureaucracy' and 'bureaucratic' statism." The
LCY, Renmin ribao declared, "has viciously slandered proletarian
dictatorship, alleging that it 'leads to bureaucratism, the ideology
of statism, separation of the leading political forces from the
working masses, stagnation, the deformation of socialist development, and the sharpening of internal differences and contradic-

tions.'" In response, Chen Boda rejected the antibureaucratic, decentralized, worker-input innovations of Tito and revived the orthodoxy of Stalin. With regard to collectivization, Chen wrote,

Stalin rightly said, "Everything depends upon the content that is put into this
form." All organizational forms, political or economic, remain mere organizational forms. The question is who runs them, who leads?

For Chen Boda, what was needed to assure a continuing transition
to communism was not democratic, antibureaucratic institutions or
continuing material progress, but making certain that real Communists controlled the levers of state power and used that concentrated
force to destroy all obstacles to the transition. The real Communists, of course, were, Chen and Mao and their allies.

Chen cited a passage from Lenin in defense of his view of the
transition. "A Marxist is one who extends the acceptance of class
struggle to the acceptance of the dictatorship of the proletariat."
Based on this analysis, Maoists explicitly reaffirmed as true and
just the June 1948 Stalin-orchestrated resolution of the Information
Bureau which made Titoism the enemy of socialism.[129]

The Yugoslavs pointed out this Stalinist theoretical essence of
Chen's Maoism at the time. In 1958 they pointed out that Maoist
attacks on the Titoist path "do not proceed from some new critical
'revelations'...but more or less rewrite the [1948] Resolution of
the Information Bureau instead."[130]   Maoism contained Stalinist
elements.

What is at issue here is not an accurate assessment of the dynamics of Yugoslav society. Surely Khrushchev was not all wrong
when he mocked the Titoist critique of Stalinism as charlatanism,
pointing out that Yugoslavia's ruling groups, like those in the USSR,
insisted on controlling the mass media and on jailing even theoretical opponents such as Djilas.[131]

There is something to be said for treating Maoism, Titoism, and
Stalinism as heuristic devices, highlighting three strategies of the
socialist transition. Stressing only what distinguishes the strategies, however, obscures what they shared. All three movements
held state power in conditions which presented problems which
Marx assumed would be solved before socialists smashed the remaining impediments to a full transition.

All three had to create the economic prosperity that Marx assumed capitalism would create. None inherited the democratic institutions that Marx assumed would also have been created by bourgeois democrats before socialists won state power and imparted genuine democratic content to these forms. Maoists damned as capitalist restorationists people seeking clues in Titoism as to how to build democracy in a state whose levers of power were held by groups committed to a socialist transition. They never discovered any genuine socialist democratization in Yugoslavia.

Surely this critique of Titoism from the perspective of Stalinism must be taken seriously. It claims that Titoism is inherently incapable of solving the problem it poses. Chen Boda aside, many social scientists argue that a Leninist party state with a planned economy can neither be politically democratized nor economically rationalized. Titoism is a promise which decays into a lie.

Titoism is not a solution. It is the posing of a question which challenges societies which claim to be socialist, the question of whether it is possible to democratize and devolve power in a Leninist party state. While the Chen Yun path preferred commodity socialism to product socialism, the law of value to ignoring the law of value, and indirect planning to direct planning, both alternatives "use compulsory means to force enterprises to follow state plans."[132]

What is at issue is the right and ability to compel, that is the uses of state power. Can it be democratized? Maoism reviled people who asked that question; but the question and challenge to antidemocratic Stalinism first explored in Tito's Yugoslavia will not go away.

In China, the 1956-57 search for democratic, market institutions was supplanted by a struggle to rid the state of people committed to that democratic quest. Surely in 1958 Chen Boda's regurgitated Stalinism of 1948 did not do justice to this quest or to Yugoslav reality. The Chinese group pressing this swift transition to communism, a revolution after the revolution, held to a perversely flawed analysis. It argued that the negative model, that which had to be avoided, was not Stalin's overcentralized, terror state, but Tito's more decentralized economy with its institutions of worker self-management. In 1957-58, precisely at the moment when Chen Boda, Zhang Chunqiao, and other Chinese stalwarts of the rapid transition thesis directed their theoretical arrows against the Yugoslav target, the American Marxist Paul Sweezy returned from a trip to Yugoslavia and described "their great experiment" of combining "planning plus workers' control." Sweezy saw the Yugoslav partisans in power struggling to build an alternative to USSR-style socialism which "was an extreme form of <u>centralized</u>, <u>administrative</u>, and <u>bureaucratic</u> planning." Sweezy worried that, in going too far in a decentralist direction, the Yugoslavs would not "reap the full benefits of modern technology and the managerial arts." He concluded that "the new Yugoslav system ... proves that a socialist economy can be radically decentralized and debureaucratized." Yugoslav practice negated the assumption of ruling groups in Moscow that theirs

was the only possible form for a socialist economy to take. The Yugoslavs have refuted this assumption once and for all, and in doing so they have opened up new vistas to the human race.[133]

Other sympathetic students of Yugoslavia's anti-Stalinist strategy mention the Chinese Maoist critique of Titoism, but only to show that it ignores what is special about Yugoslavia. Such people then move on to a more serious consideration of the Yugoslav path.[134] Anthony Giddens finds that in contrast to capitalist societies, there is in Yugoslavia a greater amount of on-the-job training which eases movement from nonskilled to skilled factory jobs and much more promotion of managers from people of peasant and worker backgrounds.[135] One analyst notes that

contrary to conventional descriptions of Yugoslavia as the most "capitalist" of contemporary socialist societies, its social organization has mediated technology in a manner not dissimilar to descriptions of "technological nativism" in China.[136]

Quite naturally, therefore, many people — not least important those in Leninist party systems already in power — seeking alternatives both to the perceived flaws and inhumanities of contemporary capitalism and to those of Stalinist socialism would closely examine the positive features of the Titoist alternative.[137] That would no longer be possible in China from 1958 until the left Maoist coalition lost power in 1976.

Just as Maoism distorts China's real domestic situation, so it obscures what was actually going on in Chinese foreign policy.

It was a bit perplexing to the Yugoslavs that even while the Chinese had praise for Stalin's attempt to oust Tito and for Khrushchev's success in crushing the Hungarian revolution, the Chinese also continued to criticize the unfair terms of their economic bonds to the Soviet Union. Liu Xiao, China's ambassador to Moscow, complained about the high cost of Soviet experts in China and of Chinese students in the USSR and "asked how we [Yugoslavs] had found this prior to 1948." The Chinese continued to seek out the Yugoslavs to point out the details of Soviet exploitation of China.

Even while Maoists denounced Titoists, it soon was almost impossible to disentangle a Chinese view of the international world from a Yugoslav one. Albania's Stalinist ruler, Hoxha, was quite confused (although he also was quite clear that Zhou Enlai was not on the side Hoxha preferred and that Chen Boda was).[138] By 1964, just after the Chinese had spelled out "Why Yugoslavia Is Not a Socialist Country," they also wanted to join with Yugoslavia. Hoxha complained,

Yesterday Tito was a traitor to the Chinese; later he was rehabilitated; then he became a traitor again; and now ... this great traitor has become a "minor devil."[139]

Hoxha, sticking to his Stalinism of 1948 which promised all power in his hands and independence from Yugoslavia and from subordinate integration into the Soviet economic bloc, CMEA,[140] found the Chinese sounding just like Tito: (1) Stalin was "a plunderer and an imperialist"; (2) "Tito was not wrong, but Stalin was wrong about him"; (3) Tirana should join with Belgrade, Beijing and all others against Moscow; (4) "The Chinese have a special ... admiration for the policy of Tito in the 'third world.'"[141]

Actually this would amount to a Chinese-style Titoist foreign policy. In the 1960s Mao, like Tito in 1948, did come to see the Soviet Union as a greater threat to China than was the United States. Mao too advocated gaining military leverage from one hegemonic power to survive the other. Mao too, like Tito, promoted a special Chinese role in the Third World. Tito, before Mao, stood for "international cooperation, particularly among the small and medium-sized countries."[142] The Titoists identified with and worked for the economic interests of newly emerging nations in Asia and Africa in international organs such as UNCTAD, SUNFED and the Group of 77. The goal was genuine national independence for all, the goal denounced by Stalin as a betrayal of proletarian internationalism.

The enemy was superpower hegemony.

The peoples of Yugoslavia cannot accept the assumption that mankind must today choose between the domination of one great power or another. We consider that there is another path, the difficult but necessary path of democratic struggle for a world of free and equal nations . . . against foreign interference in domestic affairs. . . . [143]

This meant seeking maximum room for maneuver by strengthening ties to other developing nations while getting the best terms possible in trade and other economic realms both from CMEA and GATT. [144]

That's not how Chen Boda saw it. Explicating a May 17, 1958, Saturday Evening Post article by Ernest Hauser, "Will Our Yugoslav Gamble Pay Off?" Chen used it to argue whether Tito was "a tool of imperialism or a servant of the Yugoslav people." Hauser had found that Tito "would be independent of both Moscow and Washington," that "where socialism was at stake, he simply could not compromise," that "Tito is a Communist," that when he found the U.S. Congress in the process of putting strings on U.S. military aid to Yugoslavia, "Tito asked us last year to discontinue our shipments." Hauser concluded, "He's not on our side." Nonetheless, Hauser contended that the "marriage of convenience" between Belgrade and Washington was very much in U.S. interests because Tito successfully challenged Moscow's hegemony in Eastern Europe and because Tito's prestige and example helped threaten that control. Hence "Tito's interests" in national independence of the USSR "run parallel to ours" in weakening the Soviet empire.

But, as Chen saw Hauser's argument, it was saying that Tito was a slave whom American imperialism had bought. Chen insisted that Hauser's article showed that Tito was not independent because, as Hauser said, "seven tenths of the flour in every loaf of bread consumed in Yugoslavia comes from the United States." Maoists insisted that national independence required self-reliance in grain, a policy which would ravage China's complex rural economy. Meanwhile Chen excoriated Tito for purchasing U.S. wheat. Tito responded to this claim that "socialism cannot be built with American wheat," declaring, "Those who know how can do it, while those who do not know will not even be able to build socialism with their own wheat." [145] By the early 1960s both China and the Soviet Union became far larger purchasers of Western bloc wheat than was Yugoslavia. China's dire need for imported grain was made extreme by the disaster and decline caused by the anti-economic irrationality of the Maoist Great Leap Forward, one of whose goals, ironically, was self-reliance.

Tito's foreign policy, Chen wrote, proved Tito was a tool of imperialism. He had sold out the Greek rebels, encouraged the Hungarian rebels, and refused in November 1957 to participate in the Moscow Conference. Chen concluded, following Hauser, that Tito's ultimate service was the promise of more Titos in the Soviet-led camp. Chen doubted it could happen.[146]

Yet China less than two years later was encouraging Albanian and then Romanian independence from the Soviet-led camp. Tito had been right in noting the identities in Belgrade's and Beijing's situation vis-à-vis Moscow. Even at the time that Chen wrote how Yugoslavia in contrast to China was a tool of imperialism, in fact, both China and Yugoslavia had committed themselves to aid the Algerian war for national independence from France, the most important liberation struggle of that moment. The Soviet Union, on the other hand, wanting to keep France strong enough to balance a potentially revanchist West Germany, would not act so as to weaken France. Tito, meanwhile, provided arms aid to the Algerian rebels, let them care for their wounded in Yugoslavia, and put out their publications in Yugoslavia.[147] The Maoist critique of Yugoslavia for being a tool of imperialism from 1948 to 1958 was a gross distortion. So much was the narrowest of clique power politics defining the categories of concern that it didn't even accurately comprehend Chinese national interests.

If we want to understand what is valid in Maoist comprehension of world forces, we must also understand its distortions of reality. In 1960, after Khrushchev tried viciously to squeeze the Chinese economy to surrender to his purposes, the Chinese leadership came to argue that the Soviet Union since the death of Stalin, and as exemplified by its economic bloc relations, CMEA, was an imperialist country. To be sure, Khrushchev was now cruel to China, but virtually all historians of CMEA find that, Maoists to the contrary notwithstanding, while Stalin plundered Eastern Europe, Khrushchev tried to buy the nations off, acting more as a world empire subsidizing its political dependencies. On international criteria as on domestic ones, the notion which legitimates the Maoist critique of Tito for wrongly splitting with Stalin in 1948 and of China for rightly breaking with Khrushchev after 1958, the notion that Khrushchev had led the Soviet Union from socialism to capitalism as Tito had earlier done in Yugoslavia has precious little to support it.

Understanding Maoism within a spectrum of Chinese political alternatives as an ill-conceived critique of Titoism has permitted us to see how much of Maoism stems more from international realpolitik, Chinese history and concomitant Chinese domestic power struggle, and universal Maoist abstractions more closely associated with Stalinism — cult of the leader, secret police terror against the Party, slighting the requirements of democracy, imposing collectivization against peasant interests, neglecting the material concerns of workers and peasants, using class struggle as a legitimation to attack adversaries, betraying other nation's interests, etc.[148] — than from the real needs and situations of China. Maoism precluded consideration of the more decent initiatives sparked by Titoism and other East European societies confronting problems similar to China's. Once made into ideas of steel, the notion of Titoism as capitalist restoration chained Maoism.

CONCLUSION: SOME SOURCES OF THE MISUNDERSTANDING OF MAOISM

In 1958 much of the Chinese leadership welcomed this Maoist approach to the socialist transition. By the 1960s the situation was different. Then, after Mao's 1959 purge of Peng Dehuai and with the disasters of the Great Leap known to all, many people saw the wisdom of the Chen Yun more Titoist position. A large number fearfully kept silent or bent with the wind or fought their battles in a subterranean way. Others kept silent because of a felt patriotic need for unity in a world where China was isolated, where it was opposed by both the Soviet-led bloc and the American one.

But in 1958 it was different. Then Mao was experienced as an omniscient genius. According to Chinese Party people with whom I talked in Beijing in the summer of 1980, that experience was almost inevitable given what led up to it.

China's revolutionary armies in the late 1940s seemed isolated and vulnerable. Mao said fight on, victory would be ours. And, unbelievably, victory was swiftly won over the dispirited troops of Chiang Kai-shek. What couldn't be won?

But then it seemed that the economy would fall apart. That's what had happened after the Bolshevik Revolution. And China was so much poorer. Its tillers might hold back food. Its trained people might flee to Hong Kong or Taiwan or elsewhere. But Mao advised promoting new democratic appeals to peasants, intellectuals, and entrepreneurs. Few fled. Sabotage was minimal. Despite war

with the United States in Korea, despite blockade and embargo by
the United States, by 1952 China's economy was stable, growing,
surging forward. This was beyond everyone's wildest expectations.
Could new China realize all its dreams?

In 1955-56, Mao urged immediate collectivization of Chinese
agriculture. That was scary. Peasants were conservative, tied to
their soil. The inhuman horrors and production declines which
accompanied Stalin's collectivization were well known. Yet, mir-
acle of miracles, Chinese collectivization went ahead bloodlessly,
went ahead far faster than even the Soviet Union's experience or
Mao's expectations. Clearly China could do what had never been
done. Clearly this revolution with Mao's inspiration and leadership
could move forward through socialism with fantastic successes such
as the world had never seen. Weren't the Chinese people capable
of Maoist miracles?

With these high experiences as background, going from one peak
to another, with faith in Mao and belief in the miracles performed
by the people, with the need for unity and greater effort to win independence from the Soviet Union and not fall into the hands of the
United States, virtually all Chinese leaders could dismiss the more
Titoist strategy proposed by Chen Yun which required cutbacks,
slow growth, and international maneuver. Most could agree that
Deng Zihui was too conservative on agricultural policy, tottering
forward, just as Mao said, like an old woman with bound feet. Who
then could doubt in 1958 that China could leap forward toward communism in a new way, a Maoist way, on the basis of mobilized mass
energies?

But Chen Yun and friends were right. The Great Leap was a
disaster. Nonetheless, few would take on Mao openly. China's international isolation required patriotic unity. The belief that Mao,
beginning with the strategy of surrounding the cities from the countryside, had made globally important contributions to liberating
colonial and semicolonial peoples made Maoism in China a matter
of both nationalistic pride and socialistic dedication. The unity
around Mao held together for a long time despite the destructive
consequences of his post 1955 policies.

As the prestige of the Bolshevik revolution led China's leaders
to measure Chinese collectivization against a foreign standard not
appropriate to the Chinese setting, 149 so their own situation and
the international situation could mislead non-Chinese about the
nature of Maoism.

Tito from 1948 through 1956 wrongly saw Maoism as an alternative to Stalinism. By 1968 many non-Chinese progressives saw Maoism as a non-Stalinist alternative. Ignoring the unpersuasive, albeit central Maoist idea that Stalin was building authentic socialism, people such as Samir Amin put this erroneous, positive evaluation of Maoism most forcefully.

The orientation of China since 1950 (very different from that of the USSR) culminating in the Cultural Revolution, permitted for the first time a critique from the Left of the Soviet experience. This appears to us to have been fundamental.[150]

The independent Marxist socialist Paul Sweezy wrote that with Mao on the socialist transition and on avoiding capitalism, "for the first time the problem has been fully recognized and correctly posed."[151] His co-editor of Monthly Review, Harry Magdoff, added that China "has already taught the world about what the path to socialism really is...."[152] Sweezy expressed what many then believed, that "China is the bell-weather for the Third World as a whole — and ultimately... for the rest of us too."[153]

Even conservatives who are not even critical friends of Leninist party states like China saw solutions where actually there were problems. While we now know of huge pockets of poverty, stagnation, and malnutrition in large regions of China, regions which suffer extreme protein deficiencies and shortages of milk for children, Donald Zagoria in spring 1975 insisted that in China there was no "hunger, and destitution; this undoubtedly is one of the notable achievements of the Communist regime."[154] The New York Times agreed.

The greatest progress toward increasing food production has been achieved by China in recent years. Not only have its more than 800 million people eliminated hunger, but they have also increased food production to the point of building surpluses against poor crops.[155]

As with Tito's 1948 and after misunderstanding of Maoism, as with the 1958 misunderstanding of Maoism by so many Chinese who later opposed it, so the 1968 misunderstanding of Maoism elsewhere should be explained. The revolutions of 1968 promised a fundamental transvaluation of human values. In Vietnam, the Tet Offensive shattered Lyndon Johnson's dreams of dragging the American people with him till light could be found at the end of an infinite tunnel. The new, fantastic reality seemed to be that even the mightiest of industrialized nations could not prevent the liberation of a poor people capable of fighting a people's war, of taking the path pioneered by Mao in China. In Czechoslovakia, the Soviet Union further discredited itself as an alternative beacon of progress as its invaders militarily crushed the hope for "socialism with a human face," as some Czechs dubbed their goal. That there was a humane alternative to the distortions of capitalistic and statist bureaucratic civilization was further proved by the events in France in May 1968. All the notions of a permanently stable, pragmatic end to ideology were buried behind French barricades which built a promise that even the richest of industrial societies could have its bureaucracies, hierarchies, and centralized, elite organizations replaced by autonomous human beings democratically and authentically determining their own destinies in their own communities and workplaces. For many, all doubt was erased that the notion of nonbureaucratic, decentralized alternatives to behemoths east and west was practicable because the Chinese — pioneer and friend of people's war, enemies of bureaucratic socialism and statist capitalism — in their Cultural Revolution had already begun to make the alternative real. So the Maoists said. In retrospect, it seems overdetermined that very many good people of diverse concerns would by 1968 assume that China held the answer to pressing human problems, certainly to the socialist transition.

It was an erroneous assumption. There was precious little hard evidence to buttress the claim. China's diverse regions were off limits to serious study. That is why I have tried to analyze how those assumptions came to be and what they omitted or distorted.

To understand the abominations in the 1968 theory and practice of the Chinese Cultural Revolution left, of Maoism, one must return to the decade of events leading up to the 1958 formulation of Chen's Maoist position in which Stalinism was to be preferred to Titoism. Only by comprehending the major rationalizations, irrelevancies, parochialisms, and Stalinist strands woven into the red banner of the Chinese group committed to a swift socialist transition to communism can we understand why it was colored with the spilled blood of so many innocents, heroes, and martyrs.

NOTES

1. For two excellent approaches to these three paths through socialism, see Dorothy Solinger, "Marxism and the Market in Socialist China," in Victor Nee, ed., State and Society in Contemporary China, forthcoming, and Peter Van Ness and Satish Raichur, "Dilemmas of Socialist Development: An Analysis of Strategic Lines in China, 1949-1980," a paper delivered to the Regional Seminar at the Center for Chinese Studies, University of California, Berkeley, March 21, 1981. These approaches which focus on Maoism as the antithesis of Stalinism defined as bureaucratism forget that Titoism and most other socialist isms also oppose bureaucratism. No comprehension of Stalinism is nearly complete if it omits the issue of unchecked state power which makes for Stalinism's state terrorism.

2. Because Mao himself eventually attacked and discredited Chen in 1970-71 and because Kang Sheng's security apparatus is a major obstacle to China's past-Mao Titoists, these Titoists ahistorically stress Kang's role in 1958 and slight Chen's.

3. The most brilliant argument that there is no alternative to Stalinism in the Marx-Lenin tradition is L. Kolakowski, Main Currents of Marxism, vol. 3, (Oxford: Oxford University Press, 1981).

4. Yu Guangyuan, "Several Theoretical Problems Concerning the Socialist Economy," Jingji yanjiu (Economic Research), January 20, 1981, p. 18.

5. Instead a vicious and murderous secret police apparatus grew cancerously at the heart of state power.

6. Collected Works of Liu Shao-ch'i 1945-1957 (Hong Kong: Union Research Institute, 1969), pp. 129, 141.

7. Wang Ming, Mao's Betrayal (Moscow: Progress Publishers, 1979 [1975]), p. 38.

8. Quoted by Roy Medvedev, "New Pages from the Political Biography of Stalin," in Robert C. Tucker, ed., Stalinism (New York: W. W. Norton Company, 1977), p. 230.

9. James Hsiung, Ideology and Practice: The Evolution of Chinese Communism (New York: Praeger, 1970), p. 177.

10. Detailed in a book manuscript by Blum tentatively titled Drawing the Line, in Blum's fourth chapter, "Prospects for Titoism." Chen Yi, later to be China's foreign minister, is said to have stood with Zhou.

11. Wusi qianhou Zhou Enlai tongzhi shi wenxuan (Writings of Zhou Enlai in the May Fourth Era) (Tianjin: Tianjin renmin chubanshe, 1979), pp. 373-379.

12. Collected Works of Liu Shao-ch'i, pp. 145, 149.

13. Robert Bass and Elizabeth Natbury, eds., The Soviet-Yugoslav Controversy, 1948-58 (New York: Prospect Books, 1959), p. 42.

14. Observator, "China 1950," Review of International Affairs 1.15 (December 20, 1950): 4.

15. Ibid.

16. "Soviet-Chinese Joint Companies," Review of International Affairs 1.1 (June 7, 1950): 26.

17. John C. Campbell, "Yugoslavia and China: The Wreck of a Dream," in A. M. Halpern, ed., Policies Toward China (New York: McGraw-Hill, 1965), p. 371.

18. Review of International Affairs 1.1 (June 7, 1950): 23-24.

19. Joyce and Gabriel Kolko, The Limits of Power (New York: Harper & Row, 1972), p. 195.

20. Ibid., pp. 398, 399, 400.

21. W. W. Rostow, The Diffusion of Power (New York: Macmillan, 1972), p. 16.

22. Kolko, The Limits of Power, p. 409.

23. World View 15.5 (May 1972): 31-32. Lukacs' point was that realpolitik might justify a temporary Hitler-Stalin pact but legitimating it with a theory which made socialists worse than fascists was an antisocialist evil.

24. Cited in Review of International Affairs 1.14 (December 6, 1950): 14.

25. Z. Peckar, "Defenders of Soviet Bureaucratic Caste and the Most Important Decree of the Paris Commune," Review of International Affairs 1.8 (September 13, 1950): 10-11.

26. Cf. Gerson Sher, Praxis (Bloomington: Indiana University Press, 1977), pp. 3-29.

27. Leon Gershkovich, "On the Real Road to Socialism," Review of International Affairs 1.3 (July 5, 1950): 10.

28. V. Milenkovic, "Economic Development in Asia and the Far East," Review of International Affairs 6 (February 16, 1956): 13.

29. Vlada Milenkovic, "Eastern European Foreign Trade, An Instrument of USSR," Review of International Affairs 2.22 (October 24, 1951): 10.

30. "Now That They Have Crossed the Thirty-Eighth Parallel," Review of International Affairs 2.2 (January 17, 1951): 3.

31. Mao Zedong sixiang wansui (Long Live Mao Zedong Thought), 1969, p. 432.

32. Frances Fejto, "People's Republic of China — A Potential Rival of the USSR," Review of International Affairs 5 (June 16, 1954): 4.

33. Edward Friedman, "Nuclear Blackmail and the End of the Korean War," Modern China 1.1 (January 1975): 75-91.

34. "The Russians and the Chinese," Review of International Affairs 3.22 (November 16, 1952): 11.

35. Strobe Talbott, ed., Khrushchev Remembers: The Last Testament (Boston: Little, Brown, 1974), pp. 243-244.

36. Issues & Studies 16.6 (June 1980): 94.

37. Rice, Mao's Way, p. 141.

38. Wang Ming, Mao's Betrayal. Wang described the murderous 1943 "Emergency Salvation" campaign as "a dress rehearsal" for the Cultural Revolution (p. 163). One difference between Wang's account and contemporary Chinese accounts of the campaign is that Wang links Liu Shaoqi to Kang Sheng. With China's post-Mao rulers properly considering Liu a martyr of the vigilantism of the Cultural Revolution, contemporary Chinese historiography does not discuss black marks on Liu's record. I believe there was a longer, stronger, closer tie between Kang and Liu than is convenient for contemporary Chinese historiography.

39. Chen Pai-ta, Critique of Chiang Kai-shek's Book "China's Destiny" (New York: The Communist, 1944), pp. 27-30. Chen continued to be concerned about these Chiang Kai-shek agents in 1949 (Chen Boda wenji [Selected Writings of Chen Boda], pp. 3-4.

40. None in Zhou's French group were ever in any of the purist left groups.

41. Cf. Cyril Chihren Lin, "The Reinstatement of Economics in China Today," The China Quarterly 85 (March 1981): 1-48.

42. Solinger, op. cit., makes "marketeer" the essence of the Chen Yun position.

43. Cited by Michael Barratt Brown, Economics of Imperialism (Baltimore: Penguin Books, 1974), p. 290. Brown correctly has the Bettelheim position as the antithesis of those who would build on this aspect of Stalin.

44. For more on Yang's position see the sources and explication in my "Cultural Limits of the Cultural Revolution," Asian Survey 9.3 (March 1969): 188-201.

45. Unpublished Ph.D. dissertation, University of Wisconsin, Madison, History Department, chapter titled "Debate on the Soviet Model."

46. Huang Zhenji et al. in Xinhua yuebao (New China Monthly) 12 (1979): 59-60. For a discussion of Sun's position see Jingji yanjiu 1 (1980): 45, 60, 61, and Sun's description of his own position in that journal, pp. 28-37. Sun also promoted his position in issue 6 (1956) of Jingji yanjiu.

47. Chen Boda, "Explanatory Notes to the Draft Decisions on Agricultural Cooperation" in Decisions on Agricultural Cooperation (Beijing: Foreign Languages Press, 1956), p. 37.

48. Ibid., p. 52.

49. Cited in Renmin ribao, November 1, 1964; translated in SCMP (Survey of the China Mainland Press) 3337, p. 14.

50. Cited in Renmin ribao, November 1, 1964; translated in SCMP 3337, p. 11.

51. Guangming ribao (Guangming Daily), February 19, 1965; translated in SCMP 3428, p. 5.

52. Yang's position was again defended on July 3, 1980 (Guangming ribao, p. 4, "A Review of 'The Theory of the Composure Economic Base'"), because even today in China without relying on those elements which could be regarded as totally socialist, the economy would be drastically set back and the material interests of most Chinese would be seriously injured.

53. A. Nove, Political Economy and Soviet Socialism (London: George Allen & Unwin, 1979), ch. 7.

54. Lin, "The Reinstatement of Economics," p. 24.

55. For an introduction to the untoward consequences of the frantic pace of socialist transformation, see Christopher Howe and Kenneth Walker, "The Economist," in Dick Wilson, ed., Mao Tsetung in the Scales of History (Cambridge: Cambridge University Press, 1977), p. 192.

56. I read only the first page of this document on June 20, 1980, at the Revolutionary History Museum in Beijing. I was not granted permission to see the remainder of the document. For Liu's view that "the Chinese should learn from Yugoslavia" see Roderick MacFarquhar, The Origins of the Cultural Revolution (New York: Columbia University Press, 1974), p. 368.

57. Klaus Mehnert, Peking and Moscow (New York: Mentor Books, 1964 [1962]), p. 367.

58. Enver Hoxha, Reflections on China (Tirana: The '8 Nentori' Publishing House, 1979), p. 85.

59. Stane Pavlic, "Yugoslavia and China," Review of International Affairs 6 (December 16, 1956): 12.

60. JD, "Economic Agreements with East European Countries and China," Review of International Affairs 6 (March 1, 1956): 14.

61. NCNA, Guangzhou, October 25, 1956. SCMP 1400, p. 30.

62. NCNA, Beijing, October 4, 1956. SCMP 1386, p. 4.

63. Interview, China, July 1980.

64. V. Milenkovic, "Economic Development in Asia and the Far East," Review of International Affairs 6 (February 16, 1956): 13.

65. F. Schurmann, Ideology and Organization in Communist China (Berkeley: University of California Press, 1966), pp. 195-210. Schurmann went on to chart the return of the Chen Yun policies in the early 1960s after the next disaster caused by Chen Boda's anti-economic Maoism of the Great Leap. Cf. Franz Schurmann, "China's New Economic Policy," in R. MacFarquhar, ed., China Under Mao, pp. 211-237.

66. Stane Pavlic, "Yugoslavia and China," Review of International Affairs 6 (December 16, 1956): 13.

67. Xinwanbao (New Evening Paper), December 7, 1980, p. 1; translated in JPRS 77, 162, p. 47.

68. Zhengming, No. 43 (May 1, 1981): 43-47.

69. Milenko Markovic, "Eighth Congress of the Chinese Communist Party," Review of International Affairs 7 (October 15, 1956): 17, 18.

70. For an introduction to Chen's early writings, see Raymond Wylie, The Emergence of Maoism (Stanford: Stanford University Press, 1980).

71. Chen Boda, Notes on Ten Years of Civil War (1927-1936) (Beijing: Foreign Languages Press, 1954), pp. 8, 19, 39, 47, 67, 68, 69, 100.

72. Chen Boda, Stalin and the Chinese Revolution (Beijing: Foreign Languages Press, 1953), p. 18.

73. "Stalin's 79th Birthday Warmly Celebrated in China," People's China 1.1 (January 1, 1950): 23.

74. Claudie Broyelle et al., China: A Second Look (Atlantic Heights, N. J.: Humanities Press, 1980), p. 79. After Chen fell he was said to have been too accommodating.

75. Borisov and Koloskov, Sino-Soviet Relations, p. 120.

76. Zdenek Mlynar, Nightfrost in Prague (New York: Karz Publishers, 1980), p. 28.

77. Chen Boda wenji, p. 23.

78. Included in Chen, Stalin and the Chinese Revolution, pp. 31-3, 44, 47-48, 49, 51.

79. Chen Boda wenji, p. 20.

80. Ibid., p. 159.

81. Ibid., p. 5.

82. Ibid., p. 22.

83. Ibid., p. 97.

84. Ibid., p. 41.

85. Cf. Chen Boda, A Study of Land Rent in Pre-Liberation China (Beijing, Foreign Languages Press, 1958 [1947]).

86. Chen Boda wenji, p. 41.

87. Ibid., p. 69.

88. Ibid., p. 68.

89. Ibid., p. 95.

90. Adam Ulam, Stalin (New York: Viking, 1973), p. 669.

91. Hamilton Fish Armstrong, Tito and Goliath (New York: Macmillan, 1951), p. 278.

92. Adam Ulam, Titoism and the Cominform (Westport, Connecticut: Greenwood Press, 1971 [1952]), pp. 114-20.

93. Xuexi (Study) 8 (1955): 21.

94. Armstrong, Tito and Goliath, p. 278.

95. Veljko Micunovic, Moscow Diary (Garden City, N. Y.: Doubleday, 1980), p. 265.

96. Interview, Shanghai branch, Chinese Social Science Academy, July 12, 1980.

97. Ulam, Stalin, p. 664.

98. Adam Ulam, "Soviet Ideology and Soviet Foreign Policy," in Philip Mosely, ed., The Kremlin and World Politics (New York: Viking, 1960), p. 147.

99. Edward Rice, Mao's Way (Berkeley: University of California Press, 1974), pp. 133-134.

100. General Office of the CCP CC, "Forever Bear Chairman Mao's Teachings in Mind and Persevere in Continuing the Revolution Under the Dictatorship of the Proletariat," Renmin ribao, September 8, 1977; translated in CMP-SPRCP-77-38 (September), pp. 32, 26, 27. This group may in October 1954 have linked up with Hua Guofeng (cf. Renmin ribao, September 13, 1978, p. 3).

101. Mao Zedong, "On the Co-operative Transformation of Agriculture," in Selected Works of Mao Tse-tung, Vol. 5 (Beijing: Foreign Languages Press, 1977), pp. 197, 196, 198, 199, 202, 201.

102. A politics of historical economic geography would have been far more meaningful. There were rich and poor regions.

103. Mao Zedong sixiang wansui (1967), p. 242, a 1960 statement.

104. Schurmann, Ideology and Organization in Communist China, p. 437.

105. Jack Chen, New Earth (Carbondale: Southern Illinois University Press, 1957), pp. 69 and 72.

106. Chen Boda wenji, p. 70.

107. Su Xing, Jingji yanjiu 8 (1965): 18.

108. Ho Zhun, "Concerning the Problem of Rich Peasants," Zhengzhi xuexi (Political Study) 7 (July 13, 1955); translated in ECMM 12, p. 25.

109. Su Xing, "Only Socialism Can Save China," Lishi yanjiu (Historical Research) April 20, 1977; translated in CMP-SPRCM-77-27. No. 938 (August 22), p. 7.

110. Chen Boda wenji, p. 77.

111. Ibid., pp. 77-78.

112. Cf. Friedman, Johnson, Pickowicz, Selden, A Chinese Village in a Socialist State, forthcoming.

113. Deng Zihui, "Changes in China's Rural Economy and Problems in the Agricultural Cooperation Movement," in New China Advances to Socialism: A Selection of Speeches Delivered at the Third Session of the First National People's Congress (Beijing: Foreign Languages Press, 1956), pp. 118-136.

114. Cited in Michael Yahuda, China's Role in World Affairs (London: Croom Helm, 1978), p. 82.

115. Philip Mosley, The Kremlin in World Politics (New York: Vintage, 1960), p. 474.

116. Micunovic, Moscow Diary, pp. 128 and 133.

117. Bass and Marbury, eds., The Soviet-Yugoslav Controversy, pp. 70, 71, 72, 89, 90, 98, 99, 101.

118. Renmin ribao, September 6, 1963.

119. Micunovic, Moscow Diary, p. 135. Most of the few people executed by the Hungarian rebels were the worst secret police murderers.

120. ECMM 64, pp. 6-7.

121. People's China, Supplement No. 2, No. 22 (November 1, 1956).

122. For a political history of the origins and end of this policy, see my essays, "Power and Progress in Revolutionizing China," Journal of Asian and African Studies 1.2 (April 1966): 118-128, and "The Revolution in Hungary and the Hundred Flowers Period in China," Journal of Asian Studies 25.1 (November 1965): 119-122.

123. JPRS 36, 136, p. 5.

124. Micunovic, Moscow Diary, p. 197.

125. Ibid., p. 188.

126. Ibid., pp. 322, 266.

127. Chen Boda, "Under the Banner of Comrade Mao Zedong," Hongqi 4 (July 16, 1968); translated in SCMM 138, pp. 5-17.

128. Maoism includes elements of Titoism, too. Maoism saw that the contradictions between leaders and led could grow antagonistic; it never dropped a verbal commitment to more stress on agriculture and light industry. Despite the fact that Maoism overlaps in many ways with Stalinism and in a few with Titoism, the Maoist stress on class struggle, many enemies to socialism, campaigns, unbalanced growth, moral incentives, grain self-reliance, anti-economic calculus, lack of interest in democratic institutions to check a central, bureaucratic concentration of power, etc., does in combination sharply distinguish Maoism from Titoism.

129. Vackac Benes et al., eds., The Second Soviet-Yugoslav Dispute (Bloomington: Indiana University Press, 1959), pp. 131-135 and 170-180.

130. The Second Sino-Soviet Dispute, p. 222.

131. Micunovic, Moscow Diary, p. 158.

132. He Wei, "A Tentative Discussion of the Stages of Commodity Development in Socialist Society," Jingji yanjiu, October 20, 1980, pp. 43-47.

133. Paul Sweezy, "The Yugoslav Experiment," Monthly Review, March 1958, pp. 362-374.

134. David Lane, The Socialist Industrial State: Towards a Political Sociology of State Socialism (London: George Allen & Unwin, 1976), pp. 143-153.

135. Anthony Giddens, The Class Structure of the Advanced Societies (New York: Harper and Row, 1975 [1973]), pp. 232-237.

136. William Dunn, "The Social Control of Technology Assessment in Eastern Europe," in F. J. Fleron, Jr., ed., Technology and Communist Culture (New York: Praeger, 1977), p. 369.

137. E.g., Charles Lindblom, Politics and Markets (New York, Basic Books, 1977); Carole Pateman, Participation and Democratic Theory (Cambridge: Cambridge University Press, 1970); Roger Garaudy, The Crisis in Commu-

nism (New York, Grove, 1970), Ch. 4, "Alternative Models of Socialism."
   138. Hoxha, Reflections on China, pp. 482, 483, 525.
   139. Ibid., pp. 91-92.
   140. William Ash, Pickaxe and Rifle (London: Howard Baker, 1974),
pp. 94, 95, 182, 185, 195.
   141. Hoxha, Reflections on China, pp. 112, 420, 421, 572.
   142. Josip Broz Tito: Selected Speeches and Articles (Naprijed, Yugoslavia, 1961), pp. 232.
   143. Kardelj in September 1950 at the UN as cited by Alvin Rubinstein,
Yugoslavia and the Nonaligned World (Princeton: Princeton University Press,
1970), p. 29.
   144. Ibid., pp. 168, 176.
   145. Cited in Nenad Popovic, Yugoslavia: The New Class in Crisis (Syracuse: Syracuse University Press, 1968), p. 98.
   146. Hongqi 2 (1958), in Chen Boda wenji, pp. 93-96.
   147. Rubinstein, Yugoslavia and the Non-aligned World, p. 87; Popovic,
Yugoslavia, p. 94.
   148. Other horrors such as the extreme anti-intellectualism and the mass
vigilantism were peculiarly Maoist.
   149. For explanations of the supposed success of Chinese collectivization,
compare Thomas Bernstein, "Leadership and Mobilization: the Collectivization of Agriculture in China and Russia," Columbia University, unpublished
Ph.D. dissertation, 1970, and Vivian Shue, Peasant China in Transition: The
Dynamics of Development Toward Socialism, 1949-1956 (Berkeley: University
of California Press, 1980). Mark Selden's essay in this volume is a more
compelling and perceptive reexamination of the problem based on recent field
work which questions the matter of success. I find Chou Lipo's novel Great
Changes in a Mountain Village (Beijing Foreign Language Press, 1961) most in-
sightful. There was a legitimate and effective local government apparatus in
the villages backed up by an active police (militia) force to prevent sabotage.
The state therefore had the power and authority to impose collectivization despite its injury to the interests of a large minority.
   150. Samir Amin, "Marxism," Monthly Review 26.2 (June 1974): 19.
   151. On the Transition to Socialism (New York: Monthly Review Press,
1971), p. 122.
   152. Magdoff, "China: Contrasts with the U.S.S.R.," Monthly Review (July-
August 1975): 56.
   153. Sweezy, "Socialism in Poor Countries," Monthly Review 20.5 (October
1976): 13.
   154. Zagoria, "China by Daylight," Dissent (Spring 1975): 139. Zagoria, in
general, was attacking China as an ugly totalitarian state.
   155. January 25, 1976, p. 55.

Andrew Walder
SOME IRONIES OF THE
MAOIST LEGACY IN INDUSTRY

Since the Cultural Revolution, it has become standard practice in
Western academic circles to refer to China under Mao Zedong as
an alternative to Soviet patterns of organization and development.
In the administration of industrial enterprises, we are told, Maoists
in China have implemented forms of decentralization which have
overcome the rigidities and inflexibility characteristic of overcentralized Soviet bureaucracies. Instead of bureaucratic domination,
Maoists have pushed for forms of mass participation which have
afforded workers control over industry at the point of production.
Instead of encouraging competitive, individualistic values antithetical to socialism, Maoists have deemphasized individual material
incentives and have used collectivist and moral appeals to tap hidden sources of worker motivation. According to this view, China
under Mao was unique in its egalitarian, participative, and collectivist
solution to problems which other socialist states tried to resolve
through the increased use of market mechanisms, rational economic
calculation and profit criteria, and graded material incentives —
solutions which served only to remove them from the socialist path.
This, at least, is the construction of reality to be found in the
writings of Andors, Bettelheim, Gurley, Hoffmann, and Riskin, to
name only a few.[1]

Alec Nove, a long-time analyst of Soviet-type economies has argued, in his criticisms of Bettelheim and Sweezy, that the Maoist
approach outlined above never offered a truly coherent alternative
model to Soviet patterns. To contrast "centralized bureaucracy"
with "the mass line," he asserts, is to counterpose an intractable
reality with a mere slogan.[2] The only way workers can even begin
to exercise control over industry, he argues, is to decentralize economic decision-making and planning to the enterprise level. The
only way to coordinate the economic activity of these discrete en-

terprises, and the only way for participating workers to evaluate alternatives, is to use markets and market prices as the basis of decisions. According to Nove's view, Maoist theories never offered a coherent alternative because they preclude as "revisionist" the only possible mechanisms — markets and profits — through which genuine decentralization can be effected and worker control exercised in a socialist economy.

The acid test of these two opposing views about China's experience is the actual outcome of institutional reforms in industry, especially those of the decade after 1965. In retrospect, the evolution and performance of China's administrative system appears to have borne out Nove's view — the problems characteristic of centralized Soviet-style economies were intensified, not alleviated, by Maoist efforts at reform. This ironic outcome has broad implications for what has hitherto been perceived as a pathbreaking Chinese model — especially for the extent to which we view it as a genuine departure from Soviet patterns established under Stalin. We limit ourselves here to a rather narrow empirical analysis, the initial step in a badly needed dismantling of the "construction of reality" used to perceive China by so many over the past decade.

REFORM IN SOCIALIST ADMINISTRATIVE SYSTEMS

Beginning in the mid-1950s, administrative reform was on the agenda for the industrial systems throughout the communist bloc. Khrushchev's denunciation of Stalinist rule at the Twentieth Party Congress in 1956 not only legitimized the critique of existing communist institutions, but jolted all of those faithfully following the Soviet path into a provoking reexamination of their form of political and economic administration. The universal diagnosis was that the administration of Soviet industry under Stalin suffered from over-centralization. The issue throughout the communist bloc was not whether or not to decentralize, but how.

The phenomenon of overcentralization in enterprise management was subtle and complex, but had two distinct aspects. The first was that it led to widespread economic irrationality — what should have been purely economic decisions were bureaucratic ones. The Soviet industrial manager was not an entrepreneur of an economic enterprise, but an administrator of a social institution, who oversaw the employment of capital "in trust" for the Party and state. Virtually all major economic decisions — investment, expansion, renovation, product lines — were set by bureaus above the enterprise level. The efforts of the industrial administrator were focused on meeting planned output indicators, since administrative performance was evaluated, and substantial bonus income derived, according to success in meeting targets.

This tended to deform the process of managerial decision-making in the enterprise. The resulting organizational syndrome has been well documented by such writers as Joseph Berliner and János Kornai.[3] The setting of targets for the factory becomes the object of a subtle form of political bargaining. Managers are sure to over-fulfill targets just enough to achieve maximum bonuses, but not so much as to provoke a substantial upward readjustment of the target for the next period. Toward this end, a variety of stratagems are perfected — the concealment of excess output, the juggling of the time periods in which goods are recorded as complete, the over-production of half-finished articles poised for completion in the next period, the quasi-legal acquisition and stockpiling of spare parts and excess machinery — all as a safety factor to gear output just above targets and assure maximum bonuses both in the short and long run. Great "leaps" in production are anathema to managers. Startling new innovations or increased efficiencies might threaten the delicate bargaining process over supplies and output targets. In a very real sense, management initiative is bounded — indeed fettered — by the contours of rigid plans. The name of the game was to limit target demands while obtaining more resources through the supply system. It was a prescription for waste and inefficiency.

The second disturbing aspect of overcentralization was quite a paradoxical one. Excessive formal centralization made control of the actual <u>behavior</u> of industrial managers very difficult. Berliner, through his interviews with industrial émigrés from the USSR, documented a subculture of managerial behavior during the late Stalinist era that was immune to the incentives — both remunerative and coercive — offered by the state. Under conditions of overcentralized planning of investment, production, and financial decision-making powers, gearing managerial bonuses closely to plan fulfillment could not solve the problem — indeed, as outlined above, it was a major cause of the problem. The draconian criminal penalties set aside for such behavior in the Soviet system, further, could not be applied on a large scale. Despite official disapproval of this managerial subculture, most officials realized that in practice this informal realm of behavior was necessary to make rigid plans work. So underlying this formal centralization of decision-making was hidden an operational decentralization, embedded in a subculture of behavior that proved impossible to control through administrative measures.

One solution — widely discussed in the satellites of eastern Europe, proposed by people like Lieberman in the Soviet Union, Chen Yun and Sun Yefang in China, and acted upon in Yugoslavia — was straightforward and ideologically daring: Dismantle portions of the industrial bureaucracies and loosen Party supervision of economic administration. Give greater planning, financial, and investment powers to the managers of enterprises. Make profit and enterprise growth the criteria for success. Then control managerial behavior through economic measures — the manipulation of taxation, loans, interest rates, and profit retention schedules — not through administrative plans and orders. The logic behind this proposed path of reform was to undercut the bureaucratic subculture of management by subjecting management behavior to clearly defined, objective economic measures. By giving managers greater powers, they simultaneously take on fuller responsibility for the entire range of economic performance of the enterprise. Despite the loss of centralized control over detailed investment and production decisions, the state can achieve increasingly direct control over the actual behavior of administrators. Managerial initiative and innovativeness increase; the troublesome bureaucratic subculture disappears. If all works well, the industrial economy is unfettered.

THE MAOIST ALTERNATIVE

From the perspective of what would later become widely known as the alternative Maoist critique,[4] this course of reform was the very essence of revisionism, a policy which threatened to end the revolution. Considerable economic, and ultimately political, powers would, in effect, be handed over to a managerial stratum that operated according to the principles of capitalist economics, not Marxist thought. An element of anarchy, it was feared, would be introduced into the economy, and full employment and price stability might be threatened. The emphasis on objective economic criteria would place in doubt the Party's ability to control society and act as a vanguard of continuing social change.

The alternative Maoist critique asserted that the main problem with the Stalinist industrial system was not the unified administrative apparatus itself but the behavior of those who filled it. The Soviet system suffered from the problem of bureaucracy because it had offered only massive monetary bonuses to managers and workers, and had neglected political education and mobilizational appeals. The counterproductive subculture was just one symptom of creeping revisionism in the USSR which began in the last years of Stalin's rule — a loosening of Party vigilance over undesired behavior, a reliance on material inducements rather than commitment to the goals of state and revolution. Thus market reforms, from this perspective, legitimate this revisionism and hasten the decay of the revolution. The Maoist answer was not to dismantle centralized planning bureaucracies through decentralizing market reforms, but to change the behavior of those within them through increased revolutionary vigilance by the Party apparatus.

For Maoists, the precondition to any kind of administrative decentralization was this transformation of behavior and values. The reduction of office staffs, of fixed procedures and rules and regulations, and the dismantling of cumbersome systems of administrative control were all predicated on this transformation. If the behavior of people was not to be controlled through material reward and administrative sanction, then the controls had to be embedded in the minds of each individual. Managers and workers would work hard and efficiently and fulfill obligations because they felt morally and politically committed to do so. It did not seem to bother Maoists that this behavioral transformation itself required the growth of an increasingly powerful security and propaganda apparatus to remold people, evaluate thought patterns, and deal with deviants. Unlike the more liberal contemporary trends in Poland and Hungary, Maoists identified strong Party guidance over all aspects of economic and political life with defense of the revolution. In this sense, as the Maoists' spirited defenses of Stalin indicated,[5] they wanted not a dismantling of the Stalinist administrative system but a return to its purer, revolutionary past, before it was beset by routinization and a loss of revolutionary vigor.

The recreation of this vigorous, effective form of revolutionary administration, and the remolding of those individuals who were to staff it, was the goal which inspired the increase in political education, the stimulation of worker participation and political activism, and the continuous campaigns against various forms of privilege, administrative sloth, and inefficiency of the 1957-1976 period. The period of this "Maoist experiment" is now history. With 1978's rapid shift back to some of Chen Yun's original reform policies of 1955-56, not only Maoist solutions, but the Maoist definition of the problem of bureaucracy, have been rejected.

Yet we are left with the task of evaluating the successes and failures, the organizational outcomes of this period of history. Such evaluation has in the past been hampered by an excessive pre-occupation with the obvious relevance this Maoist effort has for theories of administration and economic development. Too often debate over Maoist administration has taken the form of a confrontation of moral and theoretical world views — "malleable man" vs. "economic man," "revolutionary development" vs. "technocratic convergence." We have placed too great a scientific burden on postrevolutionary Maoism. The Maoist "experiment" was inspired by at best half-formed ideas and by vague principles which were subject to widely varying interpretations in practice. They were implemented piecemeal in rapid, unplanned bursts which were accompanied by political cleavage and widespread opposition by administrative actors. As an "experiment" it was an extremely messy affair, with too many uncontrolled variables. It makes for a poor test of theories.

When we have on rare occasion descended from the realm of ideas to the job of gathering and evaluating evidence on organizational outcomes, the dominant issue has been the extent to which Mao and his followers were able to induce lasting, desired changes in industrial organization. Some, working largely from Chinese newspaper sources, optimistically accepted the press image of forward progress in the direction of desired institutional change, even though they realized they could not accept all the assertions in the Chinese media. Others, often those with émigré interviewing experience, have stressed the impermanence of change, the rapid reemergence of old organizational patterns and behavior.

The accumulating evidence from recent visitors' reports, Chinese press articles since the death of Mao, and especially from my own interviewing project with former industrial employees suggests that there was profound, sustained change in industrial organization over these twenty years.[6] The irony is that these changes have consistently been in precisely the opposite direction from that which Maoists intended and Western observers expected. First, in the area of work incentives and motivation, the Chinese work force in

1976 was far less responsive to mobilizational appeals, and far more preoccupied with pay, than had been the case in 1957. Second, in the area of leadership, despite participative innovations, power became concentrated more completely in the hands of a single administrator at each level of the factory, especially after 1967. At the same time, white collar staffs became proportionally larger, more inefficient, fearful of risk, and evasive of responsibility than appears to have been the case in 1957 or even 1965. Third, the same syndrome of organizational waste and inefficiency — the managerial "subculture" that plagued enterprises in the old Soviet system — appears to have been greatly intensified in Chinese industry over the last twenty years of Mao's life. Why and how did these unintended outcomes come about? We consider, in turn, each of these three areas.

WORK INCENTIVES AND MOTIVATION

Maoists sought to transform calculative employee orientations into committed involvement — to move from remunerative to normative incentives. This is the kind of involvement one finds most often in social movements, not in routine administrative organizations. There are two dimensions to the issue of work incentives in Chinese industry. The first is the extent to which employees in routine situations can be motivated by concerns other than pay — by "moral" rather than material inducements. The second is the effectiveness of material benefits distributed at the collective, rather than individual, level. In China under Mao, there was a clear move toward a greater reliance on nonmaterial incentives, while remaining material incentives were to be offered at the collective, rather than individual, level. These, at least, were the general principles as enunciated by Maoist leaders, and as elaborated and reconstructed by Western observers.[7]

There should never have been any question in theory whether industrial employees can be motivated by concerns other than pay, or by incentives geared to collective welfare and performance. The efficacy of informal group cohesion, diverse leadership styles, and a sense of involvement in group decisions has been well documented in Western industrial psychology for decades. Collective incentives, moreover, are the driving force which impels people to become active in trade unions, political parties, or any other form of collective action.[8] The question is not so much whether collective

incentives can motivate, but to what extent specific collective incentive schedules are perceived as fair and offer sufficient inducement in given situations. The theoretical questions are in large
part settled. We are left with concrete questions about China's
experience.

The creation of the kind of collectivist industrial community embodied in Maoist writings would be a difficult, but by no means impossible, task. Such a community would require a careful blending
of material and nonmaterial appeals. And collective incentives
would have to be based on a fragile web of shared perceptions
that the distributional arrangements were both equitable and fair.
With regard to China's specific experience, the issue is, first,
what were the specific nonmaterial incentives offered and what
were employee responses? Second, were the specific collective incentives offered to employees sufficient and were the
distributional rules implied considered fair? These questions
cannot be addressed through reiteration of the stated principles
of Mao and other leaders, or through reiteration of press reports extolling outstanding models said to embody those principles.

In retrospect, there is little doubt that the Maoist attempt to
create an effective collectivist industrial community failed badly.
The reasons for this are fairly straightforward. Despite all the
elaborations by Western observers of Maoist incentive principles,
most workers experienced the much-vaunted experiment as little
more than (1) discontinuation of regular wage raises, (2) cancella-
tion of bonuses tied to work performance, and (3) intensification of
political study, campaigns, and criticism sessions. In actual practice, there was never any attempt to blend moral with material incentives, to balance collective and individual material incentives.
The mixed collective and individual incentive structure already in
use in the early 1960s was dismantled during the Cultural Revolution, and nothing at all put in its place. The consequence was not
only a complete severing of the link between work performance and
either collective or individual pay, but also, over time, a growth of
new kinds of inequality, perceived inequities, and real economic
difficulties for certain age cohorts within the labor force. The ultimate effect was a quite predictable erosion of employee motivation and work discipline. Increased ideological appeals as a remedy
appear only to have bred growing political cynicism or indifference.

The pre-Cultural Revolution incentive structure did contain a

complex blend of nonmaterial, individual, and collective incentives.
Monthly or quarterly bonuses were generally geared to the performance of the individual, the work group, and the shop as a whole in
completing planned quotas.[9] Individuals received bonus payments
composed of components that reflected both individual and group
performance. Individual performance was collectively assessed
every month in small group meetings and included not only one's
output but also one's work attitude, attendance record, relations
with co-workers, and activism in political study. Wage raises were
to be had during national wage readjustments, which before 1964
came once every two or three years. Only a fixed percentage of
workers could receive raises in an enterprise, and the nominations
were made in small group meetings where co-workers assessed
one another's performance over the years. If someone's work behavior was still notably wanting, group leaders first tried personal
consultation, and if ineffective, collective criticism and self-criticism within the small group would follow.

This pre-Cultural Revolution incentive system thus already contained a blend of different kinds of incentives. In the short run,
bonus pay depended on both individual and group performance. In
the long run, the base salary depended on individual performance.
For both bonuses and raises, the initial assessment of individual
performance was a collective one. The Party and union regularly
appealed to civic duty during campaigns to increase output and
practice economy. One's work performance was regularly evaluated
by one's peers. And for particularly poor performance, the disin-
centive of group criticism and censure could be applied.

The Cultural Revolution dismantled this incentive blend, affecting
not only the material incentives but some key nonmaterial ones as
well. Bonuses were abolished during 1966-67, and in their place
was a monthly wage supplement of roughly 5 yuan per month,
usually distributed equally to all employees. (Monthly bonuses had
earlier ranged from around 3 yuan up to around 12 yuan, or about
8 to 35 percent of the base salary, but this varied widely by enterprise.) Bonuses of this sort were not widely restored until 1977-78.
Furthermore, there were no regular wage readjustments after the
one in 1963 up until after the death of Mao — eighteen years. Thus
for both the long and short run, there was no link between either
individual or group performance and pay. But perhaps equally
damaging, workers did not regularly assess one another's work
performance in small group meetings during the entire Cultural

Revolution decade. The monthly group assessments stopped with the bonuses. Most group criticism was reserved for ideological deviance, while after 1972 some factories did restore annual group assessments of performance for model worker awards. Thus the Cultural Revolution hit collective and important nonmaterial incentives equally hard.

These ill-considered, almost unthinking changes were in themselves sufficient to erode worker motivation in the long run. In retrospect, it seems remarkable how little thought went into these incentive changes, especially since they often go directly against the grain of the Maoist principles embodied in the intellectual reconstructions of this "experiment" by Western scholars.[10] Bonuses and raises were abolished because there was a political stigma attached to them — period. It did not seem to matter that in abolishing these two pillars of the old incentive system the most important collective incentives were destroyed also, and that with this the system of mutual supervision and appraisal in the work group fell into disuse. The links between both individual and collective effort, both long and short run, and individual and collective income were completely severed. Workers were asked to work hard for the good of the nation and its people or, increasingly, for the sake of the revolution and the dictatorship of the proletariat. But whether they did work hard or not, their income would not vary as a result, either as individuals or as collectives.

In addition to this destruction of key collective and nonmaterial incentives, these incentive changes also created, in the long run, new forms of inequality, economic hardship, perceptions of inequity, and active dissatisfaction within the work force. Consider, for example, the long-run impact that this freezing of pay raises had in the changing age structure of the labor force. In China's eight-grade wage scale for workers, the promotion from grade 1 to 2 is usually automatic and takes place after one is on the job for one year. After that one must wait for a national wage readjustment. After 1963, the last one before readjustments were discontinued, workers began to pile up in the grade 2 category, with no immediate prospects for advancement. As these workers aged over the next decade and a half, they married and started families, yet their income was effectively frozen. This meant for this growing post-1962 cohort in the labor force, per capita family income was declining over time. The government recognized this problem and had a supplementary readjustment in 1972 of one grade for some of those who had been stuck at grade 2 for a number of years, but this was a stopgap measure and did not alleviate the basic problem. This declining per capita income is not an encouraging development for a system where moral incentives are geared to collective material advancement. These people were experiencing the opposite.

The problems were not limited to welfare. The distortion introduced into the wage structure created new forms of inequality based on seniority of which workers were acutely aware. The wage spread over the eight grade scale is roughly 3 to 1 — from a little over 30 yuan to around 100 yuan per month (varying, of course, by region and by industry). This means that a worker with twenty years of experience and at grade 7 can in theory have a wage level around 300 percent higher than a new worker performing the same job in the same work group. Since there are large differences in skill and experience involved, and since the new worker could normally expect to advance to higher wage levels over the years, these inequalities were not usually keenly felt. But the freezing of wages after 1963 changed these perceptions. By the early 1970s, workers with a decade of experience would usually have wages in the 40s (grade 2 or 3), while those who had begun work about seven years earlier, and who had gone through several wage readjustments, usually made about twice as much (grade 5 or 6). Very often this meant workers performing the same job, both with long experience and high skill levels, would have a wage differential of about 200 percent, with no prospect of ever catching up for the lower paid worker.

The equality that resulted within the post-1962 generation of workers, in addition, tended to be perceived as inequitable. By the early 1970s, a worker with ten years of experience and a family to support usually made the same amount of money as a young unmarried worker only one year out of secondary school. Because of the wide differences in skill levels and family responsibilities, this was widely perceived by the middle-aged generation as unfair.

The abolition of bonuses also had unforeseen consequences of a similar nature. The giving of equal wage supplements to all personnel might seem to some to be an egalitarian measure. Yet this change had the effect of eliminating an avenue to increased income on which the lower paid depended far more than the higher paid. For the higher paid, bonuses might be desirable. But for the lower paid, a bonus of 5-10 yuan per month is more likely to be crucial to family livelihood. Just as for the freezing of wage raises, the abolition of bonuses hurt the lower paid more than the higher paid. The higher paid were already relatively comfortable and did not need bonuses or raises, but the lower paid were those who most depended on bonuses and wage raises.

So in addition to the severing of the link between performance and income, at both the collective and individual level, some new kinds of inequality, inequity, and financial hardships were introduced with the abolition of bonuses and raises. To the social scientist, armed with standard deviations and Gini coefficients, everything would seem to be just fine, gradually evolving toward greater mathematical and abstract equality.[11] But equality does not ineluctably translate into equity, and on the shop floor, in ways that mattered to workers, the scholar's notion of what equality means was often less than satisfactory.

The result was a striking long-run decline in worker motivation and work discipline. This has been confirmed not only by the post-Mao Chinese press, but also by virtually every former industrial employee interviewed by this writer in Hong Kong — be they production workers, office staff, line managers, technicians, or factory doctors. A rich vocabulary has grown up in China to describe this endemic behavior — daigong (slowdown), tuotuo lala (stretching out), moyang gong (loafing). Sometimes such behavior was a deliberate and conscious response — although always with a minimum of organization among the workers involved — to short-run grievances or issues within the plant. But most often this was simply a long-run change in labor force work habits over a decade when work performance did not influence pay. Workers typically worked just to the quota (which usually was rather easy to meet for the average worker) and sometimes purposefully worked below quota if there was a possibility of pay for overtime work. Construction and installation jobs might be stretched out to twice the time actually necessary. Workers became less responsible about cleaning and maintaining their machines and tools. Lateness and early departures became a common problem. Absenteeism through the abuse of paid sick leave (by faking illnesses or by cultivating good relations with plant doctors in order to get sick leave certificates) became an almost accepted way of obtaining rest or time off for shopping and household chores.

We do not contend that this kind of work behavior was typical of every employee or that such problems did not exist before the late 1960s — this is clearly not the case. But it is the case that this kind of behavior gradually became much more common and grew into a widely perceived problem in the 1970s. In a situation where this kind of behavior was to some extent typical of a large portion of the labor force, small group criticism of individual offenders became an empty ritual. This sanction might work well when only individuals are lagging behind, but not when a large portion of the work force is doing so.

The extent to which the work force had been transformed soon became evident to a post-Mao leadership that emphasized increased productivity. Moral appeals to work hard for the "four modernizations" were treated with indifference until accompanied by sizeable bonuses. But these bonuses, in turn, were relatively ineffective until ways were found to link these closely to individual performance. When wage readjustments began, arguments and divisions arose within workshops over who should be first in line after such a long wait. Should it be those who had waited the longest, those with the highest skill and richest experience, or those with the lowest pay? The intervening decade anesthetized workers to moral appeals and heightened concern over standards of fairness in matters of pay.

Thus in the area of work incentives, there are two ironic aspects to the legacy of Maoism. First the Maoist "experiment" succeeded in dismantling those previously effective collective and nonmaterial incentives which so many Western observers perceived as central to Maoist principles. Second, the long-run effect of this experience was to make workers less, not more, motivated by moral and civic appeals, and more, not less, concerned with matters of pay.

LEADERSHIP AND PARTICIPATION

The Maoist conception of industrial administration was that of vigorous leadership. Industrial administrators were not to be administrators who elicited compliance through rewards and sanctions, but "leaders of men" who elicited compliance by being models of hardworking, selfless behavior; by being close to the masses in dress, speech, and habits; and by listening sincerely to the opinions of those being led. It was the leader, not the administrator, who was in touch with the masses and with actual conditions, and who could elicit mass enthusiasm. The more that mass enthusiasm and participation is stressed in China, the more the role of strong, vigorous leadership increases. Mass participation and enthusiasm is

predicated on the ability of strong, skillful, and ideologically correct leadership to elicit, shape, and direct mass responses toward
desired ends.

Mass participation and strong, decisive leadership are thus two
sides of the same coin. Western observers have perhaps over-
stressed the former and neglected the latter. Yet it is hard to
overemphasize the role of strong leadership in the Maoist conception of administration. It is the strong, decisive leader, enjoying
an elemental relation with the masses, that makes possible all the
organizational innovations associated with Maoism. The leader in-
spires the masses to work hard without having to offer them material inducements. The leader performs his tasks and fulfills his
responsibilities because he feels it is morally right to do so — thus
making unnecessary all the bonuses, inspections, red tape, and administrative rules and sanctions characteristic of the Soviet system.
The good leader by definition enjoys close relations with the masses
and listens to their suggestions, thus making unnecessary the formally specified rights and independent organization among the
masses that one finds in bourgeois trade unions, which assume a
difference of interests between leaders and led. Because of his
loyalty to Party and state, and his close relations with the masses,
the leader reaches decisions quickly and effectively, making unnecessary the bulky stratum of deskbound staff personnel. Maoism
may represent a celebration of mass enthusiasm, but at the same
time it propagates a cult of leadership.

This conception of leadership contrasts sharply with the conception of administration embodied in the system that China inherited
from the Soviet Union. The Soviet system assumed that there was
not only a division of labor between different industrial administrators but also a resulting division of interests. It was the responsibility of line management — plant directors, shop directors, section chiefs — to turn out goods to meet quotas. But it was the job
of staff management — finance departments, quality inspection departments, etc. — to make sure that the expenditures of line managers did not lead to unprofitable operations, and that the goods
turned out were of specified quality. Recognizing this conflict of
interests, quality control departments were put under the direct
leadership of the bureau, not of the plant director. This meant
that the line management of the factory could not override quality
norms in order to meet quotas if the plant was behind schedule.
By the same token, finance departments reported directly to the

bureau, not just to the plant director, and had the power to approve or disapprove financial dealings according to set regulations. In a sense the financial departments acted as representatives of the bureau that made sure that on a day-to-day basis the plant director did not engage in questionable fiscal practices — like trading away fixed capital equipment for raw materials — in order to meet quotas.

With the Cultural Revolution, the Maoist conception of leadership won out over this conception of administration. Virtually all industrial enterprises drastically reduced in number, size, and power all these staff departments. The excess office personnel and department heads were sent to production shops for a "remolding" that usually lasted from one to four years. At the same time, the complex systems of regulations, inspections, and reports were largely abolished.

But the effect of these changes, "antibureaucratic" as they might seem, did not serve to liberate mass enthusiasm and participation. Their sum effect was to liberate the line managers (or those activists or branch Party secretaries who acted as line managers at different times in the Cultural Revolution decade) from the bothersome quality, financial, and other regulations and inspections which hampered them in their task of turning out a specified number of products. The immediate, almost unavoidable, result, which was to plague China's factories until after the death of Mao, was an increasing proportion of industrial output which was flawed or useless, and increasing financial losses in enterprise operations.

In a system-wide sense, this "antibureaucratic" reform had the effect of concentrating power in the hands of the hierarchy of leaders that started with the plant director[12] and stretched down to the shop floor. This concentration of power was in no way checked by institutions like the highly publicized revolutionary committees, which were created in factories beginning in 1967. The revolutionary committees were headed by the top line managers in the plant. Worker delegates were chosen after consultation between military control committees and mass organizations. The delegates at this stage usually came from the leadership of one or both of the mass factions in the plant. But these independent mass organizations, which lent real power to the voice of workers for a fleeting period, were disbanded, often coercively, at the same time as revolutionary committees were formed.[13]

Soon after these revolutionary committees were formed, military control committees, the highest organ of power in factories (except in Shanghai), conducted a series of purge campaigns which struck workers as well as former managers. People were investigated, criticized, placed in makeshift cells, interrogated, and if judged by plant investigators to be guilty, sent to their native villages or to labor reform camps. During the "cleaning of the class ranks," the "anti-May 16 elements," and "one strike, three anti" campaigns, and others, absolute loyalty to Mao — and in practice to his loyal leaders in the factory — was enforced in both thought and action, past or present. Former leaders of mass organizations, originally chosen to be on revolutionary committees, were often removed and more pliable "mass representatives" put in their place. The membership of revolutionary committees evolved without elections. People were simply shuffled in and out.

By 1971, revolutionary committees had evolved into groups led by the top military or Party leaders in the plant, composed of pliant delegates who had survived the previous years of investigation and purge by not rocking the boat. They met irregularly, at the choosing of the committee head. There were no provisions for regular elections, for accountability to workers, for democracy within the committee itself. These trappings of bourgeois democracy were unnecessary because the top leaders that had survived the Cultural Revolution had "passed the revolutionary test," had been "steeled in struggle," and thus could be counted on to listen carefully to the masses. In actual practice, mass participation was canceled out by the cult of leadership that arose hand in hand with it.

By 1971, revolutionary committees had thus emerged as empty institutional shells which consecrated the expanded authority of line management. In the intervening years former staff functions had been performed by consolidated, skeleton staffs made up primarily of workers who had been rewarded for their earlier political activism by being placed in office jobs. But by this time it had become evident that these skeleton staffs could not handle all the necessary administrative work. Part of the problem was that these former workers were not trained for these jobs. So throughout the entire 1971-73 period, former staff workers were returned to their office jobs, and the former structure of staff departments was gradually rebuilt.

With the rebuilding of office staffs, an unanticipated consequence arose. The old staff workers, now ideologically cleansed by their years of manual labor in the shops, virtually all returned to their jobs. But the workers who had been promoted to take their places

during the intervening years did not return to the shop floor. Maoist leaders could accept the idea that these staff should return and
help out in office matters, but to have them replace these new proletarian administrators, one of the "newborn things" of the Cultural
Revolution, was too much. This was considered "restorationism,"
a resurgence of revisionism sure to lead China down the capitalist
road. So by the early 1970s, one of the ironic legacies of Maoism
was a stratum of office workers which was bloated beyond what it
had been in 1965. This increase outpaced the growth of the labor
force.

Not only did the size of the staff departments experience a proportional increase — the composition and experience of these staffs
meant that administrative behavior would change in profound ways.
First, there was very often ill feeling between the older staff
workers and technicians and the newer proletarian administrators,
and a subtle day-to-day jockeying for power and status took place.
Second, because of their experience during the Cultural Revolution,
staff administrators and technicians, upon their return to the offices,
were often quite hesitant to offer solutions to problems or argue for
their alternative over that of others. When the time came to make
a decision, it was referred whenever possible to the head of the department or of the revolutionary committee — the people who had
the political authority to take responsibility for their decisions.
Having gone through several years when their mistakes at work
were declared as evidence that "the working class is the most intelligent," these staff workers were understandably very hesitant
to risk taking responsibility for a decision. The final decision was
too often referred to the top leaders who had the real authority but
not the expertise to evaluate alternatives. So decisions were typically made only after a series of meetings in which the "experts"
were coaxed into offering their tentative opinions. This "committee-
ization" of decision-making was sometimes rationalized as collective leadership, but it meant that decision-making was a more time-
consuming process, with all parties trying to avoid direct responsibility. There were plenty of cadres in the staff offices, but no
one was clearly in charge of specific decisions.

By the mid-1970s, therefore, there were three ironic aspects to
the Maoist legacy in the area of leadership and administration.
First, there was a net concentration of power in the hands of industrial managers — specifically line managers. Second, over the
long run, office staffs did not decrease in size, but increased,

leaving factory organization more top-heavy than it had previously been. And third, decision-making in the rebuilt staff departments became increasingly characterized by conservatism, evasion of responsibility, and time-consuming meetings and committees — more "bureaucratic" than had been the case before the Cultural Revolution. The "cult of leadership" characteristic of Maoist thinking did not alleviate the problems of Soviet administration, but intensified them.

ENTERPRISE ORGANIZATIONAL PROBLEMS

Central to the subculture of managerial behavior in the Soviet system was the consistent bias toward reducing one's planned output responsibilities while striving to increase one's supplies of raw materials, fuel, equipment, and spare parts. Soviet industrial managerial behavior was "bureaucratic" because managers tended to restrict output per unit input as part of a subtle bargaining process. The Maoist administrator was to cut through this problem by exercising "self-reliance" as did Red Army units in the guerrilla days. Workers were to be mobilized to save every scrap of material, waste not a drop of fuel. The Maoist administrator would constantly shake down the plant in search of slack resources, striving for the sake of state and revolution to increase output per unit input. The result would be lean, efficient organization.

In this area of organizational operations, as in the previous one, the outcome of the Cultural Revolution era was to intensify, not alleviate, the problems characteristic of the Soviet system. The major weakness of the Soviet system was that finance, quality control, and other staff departments would not or could not always exercise an effective check on line management. Plant directors found loopholes in the system or enlisted the informal support of department heads. By repudiating this conception of administrative control, and by abolishing the staff departments' role as a formal check on top plant leadership, Maoists opened the door for an intensification of this kind of behavior right down to the shop level. This, in turn, created new organizational problems for the enterprise.

First, the weakening of staff departments and the strengthening of line management meant that each shop director gained increasing control over the resources in the shop — personnel, tools, equipment, parts — and that he took on increasing responsibility for managing and allocating them. With the gutting of the administrative staff departments early in the Cultural Revolution, and their later reemergence in bloated but weakened form, shops increasingly developed their own staff of technical designers and repairmen, their own stores of parts, materials, and fuel. Shops themselves were becoming increasingly "self-reliant." In some large plants, shops even did their own work in procuring supplies outside the plant.

But such self-reliance did not promote efficiency. To protect themselves from chronic shortages and unstable sources of supply, shop directors began themselves to hoard resources — supplies, skilled personnel, parts. At the same time, shop directors became more directly involved in the bureaucratic game that characterized Soviet management — increasing supplies while restricting output. Over time, the subculture of managerial behavior spread down to the basic levels of the factory. In China, not only enterprises as a whole kept resources slack as a "safety" factor, but also each shop kept such slack whenever possible, intensifying the original problem.

A second aspect to this problem is that these slack resources, embedded in each shop, became with the weakening of staff departments increasingly bottled up in the shops that held them, making it difficult for departments to reallocate resources where needed. Before the Cultural Revolution, various staff departments monitored supplies of fuel, raw materials, and parts, allocating them where needed, and could do the same with skilled repairmen, workers, or pieces of machinery or capital equipment. But with the weakening of departments, shop directors could resist the transfer of these resources to another shop. The plant as a whole could now experience both surplus and shortage at the same time. Imbalances in the production process occurred with increasing frequency as shops had to shut down to wait for the needed material. In the last analysis, appeals to the head of the revolutionary committee, who in effect occupied the role of plant director, could resolve an impasse over an inter-shop resource transfer, but this would involve several meetings, much bureaucratic maneuvering, and even more time. Overall, the plant organization became more inflexible, less capable of coordinating the activities of its component parts, and more ridden with new kinds of red tape and bureaucratic inefficiency.

At the enterprise level, the pursuit of the ideal of self-reliance led to other unintended consequences. One of the changes the Cultural Revolution wrought in national administration of industry was the large-scale transfer of enterprises from ministry systems in Beijing to provincial control. Provinces were to make annual plans for those enterprises within their boundaries. The problem was, however, that unlike ministries, each province did not have a comprehensive industrial system. This meant that when enterprises received their annual output targets, often a much lower proportion of their sources of supply than previously was prearranged for them. This is because a given province might have textile plants but no knitting machinery plants, steel mills but no manganese mines, or a general shortage of basic metals, machinery, or fuel production relative to the needs of local industry.

This meant that factories had to increase their corps of procuring agents to go out to other provinces and get the supplies needed to complete their plans. While always present in Chinese industry, as in any Soviet-style system, this subculture of back-door dealing and petty corruption grew to new proportions and flourished during the period after 1969. The procuring agent (caigou yuan) became a crucial operator, creating networks of guanxi ("connections") with other plants and fertilizing these relationships with watches, bicycles, admission to college for a nephew, or whatever scarce good or service he or his plant might have access to. Those whose plants produced scarce industrial goods — petroleum products, steel, and other metals — could and sometimes did require larger cash kickbacks for sealing a deal. Particularly strapped plants even traded away some pieces of fixed capital equipment in exchange for urgently needed parts or fuel. This kind of behavior was made harder to detect by the stripping of powers away from financial departments in enterprises, which earlier had acted as financial watchdogs over the plant director and his sales and supply departments.

By the death of Mao, therefore, there were these two additional ironic aspects to the Maoist legacy in industry. The subculture of managerial behavior characteristic of overcentralized administrative systems intensified and spread down to the shop level in Chinese factories, creating new kinds of bureaucracy, inflexibility, and waste. And the quasi-legal underside of backdoor deals and petty corruption characteristic of Soviet-style systems — and decried by Maoists as symptomatic of revisionism — grew to new proportions in China as a direct result of administrative changes made during the Cultural Revolution.

CONCLUSION

The irony of the Maoist legacy is that industrial organization was profoundly transformed in ways quite the opposite of original intentions. The problems characteristic of Soviet-style systems were intensified. We can debate to what extent Maoists were actually in control of events, to what extent they were able to make completely the changes they desired, to what extent their efforts were opposed and sabotaged — and therefore, in a larger sense, to what extent Maoists are "to blame" for actual outcomes. But these considerations would only qualify a broader pattern of evidence which suggests that the outcomes were a direct and logical result of the key policies associated with Maoism — the unwitting destruction of key collective and nonmaterial incentives in the name of abstract equality, the nurturing of a cult of leadership, the destruction of administrative staffs which checked the power of line management, the increasing pressures to conform not only in action but in thought.

One is struck, in looking back at this period, at the extent to which so many of these changes were unplanned, piecemeal, in reaction to vilified abuses rather than as part of a well-articulated conception of an alternative form of organization. One is arrested by the gnawing realization that the only "Maoist experiment" that ever existed was to be found in the intellectual reconstructions of Western observers. There were policies, there were rapid changes, but there were no coherent alternatives offered, and particularly no sense that principles of organization, once articulated, could be tested, challenged, and revised. To challenge these principles by pointing out their shortcomings in practice would be to challenge the genius of Mao and his correct followers in the factories — to challenge continuing the revolution, to espouse revisionism. In this sense the outcomes that occurred were truly unexpected; yet despite these unwanted outcomes, their existence could never be admitted, much less communicated to levels of administration above the enterprise.

One final irony is the almost unavoidable realization that Maoist ideals for industrial administration were not so much radical departures from the Stalinist tradition as profoundly conservative reactions to a proposed set of market-oriented reforms that would

move away from the Soviet framework established under Stalin.
When Mao, Chen Boda, and Kang Sheng said revisionism, they
meant it. They were opposed to any notion that the Party step back
from control over all aspects of administration of the economy,
they opposed any notion that the Party should not seek actively to
reshape human beings, and they were willing to accept the consequences of surveillance, punishment, and purge that this entailed.
The problem with the Soviet Union under Stalin, in their view, was
not that the Party and its subordinate administration was too strong,
choking off initiative and distorting rational decision-making, but
that the Soviet Communist Party drifted away from the principles
and revolutionary ideals still espoused during the 1928-1937 period.
The Maoist answer was that China should never deviate from the
correct principles of this earlier era. This was not so much a
call for a radical departure from Soviet patterns as an idealization
of a bygone era. This, perhaps, is the greatest irony of all —
Maoism as a Chinese offshoot of primeval Stalinism.

NOTES

1. See Stephen Andors, China's Industrial Revolution: Politics, Planning,
and Management, 1949 to the Present (New York: Pantheon, 1977); Charles
Bettelheim, Cultural Revolution and Industrial Organization in China (New
York: Monthly Review Press, 1975); John Gurley, "Capitalist and Maoist
Economic Development," in Edward Friedman and Mark Selden (eds.),
America's Asia (New York: Pantheon, 1969), pp. 324-356; Charles Hoffmann,
The Chinese Worker (Albany: State University of New York Press, 1974); and
Carl Riskin, "Maoism and Motivation: Work Incentives in Chinese Industry,"
in James Peck and Victor Nee (eds.), China's Uninterrupted Revolution (New
York: Pantheon, 1975), pp. 415-461.
2. See Alec Nove, " 'Market Socialism' and Its Critics," in Alec Nove,
Political Economy and Soviet Socialism (London: Allen and Unwin, 1979), pp.
112-132. Bettelheim's theoretical formulations are to be found in his Econom-
ic Calculation and Forms of Property: An Essay on the Transition Between
Capitalism and Socialism (New York: Monthly Review Press, 1976).
3. Joseph Berliner, Factory and Manager in the USSR (Cambridge, Mass.:
MIT, 1957); Janos Kornai, Overcentralization in Economic Administration: A
Critical Analysis Based on Experience in Hungarian Light Industry (London,
1959).
4. See Martin K. Whyte, "Bureaucracy and Modernization in China: the
Maoist Critique," American Sociological Review 38 (April 1973): 149-163.
5. See Editorial Departments, People's Daily and Red Flag, On the Question of Stalin (Beijing: FLP, 1963); also Liao Yuan, "The Truth about Yugoslavia's 'Enterprise Autonomy' " Hongqi (Red Flag) 11 (1961): 31-37, for the
critique of market oriented industrial reform.
6. This article is based on the major findings of my research in Hong Kong

from September 1979 to August 1980. This research included over 500 hours of interviews with 70 individuals who had experience in a wide range of occupations in Chinese enterprises. We present these findings here in simplified and preliminary form. Fuller documentation and analysis for the claims made here will appear in future reports.

7. The most elegant such reconstruction is Carl Riskin's "Maoism and Motivation."

8. See Mancur Olsen, The Logic of Collective Action (Cambridge, Mass., 1965).

9. Piece rates were apparently only rarely used, largely limited to selected kinds of jobs and industries. They were tried out widely during 1961-62, but were discontinued soon thereafter because workers boosted output by so much that it put a strain on supplies and wage funds. The ensuing readjustments in the setting of rates brought conflict. Time rates plus bonus turned out to be a more stable, less divisive system.

10. See Riskin, "Maoism and Motivation," and Hoffmann, The Chinese Worker.

11. The analysis of such income equality is pursued with particular rigor in Marc Blecher, "Income Distribution in Small Rural Chinese Communities," The China Quarterly 68 (1976): 797-816.

12. After the Cultural Revolution began, two changes took place in line management which serve to confuse terminology here. First, in many cases, new people were promoted to line management positions. Second, by 1971, all line management positions effectively combined two roles which before the Cultural Revolution were usually kept separate — the line manager and the corresponding level of Party branch secretary. Thus the head of the revolutionary committee combined the role of the plant director and first Party secretary. We are concerned here with their role as line managers.

13. The exception appears to be Shanghai, where branches of one particularly well-organized mass organization, the General Workers' Headquarters, in effect replaced the shattered Party hierarchy throughout the industrial system. With subsequent changes in its personnel, leadership, and forms of discipline, it eventually functioned quite similarly to the ways that the Party had previously.

Kojima Reiitsu
ACCUMULATION, TECHNOLOGY, AND CHINA'S ECONOMIC DEVELOPMENT

I. INTRODUCTION

More than thirty years have passed since the founding of the People's Republic of China. In that time China has not only emerged from total disruption to achieve independence and unity but liberated its people from starvation and disease and achieved a position of influence in world politics.

These thirty years have not been a smooth road, however. The road rocked to the "right," rocked to the "left," and again rocked to the "right." Each time it rocked, division and struggle emerged among the warriors of China's revolution. In 1978, for instance, just as China began to take the way of the "Four Modernizations," which was called the "new Long March" of nearly one billion people, the plan for accelerated growth was substantially modified. It became necessary to establish the three years beginning in 1979 as a period of readjustment, a period which has subsequently been extended indefinitely. During this process, the leaders who had survived the Cultural Revolution receded, and the Chen Yun-Peng Zhen group, a group in the Party committed to the use of market forces, reappeared on stage.

To assess the significance of the readjustment period in China's postrevolutionary economic history, I will focus primarily on the history of capital accumulation for socialist construction. I would like to argue that growing demands on the state budget have created severe strains on the existing sources of funds for accumulation, and that the search for new sources has been a principal factor

---

*Translated by Kyoko Selden with the assistance of Mark Selden. This article is a revised version of the final chapter of the English translation of Chugoku no keizai to gijutsu (China's Economy and Technology).

underlying economic policy shifts over the past thirty years.

II. FORMS OF ACCUMULATION

The principal forms of accumulation can be summarized in the following seven categories:

1. Utilizing the productive power of the old society
2. Utilizing unused or underutilized resources of the old society
3. Value transferred from villages
4. Value transferred from workers and labor investment of the people
5. Foreign aid
6. Accumulation within heavy industry
7. Accumulation through export of minerals and fuels.

The first means placing under people's government control the productive power of foreign capital, compradore bureaucratic capital, and the landlords. There is no reliable estimate of the value of this productive power. However, partial estimates include Chen Boda's statement that the wealth of the four great families amounted to 20 billion yuan.[1] This expropriated capital may be considered the heritage of productive power of the compradore bureaucrats. According to another source, the total fixed assets of enterprises constructed in China between 1888 and 1949 amounted to 20 billion yuan.[2] In passing, we can note that the total of the newly increased fixed assets during the First Five-Year Plan was 44 billion yuan. Of the productive power Japan constructed in the Northeast, the value of the equipment the Soviets carried off in 1946 is estimated at U.S.$2 billion.[3] Japanese factories south of the Great Wall were taken over by the Guomindang. The total value of these fixed assets has not been estimated.

Since the landlords were a parasitic class, aside from the land, the value of their productive power was small. Gold and silver confiscated went to the national treasury, the debts of tenants were written off, and land and food were distributed to the peasants.

The factories and other facilities of the national capitalists who were classified as being among the people were to be rehabilitated and utilized. By 1956 most of these had passed to the control of the people's government. However, this was a form of government purchase rather than confiscation, for "fixed interest" was paid.

The second category is the increase of accumulation by putting into production resources which were idle or wasted in the old society. Consider, for example, the Great Wall. According to a pamphlet I obtained during a 1975 visit to Badalin, the extant wall extends 6,000 kilometers; the volume of bricks alone comes to 180,000,000 cubic meters. (A Chinese research committee recently estimated the length at 5,000 kilometers.) The funds, materials, and labor power employed to produce, transport materials, and build the wall were astronomical. The wall would actually be far longer if sections now ruined were included. Similarly, Thais make gold leaves and contribute them to shrines when they save small amounts of gold. In other words, they save but don't invest. Generally, in highly civilized Asian countries such waste was immense since the landlord system was firm. If these idle funds, resources, and labor power were mobilized for water conservancy, forestry, and road-building, then accumulation would increase considerably. This is an important element for intensifying accumulation at an early stage of development. Except for labor power, however, the transfer to production of wasted or abandoned resources ends once it is done. We can call this nonrenewable accumulation.

Lenin and particularly Stalin established the third form, expropriation from the villages, in the process of primitive accumulation in Soviet socialist construction. There are three pipelines: the agricultural tax, scissors pricing, and siphoning resources from the villages through the purchase of agricultural producer goods from the industrial sector.

Agricultural taxes need no explanation. Scissors pricing refers to the establishment of low prices for agricultural commodities in comparison with industrial products. For peasants, this means selling cheap agricultural products and buying expensive industrial products. Whether in Russia or in China, the government sets agricultural prices and — with the exception of a restricted private market — peasants must sell under a strict policy of state purchase. The government processes the agricultural products in state-run factories and sells them to consumers at high prices. In China, 80 percent of the consumers are peasants. The processing is done by light industry. Therefore light industry becomes an important link in the accumulation process.

I will explain below the method by which the government siphons off funds by the sale of agricultural producer goods (fertilizers, agricultural machinery, and so forth), since this is the most important problem in China today.

Value transferred from workers means that workers' wages are depressed in order to finance accumulation. For example, in factories workers may work overtime with no overtime pay, or a freeze on wages may prevent raises to which workers would otherwise be entitled. Labor investment of the people refers to the mobilization of people to work on construction projects, again with depressed pay or even without pay. In the case of peasants, communes or cooperatives organize water conservancy or forestry work. These peasants are paid not by the state but by their own units out of agricultural income. Their work time increases but their income does not (although the value of their labor time may increase in the future if the projects contribute to greater output). This means that current income per work day or work hour tends to decline, as it has in China over the past twenty years. To use a Japanese expression, this is accumulation by "labor intensification." In Dazhai, which became the model of China's rural construction during the Mao Zedong period, since the early 1950s, eighty-ninety days per laborer was employed in this way outside of agricultural production. This enabled that poor, bleak village to succeed in constructing beautiful terraced fields.

The fifth, sixth, and seventh forms of accumulation require no explanation.

III. THE LINE ON CONSTRUCTION AND
THE TRANSITION IN THE FORMS
OF CAPITAL ACCUMULATION

Throughout the past thirty years, the line on construction has alternated between the Soviet and Maoist approaches to socialism, but how have the forms of accumulation changed? During the First Five-Year Plan period, China utilized forms 1, 2, 3, and 5. Needless to say, the most important forms were 1 and 3. No. 5 was Soviet aid, which occupied 2.3 percent of the central government budget during this period.[4] Although the amount was not high, it was invested in the major sectors of modern industry. The transfer of underutilized resources (2) grew with the development of rural cooperation.

During this period, most of the heritage of forces of production from Guomindang days was siphoned off. Also, the repayment of the Soviet debt began in earnest in 1955, and after 1956 China ex-experienced a net capital outflow to the Soviet Union.[5] This meant an outflow of domestic resources, intensifying problems of accumulation within the country.

The Great Leap Forward movement can be understood as a movement to create new modes of accumulation. During this period, besides 3, 2 and 4 became increasingly important. In particular, labor investment (4) came to play a major role. In 1958 the value of labor investment in water conservancy alone exceeded the value of the state's basic construction investment. While total state investment was 21 billion yuan in 1958, the value of labor invested in major water conservancy projects amounted to 58 billion yuan according to government cost standards, and 17.4 billion yuan according to the lower cost standards provided by people's communes;[6] whichever calculation is more accurate, the scale of accumulation based on labor investment was vast. Considering the inadequacy of the water conservancy construction methods at that time, one must subtract 20 or 30 percent from these sums. However, the mode of "bare-handed" construction centered on the peasants was an important pillar of the economy. The sums of accumulation introduced here involve only one sector, water conservancy; during the Leap, work of this kind was seen in every sector.

The success of this mode of construction depends upon the effective implementation of the mass line. Whether or not such a mode of construction can be adopted is influenced greatly by the leadership of the cadres at the work site. Since the people mobilized must supply "a certain amount of unpaid labor," if cadres live well and wield the baton while sitting at their desks, people will not follow them. That was the reason for the demand for the "three togethers," a work style demanding that cadres eat together, live together, and work together with the people. Again, if the remuneration to the participants is based on differences in the quantity of rocks moved or the viscosity of the dirt, endless numbers of record-keepers will be necessary. In order to avoid that, equality in distribution is essential. If equality is to produce no discontent, there must be enhanced morality; the transformation of consciousness toward that end becomes necessary. The Great Leap Forward, drawing on the spirit of self-reliance of the earlier wartime liberated areas, embodied each of these aspects.

In the 1960s, the forms of accumulation changed dramatically.

Underutilized resources (2) were for the most part already utilized during the Leap. Collective labor investment (4) rapidly declined at the start of the decade as China's production fell to the level of the first half of the 1950s. The transfer of village resources (3) declined sharply owing to crop disasters. Despite this situation, China began providing foreign aid to Third World countries in Africa and elsewhere. By 1975, the amount of aid committed exceeded $3.7 billion.[7] Even if we estimate the value of the aid actually provided as two-thirds of this amount, the strain was great in view of the country's limited capacity for accumulation.

China also started military modernization. The Soviet Union had been expected to supply China with a sample of an atomic bomb in 1959 but refused to do so when relations between the two states deteriorated. After the Sino-Soviet rift, Chinese leaders, in order to counter American and Russian nuclear weapons, chose to construct nuclear weapons with their own resources. The first atomic bomb experiment in the fall of 1964 was successful. It was the result of efforts which followed this decision. Nuclear weapons systems require vast sums of money. This has remained a great source of pressure on the entire national economy. Thus, while traditional sources of accumulation were drying up, competing claims for resources were increasing.

The effort to break through the bottleneck in the area of accumulation appears to have been one of the important factors underlying the Cultural Revolution. China returned to the original point of Yanan and also groped to develop the Great Leap Forward movement, which is likewise a nationwide adaptation of the Yanan approach. Mao Zedong again advocated labor mobilization (4) as the core of an accelerated accumulation drive. And just as the liberated Yanan region was blockaded by Guomindang and Japanese forces during World War II, China in 1960 was blockaded by the United States and the Soviet Union, producing a situation of international isolation. These circumstances required emphasis on self-reliance, equality, toil, and struggle. It was precisely the crisis of accumulation domestically and internationally which made Mao's spartan leadership acceptable to large numbers of people. We can understand why Dazhai, where people worked without pay eighty to ninety days a year to reconstruct land and village, was selected as the national model in agriculture, and why the oil field whose 1960 discovery broke through the cut-off of Soviet oil was called Daqing (great celebration).

Much has been written on the political struggles underlying the defeat of Lin Biao and later of the Cultural Revolution group. It has not been widely recognized, however, that one of the major factors underlying their defeat was the issue of accumulation for economic construction, since they could not create a mode of accumulation to satisfy the new situation after 1969. What was the new situation? It was characterized by growing pressure to increase simultaneously both general consumption and defense spending. In a sense we can say that the Cultural Revolution group was crushed by increased demands for both guns and butter. This can only be stated hypothetically at this point. In the absence of conclusive data, I will simply explain the hypothesis.

(1) Increased Consumption
   Pressure

The increased consumption pressure stemmed from three principal sources. First, by 1969 more than half the population had never experienced the misery of the old society. Second, population increase raised demands for consumer goods. Third, the international blockade against China disintegrated.

From the time the Chinese Communist Party came to power, serious food shortages existed only during the few years after liberation and the years 1960-62. In other periods, food problems were solved, although not always satisfactorily. The Chinese leaders publicly announced complete liberation from starvation in Zhou Enlai's report to the National People's Congress in January 1975. Those familiar with the situation in preliberation China can recognize the magnitude of this achievement. Every year, somewhere in that spacious country, tens of thousands of people used to starve to death. When drought covered a vast area, hundreds of thousands and more died of malnutrition and disease. This situation improved in the early 1950s at unusual speed. With 1956 as the high point, however, there has been no subsequent major improvement. The same is true with regard to the provision of clothing.

The rapid improvement of living standards up to 1956 can be readily seen if we examine Figure 1. Up to 1957 there were four sources of accumulation (including the inheritance from the forces of production of the old society and foreign aid). In addition, the Soviet Union's umbrella provided for China's secu-

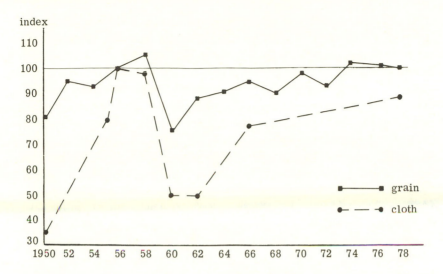

Figure 1. Developments in per capita availabilities of grain and per capita consumption of cloth (1956 = 100).

Sources:

Grain. J. Groen and J. A. Kilpatrick, "Chinese Agricultural Production," in Chinese Economy Post Mao (Washington, D.C.: U.S. Government Printing Office, 1978), p. 649.

Cloth. Author's estimate. Main sources for the estimates are

1) R. M. Field, "Chinese Industrial Development 1949-70," in Joint Economic Committee, Congress of the United States, People's Republic of China: An Economic Assessment (Washington, D.C.: U.S. Government Printing Office, 1972).

2) K. Nakagane, Chogoku no shoki suijun to shohi kozo (Chinese Consumption Standard and Its Structure), in S. Ishikawa, ed., Chugoku keizai no choki tenbo II (Long-term Projection of Chinese Economy II) (Tokyo: The Institute of Developing Economies, 1966), pp. 150-152.

3) Tan Zhenlin's article, Renmin ribao (People's Daily), May 5, 1957.

4) State Statistical Bureau, "Wuo guo gangtie, dianli, meitan, jixie, fangzhi, zaozhi gongye de jinxi" (Our Country's Iron and Steel, Electricity, Coal, Machinery, and Textile Industries), 1958.

rity. This enabled China to limit its military budget which in turn was the background for the rapid improvement in living standards.

In the early to mid-1960s, accumulation came overwhelmingly from the agricultural sector. Moreover, China had to shoulder the

costs of debt repayment to the Soviet Union as well as to pay for
its own foreign aid to other countries while developing expensive
nuclear weapons. The influence of these increased costs is clearly
exhibited in cloth consumption levels. In the first half of the 1960s,
cloth exports were pressed to the limit in order to repay the Soviet
loans. Textiles accounted for as much as 40-45 percent of China's
total exports (by 1980 their share had fallen again to about 20 percent). It appears that China did not achieve 1956 per capita cotton
cloth consumption levels again until 1978. A Chinese writer states
that there was no change in the cotton cloth ration between 1969 and
1979.[8] As to food consumption, it neither rose nor fell between
1956 and the late 1970s, according to another writer.[9] Such consumption stagnation derives not only from the increase in population but also from the important fact that capital requirements per
unit of output were rising. In the absence of new sources of capital,
domestic or foreign, the main burden of accumulation continued to
rest on the peasants.

After the Tet offensive in Vietnam in January 1968, the United
States was forced to retreat militarily from the Asian mainland.
At the same time, the 1971 invitation to Nixon and the subsequent
development of U.S.-China relations decisively broke the international isolation of the 1960s. Thereafter, the threat to China from
the east decreased year by year, easing tensions within the country. The production of some consumer goods began to reach mass-
consumption levels, but the aspirations for such goods as radios,
bicycles, sewing machines, and wristwatches grew much more
rapidly than their output.

*(2) Increase in Military
    Expenditures and
    Bureaucratization*

Since direct materials concerning the size of military expenditures are unavailable, I will simply survey the evidence concerning
the scope of China's nuclear development program to indicate the
extent to which it diverted resources which might otherwise have
served accumulation or consumption.

In order to counter the United States at first but from the 1960s
increasingly the Soviet Union, China began to construct ambitious
defense systems. In the 1970s, it is conjectured that the impact
of the military budget on the entire national economy had increased
immeasurably over the 1960s.

Table 1

A Chronology of China's Nuclear Development

October 1964	The first successful atomic bomb experiment
October 1966	Nuclear missile experiment
June 1967	Hydrogen bomb experiment
December 1968	Experiment on a new model hydrogen bomb
April 1970	Orbit of the first manmade satellite
March 1971	Experiment on a manmade satellite for scientific purposes
November 1971	A new model nuclear experiment (perhaps hydrogen)
September 1972	Installation of IRBM. The British Institute of Strategy Studies commented: A remarkable development both qualitatively and quantitatively in the past year in the nuclear armament sector. Installed approximately 100 middle-distance bomber TU16s, 15-20 IRBMs, 20-30 MRBMs to carry nuclear bombs (The Asahi, September 1972).
June 1973	Hydrogen bomb experiment
1973	The first ICBM experiment
June 1974	Sixteenth nuclear experiment
October 1975	Underground nuclear experiment
November 1975	Launch of fourth manmade satellite
December 1975	Fifth satellite
October 1976	Underground nuclear test
1976	Active development of ground-to-ground missiles
January 1977	Success in creating a nuclear missile
September 1977	Nuclear test

Source: Except for the information of September 1972, Kojima Reiitsu, Chinese Economy and Technology, supplementary table of chronology, and Annual Report on Developments in Asia (Tokyo: Institute of Developing Economies).

The political power of the military increased dramatically from the time of the Cultural Revolution when the Party and government were paralyzed, and national unity was barely maintained through military intervention. After 1971, the military retreated from the arena of power, but is it rash to suspect that the military technocrats promoting ultra-modern weapons have begun to multiply? If this is the case, it would suggest that the early idea of arms sufficient for self-defense against Soviet and American surprise attack may shift to the buildup of an arms system serving the self-perpetuation and status of military technocrats.

This is only an anticipation; the point remains conjectural. The result of fostering technology divorced from the people, however, is the creation of a military-bureaucratic group remote from the people. The great tradition of the Chinese Red Army was "soldiers like fish in the water and the water is the people." This relationship will decline if our understanding of the consequences of modern weapons is correct.

(3) Modern Technology and the
Cultural Revolution Group

One factor in the defeat of the Cultural Revolution group was the introduction of foreign plants after Zhou Enlai triumphed over Lin Biao in the early 1970s. In the three years starting in 1972, China imported plants valued at as much as U.S.$2.8 billion, mostly from Japan, the United States, and Europe. It seems that the Cultural Revolution group's effort to sustain economic development on a largely self-sufficient, self-reliant basis was compromised by these purchases.

Since liberation, China has imported massive amounts of foreign technology on four occasions: the first half of the fifties, the first half of the sixties, the first half of the seventies, and finally after 1978. During the first period, China imported high-technology plants, including steel, coal, electric power, and heavy machinery. During the second period, it imported chemical fertilizers, synthetic textiles, and oil refinery plants, mostly from Europe. The strong will to overcome the agricultural disasters of the early sixties can be seen clearly when the items imported in the sixties are analyzed. During the third period, China imported plants for the production of chemical fertilizers, synthetic textiles, and petrochemicals, as well as oil-drilling equipment, steel, aircraft, and ships, mostly from Japan and Europe.

The introduction of foreign plants exerted great influence on internal economics and politics. Since China's economic construction relies on limited capital, resources, and personnel, all generated domestically, these were concentrated in order to purchase imported plants. The key personnel in this construction were technically trained intellectuals who thus became socially important. As the modernization of the economy made it increasingly dependent on those with technical skills, the Cultural Revolution group's denigration of intellectuals became increasingly anachronistic and difficult to sustain. The import of foreign technology in the early seventies especially, when foreign technologies were so much more sophisticated as to represent a qualitatively new stage in technological development, played an important role in undermining the leadership of the Cultural Revolution group.

(4) The Failure of the Cultural Revolution Group to Create a New Form of Capital Accumulation

In addition to new technology, the development of the national economy came to require by the 1970s new sources of accumulation. Under these circumstances, the Zhou Enlai-Deng Xiaoping group sought to increase exports of mineral resources as a source of accumulation as well as of foreign exchange. The Cultural Revolution group had opposed such a strategy on the grounds that the export of resources would turn China into a colony of capitalism again.[10] Behind this dispute was a difference of opinion concerning whether or not it was possible to further intensify the major form of accumulation, value transferred from villages (3), and whether or not it was possible to intensify value transferred from workers and collective labor investment (4). The empirical evidence suggests that both sources of accumulation had reached their limits.

I have already indicated that the government has three ways of raising funds from the villages. By siphoning off peasant purchasing power through supplying large amounts of agricultural producer goods (3), the government seems to have reached a point at which peasant living standards stagnated or even declined. It seems that the state supplied relatively expensive producer goods to the extent that per capita peasant incomes remained largely unchanged even while output was rising appreciably.

Japan had the experience in the 1930s of supplying relatively expensive chemical fertilizer to peasants and greatly contributing to accumulation in the chemical industry. In Taiwan in the fifties the government was the sole agent of the sale of chemical fertilizers, and it expropriated funds from peasants by selling at prices which were high relative to the price of rice. In Japanese villages today, the expression "landlord before, agricultural cooperative now" is often used. In the old days, the landlord took away half of the output, but now the agricultural cooperative does the same

through its control of high-priced inputs. The majority of agricultural producer goods is supplied through the cooperative, and half
the income from the sale of agricultural products disappears into
purchasing them. It seems that a similar situation in China has
been growing for the past ten years or so, with the state siphoning
off much of the surplus in this way.

The increase in the supply of agricultural producer goods is
shown in Table 2. Since these producer goods were paid for by the
peasants and since the increases in quantities dwarfed reductions
in prices, the table indicates a growing flow of resources out of the
agricultural sector to pay for the means of production.

While the cost of agricultural producer goods has been brought
down over the years, the study by Victor Lippit in this volume suggests that such costs remain high relative to the prices received
for agricultural products. Further, the problems are compounded
by the fact that although Chinese agriculture has become increasingly capital-intensive, labor productivity has not risen commensurately. Multifaceted study is necessary to explain why labor
productivity has not increased faster than the increase of modern
inputs. We note here, however, that even if modern inputs increase,
if labor productivity does not rise correspondingly then peasants
become poorer since the marginal cost of agricultural products
increases annually. Unless labor productivity is raised, price increases for agricultural products can provide only temporary relief for the peasants. From the standpoint of the national economy,
price increases add to the burden on the national budget in the long
run. Japan's high rice-price policy of the past thirty years is an
example of this. In China for the past ten years it seems that the
increase of modern inputs raised marginal costs which impoverish-
ed the peasants. Compare the years 1956 and 1972 in the following
survey of 2,162 production brigades:

The yield of six grains increased from 1,740 to 2,370 kilograms per hectare.
Production increased by 36 percent, but production costs, excluding labor, increased from 39.3 to 60.8 percent of the value of the grain. This was a 54
percent increase. As a result, the net agricultural income declined, the
average distribution per work day going down 20 percent.[11]

When I visited China in May 1979, the vice-chairman of the State
Planning Commission cited a recent large-scale survey of production brigades which showed that the state purchase price was as
much as 10 percent below production costs. These two items

Table 2

The Supply of Agricultural Producer Goods
(1957 = 100)

Year	Tractors	Fertilizer	Drugs	Village electric power	Village irrigation & drainage
1957	100	100	100	100	100
1958	184	129	128		
1959	(240)	210	214		248
1960	(321)	(317)	(236)		
1961	(400)	(396)		(810)	
1962	(408)	(556)	(156)	(1700)	(354)
1963		(741)	(177)		
1964	(504)	(1109)	(207)	(2270)	
1965	(548)	(1428)	(311)	(2500)	
1966				(3400)	
1967					(500)
1968					
1969					
1970		(2028)			
1971		(2583)		(10210)	
1972	(1520)	(2854)			
1973		(3603)			
1974		(4780)			
1975					
1976					
1977	4420	(5750)	714		5310
1978	5290	(6870)	833	24300	5800

Note: The numbers in parentheses are my own estimates. In the numbers of tractors in 1977 and 1978, two hand tractors are calculated as one regular tractor.

Sources: 1957-73: Kojima, "Chinese Economy in the Past 25 Years Seen From Economic Statistics (II)," JETRO, Chugoku Keizai Geppo (Study of Chinese Economy Monthly), July 1974.

1977-78: State Statistical Bureau, A Report on the Results of the National Economic Plan, 1978.

1974-76: Zhou Enlai, "Report on the Work of the Government," Renmin ribao, January 21, 1975.

clearly demonstrate the cycle from the increase of modern inputs to the rise of the marginal cost of agricultural products to the impoverishment of the peasants.

There is another serious problem: the agricultural machinery industry, an important agricultural producer goods industry, operates at a loss. This situation appears to indicate that the third form of accumulation, drawing off resources from the villages via the sale of agricultural producer goods to them, is approaching a limit. It suggests that the state can no longer raise funds from the villages in this way. If this is so, what form of accumulation can be created in its place? The Cultural Revolution group seems to have neither thought about this nor made efforts to create one. Though only a hypothesis, we see in this a possible cause of its defeat viewed from the perspective of accumulation.

In order to break out of the cycle from a deficit in agricultural producer goods to a deficit in the entire agricultural sector to impoverishment of the peasants, in April 1979 the administration raised the purchase price of agricultural commodities by an average of 2.5 percent. This is said to have amounted to financial aid of 7 billion yuan. Additional price reductions of agricultural producer goods announced bring the total aid to 8 billion yuan, more than 7 percent of the 1979 central government budget.[12] While this helps to reform a system which weighed heavily on the peasants, we see that agriculture is becoming a burden on the national economy.

IV. THE 1979 ECONOMIC PLAN

(1) The Ten-Year Plan of
*   February 1978 and the*
*   Targets of the Adjustment*
*   Policy*

In February 1978, following the conclusion of the struggle against the Cultural Revolution left, the National People's Congress was held. There Hua Guofeng announced the framework of a long-term economic plan, which proved to be short-lived, meant to cover the years up to 1985. It set targets for 1985 of 60 million tons of steel (compared with 23.7 million tons in 1977) and 400 million tons of grain (compared with 282.8 million tons in 1977). The rate of

industrial growth was set at 10 percent. The targets included the
construction of fourteen major industrial bases and more than 120
large-scale projects all over the country; these included 10 large-
scale iron and steel bases, 9 large-scale nonferrous metals bases,
8 large oil fields, 10 large oil and gas fields, 30 large power plants,
6 new railroad lines, and 5 large-scale ports. The plan sought to
raise the rate of agricultural mechanization from 20 percent to
85 percent. Its grandiose scale can be fathomed from the grand
total of U.S.$13 billion in inquiries to Japan alone concerning the
purchase of plants prior to 1985. Of this, contracts were actually
finalized for U.S.$3.7 billion. The December 1978 Third Plenum
drastically cut the plan's overambitious targets, and other contracts
were shelved as China initiated a prolonged period of "readjustment."

There was significance in the appearance of the Chen Yun group
at the Third Plenum. Chen Yun belonged to the group which had
been critical of the Great Leap Forward policy. In 1978 he favored
balanced growth, cutting back the scale of accumulation to permit
immediate increases in consumption and the limited introduction
of market allocation to reduce the bureaucratization of economic
decision-making. The Congress agreed to designate the three
years from 1979 as an adjustment period and only subsequently
to resume intensive heavy industrialization. By 1980-81, however,
it became clear that the readjustment of the economy would require
far more than three years.

Why did the long-term plan of February 1978 go bankrupt in its
first year? It is owing to the Hua Guofeng-Deng Xiaoping administration's decision to promote intensive heavy industrialization
requiring vast investments before placing the new form of accumulation on firm foundations. I have already pointed out that the third
form of accumulation has reached its limit. The seventh form,
seeking capital through exports of oil and coal, had just begun, and
it seems that the initial expectations concerning how much capital
could be raised from this source were overoptimistic and unreal-
izable. The February 1978 long-term trade agreement between
China and Japan projected total trade between the two countries of
U.S.$20 billion (10 billion each way) by 1985, with Japan expected
to export U.S.$10 billion-worth of plants and construction materi-
als in the five years up to 1982.[13] In turn, Japan was to import in
the same five-year period 47.1 million tons of oil and 8.45-9.2
million tons of coal. As for the years 1983-85, trade figures were

to be balanced subsequently. The agreement anticipated the export of more than 3 million tons of oil by around mid-1980.

In the process of gradually enlarging the seven forms of accumulation, the Chinese economy is oriented toward changing into one that allows heavy industry to expand and reproduce by accumulation within the heavy industrial sector itself. Accumulation within heavy industry will become possible at the point when heavy industrial products achieve the capacity to compete internationally. The third form of accumulation remains important. It seems that the three-year adjustment period starting in 1979 was designed to place forms (3), (6), and (7) on the right track.

*(2) A New Choice of Industrial
    and Agricultural Policy*

Agriculture (hence light industry) still remains the sector with the greatest accumulation potential. The more China tries to intensify heavy industrialization, the more critical the support of the agricultural sector becomes. Thus when investments in heavy industry rose suddenly and accumulation reached a limit, as happened during the Great Leap Forward, it became necessary to adopt policies emphasizing agriculture to restore balance in the economy. Table 3 indicates the changes in the central government's investment in agriculture and light industry as proportions of its total basic construction investment.

The short-lived attempt to speed up industrialization in 1978 once again made apparent the reliance on the agricultural sector to provide essential support and its inability to provide such support. It became clear that rapid industrialization would have to await putting agriculture on a sounder footing; agriculture would have to receive priority. Under these circumstances, the government hammered out the following agricultural policies:

(a) The government purchase prices of agricultural commodities were raised by an average of 25 percent.
(b) The elimination of egalitarian measures which reduced production incentives.
(c) The encouragement of free markets.
(d) The autonomy of production brigades and particularly teams was to be respected.
(e) Twelve commercial grain bases were to be established in

Table 3

Investment Rates in Agriculture and Light Industry as a Percentage
of the Central Government's Basic Construction Budget

Year	Agriculture (including water conservancy and meteorology)	Light industry
1953	9.7	2.5
1954	4.6	7.4
1955	6.7	5.7
1956	8.0	6.4
1957	8.6	8
1958	9.9	8.2
1958-60	n.a.	3.9
1966-70	n.a.	4
1971-75	n.a.	2.1
1977	n.a.	2.0
1978	10.7	5.4
1979	14	5.8

Sources:

1. 1953-58 figures calculated from Ten Great Years, pp. 46, 52.

2. 1958-75 figures for light industry from Fan Yan, Renmin ribao, May 25, 1979, p. 3.

3. 1977-79 figures from Zhang Jingfu, "Report on the Final Accounts of the State Budget and Preliminary 1979 State Budget," June 1, 1979. 1979 is a budget figure.

different parts of the country. They would receive investment priority over other regions.

Missing from these policies is Dazhai-style labor mobilization for construction. Policies (a) through (d) represent concessions and compromise toward the peasants. They aim at increasing production by enlarging material incentives. More than 30,000 free markets are already in existence all over the country, and under certain conditions the sale of grain, forbidden even when free markets were allowed in the past, has been recognized. These can be considered policies to cure "impoverishment."

Policy (e) is directed to making agriculture capable of supporting industrialization. In general, there are two principal functions of agriculture at an early stage of modernization. One is subsistence agriculture, which in China is directed toward feeding one billion people, 80 percent of whom live and work on the land. The other is agriculture which can support industry. The former requires raising the productivity of land mainly. The latter, by contrast, requires raising <u>labor</u> productivity. The Maoist approach overwhelmingly stressed the former. China's primary aim, accordingly, was to produce grain everywhere and to attempt to achieve self-sufficiency in every locality. At present, this policy has been revised, and appropriate specialized production in different areas is advocated. This revised orientation seeks to create an agriculture capable of producing a high percentage of marketable commodities. Its concrete policies are as follows. Suburban areas are to concentrate on producing nonstaple foods for the cities. Suburban land conditions are favorable, and productivity is apt to rise. Producer goods are to be selectively introduced in these areas with the intention of holding down the increase in marginal costs.

In the twelve delta and valley regions designated as commercial food supply bases, regions occupying 15 percent of the entire arable area, large-scale cultivation with the highest capital-intensity will be emphasized in order to produce agricultural products for the cities and for export.[14] Cultivation is under way on the Heilongjiang border, opening up arable land on a scale which corresponds to 80 percent of Japan's total arable land area, 6 million hectares. In such especially important areas, mechanization promises to raise the productivity of agricultural labor considerably; it will be accompanied by efforts to divert peasants into local or service industries to the extent possible. The twelve commercial bases are listed in Table 4.

Table 4

China's Twelve Commercial Grain Bases

(1) The Changjiang delta
(2) The Pearl River delta
(3) The Two Lakes plain (Jianghan, Dongting Lake)
(4) Xiangyang Lake plain, Jiangxi
(5) Chuanxi plain, Sichuan
(6) Hotao plain, Ningxia, Inner Mongolia
(7) Hexi corridor, Gansu
(8) Guanzhong plain, Wei River, Shaanxi
(9) North Jiangsu-North Anhui plain
(10) Sanjiang plain, Heilongjiang
(11) Songlan plain, Jilin
(12) Liao River plain, Liaoning

Regions (10) and (11) are newly cultivated ones. Compared with the regions emphasized during the 1961-65 adjustment period, these areas and the Sichuan Valley, the Yinho district of Ningxia, and the Hexi district of Gansu have been added.

How will this new agricultural investment affect areas which are not supporting industry directly? To the extent that the base areas are favored by the state, differences in productivity and in income between the twelve agricultural bases and suburban areas on the one hand and the remaining agricultural areas on the other will inevitably grow. The result is likely to be growing regional inequality in the countryside, even though income differences between peasants in favored areas and urban residents appear likely to diminish.

(3) Industrial Policy

(a) Priority industries. In order to overcome bottlenecks in industry, highest priority is to be given to the energy and transportation sectors. These include coal, oil, natural gas, and electric power industries, and the construction of infrastructure. Of these, electric power output is said to be 20-30 percent below demand.[15] Electric power therefore receives highest priority.

Another key item is export industry. Mao Zedong was critical of selecting certain export industries for emphasis. In the old society, foreign settlements or colonized areas became industrialized regardless of the domestic market. The Northeast developed as a sector of Japan's imperialist economy, and Qingdao, Tianjin, and Shanghai were appendages of the economies of such powers as the United States, England, and Japan. Politically, this unequal industrialization formed a barrier to national unification. This situation was changed during the Mao period, with state policy directed toward the formation of an organic and unified national market. Policies to industrialize certain areas to satisfy the demands of foreign countries were strictly avoided. This policy has now been revised, and export industry is being fostered. Policies similar to the tax-free-zone policy adopted by Korea, Taiwan, Hong Kong, and Singapore for the past fifteen years have been adopted or are under consideration. At present, China is in the trial stage in implementing policies of this type.

Promoting the tourist trade is another link in Chinese efforts to earn foreign exchange and obtain resources to support accumulation. China received 400,000 overseas Chinese in 1978 and 100,000 other foreign tourists on its way toward a target of 3.5 million visitors by 1985. By 1981 the number of foreign tourists (excluding overseas Chinese) had risen to 529,000.[16] In this way, the correction of imbalances among sectors and fostering industries to obtain foreign currency influence the decisions as to which industries to foster.

(b) The choice of technique within industry. During the First Five-Year Plan period ending in 1957, China stressed the development of large-scale, heavy industrial complexes. During the Leap and the Cultural Revolution, since native techniques received greater emphasis, large, medium, and small-scale technologies were all developed and competed for resources. When emphasis is placed on labor productivity, medium and small industries are not as likely to be encouraged. The reason that large-scale unemployment has not surfaced in China lies in the Party's power of organization and control within the villages and the approach to construction of medium and small-scale factories which have a large capacity for employment. Since 1976, raising labor productivity has become categorical. Policymakers have as a consequence closed down or threatened to close down, merge, or otherwise reorganize factories which persistently operate in the red. The majority of these factories are medium and small plants located in villages and small cities, especially in such industries as iron, coal, chemical fertilizers, and cement. However, it will not be possible boldly to allow them to collapse as in the period between 1961 and 1965, for employment problems would then become acute.

(c) Accelerating basic construction and formulating new incentive policies. Up to the end of 1979, basic construction investment has been carried out by the state in the absence of institutional indices to measure the period and effectiveness of construction. Beginning in 1980, the People's Bank began charging interest on the funds it advances, and the record of the construction industry is to be measured in part by its success in keeping interest costs down. This means that the longer the period that construction enterprises take to complete their assigned tasks, the greater the interest charges they will have to pay and the less their profits. Since they are to be allowed to keep a share of the profits for worker welfare expenditures (e.g. housing), bonuses, and investment (in this regard they are just like other state enterprises), the construction enterprise employees will have a direct material interest in completing their assigned tasks in the shortest time possible. Similar profit-sharing schemes have been widely introduced to raise labor productivity in many other industries.

(d) Fostering industrial specialization. Chinese factories, unlike Japanese, are of the General Motors type. The production ratio within the same factory is extremely high. The ratio of production within the same factory is approximately 30 percent in Japanese automobile factories, but in China almost all parts are produced in the same factory. Consequently, within the same area, each factory has similar work processes and parts production. Thrusting an operating knife into this mode, China aims to foster specialized factories in each locale. This means dividing the work processes and the parts, and arranging them linearly.

(e) Changing independent budgetary units. Chinese industrial organization goes from company to factory to workshop to work group to production team. Formerly the company was a coordinating organization, and the factory was the unit of independent budgeting. But current reform efforts include trying to introduce a budget system in the workshop. For example, when an entire group of workshops improves its performance, the logic of rewarding workers in all of the shops is clear. However, if upstream workshops fail to provide sufficient processing materials, is it appropriate to penalize the entire factory? A system of circulation has to be designed so the workshops can independently procure additional materials when necessary from different factories in the market outside of the factory. This requires wholesale economic reorganization, involving great difficulty.

(f) Emphasizing profits. Factory achievement had been evaluated on the basis of eight categories of performance. These were based on a concept of the gross value of production. This encouraged such behavior as increasing gross production by putting a mink collar on a cotton overcoat or aimlessly stockpiling semifinished goods. A mink collar is far more expensive than a cotton one. Hence the enterprise can report increased value of its product. This encouraged factory managers to use unnecessary and expensive materials. To deal with such problems, current economic reforms are stressing the role of profit as an indicator. As Carl Riskin's essay in this volume shows, however, prices remain an inadequate indicator of real social costs and cannot, moreover, be reformed readily. Thus reforms which allow enterprise officials to pursue profits will create some new problems in economic decision-making.

Taken together, these reforms represent a wide-ranging change in the entire economic system. We can, accordingly, anticipate difficulties which go to the roots of the economic system, much as did the innovations in the Soviet Union and Eastern Europe in the sixties and seventies. The principal objective of the reforms is to make economic activity more efficient and thereby reduce the capital requirements per unit of added output, to deal with the accumulation problem by reducing the scale of accumulation required to attain China's economic growth and modernization targets.

(4) Population Policy

In Chinese cities, as late as 1977 there was still a saying: "One's too few, two's fine, three's okay, four's a mistake."[17] One child is too few, two children are good, three are passable, four won't work. In 1979 it changed to "one's good, two's okay, three's a mistake, four's a nuisance." One is fine, two is passable, three is a mistake, and if you have four, you're in trouble. More recently still, overwhelming stress has been placed on limiting each couple to one child. The state now pays 5 yuan per month to a couple with one child, but fines families with more than three children 5 yuan per month (families with many children prior to the institution of the new policy are not penalized). The system of fines of course reduces opportunities for education and jobs for these families.

What is the target of this population policy? Considering the critique of egalitarianism in distribution systems in the villages and the policy of raising the wages of city workers, this population policy can be understood as seeking gradually to raise per capita consumption levels by controlling the rate of increase of consumption in the national economy as a whole. This population policy represents an effort to find a way out of the increased demand for butter. To control the rate of increase of total consumption is one way of reconciling the requirements for increased living standards with sustained high levels of accumulation. To the extent that economic reforms can increase efficiency, population control may even contribute to reducing the levels of accumulation required. The policy for raising per capita consumption standards abandons the Dazhai construction approach based on arduous labor and seeks to employ material incentives to secure active participation in national construction.

The rate of population increase in the fifties is estimated at approximately 2.3 percent. In the 1960s, population control policy began to be adopted as a unified Party policy. Even so, the rate fluctuated between negative increase and 3 percent, averaging 2.23 percent, though the statistics are unreliable. Total population in 1959 was 662 million which increased to 825 million in 1969.[18] In 1977, China succeeded in lowering the rate to 1.2 percent.[19] The national target is to lower it to 0.5 percent by 1985.

(5) Acceptance of Foreign Aid

After 1961, China's policy of self-reliance dictated a refusal to go into debt internationally. But China now receives long-term loans with special terms. This can be called a Copernican reversal. The Central Committee seems to have resolved the issue of foreign aid around the summer of 1978. As of September 1979, the sums signed for long- and short-term loans totaled U.S.$2.5 billion; this includes U.S.$600 million in Japanese short-term loans and U.S.$400 million in long-term loans.[20] The total debt under negotiation was as high as U.S.$20 billion. The accumulated public debts of the Third World at the end of 1978 amounted to U.S.$348 billion dollars, the largest being Brazil's U.S.$33.3 billion. Mexico had borrowed U.S.$31.2 billion, India U.S.$20.6 billion, and South Korea U.S.$18.2 billion.[21] Had China gone through with the scale of foreign borrowing initially contemplated, it would have become a major debtor nation. The cancellation of foreign orders in 1980, however, suggests wariness over falling into the "debt trap."

V. CONCLUSION:
   ANTICIPATED CONTRADICTIONS

The Mao period was one which achieved national independence and unification and liberation of the oppressed from starvation and exploitation. The 1970s struggle between the Cultural Revolution group and advocates of the "modernization" strategy can be called a struggle over what kind of society to build following these achievements. The defeat of the Cultural Revolution group seems to derive from the belief that the egalitarian strategies of accumulation developed during the Yanan period and the era of isolation in the sixties could not be sustained after the early objectives of liberation and revolution were basically achieved.

The theory that the contradiction between "advanced relations of production and underdeveloped forces of production" must be resolved by developing the forces of production seems to have triumphed over the earlier emphasis on further developing advanced relations of production as the basis for material change. I will conclude by pointing out some contradictions that can be anticipated in the modernization strategy from the perspective of capital accumulation.

The administration is relying on the following forms of accumulation: transfer of value from the villages (3); foreign loans (5); accumulation within heavy industry (6); and export of mineral resources and import of capital goods (7). Of these, (6) and (7) are secondary. The success of the government depends on whether it can smoothly materialize (3) and (5).

(1) Is It Possible to Increase
Labor Productivity in
Agriculture?

The major domestic source of accumulation remains the transfer of value from the villages. I have already stated that labor productivity must be raised in agriculture in order for it to support further the development of heavy industry. Since 1949, China's arable land area has hardly increased, although double and triple cropping has increased utilization rates. This means that newly tilled areas are approximately the same as the amount of land taken out of cultivation. For one thing, marginal lands become wastelands owing to drought and the encroaching desert. More important, however, is the land transferred to use for factories, roads, water conservancy, schools, housing, and so forth. New cultivation is carried out in marginal areas while the transfer of existing farmland to factory and other uses takes place in fertile areas. In the future, as industrialization proceeds, more fertile land will be destroyed. Food production has increased despite the fact that the arable area was fixed because the crop index and land productivity have increased.

How will this situation change in the future? The land utilization index has probably reached capacity at about 1.6 crops per year. It was 1.41 in 1957. The highest in Japan's history was 1.45. Today in Japan it is below 1. It is not easy to increase it further in China which has vast regions of inferior agricultural conditions in areas such as the Northeast and Northwest.

China has also approached the limits of land utilization. The planting of three crops per year is an example. Before the earlier crop is harvested, the new crops are planted between the furrows. This planting system hinders mechanization. Japan has been able to achieve rapid mechanization in agriculture over the past twenty-five years because it stopped planting wheat, formerly the secondary crop, in the rice fields. China's Ministry of Agricultural Machinery has experienced difficulty in designing machines suitable to the intercrop system; for example, I have heard reports that combines could not be used because corn is interplanted between rows of wheat.

(2) Employment Problems

Every year 14 to 16 million people enter the working-age population. Large-scale plants imported from foreign countries have extremely low employment capacity. Raising labor productivity in industry, moreover, a principal goal of economic reform, will put further pressure on employment opportunities. Imaginative policies seeking to develop urban cooperative industries have been adopted in the last few years, policies oriented toward the development of urban services especially. At least in the early stages of reform employment problems can be expected to increase even though they may take the form of disguised unemployment of workers within enterprises.

(3) The Destruction of Nature and the Environment

In May 1979, when I visited Beijing, water was said to go up only to the second floor in the eleven-story workers' apartment on Qianmen Street in Beijing. One problem is insufficient electric power. The other is lack of water. The level of underground water in Beijing is said to fall annually by 50cm to 1m.[22] At this rate, won't Beijing become a desert? Similar things are happening in various places. Dongting Lake lost one-third of its original natural reservoir and water surface owing to cultivation. Although there are areas where surface erosion has decreased, there are more where it has increased.[23] As in other societies where economic growth has been accorded such a dominant position among social priorities, preservation of the environment will be increasingly difficult to maintain.

(4) Problems of Bureaucratization
and the Creation of an
Elite Class

This is the greatest challenge China will have to face in the 1980s, and one which appears the most difficult to solve. It seems to me it will hang like a dark cloud over the entire social development of the nation. The bearers of society in the future will be the graduates of the higher education system. In order to enter that route, a stable social order has to be born. This order and the military will become the soil for bureaucratization. Although China's economic reforms promise to decentralize decision-making to the enterprise level and thereby check the power of the bureaucratic state, and although its social reforms promise to protect individual rights and democratize the selection of officials, also checking the power of the bureaucratic state, the emergence of a new technocratic-bureaucratic elite of educated people appears almost inevitable under the current system. The nature and forms of power will shift under the new system. But following the Cultural Revolution's inability to solve either the problem of power or that of bureaucracy, it remains unclear how the immediate producers will be able to establish their authority at every level of society.

(Text completed Spring 1980)

NOTES

1. Chen Boda, Jiang Jieshi, Enemy of the People (Beijing: Xinhua Bookstore, 1949), p. 1.
2. "State Construction Funds Are Raised Internally: Foreign Debts Are Already Paid Prior to Term," Correspondence with the Central Committee of the Soviet Union, January 11, 1966, p. 2.
3. Edwin Pauley, "Report to the President of the United States."
4. Akira Fujimoto, Shin Chugoku no Kokka Zaisei no Kenkyu (A Study on the National Budget of China) (Tokyo: Yuhikaku Book Publishing Company, 1971), p. 84.
5. C. Y. Cheng, Economic Relations between Peking and Moscow, 1949-1963, New York, 1964. F. H. Mah, "Foreign Trade," in A. Eckstein et al., eds., Economic Trends in Communist China, Chicago, 1968.
6. Kojima Reiitsu, "Daiyakushin Seisaku no Keiseikatei" (Formation of the GLF policy), Ajiya Keizai, 12 (1969): 57. Cost standard per cubic meter

is one yuan in the national projects, while it is from 0.3 to 0.6 yuan in commune projects.

7. Collected Statistical Materials on the Chinese Economy, Sino-Japanese Economic Association, March 1977, p. 153.

8. Fang Yan, Renmin ribao (People's Daily), May 25, 1979.

9. Hu Qiaomu, Renmin ribao, October 6, 1978.

10. Article by Fang Hai, Hongqi (Red Flag), 1976, no. 4.

11. Article by Yao Lanfu, Jingji yanjiu (Economic Research), 1978, no. 12, pp. 17-18.

12. State Planning Commission briefing to Japanese delegate, Sino-Japanese Economic Association, May 1979.

13. As to the full text, see Nichu Keizai Koryu 1979 Choseika ni Sogoizon o Motomete (Japan-Sino Economic Exchange 1979 Mutual Interdependence in the Adjustment Period), Sino-Japanese Economic Association, 1980, p. 12.

14. Agricultural Ministry briefing, May 1979.

15. State Planning Commission briefing, May 1979.

16. Beijing Review (Japanese edition), 1979, no. 2, p. 37.

17. Explanation by a worker, May 1979.

18. Wang Jiamo, "Wenti shi fou zaiyu jileirui guogao" (Is the Accumulation Ratio Too High or Not? This Is the Point.) This seems to be a paper distributed to the participants of a scientific discussion meeting. The date of the meeting remains unclear. This covers basic data on population, GNP, rate of accumulation, and so on.

19. State Planning Commission briefing, May 1979.

20. The figure is calculated from information in Japanese newspapers since 1978.

21. World Bank, Annual Report 1980, pp. 132, 134, 135.

22. Article by editorial writer, Renmin ribao, May 31, 1979.

23. Guangming ribao, May 23, 1979.

Tang Tsou, Marc Blecher, and Mitch Meisner[1]

NATIONAL AGRICULTURAL POLICY: THE DAZHAI MODEL AND LOCAL CHANGE IN THE POST-MAO ERA

Events since the death of Mao Zedong on September 9, 1976, to the present have made it clear that the Third Plenum of December 1978 was a decisive turning point in the history of the Chinese Communist movement.[2] The revolutionary impetus has yielded to a search for a distinctively Chinese path toward economic development, "socialist democracy," and "socialist legality." The progressive expansion of political control over all spheres of social life and individual activity has been superseded by a trend toward giving various social groups and individuals a larger sphere of autonomy free from arbitrary interference by the Party or the government. This trend has been accompanied by a drastic change in the substance of Party policies and the methods of Party leadership in the direction of paying greater heed to the felt needs and immediate material interests of groups and individuals. The Party's deeply rooted practice of using political movements and administrative fiat to promote economic development has come under repeated criticism. It has been replaced by an emphasis on "objective economic laws" and "natural laws" in the formulation of economic policies and in the reform of the economic system. The use of material incentives, the assignment of an increasingly larger role to market mechanisms, the acceptance of limitations imposed by existing economic conditions, the recognition of the severe constraints of China's high population-land ratio, and the constant emphasis placed on the variations in natural environment in different parts of China have become prominent ingredients in the making of decisions. In virtually every sphere of concrete policies in domestic affairs, the programs initiated by Mao since the second half of 1957 have been drastically reversed. The mistakes of the Cultural Revolution, now called the "ten years of calamity," have been traced not only to certain tendencies within the Party from the very beginning but also to certain aspects of Leninism, not to mention Stalinism. Few nations have undergone such a drastic reversal of direction and such a comprehensive search for answers in so short a period of time.

This period of reversal of policies gives us an opportunity to observe the relationship between macro-political changes and the responses which these evoke at micro- and individual levels.

1. THE RISE AND FALL OF THE
LEADERS OF DAZHAI AND XIYANG

Among the best places to observe this linkage are Dazhai Brigade and Xiyang County. As national models, Dazhai and Xiyang reached the zenith of their prominence in the period after the two national conferences on building Dazhai-type counties held in September 1975 and December 1976.

Chen Yonggui, the Party secretary of Dazhai Village since 1952 or 1953, had been the most powerful figure in Xiyang since 1967 in his capacity as the chairman of the Xiyang Revolutionary Committee and a member of a Party core group. In March 1967 he was identified as one of the vice-chairmen of the Shanxi Revolutionary Committee, one of the first two revolutionary committees organized after Mao's call for the seizure of power in January 1967. From 1971 on and after the system of Party committees was reestablished, he also served as the secretary of the Xiyang County Party committee, the Party secretary of Jinzhong District,[3] and a secretary of the Shanxi provincial Party committee. At the national level, he was elected a member of the Ninth Central Committee of the CCP in April 1969, and a member of the Politburo of the Tenth Central Committee in August 1973. He was appointed a vice-premier in January 1975, at the time of the first session of the Fourth National People's Congress (NPC). In August 1977 he was reelected a member of the Politburo of the Eleventh Plenum.

But in December 1979 Chen Yonggui was removed without any publicity from his position as the secretary of the Party Committee of Xiyang County to be replaced by Liu Shugang, who had served for several years prior to that time as a deputy secretary in charge of industry. In August 1980, he was only identified as a member of the Party branch at Dazhai.[4] In September, Chen's resignation from his position as vice-premier was approved at the Third Session of the Fifth NPC amid severe criticisms of Dazhai and Xiyang made by the delegates, some of which were published in the official news-papers. During this period of time, important changes in personnel occurred at all levels of Dazhai Brigade, Jinzhong District, and Shanxi Province. Chen lost his positions in the provincial and district Party committees. So did his deputies on the Xiyang and Jinzhong Party committees and many of his supporters in the provincial-level units and other counties of Shanxi, including Guo Fenglian.

From mid-June to November, the Xiyang Party committee and later the "principal responsible person in Xiyang County,"[5] i.e. Chen Yonggui, were accused of all sorts of mistakes in methods of leadership, principally but not exclusively revolving around two major decisions made by Chen: first, the inauguration in 1975 of the project of diverting a large part of the water of a river flowing westward to the east to benefit Xiyang County and, second, the falsification of the total grain production figures of the county from 1973 to 1977.

According to a broadcast in Beijing reported in the Foreign Broadcasting Information Service (FBIS) on April 16, 1981, Dazhai's Party members had by secret ballot elected in December 1980 a new Party branch committee. The former deputy brigade leader Jia Changsuo, who had been dismissed for experimenting with small work contracts, was elected secretary of the Party branch. Three members of the old Party branch (Song Liying, Liang Bianliang, and Jia Laigeng) were reelected. The other three of the new seven-member Party committee were newcomers. Referring indirectly to Chen Yonggui, the broadcast said that because he had committed leftist mistakes and had not made a self-criticism, "naturally he was not elected this time."

On February 12, 1981, Renmin ribao published a report on the self-criticism, made by the provincial Party committee of Shanxi under its new first secretary, of the "leftist" errors which it had committed in guiding the movement to learn from Dazhai in that province. But it also criticized both Dazhai and Xiyang for having pushed forward the "so-called continued revolution under the dictatorship of the proletariat." A commentary by the Party Center was published alongside this self-criticism. It asserted that since the beginning of the Cultural Revolution, Dazhai had become a model in "implementing 'the leftist line' and that the movement to learn from Dazhai had created serious consequences."[6] Dazhai was finally and definitively repudiated.

Thus, the cycle of the rise and fall of Xiyang County and of Dazhai Brigade as the sole national models at two different levels of governance and production has been completed. So has the reversal of Mao's policies of agricultural and rural development throughout the nation.

2. DAZHAI AND XIYANG IN NATIONAL POLITICS: THE SPECIFIC FEATURES OF DAZHAI AS DISTINGUISHED FROM THE "BASIC EXPERIENCE" OF DAZHAI AND THE CRITERIA OF DAZHAI-TYPE COUNTIES (1964-1975)

The seeds of the total repudiation of the "movement to learn from Dazhai," Xiyang as the first Dazhai-type county, and Dazhai itself for the period during and after the Cultural Revolution must be sought in the political processes which gradually developed after the antirightist campaign of 1957, which took definite shape during the Cultural Revolution from 1966-1976, and which had their roots deep in the history of the CCP and indeed in Imperial China. When in 1964 Mao called on the nation to learn from Dazhai,[7] Dazhai not only became a national model, but was also pushed into the maelstrom of national politics which was then rapidly developing and was to engulf the whole nation during the Cultural Revolution. The point of departure of this political development was the slogan "never forget class struggle," a slogan distilled from remarks made by Mao at the Tenth Plenum in 1962. Later, this class struggle was specified as a struggle between two lines, socialism and revisionism, and its targets were first identified as "the capitalist-roaders in authority within the Party" and still later as "the bourgeoisie within the Party."

Among other reasons, Mao elevated Dazhai into a national model in 1964 in order to counter the "Taoyuan Experience," an experiment to revitalize agricultural development and to reimpose order and discipline in the rural areas. This experiment was undertaken by Wang Guangmei, the wife of Liu Shaoqi, at a brigade in Funing County, Hebei. In retrospect, it was inevitable that Dazhai's position would suffer once Mao's ideological and political lines, as well as his specific policies on agricultural development, were reversed.

Dazhai and Xiyang represented a specific approach to agricultural and rural development at a definite stage of China's economic growth. The specific features of this approach are outlined by us in an earlier article.[8] Briefly summarized, these were: the use of the brigade, rather than the production team, as the basic unit of account; the collective cultivation of private plots; the sharp restrictions imposed on rural markets and their total elimination in some places; the attempt to develop collective raising of pigs; the prevention of the outflow of agricultural labor to the towns and cities seeking gainful employment either as individuals or under collective auspices; the total mobilization of underemployed labor to undertake basic farmland construction; the system of labor management and remuneration known as "self-assessment and public discussion" to determine the number of work-points earned by a peasant; the use of the same system for grain distribution; the building of collectively owned housing; the imposition of an upper limit on work-point values to enlarge public accumulation for the purpose of reinvestment and collective provision of public welfare; and finally (and specifically confined to Dazhai commune), preparation for a transition to the commune as the basic unit of account.

These measures formed a coherent whole. In the sphere of organization, the idea behind these measures was that the collective unit should assume as many functions as was feasible in production, distribution, the supply of facilities and services to satisfy individual needs (such as housing, medical care, sewing, etc.), and the provision of social welfare, while the role of individuals should shrink except insofar as they work through organizational channels for the collective unit. To put it simply, the collective sector of socioeconomic life should expand and the private sector should contract as much as possible. In terms of the relationship between production and income, the major principle was that economic growth had to go hand in hand with "common prosperity" for everyone, which was to be achieved not merely by the provision of a floor under the most disadvantaged groups and individuals but also by narrowing the gap between the most productive and the least productive persons, by expanding the scope of collectively provided goods and services, and by keeping the cash income of the individual peasants in the richer villages at a lower level than warranted by the rise in the collective income of these villages as a result of economic growth. The relationship of growth and increased equality was seen to be reciprocal; economic growth would

provide the material base for increased equality, while the latter
was also considered to be a positive factor in contributing to a rise
in production. An idea implicit in both the ideals and the organizational structure was that the larger the unit of account, the higher
was the level of equality and production which could be achieved.

Dazhai Village, which adopted these specific measures in agriculture and rural development over a period of seventeen years
starting in 1960, was a product of very special historical, political,
and ecological factors which did not necessarily exist elsewhere.
But after 1964, particularly after the beginning of the Cultural Revolution, the notion that there should be only one national model in
agricultural development became a "guiding idea." The idea of one
national model was extended to industrial development through
Mao's slogan, "in industry, learn from Daqing [oil field] ." The
eight model works in the sphere of theatrical performances reflected the same mentality. This idea of "one model" stood in
sharp contrast to the wide variations in China's natural environment, the complexity of modern socioeconomic life, and the diverse
strands in China's own tradition. The renewed recognition of
China's great diversity accompanied by a reemphasis on the importance of tailoring policy to local conditions, specific circumstances, and special characteristics in various areas of human
activities, all themes in Mao's own thinking in his early years, led
to the downgrading of the Daqing approach to industrial development
and the virtual disappearance of the eight model works as well
as the repudiation of Dazhai and Xiyang as the only national
models.

Insofar as the movement to learn from Dazhai was concerned,
the moderate Chinese leaders at the very top, economic planners,
many cadres at the local levels, and most peasants at the grass
roots had realized from the very beginning that many of the specific
features adopted by Dazhai at different periods could not be successfully implemented elsewhere in China. Thus, attempts were
made to interpret the model of Dazhai at a very high level of gen-
erality without mentioning its specific features. This interpretation
of the meaning of Dazhai as a national model had to satisfy at once
Mao's call for "learning from Dazhai" and allow the various local
units to adopt programs suitable to their natural environment and
the stage of their economic and political development. The first
attempt was made by Zhou Enlai. In his "Report on the Work of
the Government" made to the first session of the Third National

People's Congress held in late 1964, Zhou made what was called a "scientific" summary of the Dazhai experience in terms of three very broad principles: first, the principle of putting politics in command and letting ideas take the lead; second, the spirit of self-reliance and hard struggle; third, the Communist style of loving the state and loving the collective units.[9]

In 1967, Chen Yonggui seized power in Xiyang County, not with the support of students from outside or even in that county itself but by organizing a coalition of local cadres, mainly at the commune and brigade levels, and local peasant leaders, and by coopting some cadres at the county level. By 1970, Xiyang had become the first county in the nation which had, in the view of the more radical leaders, successfully learned from Dazhai in the preceding three years. A conference on Agriculture in the Northern Region was held in 1970 to push forward the movement to learn from Dazhai and Xiyang County. What occurred at this conference remains something of a mystery to outside observers. But it is clear that many leading officials opposed the extension of the specific measures of Dazhai to the whole country. In a report on the conference, the State Council, where the influence of the moderate leaders remained strong, made a basic distinction between the fundamental experience of Dazhai, which should be emulated, and its concrete measures, which should not be copied by other units "without regard to their own conditions."[10] This warning was reiterated in a directive issued by the Party Center on December 26, 1971.

The first national conference on building Dazhai-type counties was held in September 1975, when the conflict between Deng Xiaoping and Jiang Qing was rapidly coming to a head and when Jiang Qing was launching a fierce counterattack against Deng, as we shall show. The conference was organized under the leadership of Vice-Premier Hua Guofeng and held first in Xiyang County and later in Beijing. Chen naturally played the most prominent role in the conference after Hua.

In his concluding report at the conference, Hua listed six criteria for a Dazhai-type county: (1) the existence of a leadership nucleus in the county Party committee which firmly implements the line and policies of the Party; (2) the establishment of the dominant position of poor and lower-middle peasants and the ability to struggle resolutely against capitalist activities and to supervise and reform class enemies effectively; (3) the participation in labor of the cadres at the three levels of the county, commune, and brigade in collective production like the cadres in Xiyang; (4) rapid progress and good results in basic farmland construction, mechanization in agriculture, and scientific farming; (5) the continued growth of the collective economy, with the production and income of the poor communes, brigades, and teams reaching or surpassing the present levels of the communes, brigades, and teams in the middle range of their localities; (6) all-around development of farming, forestry, animal husbandry, sideline production and fishery, great increases in production, great contributions to the state, and gradual improvement in the livelihood of the members of the commune.[11] Of these six criteria, only the second had ominous ideological and political implications and could be used to justify ultraleftist policies and the arbitrary use of political power. But the various local units could still subtly evade these consequences by their own definitions of what constituted "capitalist activities."

In his concluding report, Hua apparently endeavored to effect a compromise among the views of the moderate leaders as expressed in the Party Center's directive on agriculture in December 1971, the ultraleftist ideas underlying Zhang Chunqiao's article in Hongqi (Red Flag) in April 1975, and the specific features of the Dazhai-Xiyang model. He carved out for himself a middle position in the political struggle. This middle position satisfied the moderate leaders because they could continue to pursue their current policies by emphasizing the fourth and sixth criteria while biding their time, further working out their own reformist ideas about agriculture, and waiting for a more opportune moment to turn these ideas into Party policies. It rallied the support of Dazhai leaders because they were now given a prominent position in the formulation and implementation of national policy in agriculture.

But the results of the conference did not satisfy the "Gang of Four." The full text of Hua's speech was not published in Hongqi, the theoretical journal of the CCP then under the partial control of Yao Wenyuan. The political significance of the First Dazhai Conference was that Hua took over leadership of agricultural development, established a close relationship with Dazhai leaders, once again identified himself as an orthodox Maoist while keeping himself some distance from the "Gang of Four," and carved out a middle position between the moderate leaders and the ultraleftists.

3. DAZHAI AND THE "GANG OF
FOUR" (1975-1976)

Shortly after the end of the first conference on building Dazhai-type counties in September 1975, the political struggle for succession took a drastic turn against Deng and in favor of the "Gang of Four." It is to be recalled that in spite of the all-out opposition of the "Gang of Four," Deng was appointed a vice-premier of the State Council in January 1975 to take charge of all its work on behalf of the seriously ill Zhou Enlai. He downgraded Mao's call for class struggle and put it on a par with the need to preserve "stability and unity" and a program of economic development. Mao, however, had serious disagreements with Deng's program of economic development which downgraded the revolutionary class struggle. In November, a campaign to "beat back the right-deviationist wind of trying to reverse correct verdicts" was launched. Deng was the target of severe criticism although his name was not mentioned. It was later said that the campaign had been personally initiated and led by Mao himself.

The death of Zhou Enlai in January 1976 made Deng's position utterly untenable. In February 1976 Hua was appointed the acting premier of the State Council. Deng disappeared into limbo. Two days after the Tiananmen incident on April 5, Deng was dismissed from all his positions but was allowed to keep his Party membership. Hua Guofeng was appointed the first vice-chairman of the Central Committee and the premier of the State Council to take over the leadership of the Party and government under Mao's general guidance. The balance of power shifted sharply to the left with the "Gang of Four" as the most united and vociferous power bloc in the Politburo. Afterward, a campaign to criticize Deng by name moved toward a crescendo in the spring and early summer.

As was the usual practice, all of the well-known units in China had to take a public position either through articles published under their bylines or through articles written by correspondents of official newspapers reporting their denunciations of Deng and his policies. Not surprisingly, an article published on June 2, 1976, in Renmin ribao under the byline of Dazhai Brigade attacked Deng's remark: "In order to limit bourgeois right, there must be a material foundation. Without the latter, how can we limit bourgeois right?" It asserted that to the contrary, Dazhai had self-consciously put a limit on "bourgeois right" even when it was extremely

poor; its cadres had always participated in physical labor in production and shared weal and woe with all its members.[12] Thus,
Dazhai adopted the slogan first raised by Zhang Chunqiao as early
as 1958 and expounded in his article prominently published in the
authoritative journal Hongqi in April 1975. After Dazhai and Xiyang
fell into line, Renmin ribao published a dispatch which summarized
the experience of the Xiyang Party committee in criticizing Deng,
"beating back the right-deviationist wind of trying to reverse correct verdicts," and promoting the movement to learn from Dazhai
in the past five or six months.[13] The publication of this dispatch
signified that the Party Center, with the "Gang of Four" as its most
united political bloc, now renewed its support for the movement to
learn from Dazhai.

4. DAZHAI AND XIYANG AT THE
HEIGHT OF THEIR PROMINENCE
(1975-1977)

Mao died on September 9, 1976. On October 16, the "Gang of
Four" was arrested according to a decision made jointly by Hua
Guofeng, Ye Jianying, and Wang Dongxing and supported by most
Party and military leaders at the top. With the removal of the
"Gang of Four," Hua and many of the leaders who had risen to the
top from the middle and lower levels during the Cultural Revolution
came to represent the Maoist ideological and political line as it had
developed during those ten years. They now occupied the left side
of the political spectrum.

From then on, political development in China revolved around the
conflict between two political tendencies. One is the tendency to
uphold the Maoist line in virtually all spheres. The other is the
tendency to reform the political process and the political system
as they have developed since 1957 and, with regard to some specific
features, even before that time. The reformists are those who had
suffered one kind of persecution or another since 1957, particularly
during the Cultural Revolution.

Following the lead of Hua, who was elected chairman of the CCP
by the Politburo in October, Chen Yonggui supported the arrest of
the "Gang of Four." Thus, his political influence was further enhanced. A second national conference on building Dazhai-type
counties was convened in December 1976. The purpose of the
conference was to combine a condemnation of the "Gang of Four"

with the perpetuation of the Maoist approach to rural development, of which "learning from Dazhai" was a key element. In repudiating the program of the "Gang of Four," Hua's speech to the conference also incorporated the moderate leaders' program of the four modernizations and rejected the ultra-leftists' contention that the program was based on the erroneous "theory of productive forces" — a theory which posits productive forces as the sole determinant of political development and, therefore, their development as the primary policy goal of socialist governments and the main criterion of their success.

Chen's speech combined an emphasis on increasing production through mechanization, scientific farming, basic farmland construction, the development of commune-owned industries and sideline production with orthodox Maoist slogans like "unless one blocks the capitalist road, one cannot take a long step toward socialism" and with the Maoist policy of firmly correcting "the tendencies to enlarge private plots, to expand free markets, to increase the number of small enterprises or collective units with sole responsibility for their profits and losses, and to fix farm output quotas for individual households" with each on its own. At this conference, the locally developed experience in Dazhai coincided with the ideological and political line which gained temporary predominance at the highest level.

After the conference, the movement to learn from Dazhai and to build Dazhai-type counties was once more in the limelight of national publicity. To push forward this movement, the People's Publishing House of Shanxi published in June 1977 a book entitled The Dazhai Experience which represented one of the best efforts to rationalize the Dazhai experience in terms of Mao's ideas as developed in his last years, but which also contained much new information on Dazhai's specific features.

At the height of its influence in 1977, Dazhai Commune began in August a serious discussion among the masses of the advantage of a transition from the brigade to the commune as the basic accounting unit.[14] The rationale given for the desirability of the transition was that brigade accounting was no longer suitable to the changed conditions brought about by past efforts in economic development. Projects of basic farmland construction which could be undertaken by a single brigade had been completed. Larger projects could only be undertaken by the commune as a whole, which had more material and manpower resources at its command. Moreover, commune accounting would enable the various brigades to specialize in certain types of agricultural tasks most suitable to their natural conditions. For example, part of the sown acreage in the hilly brigade of Nannao could be utilized to plant trees for producing fresh and dry fruits or for use as lumber, while its loss in grain production could be made up by the commune under a system of commune accounting. Self-sufficiency in grain would then become a task to be achieved not by any single brigade but a commune. The construction in 1975-76 of 500 mu of good cropland on the sandy and stony banks of a river at Gaojialing and the planting of hundreds of thousands of trees in Mengshan Brigade in August 1977 by 6,000 peasants from various other brigades were mentioned as examples of the merits of raising the level of the unit of account.[15]

In the transition, brigade enterprises would be transferred to the commune, which would compensate the brigades for these enterprises at a "fair price to be discussed." In agricultural production after the transition, the commune would assign quotas to be fulfilled by the brigades based on averages of their production for a number of years in the past. One idea advanced was that the brigades would keep everything produced above their quotas for themselves. The commune would establish a monthly wage system of 12 grades, ranging from 9 to 45 yuan with a difference of 3 yuan between each grade, covering supplementary labor and full labor. An individual's wage could be lowered or raised every three months or every year, depending on his work contribution. A system of retirement would be instituted for peasants when they reached the age of sixty. It was said that in the view of "the masses," the time was ripe for the transition. They were now waiting for the approval of the state. In an interview conducted on November 4, 1977, Vice-Premier Chen asserted that since the income of the commune enterprises consisted of more than 50 percent of the total income of the commune and brigades, further development of production would be hindered unless a transition was made to the level of commune accounting. This attempt to make the commune the basic accounting unit was sharply criticized after 1978.

5. THE EMERGENCE OF THE RURAL
PROGRAM OF THE REFORMERS (1976-1980)

Side by side with the continuous ascendancy of Dazhai and Xiyang, a political and ideological countercurrent rapidly developed. Almost invisible at the beginning, it was to become within four years a tidal wave sweeping everything before it. The political forces in this countercurrent consisted of the following elements: almost all of the leaders and cadres at every level who had been disgraced, persecuted, or pushed aside during the Cultural Revolution and during the purge of anti-Party elements after the Lushan Conference of 1959; all intellectuals, scientists, technical personnel, educators, and other professionals who had suffered from one kind of denunciation or another since 1957; and those moderate leaders who had reluctantly gone along with the ultra-leftist policies of Mao during the Cultural Revolution and had tried to keep the economy and the political system functioning as best they could under the protection of Zhou Enlai. These leaders and cadres enjoyed the diffuse and inarticulate support of the overwhelming majority of the urban population and many peasants in different localities — persons who had lost faith in the ability of the Party and government to improve their livelihood. The reformers' aim was nothing less than the restructuring of the whole system while endeavoring to maintain continuity with the past by affirming and reinterpreting the four general principles underlying the Party-regime: socialism, the dictatorship of the proletariat, the leadership of the Party, and Marxism-Leninism-Mao Zedong Thought.

The agricultural and rural program of the reformers has now gradually taken form, but many of its components are still tentatively held. This is not the place for a full discussion of this program. Only certain of those principles and practices which have direct bearing on the movement to learn from Dazhai and to build Dazhai-type counties will be briefly outlined as a prelude to an account of the downfall of Xiyang and the final repudiation of Dazhai.

First, the aim of economic development, particularly agricultural production, is to meet the immediate material interests and felt needs of the peasants, lifting them up from abject poverty and from the subsistence level and raising their standard of living as fast as the Chinese economy permits. "Production increase is a means. The improvement of the people's livelihood is the aim."[16]

Second, this aim is to be achieved not through the strengthening of the collective economy alone, but also through the encouragement of individual initiative and effort outside the collective sector of agriculture so long as the collective sector is maintained to perform those functions which it has effectively discharged in the past.

Private plots are to be protected and in some cases enlarged. Sideline production by peasant households is encouraged. All pre-existing free markets have reopened, and most of the restrictions have been removed. Peasants are permitted to seek gainful employment individually or under collective auspices in their spare time and in slack seasons. Increases in peasants' income from family sideline production or individual economic activities have been popularized and praised rather than condemned as a form of "capitalism." In short, the private sector should expand both in relative and in absolute terms as a supplement to the collective sector.

Third, in the collective sector, the production team is considered to be the key in farming activities, while the commune and the brigade take charge of small-scale enterprises in processing agricultural products and other tasks which the team is not able to undertake alone. The autonomy of the production team in planning agricultural production is protected so long as state targets and general guidelines are met.

Fourth, production teams are encouraged to divide themselves into permanent work groups so long as the land and major agricultural implements are collectively owned by the teams. Under certain conditions, a team can conclude contracts with its individual households for the delivery of certain amounts of agricultural produce. Everything produced above the quota specified in a contract belongs to the household, while failure to meet the quota is subject to penalties. The responsibility for fulfilling the state quota is thus subdivided among, and devolved to, smaller and smaller units.

Fifth, the peasant's reward must be closely linked to his work. This linkage must be immediately obvious to the peasants. "Piece-work" is preferred over "time work" whenever the former can be used in agriculture. Grain distribution to the peasants should be linked partly to work performance.

Sixth, cost effectiveness must be taken into account not only from the viewpoint of the state and collective units but also from the standpoint of the individual peasant. Cost-benefit analysis must be a part of economic planning and a basis for judging the peasants' economic activities. To decrease cost is one of the many methods used "to lighten the burden of the peasants."

Seventh, a logical corollary of cost effectiveness is that the plans of agricultural development in different localities must be guided by a realistic understanding of the vast variations in the natural conditions of China. "Adopting suitable methods in light of local conditions" has replaced the use of a single national model. "Taking grain as the key link" is given less emphasis, while "all-around development" in the planting of other crops, forestry, animal husbandry, sideline production, and fishery is underscored. Localities where the land and climate are best suited to agricultural production other than grain will be supplied with grain by the state obtained from grain-producing areas. In effect, the policy that all local units, ranging from the production team to the province, should give first priority to self-sufficiency in grain supply has been abandoned.

Eighth, the idea that mechanization is the best method for agricultural development and should thus be given the first priority in economic planning has been abandoned. Its place has been taken by the use of new seeds, better fertilizers, and the more effective use of biological and chemical methods.

Ninth, ecological considerations must be taken into account in all projects of farmland construction and reclamation.

Tenth, the trend toward the expansion of the public sector in housing, medical care, and social welfare has been checked. An individual's loss of social benefits and his increased responsibility to provide for his own needs are compensated for by raising his income.

Eleventh, mass movements and mobilization have been abandoned as methods of agricultural development. Day-to-day and routinized work by individual peasants and collective units of all levels should not be interrupted. Policy vacillation from one extreme to the other is to be avoided so that the peasants' expectations can be stabilized and regularized. Political movements are not to be launched. Tumultuous class struggle on a large scale is now considered a thing of the past. Most landlords and rich peasants have been reclassified as regular members of the teams, brigades, and communes and should no longer be subjected to discrimination. All of their descendants are to enjoy the same privileges as everybody else.

These principles and practices which are specifically related to agricultural and rural development are linked to the general economic program of "readjustment, restructuring of the economic system, consolidation, and improvement." They are ultimately justified by the epistemological principle that "practice is the sole criterion for testing truth" and the idea that economic work must be guided by laws of economics which like other laws of nature cannot be changed by human will or political decisions.

6. THE UNDERCURRENT OF OPPOSITION
TO THE MOVEMENT TO LEARN
FROM DAZHAI (1977)

The emergence, development, and triumph of the ideas of the reformers inevitably entailed the progressive decline and final repudiation of the movement to learn from Dazhai and Dazhai itself after it had been dragged into the maelstrom of national politics. This process of decline and fall began almost invisibly and gathered increasingly greater momentum until it reached a crescendo in the second half of 1980 and ended with a final judgment rendered by the Party Center in February 1981.

As early as November 13, 1976, Renmin ribao published an article which attacked the "Gang of Four" for forcibly closing the rural markets in localities where it was impossible for the sales-and-supply cooperatives to provide peasants with the necessary commodities and to purchase their privately produced goods, although it still recognized the negative effects of rural markets on the movement to learn from Dazhai. Shortly after the Eleventh Congress in August 1977, another Renmin ribao editorial urged the rural cadres to implement correctly the socialist principle that each person should do his best according to his ability, that the distribution of rewards should be proportional to his work performance, that he who labors more should receive more rewards, and that he who does not labor should not eat.

In November 1977, the Anhui provincial Party committee under the new leadership of First Secretary Wan Li adopted a regulation which permitted the production team to divide itself into temporary or fixed work groups which were assigned fixed tasks, fixed standards of quality, fixed time periods of work, and fixed work-points. Even more startling to the orthodox Maoists, it also allowed the assignment to a specific individual of tasks which could be performed by one person.[17] The above examples show that even at the height of the movement to learn from Dazhai, many localities openly adopted measures which ran directly counter to the specific features of the Dazhai-Xiyang model.

7. THE DECLINE OF XIYANG
AND DAZHAI: THE PRACTICAL
IMPLICATIONS OF TWO ABSTRACT
POSTULATES IN EPISTEMOLOGY
AND ECONOMIC DEVELOPMENT (1978)

The decline of Xiyang and Dazhai was preceded by the publication of two major articles which formed the ideological justification for the complete destruction of the Maoist line of the Cultural Revolution period. These articles also marked the beginning of the end of the movement to learn from Dazhai and to build Dazhai-type counties, although few persons realized this implication at the time. The first article, "Practice Is the Sole Criterion for Testing Truth," was published on May 11, 1978.[18] It was implicitly endorsed by Deng Xiaoping in an important speech on June 2. The significance of this article was that it provided the epistemological postulate for the refutation of the leading guideline of the orthodox Maoists that "whatever the decision made by Chairman Mao was, we will resolutely support; whatever Chairman Mao's directive was, we will unswervingly obey."[19] In other words, Mao's decisions and directives must now be judged by a basic epistemological postulate which was derived from Mao's notion of the unity of theory and practice itself. If they are found to be incorrect, they should be rejected. Mao's ideas are no longer sacrosanct. This epistemological postulate was to become the ultimate justification for a total reevaluation of Mao's role in China's political development after 1957, particularly during the Cultural Revolution. The other article was "Observe Economic Laws, Speed up the Four Modernizations," a speech given by Hu Qiaomu in July 1978 at a State Council meeting.[20] For our purpose here, its pertinent argument is that political decisions can bring enormous damage to economic development, if they are not made in conformity with "objective economic laws" which, like the laws of nature, cannot be changed by human will.

Meanwhile, the Party Center launched an indirect criticism of the specific features of the Xiyang model. In early July, the Party Center sent down a document on the "experience in Xiangxiang County" in Hunan in decreasing the burdens of the peasants.[21] Among other things, it denounced the former practice of the upper-level units in using the labor power, funds, and material resources of the production teams without compensation as well as the enormous increase in nonproductive personnel, work, and expenditures. It criticized the overextension of the scale of basic farmland construction beyond the ability of the teams and the peasants to undertake these tasks. It showed how the elimination of these abuses had led to an increase in the income of the teams and the peasants.

In response to this document, the Xiyang Party committee made its first officially published self-criticism.[22] In it, the county Party committee admitted the existence of the following problems: Its method of labor management gave rise to inefficiency in the use of labor. Many brigades did not seriously assess the work of the peasants in awarding them work-points. There was a tendency toward "equal-divisionism," i.e., granting the same number of work-points to peasants whose contributions to collective work were widely different. In many communes and brigades there were too many nonproductive personnel who, unlike the cadres at Dazhai, did not engage in labor. Obviously, basic farmland construction also imposed a heavy burden on the brigades and the peasants. In interviews conducted in August 1980, the officials of the county admitted there had been in 1978, 4,800 of the county's best workers in "the special task force for basic farmland construction" at a time when the total labor force of the county, including both male and female and full-time and part-time workers, had numbered only 76,000 persons. The work-points earned by these peasants and the food consumed by them were given by the brigades while the county paid only a daily subsidy of 0.40 yuan per person each day. By 1979, the number had been reduced to slightly over 3,000. By 1980, it had decreased to 1,600 and further reduction was being planned.

The decline of Dazhai and Xiyang as national models became obvious during this period. Although Chen Yonggui still chaired the national conference on basic farmland construction held in July-August 1978, it was Vice-Premier Li Xiannian, a moderate leader, who gave the opening speech. Although Li asserted that to develop agriculture to a higher level, the Chinese had to rely ultimately on learning from Dazhai, he also noted that many mistakes had been made in the movement. He reiterated the Party's policy of allowing the peasants to enjoy "small freedoms." He warned the cadres against arbitrary interference with the peasants' private plots and sideline production. He told them not to eliminate rural markets wantonly. It was Ji Dengkui who gave the concluding speech. He had apparently replaced Chen Yonggui as the leading official in charge of agriculture under the general guidance of Hua and Li.

Paralleling this gradual decline was a growing debate over the epistemological principle that "practice is the sole criterion for testing truth." The reformists had to win this ideological battle not only to destroy the Maoist ideological and political line of the Cultural Revolution period, but also to free the Chinese from the fetters on their thinking and to open up a new era of intellectual and institutional development. For our analysis, it is important to note that this epistemological postulate, as well as the leading idea that "objective economic laws" must be obeyed in making economic decisions and policies, was indeed used as the basic justification for a reevaluation of the movement to learn from Dazhai and to build Dazhai-type counties.

By December, the debate over the epistemological principle that "practice is the sole criterion for testing truth" had largely but not completely been won by the reformists. Between May and December 1978, over 500 articles on the subject upholding the slogan were published in newspapers and journals all over China. Wang Qian, the first secretary of Shanxi since 1974 and a strong supporter of Chen Yonggui, fell into line rather late in the debate. In an article published on November 6, 1978, in Renmin ribao, Wang directly linked the epistemological principle and the need to observe "objective economic laws" with agricultural development in Shanxi. In what amounted to a rather ambiguous self-criticism, he admitted that for many years the officials in the province had erroneously criticized the sideline production of the brigades and communes (including the sideline production of the commune members' households) as "a spontaneous capitalist tendency." He noted that although grain production had gone up, the production of industrial crops had declined and that forestry and animal husbandry had not developed very quickly. He now understood the distinction between the "basic experience" of Dazhai as defined by Zhou Enlai and its special features. He adhered to the position that in learning from Dazhai's "concrete experience" the various localities had to take account of differences in conditions and adopt only those measures which had proven effective, should not use a single standard to measure everything, and should not try to impose uniformity in all matters in every locality when local conditions were different from Dazhai's.

8. THE THIRD PLENUM: THE
ADOPTION OF TWO DRAFT DOCUMENTS
ON AGRICULTURAL DEVELOPMENT
AND RURAL INSTITUTIONS

The Third Plenum of the Eleventh Central Committee meeting from December 18 to December 22, 1978, was another important step in the decline of the movement to learn from Dazhai. According to a Hong Kong newspaper, Ji Dengkui's report on agriculture still adhered to the orthodox line. It underscored achievements and failed to mention shortcomings. In the debate on the movement to learn from Dazhai, the reformists underscored the mistakes of Ji and Chen in blindly pushing forward that movement and in using a small village of eighty households[23] as a model for 800 million people. They also noted that for China as a whole, increase in agricultural production had lagged far behind the increase in inputs such as chemical fertilizer as well as the increase in manpower in the rural areas. It was said that Ji had been forced to make a self-criticism and to submit a report asking to be relieved of his work.[24] Interviews in Xiyang in 1980 confirmed that shortly afterward Wang Renzhong replaced Ji as the person in charge of agriculture. In his capacity as a vice-premier, he also assumed the chairmanship of the State Committee on Agriculture.

More importantly, the Plenum agreed to distribute to the provincial-level units for discussion and trial use two decisions. These were: "Decisions on Some Questions Concerning the Acceleration of Agricultural Development (Draft)" and "Regulations on the Work in Rural People's Communes (Draft for Trial Use)."[25] Although the movement to learn from Dazhai was reaffirmed in the first document, many of the Party's concrete policies on agriculture and the rural economy as mentioned in its twenty-five points ran counter to the specific features of the Dazhai-Xiyang model. Point three urged the collective units at all levels to implement the principle of distributing rewards in proportion to work done, to correct the mistake of "equal divisionism," to permit the production teams to assign production quotas to work groups, and to give the latter bonuses in case they exceeded their production quotas. It gave distinct preference to the system of grain distribution under which 30-40 percent of the grain is distributed in proportion to the workpoints earned by the peasants, which was not the practice in Dazhai and Xiyang. Point four asserted that private plots, family sideline production, and rural markets are necessary supplements to socialist economy and should not be criticized as "the tail of capitalism" — a direct reference to a slogan popularized by Dazhai. Point five asserted that the production team was the foundation of the system of ownership of means of production by units at all three levels. This system should continue to be stabilized. It was impermissible to raise the basic unit of account from a lower level to a higher level when conditions were not ripe — another implicit reference to the actions of Dazhai-Xiyang leaders and other officials who pushed the Dazhai movement beyond the six guidelines adopted in 1975.

The second document was a revision of a document with the same title adopted in September 1962 which had authorized most of the concrete measures used at one time or another in the period of 1959-1961 to overcome the agricultural crisis. From the long perspective of political development, the most significant provision was Article 50. This article provided that those peasants coming from the families of landlords and rich peasants should all be regarded as members of the commune, enjoying the same rights as other members and should not be discriminated against and that all their children should no longer be treated as persons of landlord and rich peasant origins.

9. THE TERMINATION OF THE
DAZHAI MOVEMENT: THE NATIONAL
POLITICAL CONTEXT

The important but not total victory of the reformers at the Third Plenum over the question of the criterion for testing truth drastically changed the terms of the ideological and political debate, just as the Central Committee's decision to shift the stress of the Party's work to modernization and the election of Chen Yun, the veteran moderate leader specializing in economic work, as a vice-chairman of the Party, at once reflected and accelerated a fundamental change in the direction of China's economic and political development. The Plenum decided "to cancel the erroneous documents issued by the Central Committee in regard to the movement 'to beat back the Right-deviationist wind to reverse correct verdicts.'" This decision was a complete vindication of Deng Xiaoping's policies, adopted in 1975. The Plenum also rehabilitated Peng Dehuai, Tao Zhu, Bo Yibo, Yang Shangkun, and others. It declared that no revolutionary leader, including implicitly Mao himself, can be "free of all shortcomings and errors."

The reformers lost no time in exploiting this victory, in further developing their ideas, and in rapidly pushing forward their programs. In an editorial in Renmin ribao on January 16, 1979, Lin Biao and the "Gang of Four" were accused of pushing an "ultra-leftist, counterrevolutionary, and revisionist line"[26] — thus implicitly but officially repudiating the earlier characterization of their ideas, programs, and actions as "ultra-rightist" or as "leftist in form but rightist in essence." More importantly, the reformers applied the criterion for testing truth to examine Mao's decisions, to reevaluate Mao's role in Chinese politics, and to reassess the Cultural Revolution in an even more thoroughgoing manner than before. The decisions made by the Third Plenum, the adoption of two draft documents on agriculture and the commune system, the reevaluation of the Cultural Revolution, and the increasing momentum toward reform provided the context for the final termination of the movement to learn from Dazhai and to build Dazhai-type counties.

At the end of September, the Fourth Plenum of the Eleventh Central Committee took place. It made two major decisions. First, it discussed and approved the speech to be delivered by Ye Jianying on behalf of the Party Center, the Standing Committee of the NPC, and the State Council at the meeting to celebrate the thirtieth anniversary of the founding of the People's Republic. Second, it "unanimously approved" "the Decisions on Some Questions Concerning the Acceleration of Agricultural Development." Thus, the draft document approved in principle by the Third Plenum was turned into an authoritative document.

In his speech as delivered on September 29, 1979, Ye characterized the Cultural Revolution as a "calamity for our people" and "the most severe reversal to our socialist cause since the founding of the People's Republic."[27] This declaration came only nine months after the Third Plenum had decided to shelve the problem of summing up the shortcomings and mistakes of "this great revolution."[28] It meant that a new evaluation of the Cultural Revolution had been reached, even if Ye did not make detailed analyses of all the important decisions and events during those ten years. Ye observed: "Leaders are not gods. They are not infallible and should therefore not be deified." He went beyond the communique of the Third Plenum in declaring that the Third Plenum had "explicitly

confirmed the unshakable, fundamental Marxist epistemological
tenet that practice is the sole criterion of truth."

10. THE TERMINATION OF THE
DAZHAI MOVEMENT: THE DIRECT ATTACKS
ON THE DAZHAI-XIYANG MODEL
(DECEMBER 1978-SEPTEMBER 1979)

After the draft document adopted in December 1978 on the acceleration of agricultural development had been sent down to the
basic levels for study and trial use, a propaganda campaign was
launched to urge its implementation. In addition, this campaign
in the press criticized all the slogans and specific features of the
Dazhai-Xiyang model as well as the movement to learn from
Dazhai and to build Dazhai-type counties. An important editorial
in the January 22, 1979, issue of Renmin ribao asserted that all
economic units at the three levels of the commune must implement
the principle of the "distribution of rewards according to work
done" and overcome "equal divisionism." They must not wantonly
interfere with the private plots, sideline occupations, and rural
markets. They must regard these as necessary supplements of
the collective rural economy rather than as "the tail of capitalism."
They must not arbitrarily change the system of three-level ownership with the production team as its foundation and absolutely should
not attempt to make the brigade or commune the basic unit of account when the peasants and the various units were still very
poor.[29] Meanwhile, the press carried many reports which gave
specific examples in various parts of China of the disasters brought
about by "equal divisionism," by the attempt to make the brigade
the basic accounting unit in a hurry, by the adoption of leftist policies in agriculture, and by the suppression of the peasant's sideline
occupations and the rural markets. These reports also underscored the positive results achieved after the reversal of these
decisions.[30]
The propaganda campaign and these theoretical analyses fur-
nished the immediate context for the termination of the Dazhai
movement. Shortly after the Third Plenum, Guangming ribao took
the lead in openly and forcefully attacking the movement to learn
from Dazhai. It suggested that henceforth people should no longer
shout such slogans as "unless the capitalist road is blocked, ad-

vance toward socialism cannot be made." Instead, it asserted that
they should now grasp the "central task" of reforming and improving their agricultural techniques.[31] It directed its attack first
on the Dazhai movement in Shanxi Province, the most vulnerable
target among the twenty-nine provincial-level units in China. It
charged that the Dazhai model had been deified in Shanxi and that
the label of "opposing Dazhai" had been used as a bludgeon to attack many cadres from the provincial to the basic levels.

This article was published at roughly the same time that an enlarged meeting of the Shanxi provincial Party committee was held
to sum up the lessons of the movement to learn from Dazhai according to the spirit of the Third Plenum. At this meeting, the
same accusations were made against Shanxi leaders. Many participants charged that the provincial Party committee had allowed the
people in various localities to "chant only the scriptures of Dazhai
and Xiyang" and nothing else and had stressed the necessity for
the whole province to do what Dazhai did. On behalf of the standing
committee of the provincial Party committee, First Secretary Wang
Qian accepted the responsibility of the provincial Party committee
and his own principal responsibility for the problems which had
emerged in the movement to learn from Dazhai.

The position of the Xiyang County Party committee was even more
vulnerable than either the provincial Party committee or Dazhai.
For the whole movement to learn from Dazhai and to build Dazhai-
type counties could be stopped and totally refuted if it could be
shown that the first Dazhai-type county had committed many mistakes and never been a model of advanced development as orthodox
Maoists had claimed. At about the same time, the deputy secretary
of the Xiyang County Party committee, Li Xishen, made a self-
criticism on behalf of the committee even as it also affirmed its
own achievements. Most damaging of all the seven self-criticisms
was the admission that the committee had falsified the production
figure for 1973, when the county had been suffering from a serious
drought. The others dealt with the attack on leading cadres from
the provincial to the county levels in struggle meetings staged in
1967, the transition to brigade-level accounting, the suppression
of sideline production, excessive stress on production of grains,
particularly high-yield varieties such as maize, "equal divisionism"
in income distribution, and overemphasis on top-to-bottom leadership.[32]

By the time that the Fourth Plenum met in late September, the ground had been fully prepared for the termination of the movement to learn from Dazhai. The draft document on "Decisions on Some Questions Concerning the Acceleration of Agricultural Development" was adopted as a definitive statement of policy. Unlike the draft, the now definitive document no longer told "Party committees at all levels" that "they must continue to grasp well the mass movement to learn from Dazhai and to popularize Dazhai-type counties." It merely urged them to continue to guide the vast number of cadres and peasants in learning from the "basic experience" of Dazhai, which was now defined in the words of Zhou Enlai rather than the modified formulation widely used during the Cultural Revolution. In contrast to the draft document, it did not flatly prohibit the assignment of production quotas to individual households. Indeed, it said that "except for special needs of certain sideline production and single households living in remote hilly areas without easy means of transportation," the system of assigning quotas to single households was not to be used.[33] This exception turns out to be rather important, for there are many areas in China and many types of sideline production which can be easily subsumed under it, if it is interpreted liberally as is now the case. Thus, the system which had once been used during the three years of economic difficulty and for which Liu Shaoqi had been unjustly criticized was again given a measure of legitimacy. By late 1980, 20 percent of the production teams in China had adopted this system.

According to the cadres interviewed at Dazhai, soon after Wang Renzhong had replaced Ji Dengkui, he proposed that the movement to learn from Dazhai and to build Dazhai-type counties should now be discontinued in accordance with the general policy of not launching any political movements. The failure in the document adopted at the Fourth Plenum to urge the Party committees to continue to push forward the movement to learn from Dazhai and to build Dazhai-type counties merely represented the formal ratification of Wang's proposal, after the movement had for all practical purposes ceased to exist for some months. Thus the movement to learn from Dazhai launched by Mao in 1964 and the movement to build Dazhai-type counties unofficially begun in 1970 and officially proclaimed in 1975 were for all practical purposes terminated in September 1979.

11. THE REPUDIATION OF THE
DAZHAI-XIYANG MODEL
(SEPTEMBER 1979-FEBRUARY 1981)

Within a week after the Fourth Plenum and even before the official publication of the "Decision on Certain Problems Concerning
the Acceleration of Agricultural Development," the termination of
the movement to learn from Dazhai and to build Dazhai-type counties was made known to the public through a report published in
Renmin ribao. This news dispatch reported a series of nine decisions which had been made by the Xiyang Party committee in
meetings held since August when they had applied the criterion for
testing truth in examining the ultra-leftist errors committed in the
movement to learn from Dazhai.[34] First, the county Party committee had decided that all private plots were to be given back to the
peasants for self-cultivation after the fall harvest.[35] Second, the
"system of management by fixed quotas" should be adopted throughout the county, and the system of dividing a production team into
work groups which would sign contracts with the team to fulfill production quotas should be allowed. Most importantly for our purpose, the Party branch of Dazhai was reported to have said that
Dazhai would also implement the "system of management by fixed
quotas." In effect, Dazhai itself had fallen in line with the Party
Center and decided to give up its famous system of "self-assessment and public discussion" in assigning basic work-points to a
peasant. Third, rural markets had gradually been reopened in
Xiyang since July. Fourth, the county should actively promote the
industrial and sideline production of all communes and brigades.
In this context, the report revealed that according to an unwritten
rule, no other units should be allowed to surpass Dazhai in any kind
of work and thus they had not dared to develop fully their potential
or at least to claim superiority over Dazhai. Actually, many brigades had surpassed Dazhai in developing industrial and sideline
production, forestry, and animal husbandry. The county Party
committee asked: "Why should we not learn from them?" Sixth,
the privately grown trees which had been collectivized should be
given back to the peasants. Seventh, the county Party committee
had revealed that in building "new villages" according to the Dazhai
model, many brigades had torn down old houses but failed to give
the owners adequate compensation or sometimes any compensation
at all. It had decided that readjustment should be made in these

cases. It also compared residential units of a row-house style un-
favorably with old-style houses because the former provided no
space for raising chickens or pigs. Everyone knew that this was a
reference to Dazhai-type architecture. Seventh, the county committee had decided that in the distribution of rewards after the autumn
harvest, the system of "self-assessment and public discussion" both
in determining the basic work-points of the peasants and the distribution of grain should be discontinued in all brigades within the
county. Eighth, it had criticized the overextension of the coverage
of social welfare and ordered a retrenchment. Ninth, it had
decided to correct the abuse of giving too many work-points to
cadres.

On November 3, the Party committee of Jinzhong District published a thoroughgoing self-criticism of its implementation of the
movement to learn from Dazhai. The district Party committee
admitted the error that it had deified Dazhai and mistaken the
Dazhai model in agricultural development for "a brilliant model
of continuing the revolution under the dictatorship of the proletariat" and for "a model of all-around dictatorship, thus magnifying
the class struggle in the countryside." It had turned the movement
to learn from Dazhai into a political movement in class struggle
and a struggle between two lines. One of the results had been to
consider Dazhai the model in all other fields as well, for instance,
in education, public health, finance and trade, physical education,
and cultural affairs. In sum, the "Dazhai experience" had been regarded as "universal truth," omnipotent and all-inclusive.[36]

The committee also revealed several interesting details about
the Dazhai movement in the district. The percentage of the brigade-level accounting units had increased from 39 percent in 1973
to 71 percent in 1977. By 1978, 99 percent of all private plots were
cultivated by collective units. The private sideline production of
the peasants had been subjected to severe limitations. In some
places, it had been limited to "one pig, one tree, one chicken, and
one rabbit." Some kinds of trade in rural markets had been out-
lawed, and some rural markets had been closed altogether. In undertaking farmland construction in the four years up to August
1978, the district had appropriated 11 million jin of food grain,
1.4 million yuan in cash, 15 million workdays in labor power, and
1.2 million yuan worth of materials from brigades which had not
received any benefit from these public projects. Like Xiyang
County in August, the district Party committee decided to abandon

its past policies. Thus, the Xiyang-Dazhai model was in the process of being dismantled.

But Dazhai itself as distinguished from Dazhai as a model was still listed as one of the 351 advanced units in various fields throughout China in the year-end list.[37] Dazhai had a bumper crop in 1979. It was developing two new brigade enterprises. It raised its workday value to 1.80 yuan. Above all, it was in the process of trying to keep in step with the Party Center but, as we shall see, not without some difficulties.

The Fifth Plenum of the Central Committee met in February 1980. Prior to the meeting, many outside observers had predicted that Chen Yonggui would be removed from his positions as a member of the Politburo and a vice-premier of the State Council. But this did not happen. The Plenum made sweeping changes in the institutional arrangement and personnel at the summit of Chinese politics. It reestablished the secretariat of the Central Committee which had disintegrated during the Cultural Revolution and whose functions had been taken over partly by the General Office of the Central Committee and partly by the Cultural Revolution Small Group. It elected Hu Yaobang as the general secretary to head this new organization of eleven men.

After several months of silence, the official newspapers in China began on June 15, 1980, a series of sharp attacks on various policies and programs of Xiyang County. On July 7, the responsibility for all the mistakes was publicly attributed to "the former principal responsible person in Xiyang County," i.e., Chen Yonggui,[38] whereas prior to this time the published criticisms of Xiyang County and the movement to learn from Dazhai had not used this indirect reference to Chen, and all the self-criticisms had been made in the name of the Party committees concerned or by Chen's supporters or followers.

In the public attacks on Chen after June, all aspects of Chen's leadership were severely condemned. These ranged from such concrete charges as the falsification of the figures on grain production through the problems of leadership style to the basic question of his approach to agricultural development. It is obvious from these attacks that the reformists were determined to destroy the Dazhai-Xiyang model completely with or without Chen's cooperation. Since this model stood as a concrete embodiment of the ultra-leftist line, its survival would have blocked the way of sweeping reforms in agricultural development and rural life. As the Dazhai movement from 1964 onward was part and parcel of the Maoist program as developed in Mao's last years, it had to be totally discredited in the process of a reevaluation of Mao's role and a reexamination of its roots in Chinese society and history.

Thus, in February 1981, the Party Center made public its final judgments on Dazhai and the movement to learn from Dazhai.[39] These judgments were embodied in a self-criticism of the Shanxi provincial Party committee and a commentary by the Party Center. But in contrast to the practices of political struggle and its resolution during the Cultural Revolution, the provincial Party committee not only assumed publicly the responsibility for the "Leftist" errors committed in the movement in Shanxi but also absolved all the lower-level Party organizations and the "vast number of cadres" of any responsibility. In turn, the Party Center attributed the "principal responsibility" for the mistakes made in the nationwide movement to the "Party Center at that time." It affirmed the achievements in production and reconstruction of the "overwhelming majority" of the advanced units in learning from Dazhai. As for Dazhai, it used the Cultural Revolution as a line of demarcation. While it affirmed Dazhai as an advanced model in agricultural development prior to that time, it condemned Dazhai during and after the Cultural Revolution as the model in the implementation of the "Leftist" line.

In summing up the lessons, the provincial Party committee asserted that the "Leftist" tendencies in Dazhai and Xiyang had found concentrated expression in the "so-called three basic experiences," i.e., "to make an all-out effort to criticize revisionism," "to make an all-out effort to criticize capitalism," and "to make an all-out effort to build socialism." These three "basic experiences" were summed up by the provincial Party committee in one point: "so-called firmly upholding the continued revolution under the dictatorship of the proletariat." The contents of this "continued revolution" were described as follows: (1) to create "class struggle" uninterruptedly and artificially and thus to magnify it; (2) to transform relations of production uninterruptedly and to make a transition to a higher level of collective ownership and accounting in spite of the poverty of the local units; (3) "to cut the tail of capitalism" and "to block the path of capitalism" uninterruptedly; and (4) to promote "equal-divisionism" (pingjun zhuyi) and to destroy the system of distributing rewards according to work done.

On its part, the Party Center observed that like everything else, an advanced model undergoes continuous development and change. When it cannot continue to be an advanced model, it should not be maintained artificially either by outside aid or by deception which harms others while hurting oneself. The variations in conditions in China make it necessary to discover and cultivate all kinds of advanced models. To use a single model for agricultural development was a serious error. Finally, the Party Center condemned the practice of selecting labor models to fill leading posts in state and Party organs or mass organizations because they had proved unable to discharge these tasks satisfactorily and at the same time they could no longer function as labor models.

These two reports constituted a total repudiation of developments in Dazhai and Xiyang after 1966. They did not mention any redeeming merits. They represented the tragic end not only of the Dazhai model but also the inevitable outcome of the idea and practices of the two-line struggle.

12. REFLECTIONS ON THE DAZHAI EXPERIENCE

The repudiation of the movement to learn from Dazhai and to build Dazhai-type counties, particularly the condemnation of many of the specific policies of Xiyang County, should not prevent us from reaffirming the earlier achievements of Dazhai Village under the leadership of Chen Yonggui and should not blind us to some of the specific achievements of Xiyang County. Chen's early successes in leading the transformation of an extremely poor village into a relatively wealthy one through sheer human efforts while spreading the benefits fairly evenly among its various households should not be denied. Above all, the spirit of endeavoring to do what others believed to be impossible, unrealistic, or neglectful of the criteria of cost-effectiveness which has now become one of the causes of his downfall served at an earlier time the historic function of breaking the fatalistic tradition of Chinese peasants.

Similarly, the rise of Dazhai as a national model and the movement to learn from Dazhai must be further analyzed from a larger historical and political perspective. The resonance between Mao's ideas and the practices spontaneously developed in Dazhai in its early years was not a pure coincidence. Both embodied the spirit of daring to attempt apparently impossible feats. Both reflected the egalitarianism prevalent in traditional peasant rebellions, which is characterized by an author in a widely praised article as the core of "agrarian socialism"[40] in contradistinction to "scientific socialism." The major force in the Chinese revolution was the peasantry in the border regions and the interior far from the city and out of touch with modern civilization. A unique characteristic of the Chinese revolution was that the forces in the vast backward rural regions conquered the modern urban areas. In spite of his knowledge of Marxism-Leninism and his intellectual curiosity about modern science, Mao's instinctive and primordial orientation was basically rural. The vast majority of cadres, at least at the middle and lower levels, also came from the countryside. This was particularly true for the cadres in the army. The prominence of the rural revolution and the eclipse of urban values and attitudes finally culminated in the oppression of the urban intellectuals and the near destruction of science, higher education, literature, art, and other higher forms of culture during the Cultural Revolution.

Given the resonance between Mao's ideas and the peasants' demands in a revolutionary period, it is not surprising that the reevaluation of Mao's role in his last years has been an endeavor on the part of many intellectuals to seek the social roots of China's political ills in the mentality of the "small producers," or more specifically the peasants. But we submit that the ultimate source of the patriarchal style, bureaucratic practices, and methods of unrestrained intra-Party struggle which dominated politics during the Cultural Revolution must be sought not in the peasants' mentality but in the long political tradition of the Chinese ruling class which could not but influence the personal values, attitudes, and habits of the peasants at the grass roots and leaders at various levels who hailed from the peasantry.

In retrospect, the reversal since 1977 of the whole approach to China's economic and political development is probably the result of the attempts of Mao and his followers to push to the extreme their revolutionary ideas without adequate regard to reality. The new approach of the reformers may very well have rescued China from the brink of disaster. It may very well lead China successfully toward its goal of building a modern nation. But a balanced assessment of the successes and failures of the past and a proper evaluation of the role of the peasants must accompany this new approach so that it can be put on a solid foundation of mass support in the countryside. Egalitarianism in the distribution of the basic necessities of life has deep roots in China. It is also a modern ideal. It played a part in stifling individual effort and initiative in the countryside only when it was pushed to the extreme in disregard of the level of economic and political development in different localities. Shorn of their extreme manifestations, egalitarian ideals must again be given a proper place in the whole scheme of "socalist modernization." "Agrarian socialism" should not be counterposed to "scientific socialism." On the contrary, a synthesis should be achieved in the search for a distinctively Chinese path to socialist modernization. Such a synthesis would be a signal contribution to the theory and practice of economic development in an agricultural country, particularly a nation with a high population-land ratio.

NOTES

1. This paper was completed in February 1981, with new information added in April. Tang Tsou acknowledges the support of the National Endowment for the Humanities for the project "Political Leadership and Social Change at the Local Level in China from 1850 to the Present" at the University of Chicago. This support made it possible for him to make a field trip to Xiyang, Shanxi, and Loshan, Sichuan, in the summer of 1980. He also benefited from a trip made by a group of Western scholars, organized by Edward Friedman, Maurice Meisner, and Angus McDonald with the support of the National Endowment for the Humanities to study macro-political changes in China in the post-Mao era. He wishes to express his appreciation to Mr. Edmond Lee for his indefatigable and efficient help in working out the final draft. Marc Blecher acknowledges support from the Committee on Research and Development of Oberlin College. A more extended treatment of these and related issues is found in Tang Tsou, ed., Select Papers from the Center for Far Eastern Studies (University of Chicago), no. 4 (1979-80).

2. Tang Tsou, "Back from the Brink of Revolutionary-'Feudal' Totalitarianism: Some Preliminary Reflections," a paper presented at the Luce Seminar, University of Chicago, on May 30, 1980.

3. Throughout this paper, the term "district" rather than "prefecture" is used to translate the term "diqu."

4. Interview at Dazhai in 1980. At this time, Chen still retained his nominal positions as a member of the Politburo and as a vice-premier. Guo Fenglian was still an alternate member of the Central Committee. But neither had any authority or influence.

5. Sometimes the term "comrade" was used in place of the word "person" in this indirect reference to Chen.

6. Renmin ribao (People's Daily), February 12, 1981, p. 1.

7. Taiwan sources frequently give February 1964 as the time when Mao issued the call. When interviewed in 1977, Chen Yonggui said that Mao had issued the call in January 1967, but he conceded that the precise date could not be found in any published documents. It is difficult to find the precise slogan "learn from Dazhai" in documents and articles published in 1964.

8. Tang Tsou, Marc Blecher, and Mitch Meisner, "Organization, Growth, and Equality in Xiyang County: A Survey of Fourteen Brigades in Seven Communes," Select Papers from the Center for Far Eastern Studies, no. 3 (1978-79): 181-217.

9. These words have been frequently repeated, but they cannot be found in the published reports of Zhou's speech at the time. In official English translation, the term "ideology" is used to translate the Chinese term sixiang. Zhongguo shehui kexue yuan zhexue yanjiu suo xiezuo zu, Weiwu bianzhengfa zai Xiyang de shengli (The Victory of Materialist Dialectics in Xiyang — Beijing: Renmin chubanshe, 1979), p. 1.

10. Wang Gengjin, "Some Problems in Implementing Agricultural Economic Policies," Jingji yanjiu (Economic Research), 1978, no. 8, p. 19.

11. For a discussion, see Mitch Meisner and Marc Blecher, "Administrative Level and Agrarian Structure: The County (W)as Focal Point in Chinese Rural Development Policy," in Gordon White and Jack Gray, eds., China's New Development Policy (London: Academic Press, forthcoming).

12. Renmin ribao, June 2, 1976, p. 3.

13. Ibid., June 28, 1976, p. 1.

14. Interviews conducted at Dazhai in October 1977.

15. These peasants were paid by their own brigades for work at Mengshan.

16. Renmin ribao, December 4, 1980, article by Wu Chenggun.

17. Article by Gao Zhengyong et al., Jingji yanjiu, 1979, no. 2, p. 54. Article by Wang Gengjin and He Jianzhang, ibid., 1978, no. 8, pp. 16-20.

18. Guangming ribao (Guangming Daily), May 11, 1978, p. 1. See also Tang Tsou, "Back from the Brink . . . ," pp. 23-24.

19. Hongqi (Red Flag), 1977, no. 3, p. 10.

20. For an English translation of this article, see Beijing Review, November 10, 1978, pp. 7-12, November 17, 1978, pp. 15-23; November 24, 1978, pp. 13-21.

21. Renmin ribao, July 5, 1978, p. 1.

22. Ibid., July 21, 1978, p. 1.

23. By 1977, Dazhai actually had about one hundred households.

24. Ming bao, July 4, 1979, p. 3.

25. These draft documents have not been published in China. Reproductions can be found in Zhonggong yanjiu (Taiwan), Vol. 13, no. 5 (May 15, 1979): 150-162; Vol. 13, no. 6 (June 15, 1979): 139-152. We believe that these documents are genuine, although there is no way to check if they are totally accurate.

26. Renmin ribao, January 16, 1979, p. 1. These words also appear in the draft document on acceleration of agricultural development as printed in Zhonggong yanjiu, Vol. 13, no. 5 (May 15, 1979): 152. But they do not appear in the final document adopted in September 1979 and published on October 6.

27. Beijing Review, October 5, 1979, p. 15.

28. Ibid., December 29, 1978, p. 15.

29. Renmin ribao, January 22, 1979, p. 1. See also editorials, ibid., January 16, 1979, p. 1, and January 24, 1979, p. 1.

30. For example, see ibid., January 6, 1979, p. 1; January 10, p. 1; January 20, p. 1; March 1, p. 4; March 15, p. 1; March 16, p. 2; May 5, p. 2; June 9, p. 1; August 19, p. 2.

31. Article by a special commentator, Guangming ribao, June 12, 1979, p. 1.

32. Renmin ribao, March 15, 1979, p. 2. Wenhui bao, March 8, 1979, p. 3.

33. Ibid., October 6, 1979, pp. 1-2.

34. For example, see Renmin ribao, December 24, 1980, p. 2.

35. Ibid., October 3, 1979, p. 2.

36. This represented a change in its view held as late as April and May 1979. See Tsou, Blecher, and Meisner in Selected Papers, no. 4, pp. 294-295.

37. Renmin ribao, November 22, 1979, pp. 1-2.

38. Ibid., December 29, 1979, p. 2.

39. From now on in this paper, we shall use Chen's name in place of the indirect reference used in the official press. Up to early 1981, Chen has not been criticized by name. Hongqi, 1981, no. 2, p. 2.

40. Wang Xiaoqiang, "A Critique of Agrarian Socialism," Xinhua yuebao (New China Monthly), 1980, no. 5, p. 12.

Carl Riskin
MARKET, MAOISM,
AND ECONOMIC REFORM IN CHINA

The beginning of the 1980s found China in the throes of an economic riptide.* A reform-minded leadership, attempting to reverse the direction of two decades, was promoting an economic system quite different from any espoused by the late Mao Zedong — one with independent enterprises practicing "scientific management" and responding to the signals of the market. Such a system, according to the reformers, has the best chance of overcoming the still prevalent attitudes of "feudalism" in China, strengthening the forces of economic rationality, and ultimately speeding economic growth. Yet the partial reforms that were introduced conflicted with still dominant elements of the old approach to economic management, eroded central control of investment activity, and worsened long-standing problems of economic imbalance that the leadership was equally committed to solving. Economic reform was therefore slowed, and its future put in doubt.

When leaders and intellectuals dwell on the obstructive remnants of the past in today's China, it is "feudalism" rather than capitalism they mention. During the Cultural Revolution, seventeen years after the achievement of state power by the Chinese Communist Party, "feudal" habits are said to have still permeated Chinese thought and behavior sufficiently to threaten the revolution itself and bring the economy "to the brink of disaster." Implicit in this

*This article was written in early 1981, in a period of rapid change in Chinese economic policy. While some of the issues it discusses are specific to the period covered, its broader underlying theme concerns problems that China is likely to face for some time to come.

I am most grateful to the editors of this volume for a painstaking critique of an earlier draft of this essay. Helpful comments were also received from Robert Heilbroner, Tom Rawski, Dorothy Solinger and Andrew Zimbalist. Responsibility for the final result is the author's alone.

view is the idea that certain phenomena historically associated with capitalism still lie ahead for China. When Oriana Fallaci asked Deng Xiaoping in October 1980 whether he thought "capitalism is not all that bad," Deng replied offhandedly, "We must distinguish what is capitalism. Capitalism is superior to feudalism."[1]

The term "feudalism" as used in China refers generally to the means of domination of Chinese society employed by a privileged class for many centuries.[2] The Party journal Hongqi (Red Flag) put it bluntly:

[F]eudalistic ideology is so prevalent that it has permeated every corner of the society.... For instance, the concepts of respectability and inferiority, the hierarchical system and patriarchal behavior manifest themselves everywhere. At the same time ...the ideology of the agricultural small producers is characterized by the belief that they cannot take their destiny into their own hands, but rather entrust it to some "saviour."...[3]

As applied to the economy, the term embraces several current and recent hallmarks of Chinese economic organization: the overlapping of political and economic jurisdiction, permitting government organs to milk economic units for their taxes and profits; the quest for local self-sufficiency, with insufficient regard for the principles of specialization and division of labor; an overemphasis on the motivating force of loyalty, patriotism, and authority and an underemphasis on material interest; an attempt to organize production directly for use, rather than allowing and encouraging the development of the market and of production of commodities for the market; the resort to supraeconomic coercion; overstaffed and overlapping administrative structures; one-sided emphasis on mobilizing labor, to the neglect of science, technology, and intellectuals.[4] These are all modes of thought and behavior presumably rendered obsolete in the advanced West and Japan by the rationalizing power of capitalist development, but still strong in China, where such development was weak and truncated.

The metaphor of riptide is limited, however. Neither the inexorable force of the moon's pull nor the inevitability of its result has an analogue in the efforts of China's leadership to reform the economic system. The most elementary kinds of errors have been committed: building factories without first investigating the availability of raw materials, power, and transport facilities; rushing in the "foreign leap forward" of 1977-78 to import advanced technology ahead of China's needs and capacity to pay, turning enterprises loose in a market that still, inevitably, generates the wrong signals. Moreover, there has been a deliberate weakening of whatever remained of the old Maoist ethic of collectivism in favor of one of individual "material interest."[5] Enough "material" in the form of consumer goods must be found to satisfy a growing public appetite whetted by an unprecedented influx of affluent tourists, as well as by the newly discovered art of advertising and shop window display.[6] Growing sectoral imbalances and inflationary pressures, to which these problems have contributed, have now caused the leadership to adopt a stringent austerity program, pushing other objectives — including further basic reform of the economic system — temporarily into the background.[7] Austerity may not receive within China the same ringing endorsement it has won from the International Monetary Fund. It will disappoint expectations, only recently fanned by the leadership itself, of rapid improvements in living standards. It stands as a painful reminder of fiscal blundering by that leadership, and it is providing an excellent opportunity for the defenders of bureaucratic economic administration to rally their forces.

What the reformers want, on the other hand, is to free China's economy from the stultifying structure of centralized power that was copied from the Soviet Union in the 1950s and that then became congealed by a multitude of bureaucratic interests. Under this system, most important activities of enterprises — even those normally under collective ownership — were controlled by the central plan; the enterprise had only to fulfill its allotted tasks. If it made profits, they reverted directly to the state; if losses, they were subsidized. Virtually all of its capital came in the form of nonrepayable budget grants, ineffective use of which incurred no automatic penalty. Wages and salaries were fixed by the state and depended in no significant way on economic performance. Initiative was thus largely in the hands of the government, which administered the economy as something inseparable from government itself. Enterprises inevitably reacted like bureaucratic organs, doing the minimum necessary to avoid criticism, and exercising no independent initiative. As the economy grew and became more complex, the ability of the state to administer it effectively from the center declined, and the irrational consequences of the system became more pronounced. These consequences — e.g., overemphasis on quantity of output to the detriment of quality and variety, hoarding of labor and materials, wasteful vertical integration, etc. — are quite familiar to students of Soviet and East European economies.

Such is the case that is now made with tedious regularity in journal articles and to inquiring visitors. Although in some respects a caricature — especially because it altogether omits ideology from the picture — it undoubtedly contains a large if unmeasurable portion of truth. Western economists who study China's economy have long been aware of the structural characteristics described above, yet many judged on the basis of available evidence that such indefinables as organizational élan and ideological commitment, as well as forms of decentralization of economic administration worked out from the late 1950s on, were sufficient to neutralize such problems, at least in part, and permit China to chalk up a most creditable economic development record despite them. It is not clear that this is entirely wrong, despite the devastating self-criticisms coming out of China.

What lends credibility to the indictment of China's previous organizational system, however, is that much of it was shared by Mao Zedong himself. The irony is that Mao, whose cult is now being deflated and the last twenty years of whose thoughts will not in the forseeable future be published officially, was himself a most cogent critic of overcentralization and bureaucratism. Some people, he said of the Center, were always trying to lift stones too heavy for them and ended by dropping them on their own feet.

But Mao's approach to attacking bureaucratism differed radically from that of today's reformers. Rather than deemphasize political criteria governing the daily activities of economic units and replace them with "objective economic laws," Mao sought to mobilize localities precisely on the basis of political enthusiasm. For example, in criticizing a Soviet textbook for condemning "crash programs," he wrote:

If one wants to overtake the advanced, one cannot help having crash programs. If construction or revolution is attacked with executive orders... there is bound to be a reduction in production because the masses will not have been mobilized, and not because of crash programs.[8]

For Mao, the alternative to the command economy based on "executive orders" was not the market, but rather social mobilization using "mass line" methods of leadership.[9]

The proper environment for implementing this approach was an administratively decentralized one, with substantial control over economic activity wielded locally, primarily by the local Party committees. Mao criticized the same Soviet text for subordinating the Party role to that of local economic bureaus, which, he complained,

become the heads under the direct administration of the central government. Local party organizations cannot take the political lead in those areas, making it virtually impossible for them to mobilize all positive forces sufficiently.[10]

In the ideal case, the localities and collectives on which economic authority would devolve would be small enough for their members to perceive personal benefit in economic success and therefore to be more highly motivated. "Material interest" was thus a part of Mao's solution, although it operated chiefly at the group level.

Mobilization depended much on direct communication between the political center and the regions and localities, bypassing much of the state bureaucracy. Therefore, while Mao's concept of administrative decentralization heightened the authority of local areas, it simultaneously concentrated power at the very top. The Cultural Revolution, with the Chairman and the Cultural Revolution Group appealing directly to the masses, and with much of the ordinary state machinery lying dormant, was a stereotype of this arrangement.

The guiding hand of Mao's economy, unlike Adam Smith's, was a visible one. There is no idea here of the transformation of individual selfishness into common benefit; instead, the motive of individual gain was to harmonize with that of social welfare: people were to work at one and the same time for themselves, their unit, and the nation. True, Mao recognized the existence of contradictions between these various levels. But his solution was to combine ideological education with adjustments in the distributive system so as to give each level its due.

Such a view, in principle, is incompatible with a major market role in organizing and motivating economic activity. In the first place, the scale of economic organization called for by Mao's motivational system would correspond only by coincidence with that dictated by a market-guided division of labor. Second, the concern for overall social interest that is supposed, via ideology, to constrain individual and group acquisitiveness in the Maoist system is strictly at odds with the discipline of the market. Although all market-oriented societies must adopt some ethical and legal constraints, it is fair to say that the challenge to which the Maoist system submitted the market was so great as to severely inhibit any development or expression of "market mentality."

With neither center nor market guiding and regulating economic activity, Mao's administratively decentralized system relied for this purpose on the sense of political responsibility of the individual and the collective. A deeply ingrained socialist consciousness in each individual, achieved in part through education and in part through political struggle, was to lead to the internalization of Party goals and policy and their conscious acceptance as parameters within which community and individual gain were pursued.

Certain implications of the Maoist approach seem inevitable, especially in the light of hindsight. The simplification of policy into slogans easily grasped by large numbers of grass-roots decision-makers far from the centers of power is one of them. Another is the focus in propaganda and political line on ethics and world view. Both stem in part from the rejection of the market as organizer of decentralized economic activity and have the function of replacing it with alternative criteria of choice.

Implied also is the small-scale and relatively self-sufficient nature of much economic activity that characterized the periods most influenced by Mao's concepts: the Great Leap Forward (1958-1960) and the Cultural Revolution (1966-1968). There are two reasons for this: first, in a poor country with limited communications, technical skills, and planning apparatus, the nonmarket allocation of resources and coordination of economic activity require stringent limits on the scale of coordination, as well as on the division of labor; second, as a motivating force, "material interest" must be clearly linked to the collective effort — not to some elaborate web of activity that extends far beyond the group concerned and whose success is only in small part owing to that group's efforts. Both of these considerations dictated the relatively small size of the economic unit and its basic self-sufficiency.

Of course, Mao also advocated "walking on two legs," and a large-scale, modern industrial "leg" in fact grew up rapidly under his leadership. Indeed, small industry was always regarded not as a substitute for big, modern industry, but as its adjunct and supplement, to speed up the overall rate of industrialization. Ironically, however, while the adjunct "leg" fit into a fairly coherent ideological strategy, the main "leg" of big industry did not — nor did it have a clear-cut ideology of its own.[11] Through all the conflict over worker participation in management, cadre participation in labor, the elimination of rigid hierarchies and of restrictive rules and regulations within the enterprise, the fact is that little authority actually was left to the state industrial enterprise to share out among its constituent members. These issues, important as they were, had little direct economic significance because they concerned how orders from above were carried out, rather than the nature of the role performed by the enterprise itself.

Nor was there much scope for giving workers and managers — either collectively or as individuals — a "material interest" in the results of their performance. Wage and salary scales were fixed nationally, and bonuses played an ambiguous role in the Maoist schema.[12] Profitable or not, advanced or backward, efficient or wasteful, it rarely made a difference to the earnings of manager or worker, or to their collective welfare. They might be chosen as models for emulation or as negative examples, winning fame, suffering humiliation, or both (as in the case of the famous Dazhai Brigade), but this is different in principle from "material interest."

The lower the level of administrative decentralization concerned, the more the Maoist approach made sense. Commune and brigade industry is a prime example of collective economic activity with a clear tie to collective material welfare. At the county level (average population 500,000), the link is much more remote, while the average province exceeds in population most members of the United Nations. For relatively small collectives, the benefits of cooperative effort and widespread diffusion of initiative might well outweigh the allocative inefficiency of duplicative local production and limited division of labor. But this solution is applicable after all to only a small portion of the nonagricultural sector of the economy, and to agriculture, while the ideological and organizational implications of it — a high degree of politicization of decision-making and an emphasis on comprehensiveness, or "self-reliance" — is not so easily isolated in the relevant sectors. Nor did administrative decentralization solve the problems of the larger-scale economic units; in some respects it exacerbated them. As one of China's most perceptive modernizers puts it:

Reducing the question to one of centralization or decentralization does not help to clarify its essence and will not lead to fundamental solution. Neither can a way out be found by dividing power between the central government, the local government and the enterprise. Subjective designs which do not touch the heart of the matter inevitably give rise to a recurring cycle in which "centralization leads to rigidity, rigidity leads to complaints, complaints lead to decentralization, decentralization leads to disorder, and disorder leads back to centralization."[13]

To say that the Maoist system of organization contained contradictory elements does not imply that it was bound to fail, could not have resolved such problems, or did not achieve notable results despite them during its period of ascendancy — roughly 1958-1976. Indeed, during those years, an impressive rate of economic growth was achieved, averaging about 10 percent per year for industrial production and 6 percent for national income.[14] These rates are in fact higher than the current growth targets (e.g., the industrial growth target is 6 percent for both 1980 and 1981)[15] and compare favorably with the economic growth performances of other less developed countries.[16] Such an impressive record does not seem consistent with the much repeated statement that the policies of the "Gang of Four" brought China's economy to the "brink of collapse." The numbers have not been basically revised, for they continue to be used in Chinese economic writing.[17] However, they are now widely regarded as exaggerations. Ma Hong, director of the Institute of Industrial Economics of the Chinese Academy of Social Sciences, states bluntly that figures were sometimes falsified during the "Gang of Four" period. The best-known example is the case of Xiyang County (home of the now deflated Dazhai Brigade), whose past agricultural output is said to have been exaggerated by as much as 20 percent. Mr. Ma states that similar exaggeration certainly occurred in industry, although to a still undetermined extent; but that even where technically accurate, the figures concealed problems that tarnished their luster. For instance, much output was useless to consumers and industrial users. Even in late 1980, over 20 million tons of steel — almost equivalent to one year's production — lay idle in warehouses because it was produced in the wrong varieties, e.g., big steel plates high in nominal value but with no demand. Fifty billion yuan (over U.S.$32 billion)-worth of machinery and equipment was similarly stockpiled, an amount equivalent to the annual national investment in capital construction, about 60 percent of which has gone for the purchase of machinery and equipment (some of it imported). Because of such concealed flaws, the historical 10 percent industrial growth rate "does not reveal the low efficiency of our production."[18]

A comprehensive overview of the Maoist approach — which is not attempted here — would have to consider the anomalies of this

historical record in some detail. For example, despite rapid industrialization and an ideological commitment to steadily improving living standards, wages and salaries remained more or less
constant for twenty years,[19] while the investment rate soared
at times to unconscionable heights. Even the per capita food consumption level did not improve. Nor could the many political ab-
errations of Mao's last years be ignored. This is not to say that
all such things can be laid automatically at Mao's doorstep; only
that his long dominance in Chinese policy formation requires that
any full evaluation of his ideas about organization, development,
and social change must come to grips with their impact on actual
events.

Attacking accumulated economic problems in a very different
way, China's new leadership inaugurated in 1979 a policy of re-
adjusting, renovating, rectifying, and improving the national economy. Principal objectives of this policy, which will in fact be extended beyond the three years initially planned for it, include a reduced national investment rate and a higher proportion of consumer
goods and services in total output; faster development of agriculture and light industry, and slower growth of heavy industry; turning from what is now regarded as a one-sided agricultural policy
of stressing foodgrains, to encouraging the growth of other crops,
animal husbandry, forestry and fisheries; and concentration on
helping such problem sectors as fuel and power, transport and
communications, construction materials and urban housing.

Some of China's reformers believe, like their East European
counterparts, that a root cause of such chronic structural imbalances in the centralized, administrative economy itself. In principle, they argue, government has no business issuing commands
to enterprises regarding what and how to produce. Political and
economic authority ought basically to be separated, and the latter
left to those in the best position to exercise it — the enterprises
themselves, responding to market signals. Necessary government
intervention should use economic levers rather than administrative
orders. Accordingly, they would like to establish an "enterprise-
based economy."[20] But, unlike, say, in Hungary, where thorough
preparation for economic reform was followed by the simultaneous
introduction of all new laws and regulations governing it,[21] China
is proceeding by testing the water one toe at a time before taking
the plunge. This approach, while permitting experimentation, has
the disadvantage of creating severe contradictions between coex-

existing elements of the new and old systems — the "riptide" effect referred to earlier — with respect to both efficiency conditions and ethical assumptions.[22] The inherent problems of mixed
systems are still not well understood by the Chinese, who have
been forced to scramble in response to individual difficulties as
they crop up.

For example, the first step on the way to an "enterprise-based
economy" is to permit enterprises to keep a certain proportion of
their profits for investment, social welfare, and bonuses. Altogether, 6,600 enterprises were on such a system in late 1980, and
it was to have been spread in 1981 to all of the more than 90,000
state-owned enterprises.[23]

This system gives the economic enterprise a certain degree of
autonomy in decision-making and also stimulates the initiative of
workers and managers by linking their compensation to their
unit's performance. At the same time, it creates a host of new
problems, partly rooted in the still unreformed price structure.
Because some prices (e.g. oil) are fixed high relative to costs,
while others (e.g. coal) are fixed low, profitability varies over industries for reasons that have nothing to do with enterprise performance. The same profit retention rate would arbitrarily reward the high-profit industries more than the low-profit ones, a
phenomenon Chinese economists have referred to, literally, as
"inequality of happiness and bitterness" (kule bujun).[24] Formerly,
when profit was just another target, like output, and did not affect
anyone's income or control of resources, its arbitrary distribution
mattered little. Now, however, it is a potential source of widening
and unjustified inequality between industries and enterprises, and
of equally arbitrary expansion of productive capacity in high-
profit items relative to low-profit ones.

One obvious solution is to reform the price system to make
prices reflect the forces of supply and demand as amended by
government intervention in specific markets to achieve specific
objectives. But China's economic leadership feels that this reform "is a very complicated task that cannot be accomplished for
the time being."[25] The existing price structure is, after all, the
principal determinant of state revenue, since both taxes and the
bulk of the profits of state enterprises revert directly to the
government coffers. Any substantial change in price structure
would reverberate throughout the economy, changing costs and
profits everywhere to a degree that planners cannot fully predict

or control, and would thus threaten the stability of the budgetary system. Moreover, the distribution of income, as well as the relative price stability that has been one of the great successes of Chinese economic policy until recently, would also be threatened. So price reform is on the back burner.

Nevertheless, price structure adjustments have been undertaken in at least two ways. First, the widespread amalgamation of previously autonomous enterprises has permitted the replacement of the irrational prices at which these used to trade by rational internal transfer prices. Second, a large proportion of output was freed up for marketing at negotiated prices (see below). This practice, under conditions of large government deficits, overextended spending on capital construction projects, and general shortages, has helped to stimulate an inflation (officially estimated at 6 percent for 1980, including an 8.1 percent rise in the cities, and a 13.8 percent increase in state prices of nonstaple foods) startling to a population accustomed to price stability and only three decades away from one of history's most destructive hyperinflations. Accordingly, it was sharply curtailed in December 1980 by a State Council directive forbidding price increases for goods formally subject to state control and mandating the localities to set maximum prices on other goods.[26] It is clear that the whole issue of economic reform, and the inflationary pressures to which it has contributed, has been caught up in the continuing political conflict in China, and the reformers have been forced once again to backtrack to a more cautious position. They thus remain far from the announced goal of permitting freely negotiated prices for all but a small number of especially important commodities.[27]

Meanwhile, to deal with arbitrary differences in profitability between industries and enterprises, the leadership has tinkered with profit retention ratios, varying them to match profitability conditions. For instance, the oil industry, with high prices and profits, is assigned a low profit retention rate, whereas the coal industry, with low prices and profits, is permitted to keep a high share of profits. Thus an elaborate network of retention rules is effected to neutralize the errant price structure. But this is far from being a satisfactory solution, not only because the profit retention rates will have to be repeatedly altered in light of changing profitability conditions, but also because their very existence makes fundamental price reform more difficult: every change in prices must be accompanied by negotiations over the appropriate new profit retention rate.

The tax system is afflicted with similar problems. Now that enterprises are motivated to pursue profits, they also have good reason to avoid taxes, and the system in industry of a single tax on <u>sales</u> makes this quite easy. The more production steps that can be integrated within a single enterprise, the less tax that has to be paid. Where before several specialized enterprises might sell semi-finished goods to each other, paying a tax at each trans-action, now there is an incentive to group them all together in one integrated company, coordinated internally. Moreover, where the specialized enterprises still exist as such, they may be unable to compete with a less efficient integrated firm that pays lower taxes. "Integration" is one of the "three trump cards" of current Chinese economic policy, along with "competition" and "comparative advantage." But there can be little doubt that many enterprises are playing this card on their own behalf, to trump the state.

To this conflict between enterprise and state must be added one between locality and center. Under the current financial system, local governments in China get revenue directly from the profits and taxes of their own local enterprises. It so happens that the sale of processed farm and mining products generates much revenue under the current price structure and tax system. If these products leave their places of origin to be processed elsewhere, the original localities lose that revenue. Local governments therefore strenuously resist the transfer of their primary products, even when processing can be done much more efficiently elsewhere.[28]

All of these problems are manifestations of the dissonance produced when economic actors are freed and encouraged to respond to market signals that are still set by the old administrative planning system. It is as though automobile drivers were paid to observe traffic lights that produced pileups at each intersection. There are two possible results: that the traffic lights will be fixed; and that the pileups will discredit their use entirely. The latter possibility sounds remote only because the analogy omits the element of bureaucratic and ideological resistance to the new system that is openly acknowledged to exist in China.

The repair of one important signal will considerably reduce the amount of distortion in the system as a whole. The price of fixed capital for state-owned enterprises has up to now had only two values: zero and infinity. An enterprise obtained capital from the government in the form of a free budget grant. Once that was negotiated, additional capital was hard to obtain at any price. Now, however, enterprises are to be charged a fee for the use of state-owned fixed capital, or must obtain investment funds from the bank at interest. If these fees and interest rates are properly set, they will reduce or eliminate the profitability of inefficient producers (and potential producers) relative to efficient ones and generally inhibit the waste of scarce capital. This is one reform that appears to be escaping the current retrenchment in reformism.[29]

The second step on the way to the "enterprise based economy" is known as "self-responsibility for profits and losses" (zifu yinkui). Under this system, the enterprise pays a number of different taxes, formulated to correct the allocative inefficiency and disincentives of the current tax structure, after which it is free to use any remaining profits as it sees fit (although it is still presumably constrained by broad government policy). Conversely, any losses it makes will not automatically be subsidized by the state. In 1980, only a handful of enterprises experimented with this system, and they kept about half of their gross profits, on the average. In 1981, every province and municipality in China was to have such enterprises, but this step too has fallen victim to the new spirit of caution. The system of enterprise responsibility for profit and loss represents a big step toward cutting the enterprise loose from the system of administrative commands that characterizes the old central planning approach. Reformers have seen it as an escape route from the maze of profit retention regulations required by the prior stage, which have occasioned endless disputes. Better to pay taxes to the state than to share profits with it. Without price reform, however, the profit retention rules will only have to be replaced with equally unwieldy tax regulations.

The process of shifting from total reliance on plan to general orientation to the market picked up momentum in 1980. The role of fairs, exhibitions, and commodity exchange conferences was greatly expanded. Enterprises were allowed to seek customers for much of their output and to seek needed inputs from the market. Not only were goods transferred out of categories previously reserved for exclusive state control and into the category of freely marketable commodities, but control even of the former categories was relaxed. Producers of machinery, timber, or steel could market their above-quota output and the within-quota goods that the state chose not to purchase. Shanghai's "production materials market," for example, is of national scope. Factories from various parts of China list their excess and stockpiled goods there, and needy enterprises can contact potential suppliers without having to dispatch personnel to travel the country in search of supplies. Even if a shopping enterprise cannot immediately find what it needs in Shanghai, it is likely to meet there a number of potential suppliers with whom to deal. Whereas previously the busiest trade personnel were purchasing agents — nobody being particularly motivated to sell products — now the Chinese have discovered the fine art of salesmanship and publicly bemoan their lack of experience with advertising. Although the ultimate balance of plan and market is still unclear, the market in Shanghai and Chongqing was said already to handle some 20 to 30 percent of total output in 1980. (Ironically, Beijing, thrusting up new buildings everywhere in the rush to become a model "modernized" capital, lags behind in development of the market.) This burgeoning of market activity was the immediate backdrop of the December State Council directive, mentioned earlier, which clamped down on price increases.

The Chinese are currently both firmer and clearer about the need to combine planning with market than about what such a marriage will look like or the respective roles of bride and groom.[30] In fact, there appears to be some disagreement between those who think that essential goods and services should still be physically allocated by the government, and those who advocate principal reliance on the manipulation of prices, wages, interest rates, credit policies, etc., to influence the decisions of the economic actors. But the remarkable thing about the reform literature in this still planned economy is its relative neglect of planning itself. Material balances planning is still essential to the Chinese economy; if it is to evolve into other forms of planning, the transformation will require considerable thought and study. The worsening of sectoral imbalances in the economy over the last few years was due as much to neglect of planning by reformers seduced by the promises of the market, as it was to atavistic "leftist" contempt for balanced growth. The current stringent retrenchment has forced renewed attention to central planning, but more as an emergency measure than as a long-term problem demanding the attention of the best minds.

In the countryside, where most Chinese still live and work, collectivism has by and large meant far greater security than most people enjoyed in the past. But improvement in living standards has been both slow and unevenly distributed. Statistics compiled during the summer of 1980 from almost all basic-level units in the countryside show that more than one-quarter of them had average annual per capita incomes of less than 50 yuan (U.S.$30).[31] Members of the poorest production brigades and teams "could not even solve the problem of having enough to eat and wear," had to depend on subsidies for survival, and had little enthusiasm for collectivism. Some 100 million rural inhabitants are said to exist in this pitiable state — a fact which, if accurate, constitutes the severest indictment of the economic policies of the past. Perhaps chiefly responsible among these were infringement by the government on the right of basic-level farm collectives (production teams) to manage their own economic affairs; the use of this usurped authority to pressure farmers to grow food grains, even in areas unsuited to them; the corresponding suppression of other farm products important in the diets and budgets of the rural population; and a general underpricing of agricultural goods.

China's leaders could have limited their reforms in agriculture to the reversal of these policies, raising prices of farm products, emphasizing the right of production teams to decide for themselves what and how to produce in the light of their own conditions and of market demand, investing resources in potential grain surplus areas to provide the staples to be exchanged for specialized products raised elsewhere, and giving special assistance to the poorest regions and units. Such policies have, in fact, been put into effect and seem to have already brought some improvement both in farm production and peasant incomes.[32]

Beyond such initiatives, however, the leadership has taken steps to reduce the degree of collectivism in agriculture. Convinced that as early as the "socialist high tide" of 1956 collectivism was coercively enlarged beyond a scale that most peasants would willingly accept and could successfully manage, it has moved to break up the production teams into small working groups and even, in some cases, down to individual families. The teams still own the larger tools and oversee the distribution of tasks and of income, but the groups or individuals are allocated particular fields on a long-term basis and are free to keep their output beyond a quota negotiated with the team. As of late 1980, about one-fifth of the production teams in China were contracting production tasks to individual households.[33]

It is impossible to evaluate from afar this erosion of collectivism. In backward areas where it did not bring results, or in areas of sparse and dispersed population where it did not fit conditions, collective organization of production may indeed be discredited. Elsewhere, however, where break-up of collective organization has resurrected old problems of sharing water, animals and machinery, joining forces to fight natural disasters, undertaking capital construction and disseminating new techniques, there is resistance to the change, and "many of the peasants have demanded that we stick with the old system."[34] The essence of Party policy today is to let organizational forms vary in accordance with natural conditions and peasant desires, but the habit of heavy-handed bureaucratic interference dies slowly.

With all the changes occurring in economic structure and organization, Chinese theorists have been worried about transgressing the boundaries of socialism. For some months, the social science journals were dominated by articles on the relation between socialism and commodity production; these attacked Stalin's argument that, under socialism, the sphere of commodities (i.e. goods produced for sale), and the influence of market forces on production, was limited to "the exchange, chiefly, of articles of personal consumption."[35] Capitalism, they pointed out, performed the historic function of vastly expanding commodity production and circulation as an inextricable part of its industrial revolution. A country like China, adopting socialism on the basis of an underdeveloped, "semifeudal, semicolonial" capitalism, still dominated by the "natural" economy of self-sufficient producers, must replicate the historic contribution of capitalism by stimulating commodity production in virtually every sector of the economy. Otherwise, economic development would inevitably be impeded by bureaucratism and the continued, unchallenged dominance of "feudal" behavior traits. These negative features cannot be willed away; they can be overcome only by the most powerful system of organization and values associated with the market and the production of commodities for the market. Only an economy of enterprises with autonomous powers making their decisions under the discipline of the market can avoid the dilemma of choice between central, bureaucratic commandism and decentralized "feudal" chaos.

As a long transitional stage, socialism thus does not merely tolerate a limited sphere of inherited commodity production for the market (as Stalin held); under China's backward conditions, it must generate a great expansion of this sphere. Such a perspective alters the traditional view of the transitional character of socialism, because it posits that for a long time socialism must increasingly resemble capitalism in certain basic socioeconomic institutions in order to stimulate economic development and overcome still powerful precapitalist forces. Whether such a path risks capture by capitalism's powerful gravity is a question that does not seem to worry the reformers. They tend to the position that the future of socialism depends only on adhering to its two basic tenets, <u>viz.</u>, public ownership of the means of production and distribution according to work: "So long as public ownership is maintained, there can be no violation of socialist principles."[36] This unquestioning attitude toward "public ownership," quite extraordinary for a country that has been among the world's most severe critics of the USSR, is not, however, universally held. China's experience with the Cultural Revolution, in which the form of "public ownership" is now seen as masking quasi-feudal practices, has forced some people to take a closer look at the meaning of "ownership." In July 1980, a Beijing scholarly forum on economic manifestations of "feudalism" arrived at the following conclusion:

The system of ownership is the sum total of production relations. The transfer of ownership of the means of production, despite the legal recognition given to it, does not imply an overall solution to the problem of production relations.[37]

Similarly, Jiang Yiwei, acknowledging fears that leaders of independent enterprises might "become a new privileged stratum or even become capitalists," recognizes the need to look beyond the question of formal ownership to that of "who wields the power in an enterprise." Jiang advocates that authority rest in the hands of democratically elected representative committees of workers and staff.[38]

Toward the Pandora's box that is the market the reformers reveal a certain innocence. The market is for China a way out of the rigid, centralized bureaucracy, a means of instilling efficiency-mindedness and demand-orientation in the working population, and the framework for applying the spur of profit-orientation to an ideologically disillusioned work force. As the East Europeans have discovered, however, the market is wayward and unruly, pushing its own values and world view. Some reforming economists have been so infatuated with its dynamic motivational potential that they have overlooked its capacity to contradict social objectives. There is a genuine naiveté about the market.

Thus, there was surprise when official encouragement of individual material incentives for workers gave rise to endless bickering over distribution of wages and bonuses. According to Jiang Yiwei, "it was very difficult to decide the recipients of the [1979] wage increase." Jiang criticizes a wage system that sets worker against worker as being at odds with both socialism and social psychology. He has proposed establishing instead a system in which groups (enterprises, workshops) compete while solidarity is preserved among individuals within groups.[39]

Although the Chinese media daily have to deal with manifestations of the tensions between market and socialist values, the general inevitability of such conflict is given scant recognition. For example, both the profit-sharing and zifu yinkui systems are really at odds with the principle of payment according to work. Both systems pay workers partly out of profits, which vary for a multitude of reasons only some of which are associated with work done. The distribution of profitability among enterprises is affected by structural conditions (e.g., location of natural resources, transport availability, quality of inherited equipment and machinery, and the arbitrary price system) which in theory can be adjusted by using taxes, subsidies, fluctuating prices, etc. It is also a product of short-run forces of supply and demand. For example, a particular enterprise might enjoy high profits because of a shift in demand toward its product or an overproduction of its inputs, in neither case justifying superior compensation to its work force (and in only the former case calling for a shift in resources toward the enterprise).[40] As soon as income distribution is linked to profitability, the principle of payment according to work is bound to be compromised. If the state steps in to correct structurally caused inequities and compensate for disequilibria owing to shifting market forces, it is almost certain to affect also the "pure" relation that it wants to preserve between performance and income. This is not only because of the difficulty in practice of separating desired from undesired causes of profit variations; it also follows from the fact that the state is not a neutrally programed computer. The myriad of theoretically justified grounds for intervention legitimize special pleading and lobbying by affected interests, and the bureaucrats with responsibility for deciding such issues are themselves subject to social, professional (and perhaps economic) ties to those who are affected one way or another by regulation. This is all a drearily familiar story to Americans.[41]

To encourage the incentive function of the market, the state must exercise a large degree of "benign neglect," intervening only to correct the most glaring inequities but staying far from the margins of the efficiency-reward relationship. This policy runs the risk of generating such a sense of injustice among those on whom the market does not smile, as, in alliance with the disgruntled bureaucracy, to bring the experiment to a halt.

The Hungarian experience is one to which the Chinese have paid special attention. In Hungary, the conflict between the market and socialist values has led to the creation of complex formulas determining the division of profits between state and enterprise, as well as to various ad hoc interventions to ease "objective difficulties" or reduce "excessive" incomes. Almost two-thirds of gross enterprise profits have thus been taxed away and redistributed over the long run.[42]

The particular compromises between normative principles arrived at under given national circumstances depend on the constellation of social forces, which normally change but slowly. After a number of years of bargaining and redesigning, it becomes possible to identify the broad parameters within which a particular national system is normally capable of varying. Where the balance of forces is undergoing abnormally rapid change, however, as in a revolutionary situation, the ultimate limits of compromise are less easy to discern. Politically, such a period is not always a propitious time for leaders to stress the necessarily imperfect and compromise nature of the system they advocate; rather, they are likely to take an idealistic view of it, using this as a weapon in the still ongoing struggle. If anything is clear about China since 1976, it is that such a systemic conflict has been occurring; but that actual changes have still fallen far short of the fundamental shift from the bureaucratized command system to the enterprise-based, market-oriented system desired by the reform-oriented leadership.[43] At this point, the ultimate structure of the Chinese economy (including the role of the state) is still quite unpredictable.

Under these circumstances, the reformers have tended to disseminate a naive view of the wonders of the market. Xue Muqiao, a senior economic adviser to the State Planning Commission, contrasts China's continuing interregional inequalities, on the one hand, with, on the other, the situation in the United States, where "Many advanced areas vied with one another to invest in the backward areas with the result that all the states are fairly developed today."[44] Not only does this comparison ignore a large literature on the link between economic growth and regional inequality in market economies and the well-known impact of market forces on regional problems in the United States today, but it also implicitly deprecates China's own record of regional distribution, which is most creditable by international standards.[45] Similarly, Xue, in discussing the propensity of local governments to make economic decisions that maximize their own benefits at the expense of the nation as a whole, somewhat plaintively asks, "Why are they [capitalist countries] free from these problems? Because their enterprises are privately owned and the state has no right to interfere." In China, however, local administrative units intervene in the economic activities of enterprises: "Whether this interference damages the organic linkage and balance of the national economy is not their business."[46] The unmistakable implication of this argument — that private enterprise and capitalist public finance nicely reconcile local with national interest and "maintain the organic linkage and balance of the national economy" — is bound to create expectations that cannot be met and to provide the more sophisticated elements of the opposition with an obvious ideological weapon against reform.

Because Chinese history, culture, and revolutionary experience are exactly shared by no other people, the possibilities and constraints China faces in reconstructing its socioeconomic system are to a degree unique. The results of the current reforms cannot yet be perceived; neither can their full impact on people's lives. With the exception of the bureaucracy, all sections of Chinese society are promised improvements by the reformers. Everyone is to be made better off by increased supplies of consumer goods; women are to be helped by smaller families and the promise of payment according to work; urban dwellers by improved housing; poor regions by special aid; rich regions by less redistribution; peasants by higher prices for their products and more freedom to make economic choices; workers by wage increases; intellectuals by higher status and better salaries; the unemployed by freedom to establish collective and private enterprises. The recent inflationary pressures and resulting cutbacks in government spending and in reformism itself suggest that such a general advance on all fronts simultaneously will not take place. The actual distribution of true social benefits and costs has not yet emerged from the confusion of economic policy.

Moreover, China's leaders have lately reemphasized the role of central administrative planning as a means to implement readjustment and austerity. Yet it is just this approach that the reformers blame for the chronic imbalances of the past. If it is renewed, where will the constituencies favoring readjustment be found? How will the need for higher living standards, reduced investment rates, demand-oriented production be expressed? There is in current leadership directives a very Maoist strain: that rectification of planners' attitudes is the basic requirement of better planning. In fact, there is no doubt that central planning can be done much better than it has been in China. The reformers, in seeking to discredit the system at its root, have understated the responsibility of bad planning for China's difficulties. If administrative planning is strengthened and its effectiveness increased, the road ahead for structural reform may be rocky indeed.

NOTES

1. Foreign Broadcast Information Service, People's Republic of China (FBIS), November 18, 1980, pp. L6-10.

2. James D. Seymour, China, The Politics of Revolutionary Reintegration (New York: Thomas Y. Crowell, 1976), p. 180.

3. Translated in Beijing Review, 1980, no. 4, p. 16. Another discussion (Beijing Review, 1980, no. 36, p. 24) lists the following manifestations of feudal ideology in modern life: "despotism, monarchism, authoritarianism, the 'special privilege' mentality, obsession with hierarchical stratification, clanship, obscurantism...."

4. "To Combat Remnants of Feudalism in the Economic Sphere: An Important Task," Jingji yanjiu (Economic Research), 1980, no. 9, translated in FBIS, November 18, 1980, pp. L10-16. Also Xue Muqiao, "Some Opinions on Reforming the Economic System," Renmin ribao (People's Daily), June 10, 1980; in FBIS, June 25, 1980, p. L15.

5. E.g., a Renmin ribao article, decrying a prevalent "suffocating atmosphere of 'money, money, money,'" complains of "articles defending 'looking up to money' and 'preoccupation with personal gains and losses,'" while on the other hand, correct revolutionary slogans, such as 'selflessness,' and 'utter devotion to others without any thought of oneself'...have been subjected to criticism." See FBIS, January 21, 1981, p. L18.

6. The major attraction of fall 1980 in the windows of Beijing's largest department store was a complete modern kitchen, in which stood a Western mannequin hovering over a mobile serving table labeled (in English) "wifely wagon."

7. See New York Times, March 1, 1981. Articles in the Chinese media since

December 1980, when the austerity requirements of "readjustment" began to impose on "structural reform" policies, have revealed differences of opinion over whether the reforms can continue to be implemented and, if so, how quickly, during the current readjustment.

8. Mao Tsetung, A Critique of Soviet Economics, trans. Moss Roberts (New York: Monthly Review Press, 1977), p. 87.

9. For a brief discussion of this concept, which involves a continuous two-way relationship between leaders and masses, and of its Marxian origins, see Mark Selden, The People's Republic of China, A Documentary History of Revolutionary Change (New York: Monthly Review Press, 1979), pp. 16-20.

10. Mao, A Critique of Soviet Economics, p. 79.

11. The best study of the evolution of Mao's approach to industrial management is Stephen Andors' China's Industrial Revolution, Politics, Planning, and Management, 1949 to the Present (New York: Pantheon, 1977).

12. Mao wrote favorably of bonuses during the Great Leap Forward (See A Critique of Soviet Economics, p. 90), but they were abandoned as a manifestation of "economism" during the Cultural Revolution.

13. Jiang Yiwei, "The Theory of an Enterprise-Based Economy," Social Sciences in China 1, no. 1(1980): 55. Jiang, an influential reformer, is deputy director of the Institute of Industrial Economics, Chinese Academy of Social Sciences, and managing editor of the journal Jingji guanli (Economic Management).

14. Dwight H. Perkins, "Issues in the Estimation of China's National Product," in A. Eckstein, ed., Quantitative Measures of China's Economic Output (Ann Arbor: The University of Michigan Press, 1980); also National Foreign Assessment Center, "China: Major Economic Indicators," February 1980.

15. Beijing Review, 1980, nos. 38 (p. 36) and 16 (p. 18). Actual industrial growth in 1980 is put at 8.4 percent (New York Times, March 1, 1981, p. 1).

16. See World Bank, World Development Report, 1980, Table 1, p. 110, and Table 2, p. 112.

17. See State Statistical Bureau of the PRC, Main Indicators, Development of the National Economy of the People's Republic of China (1949-1979), Beijing, 1980.

18. Interview with author, September 16, 1980.

19. According to a recent source, the real wages of workers and staff members in state enterprises fell 4.46 percent between 1957 and 1978, while in the case of peasants, the average per capita income from collective sources rose 81.5 percent (from an extremely low base, however). A substantial increase in the number of working members per household enabled per capita income of worker families to rise despite the fall in wages. See Beijing Review, 1981, no. 8, pp. 8, 16.

20. The term is Jiang Yiwei's. See note 13.

21. Janos Kornai, "The Dilemmas of a Socialist Economy: The Hungarian Experience," Cambridge Journal of Economics 4, no. 2 (June 1980): 147.

22. Kornai, ibid., contains an excellent discussion of the clash between efficiency and such socialist ethical values as economic security, solidarity, and payment according to work.

23. Beijing Review, 1980, no. 39, p. 20. Because of the current retrenchment policy, the latter step has been canceled. See the State Council directive re-

ported in FBIS, February 5, 1981, p. L6.

24. See, e.g., Xue Muqiao article in Renmin ribao, June 10, 1980, translated in FBIS, June 25, 1980, pp. L12-18, where the phrase in question is rendered simply as "inequality."

25. Ibid., p. L14. See also Ren Tao, "On the Reform of Our Economic System," Renmin ribao, February 10, 1981, p. 5; in FBIS, February 18, 1981, p. L12: "At present, commodity prices are very irrational. . . . However, in order to stabilize commodity prices, we can only let things remain as they are."

26. However, some departments which had been given authority to "adjust" prices prior to December were permitted by the directive to continue such adjustments.

27. Xue Muqiao, "Regulation by Plan and Regulation by the Market," Renmin ribao, October 13, 1980. The State Council directive referred to is published in Renmin ribao, December 8, 1980.

28. The problems of the tax and financial system are discussed in a blunt article in the Chinese journal Jingji guanli (Economic Management), 1980, no. 9, by Luo Jingfen: "Price and Tax Reform Is an Important Link in Reform of the Economic System" (in Chinese).

29. See FBIS, January 6, 1981, p. L22.

30. Xue Muqiao, "Regulation by Plan and Regulation by the Market."

31. The exact percentage given is 27.3. No details are given as to how income was calculated. Clearly, the figure of U.S.$30 understates the actual living standard, as is apparent if one considers the possibility of surviving for one year on that amount in, say, New York City. (Wu Xiang, "The Open Road and the Log Bridge — A Preliminary Discussion of the Origin, Advantages and Disadvantages, Nature and Future of the Fixing of Farm Output Quotas for Each Household," Renmin ribao, November 5, 1980; in FBIS, November 7, 1980, p. L23).

32. In the aftermath of 1980's fall in food grain output, the press has been warning against permitting diversification to threaten the required growth in staple production. It seems likely that production teams will continue to be subject to nonmarket pressure to accept food grain quotas, except (as in pasture areas) where this is clearly irrational.

33. Wu Xiang, op. cit. (but not in FBIS translation).

34. New York Times, November 5, 1980.

35. J. V. Stalin, Economic Problems of Socialism in the U.S.S.R. (Beijing, Foreign Languages Press, 1972), p. 18.

36. Jiang Yiwei, "Enterprise-Based Economy," p. 67.

37. "To Combat Remnants of Feudalism in the Economic Sphere: An Important Task," Jingji yanjiu, 1980, no. 9, pp. 76-80; in FBIS, November 18, 1980, p. L15.

38. Jiang Yiwei, "Enterprise-Based Economy," pp. 69-70, and interview with author, October 3, 1980.

39. Interview with author, October 3, 1980. Jiang's wage proposal is spelled out in Renmin ribao, July 14, 1980, and translated in FBIS, July 18, 1980, pp. L11-L14.

40. The example, and much of the argument preceding it in this paragraph, is taken from Mario Nuti, "The Contradictions of Socialist Economies: A

Marxist Interpretation," The Socialist Register, 1979, pp. 265-66.

41. A recent example from China concerns the notorious Baoshan steel complex being built with Japanese help in the suburbs of Shanghai. The worst of several sites considered for this enormous project because of its swampy ground, necessitating the expenditure of large sums on underground support systems, Baoshan was apparently chosen because of the political pull of a high-ranking Shanghai Party official. Extraordinarily expensive, ridden with cost overruns, involving major environmental pollution issues that were never investigated, the project was kept alive by a powerful metallurgical lobby. Finally, after persistent criticism, the second phase of the project, involving half of its originally designed capacity, was postponed indefinitely last November. See China Business Review, January-February 1981, pp. 9-13.

42. Kornai, "The Dilemmas of a Socialist Economy," pp. 151-152.

43. Cf. Xue Muqiao, "Some Opinions on Reforming the Economic System," Renmin ribao, June 10, 1980; in FBIS, June 25, 1980, p. L13: "Over the past year or so, only a breach has been made in the old system."

44. Xue Muqiao, interviewed in Beijing Review, 1980, no. 36, p. 3.

45. See Nicholas Lardy, Economic Growth and Distribution in China (Cambridge and New York: Cambridge University Press, 1978). In contrast to Xue's rosy view of market and regional equality in the U.S. is that of the well-known Maoist Felix Rohatyn who, writing in the New York Review of Books (December 4, 1980, p. 22), warns about "the great shift in wealth from the Northeast and Midwest to the energy-producing areas of the U.S. as a result of price decontrol. This trend will ultimately turn the country into 'have' and 'have-not' regions."

46. Xue Muqiao, "Some Opinions on Reforming the Economic System," p. L32.

About the Contributors

Marc Blecher is Associate Professor of Government at Oberlin College, the co-author of Micropolitics in Contemporary China: A Technical Unit During and After the Cultural Revolution, and the author of several articles on Chinese politics and political economy. He is the coordinator of a group project which conducted field research in China and which is presently completing a monograph on urban/rural development in a Chinese county.

Edward Friedman is Professor of Political Science at the University of Wisconsin, Madison, and is presently Associate Staff Director, Subcommittee on Asia, U.S. House Committee on Foreign Affairs. He is the author of numerous works on modern and contemporary China and U.S.-Asian relations, including Backward Toward Revolution: The Chinese Revolutionary Party. Professor Friedman is presently completing a collaborative study with Kay Johnson, Paul Pickowicz, and Mark Selden, Wugong: A Chinese Village in a Socialist State, growing out of field research in China in 1978 and 1980.

William Hinton, farmer, agro-technical adviser, and chronicler of the Chinese revolution, worked as a tractor adviser in China in 1947-1952 and then wrote Fanshen: A Documentary of Revolutionary Change in a Chinese Village. In recent years he has served as a technical adviser to the Chinese government and completed a second epic volume on Long Bow village, to be published in 1982.

Kojima Reiitsu is Senior Researcher, The Institute of Developing Economies, Tokyo. He is the author of numerous works on China's economy and agrarian development and on Japanese imperialism. Dr. Kojima's most important works include Chūgoku no keizai to

gijutsu (China's Economy and Technology) and Chūgoku no toshika
to nosan kensetsu (China's Urbanization and Agrarian Development).

Victor Lippit, Associate Professor of Economics at the University of California, Riverside, is the author of Land Reform and
Economic Development in China. His study of "The Development
of Underdevelopment in China" appeared in Modern China and was
republished together with the response it evoked in Philip Huang,
ed., The Development of Underdevelopment in China.

Mitch Meisner taught Chinese and comparative politics at the
University of California at Santa Cruz and at Michigan State University. Beginning with his University of Chicago dissertation on
Dazhai, he has been a long-time student of the national agricultural
model and the author of articles on China's rural development and
contemporary politics. Dr. Meisner is presently in law school at
the University of Michigan.

Carl Riskin is Associate Professor of Economics at Queens College and Research Associate of the East Asian Institute, Columbia
University. The author of numerous articles on Chinese industrial
development and incentive systems, he is presently completing a
study of the economy of the People's Republic of China.

Mark Selden is Professor of Sociology and History and an Associate of the Fernand Braudel Center, State University of New York
at Binghamton. His work on modern China includes The Yenan Way
in Revolutionary China and The People's Republic of China: A Documentary History of Revolutionary Change. Following fieldwork
in China in 1978 and 1980, Professor Selden is completing a collaborative volume with Edward Friedman, Kay Johnson, and Paul
Pickowicz on Wugong: A Chinese Village in a Socialist State.

Tang Tsou, Professor of Politics, University of Chicago, is the
author of numerous works on Chinese politics and U.S.-Chinese
relations, including America's Failure in China, 1941-1950. In
recent years he has conducted extensive field work in China, particularly in connection with his study of the Dazhai model.

Andrew Walder is Research Fellow, Center for Chinese Studies,

University of California, Berkeley. In 1981 he completed a University of Michigan Ph.D. on the Chinese working class in the Cultural Revolution. Dr. Walder is the author of several articles on the Chinese proletariat, the Cultural Revolution, and the transition to socialism. In 1982 he will serve as Assistant Professor of Sociology, Columbia University.